THE
CONNECTICUT WITS

THE
CONNECTICUT WITS

Foreword by Kenneth Silverman

THOMAS Y. CROWELL COMPANY
ESTABLISHED 1834
NEW YORK

CONTENTS

FOREWORD

Twice after coming down from the mountain, the hero of Washington Irving's profound folktale cries in despair, "Does nobody here know Rip Van Winkle?" The village seems changed. At the tavern door where double-chinned Nicholas Vedder smoked his "fair long pipe" now stands a "lean, bilious-looking fellow, with his pockets full of hand-bills." Among the villagers Rip finds not "the accustomed phlegm" but a "bustling, disputatious tone." During his sleep colonial America has become America.

The value of this fine anthology is that the Connecticut Wits did not sleep through that passage. They were its most alert witnesses, and afterward its bitterest survivors. In the years between the Revolution and the nineteenth century, they saw the quality of their lives violated and coarsened. To their bewilderment, the new nation preferred a shrill radicalism to the civilities of the Connecticut Valley, clever freethinking to the long-maturing New England theology, the Jacobin Jefferson to the Federalist Adams. The Wits watched, shuddered, denounced, an ever more loathed remnant of the City on the Hill.

It is odd that we should owe this collection of their works to Vernon Louis Parrington. He was a progressive, reform-minded Midwesterner, while the Wits were conservative Connecticut men, among whose deepest fears was the opening of new western territory. He shared with those "men of notable ability and striking individuality," as he calls them, a genteel devotion to verse, great personal energy and learning, but little else. Born in 1871, Parrington was raised in Illinois and Kansas, and spent most of his life in the academy: a transfer to Harvard College in his junior year, graduate work at the College of Emporia and the University of Oklahoma, Professor of English at the University of Washington for twenty years afterward. He belonged to the generation of historians that included Merle

Curti and Charles Beard, who saw history moved by the forces of economics and deplored modern capitalist culture, including the polite world of the academy. Outstanding among his many influential books and articles was *Main Currents in American Thought,* in three volumes, subtitled "An Interpretation of American Literature." His introduction to *The Connecticut Wits* is an expansion of one chapter in the first volume, "The War of Belles Lettres." In *Main Currents,* Parrington surveyed the whole course of American thought up to his time. His theme was the dialectic between the forces of progress and reaction throughout American history, and its expression in American literature. *Main Currents* was the best-informed and most imaginative history of American literature written in three centuries of American experience—an act of great scholarly and critical daring, indeed a great work. The first two volumes received the Pulitzer Prize for history in 1928; the third appeared posthumously two years later.

Parrington's works continue to be read and reprinted. But a later generation of historians and literary critics, one determined to keep itself aware of its own assumptions, has questioned Parrington's methods and reputation. According to one school of criticism, his sense of the origin and function of ideas in history is confused. Sometimes he treats ideas—usually the reactionary ones he disliked—as the product of socioeconomic conditions; at other times he treats ideas—usually the progressive ones he liked—as arising independently of those conditions. In the present introduction, for instance, he traces John Trumbull's "bad"—that is, reactionary—ideas to his reactionary environment, but does not explain how Joel Barlow, who matured in the same environment, developed "good," progressive ideas. His interpretation of history tends to be moralistic, Manichean, a struggle between good and bad ideas and the good and bad men who held them. This moralism reveals itself in a pervasive metaphor of "currents." Heroes appear as men in the open air, navigators of the "maelstrom" of history; villains, such as Timothy Dwight, appear as landlocked, stultifying behind closed study windows. A further general criticism of Parrington is that he was too much the captive of literary history, and otherwise incompetent in metaphysics, theology, science, legal thought, and the fine arts.

These criticisms of Parrington's methods and competence are valid but narrow. Much of his account of the Connecticut Wits holds up despite weaknesses in his over-all design. He correctly regarded the Wits' poetry and late eighteenth-century Connecticut politics as one thing. He correctly insisted that the Wits "embodied a conception of life and society that had taken form during nearly two hundred years of provincial experience." His sketches of the Wits' complex lives and personalities are finely compressed and memorable. And he remains readable and instructive not only in these smaller instances, but on the most important count, too—on the largeness of his imagination. *Main Currents* should be placed alongside the other inspired reinterpretations of the American past that appeared between 1920 and 1930: *The Great Gatsby, The Bridge, In the American Grain,* Charles Ives' "Concord, Mass., 1840–1860." Like *The Bridge, Main Currents* is an act of imaginative spanning. It attempts to draw the connections between John Winthrop and Sinclair Lewis, or Pocahontas and Eugene Debs, to seize at once the whole pattern of American experience, and in the seeming alien-ness of the American past—the George Washingtons and John Winthrops and Davy Crocketts who seem so little like any of us—to find oneself. *Main Currents* is itself an American prose epic, not unlike Cotton Mather's *Magnalia Christi Americana,* indeed not unlike *The Columbiad* and *The Conquest of Canaan.* It belongs not only to academic history and criticism, but to American literature.

This is not to say that Parrington's introduction to *The Connecticut Wits* is unalterable or complete. The forty years since he wrote it have produced much fresh research on colonial American literature, new assessments of the romantic period and of the New England Puritan culture, international and domestic crises that have altered our sense of the pattern of the American past, of what is *the* American tradition. The Wits wrote out of deep apprehensions about social dislocation and chaos, and with a considered sense of the limitations of democracy; they speak perhaps more intimately to us than they did to Parrington. For all of these reasons, the present moment invites a more precise, or at least an updated, rendering of Parrington's main conclusion: that in their time the Wits represented the Old Guard, opposed to both romanticism and democracy.

Parrington characterizes the Wits as spokesmen for the "dead past." But it needs to be stressed that their conservative politics did not prevent them from sharing the highest hopes of the Enlightenment, in common with such advanced liberals of their time as Jefferson and Paine. Their works abound with rapturous hopes for progress and reform, with opposition to hereditary monarchy and primogeniture, with an impassioned defense of freedom and the abolition of slavery, with relish for new scientific ideas. Dwight, for one, wrote an essay on light, experimented with new agricultural methods, and founded a remarkable science department at Yale. To a man, the Wits championed the American cause during the Revolution, as did many of the old-line Congregational clergy, who were often the most vigorous promoters of rebellion.

In claiming that the Wits opposed romanticism, Parrington equates conservatism with Philistinism. The inaccuracy of his reference to "prim little Hartford" reflects his own identification with the Jazz Age writers who railed against the Genteel Tradition. The Wits did look backwards—back to the government of John Winthrop; but they were far from being e. e. cummings' "Cambridge ladies who live in furnished souls." Their reactionary ideas did not make them reactionary poets. Conservative politics is not inconsistent with radical literary innovation, for instance, Ezra Pound's *Cantos*. Despite his democratic ideas, Barlow was a far less inventive and innovative poet than, for all his reactionary ideas, was Dwight. In *Greenfield Hill* Dwight deliberately experimented with using a native literary language; he appended pages of footnotes (omitted by Parrington) to explain his Americanisms, an experiment for which both American and British reviewers ridiculed him. Barlow's language resounds with the official eloquence of British neoclassic verse, and is in that sense far more conservative, less preromantic. Like many writers in England in the late eighteenth century, all of the Wits attacked the neoclassical "rules" of composition. As undergraduates and later as tutors at Yale, Dwight and Trumbull argued strenuously to change the literary curriculum so as to include modern writers, and to overthrow the prevailing Aristotelian concept of fixed genres. In *The Columbiad,* Barlow praises Benjamin West for painting his military heroes not in Roman togas but in modern dress. In opposing neoclassical prescriptions, the Wits followed the direction of the romantic movement.

Again, it is true that from the perspective of international romanticism, the Wits seem the "dead past." They distrusted that longing for the infinite, that sense of inexhaustible human capacity, that desire for change which one associates with the romantic temper. But from the perspective of American romanticism, and New England romanticism in particular, the past they represented seems very much alive. Early American romantics like Cooper and Irving shared their Lockean views on the importance of property—what Parrington refers to as the "stake-in-society" principle. More important, both the Wits and the darker writers of the American romantic tradition make the same Puritanical assumptions about human nature. For instance, Hawthorne, in his concern for conscience, sin, guilt, paternity, and community obligation, is at least as close to Dwight or Trumbull as he is to Wordsworth or to Jefferson.

A much stronger case, of course, can be made for Parrington's related view that the Wits opposed democracy. But this also needs to be qualified. He attributes the Wits' antidemocratic views to the Calvinist notion of an elect, which he believes fostered aristocratic thinking. It seems reasonable to assume that the assurance that one was destined for Heaven, and that others were not, would foster a sense of one's superiority, or at least one's uniqueness. Actually, in the Puritan community the question of election remained open. Who were the elect? Why were they elected? How could one tell? The mandarin intricacies of such questions evoked widely differing answers, perhaps the most common being that there was no certain sign of election. The visible saint destined for Heaven is a less common figure in Puritan literature than is the poor doubting Christian, humbly uncertain of whether he is elect, but still willing and anxious to serve God. Most Puritan writers argued that one must not be so proud as to be certain of his election, nor so humble as to despair of it—hardly an aristocratic belief.

The Wits' very real opposition to democracy began rather in a fear of class extinction. They saw the pious, literate, genial life of the Connecticut Valley threatened by the widespread deism, illiteracy, and crassness of the lower classes. The lean man "with his pockets full of hand-bills" was usurping Nicholas Vedder's comfortable place. Paradoxically the Wits stated their opposition to the kind of democracy typified by Jefferson in the terms of the radical democratic individualism cherished by the nineteenth century. Like Emerson and Thoreau, the Wits would elect leaders and programs by a "majority of one." A man who is right, they said, constitutes a majority; the duty of government is simply to do the right, with or without the approval of the numerical majority. They framed their arguments against admitting the lower classes to power as convictions of conscience, determinations to do the right. Their arguments closely resemble those advanced by Thoreau in "Civil Disobedience," or more recently by Herbert Marcuse in "Repressive Tolerance." If the Wits opposed democracy and romanticism, so in their various ways did Irving, Cooper, Emerson, Thoreau, and Hawthorne.

Aside from these qualifications, Parrington's superb account of the Wits' Federalist-Congregationalist thought remains the most enlightening commentary on their poetry. To recover that poetry for oneself, as Parrington knew, is an act of both historical scholarship and literary criticism. The tone of the poetry is a guide to the spirit of the politics; the politics provide the only certain way of understanding the tone. For a new edition of his anthology it seems only fitting to clarify what his account makes it possible for us to see at all, this relation between the Wits' thought and the form and style of their verse.

The Wits wrote about only one subject: the ideal nature of American society. Again and again they debated in verse what countless citizens following the Revolution debated in taverns, newspapers, and town meetings: What should the new republic be like? Except for the internationalist Barlow, they answered this question simply by depicting the life they led in the Connecticut Valley. They felt that the way of life celebrated in *Greenfield Hill* would insure stability and happiness for all Americans. Thus they wished to nationalize Connecticut. But as they watched the progress of the late eighteenth century, they grew far from certain that the Connecticut style could take root elsewhere. Their poetry records their early hopes and their later despair. It is a mirror of cultural conflict, reflecting virtually every aspect of post-Revolutionary life from town planning to wrestling. In showing this clash of alternative visions of life and this drama of ideas and life-styles, the poems are dominated by images of triumph, conquest, defeat, conspiracy, in short of warfare—the warfare of fashion against simplicity, righteousness against infidelism, gentility against lower-class democracy, settlement against pioneering, white clapboard houses against log cabins, America against Europe, Jonathan Edwards against Voltaire, Martha Washington against Mary Wollstonecraft, and by 1800, Connecticut against practically all the rest of the world.

To express this conflict the Wits borrowed conventions and forms from contemporary English poetry. But they changed them out of their own necessities, and out of several embryonic colonial literary traditions they created their own conventions and forms. One standard form the Wits found very compelling was the epic—works such as *The Columbiad* and *The Conquest of Canaan,* or mock epics such as *M'Fingal* and *The Anarchiad.* Philip Freneau, who detested the Wits, laughed off their "Iliads begun, and finished in a day"; but it is easy to see why they often chose the epic form. Even though the genre seemed used up to most contemporary English writers, the epic, by definition, suited a country anxious to declare its nationhood. The Wits' epics are experiments in self-respect, attempts to achieve a cultural identity by finding and naming the events, persons, and values that deserve recognition and homage. Often the experiment breaks down into disconnected panegyrics on

Franklin, Rittenhouse, and West, or on the national genius displayed in commerce, science, and manufactures. The more subtle attraction of the epic lay in its sheer amplitude. The epic dimension seemed to the Wits and to other American poets the necessary expression in art of the physical grandeur and dazzling political destiny of the republic. Here, too, the fervor of the Wits' nationalism strained their talents, and often produced no further evidence of national genius than mere length and bombast. Even this gigantism, however, stamps their epic poetry as that familiar American gesture, the show of cultural maturity. Their epics imply, simply by being epics, that the attempt to prove the continuity and richness of American culture proves it—is a proof *of* it. They predict the megalithic shapes of American culture—the sprawling Leatherstocking series and the Yoknapatawpha saga, the orotundity of Thomas Wolfe and Walt Whitman, such culture palaces as Lincoln Center in New York City, the on-parade, hats-in-the-air cacophony of Charles Ives.

The epic's traditional narration of combat had the further advantage of allowing the Wits to commemorate the recent Revolution and to define its significance. Almost the whole of *The Conquest of Canaan,* although Dwight denied such an intent, is a masked description of Revolutionary events, as without the allegorical guise, is Book VII of Barlow's *Columbiad.* Primarily the Revolution seemed to the Wits a great and dignified national subject. But it also seemed a decisive precedent for national behavior. They used the Revolution ideologically. In their epics they translated their ideal program for the nation into actions and speeches suggesting the goals of the Revolution. As a result, the different treatment of the Revolution by Dwight and by Barlow indicates their different politics. In the *Conquest,* Dwight views the Revolution as a great Puritan moral struggle, a triumph of inherited plain living, sobriety, and righteousness over foreign foppishness, licentiousness, and godlessness. But in Barlow's entirely secular *Columbiad,* the Revolution marks the triumph of a Franco-American concept of "national liberty" over English hereditary monarchy. The Revolution was the Wits' "usable past" speaking to the confused present. George Washington in their epics figures not merely as a general, but as a culture hero. He epitomizes the virtues appropriate to Americans in the present moment. The Wits' treatment of the Revolution varies throughout their careers because it is always influenced by and addressed to particular political circumstances. For example, as the popularity of French philosophy increased, Dwight began to denounce the war for having brought infidelism into the country through American contacts with French troops.

As an epic model, *Paradise Lost* particularly suited the Wits' historical circumstances. The biblical events and overtones of *Paradise Lost* pervade *M'Fingal* and *The Conquest of Canaan,* and suggest the Wits' true affinity with the Puritan past. Dwight's recasting of the Revolution into the events of Old Testament history springs from the same temperament that led the Puritans to see New England as a new Canaan or a Christian Israel. The great debates in *Paradise Lost,* such as the parliament of fallen angels, restaged in the debates between Honorius and M'Fingal or between Joshua and Hanniel, patriot and loyalist, were especially meaningful for an audience that welcomed, respected, and used public debate to create a rationale for its actions. The many debates in the Wits' epics function not only as literary devices. They dramatize the flavor of American public life at the time.

The Miltonic form also produced an offshoot. During the Wits' youth, the vision of futurity that closes *Paradise Lost* had become a distinct and widely practised native genre in America. At colonial commencement exercises in the early 1770's, one young orator after another declaimed in these visionary poems his tremendous hopes for a rising people. The genre might be called the Rising Glory poem. Ultimately descended from Virgil, but more directly inspired by Milton and by English visionary odes, it includes Book VIII of *The Columbiad,* the last part of Humphreys' "A Poem on the Industry of the United States," and the final book of *The Conquest of Canaan.* The Rising Glory poem rests on the cyclical view of history, with its theory of the inevitable rise and fall of empires. The underlying metaphor of the poems is the *Translatio,* the idea

of the inevitable succession of the arts and sciences westward
from a declining to a rising empire: from the classical world
to Europe, from Europe to England, and from a moribund
England, so the Wits and others hoped, to America. The Wits
used the Rising Glory poem to project the life-style of the
Connecticut Valley into the future and on a national scale.

The Rising Glory poem is one of two native or at least
Anglo-American minor genres that the Wits and their contemporaries developed. The other could be called the International poem. In this form the poet unfolds what Dwight
called the "glorious contrast" between European and American
society. A few examples are Dwight's "Epistle from Dr. Dwight
to Col. Humphreys" (1785, omitted by Parrington), Barlow's
"The Hasty Pudding," and "American Antiquities. No. XII" of
The Anarchiad. (In the dramatic literature of the time, the
theme is represented in Royall Tyler's play *The Contrast*.)
The genre flourished into the nineteenth century, of course, in
poems like William Cullen Bryant's "To Cole, the Painter Departing for Europe"; later prose equivalents are the novels of
Henry James and the expatriate writing of the 1920's. In these
poems the Wits work out a negative ideal of nationality by
showing what America is not or should not be. Often addressed
to a young man about to depart for the old world, the poem
cautions him not to give up his sometimes nebulous native virtues in exchange for explicitly named European vices, most
often fashion and atheism. The metaphor of the "glorious contrast" is one of those most deeply embedded in all American
writing of the late eighteenth century. It was by looking at
Europe that the Wits most clearly saw themselves.

Naturally in depicting their ideal America, the Wits used
many other traditional forms—odes, elegies, hymns, topographi-
cal poems, and the like. Two themes that recur throughout their
verse call for separate notice, even though they only occa-
sionally became the subjects for whole poems. The first is a
search for the basic mechanism of social stability. The Wits
sought the one operative virtue or institution or legal principle
on which revolves the achieved happiness of Connecticut and
which, built into the nation, would set in motion national hap-

piness and tranquility. Several individual poems, such as Humphreys' poem on Industry, and many parts of longer poems
conduct this search, largely in the manner of Pope's "Windsor
Forest" and of the many eighteenth-century poems praising
English commerce. For Dwight the operative principle was "competence"—no man owning too much or too little, so that envy
is discouraged while hard work thrives; for Humphreys it was
"Industry"; for Barlow, "national liberty." The one magical
gear engages and motivates the whole complex machinery of
the perfect society. A second recurrent theme in the Wits' verse
is education. Most of the Wits taught school, and a few of them
made important innovations in American higher education,
particularly for women. In devising such heroes as the young
Irad and Dick Hairbrain, the Wits reveal a typically American
willingness to heed adolescent viewpoints. The education of
these heroes, however, only serves to illustrate the larger ide-
ology in a different form. In Barlow's "Advice to the Privileged
Orders," the university becomes the proper model for the state,
whose primary function is to teach. The pedagogical ideals the
Wits advance simply aim at creating citizens for the sort of
society foreseen in the Rising Glory poems.

These high hopes and opulent tones mark only the Wits'
earlier writing. As the century closed, they found themselves
ever more isolated in an America growing ever more unlike
Connecticut. An occasional religious revival relieved their
gloom. Otherwise they watched their magic gear grind down,
sabotaged by Shays' Rebellion, the French Revolution, the election of Jefferson, the campaigns of Napoleon, and finally, by
the incorporation of a new charter for Connecticut, granting a
wide franchise and almost ending Federalist-Congregationalist
authority in the state.

The Wits responded with a bitterness that identifies their
later, mostly anonymous works: *The Triumph of Infidelity,
The Anarchiad,* and *The Echo.* These are defiant, rear-guard
actions. They fight to salvage the Connecticut style from certain defeat by demanding that it be preserved at least in
Connecticut; even, they hint, at the cost of secession. Their characteristic device is dramatic irony, by which they expose and

defame Connecticut's enemies. In "Echo. No. XX," for example, Jefferson is made to unwittingly expose the stupidity of his policies by explaining them in transparently self-contradictory terms, with the aid of "the Goddess Reason." This use of dramatic irony is again not merely a literary device. The vehicle itself conveys the Wits' fear of a corrosive skepticism, of a nihilistic use of reason to call God and human goodness into doubt. Again and again in their late works, the sophistical arguments of skeptics like Buffon, Hume, and Voltaire not only unfrock their authors, but also explode the pretenses of the critical spirit, the means by which the Enlightenment sought to bring down Christianity. The use of dramatic irony serves to implicate the paganism of the Enlightenment in nearer, more threatening social phenomena: French meddling in American affairs, lower-class rebelliousness, the double-dealing of the Jefferson administration.

If one attends closely enough to the tone of the Wits' earliest and latest work, however, he hears not two voices, but one. That single personality is the deepest meaning of their poetry. Its language and cadences tell us, more fully than anything it openly says, what we ought to be. The righteously dignified voice that narrates *The Conquest of Canaan* itself defines a desired mode of conduct, the conduct of the Ideal American. That Ideal American is always the narrator of the Wits' poetry. In their early work he is the concerned private citizen addressing the public he's concerned for. He instructs it in what it can be, without belittling it for what it is. He speaks in a tone of grave but cordial advisement, confident of his importance in the world, but not overconfident. His voice declares moral passion tempered with cordiality; an impressive degree of learning that is never at odds with downrightness; a gentlemanliness that seems deliberately to hold off sounding aristocratic; an eloquence owning its British past but unashamed of its local accents.

The strident voice of the Wits' later work represents the voice of the same righteous, learned, cordial Ideal American; but now he thrashes or ridicules the inferiors whose rule he cannot accept. The very shrillness of his voice signifies how

FOREWORD xix

much his cordiality was the reward, as Parrington saw, of un-
challenged privilege and class exclusion. The Wits' cordiality
passed into shrillness as colonial America passed into America.
At the end they became indistinguishable from their antagonist
—the "bilious-looking fellow, with his pockets full of hand-
bills," whose presence at the tavern door left Rip Van Winkle
so disheartened.

KENNETH SILVERMAN
NEW YORK UNIVERSITY

BIBLIOGRAPHY

Several books by and about the Connecticut Wits have appeared since Parrington compiled his anthology:

Bottorff, William K., ed. *The Miscellaneous Works of David Humphries,* Gainesville, Fla., 1968.

Bowden, Edwin T., ed. *The Satiric Poems of John Trumbull.* Austin, 1962.

Cowie, Alexander. *John Trumbull: Connecticut Wit.* Chapel Hill, 1936.

Cuningham, Charles E. *Timothy Dwight 1752–1817.* New York, 1942.

Dos Passos, John. "Citizen Barlow of the Republic of the World" in *The Ground We Stand On.* Boston, 1941.

Harrington, Karl P. *Richard Alsop, A Hartford Wit.* Middletown, Conn., 1969.

Howard, Leon. *The Connecticut Wits.* Chicago, 1943.

Ravitz, Abe, ed. *Remarks on the Review of Inchiquin's Letters* [by Timothy Dwight]. New York, 1969.

Silverman, Kenneth. *Timothy Dwight.* New York, 1969.

Solomon, Barbara, ed. *Travels in New England and New York* [by Timothy Dwight]. Cambridge, Mass., 1969.

Woodress, James. *A Yankee's Odyssey: The Life of Joel Barlow.* Philadelphia, 1958.

Zunder, Theodore. *The Early Days of Joel Barlow.* New Haven, 1934.

K. S.

INTRODUCTION

For a good many years now the members of the literary coterie that forgathered in Hartford in the closing years of the eighteenth century, and proffered their wit and wisdom to all New England, have enjoyed such shadowy fame as comes from the reprinting of their names in successive school histories of our literature. Their several individualities have long since gone the way of mortality, but their composite reputation has been happily preserved by the salt of a phrase. Under the quaint title of the Connecticut or the Hartford Wits —a title which, to borrow Whitman's Gallicism, has proved to be their *carte de visite* to posterity—they are annually recalled by a considerable number of undergraduates on the eve of an examination; but what sort of men they were, and what they severally and jointly contributed to a little world sadly wanting sweetness and light, are questions about which no undergraduate ever concerns himself. Their works lie buried in old libraries with the dust of years upon them; their descriptive title alone dwells among the living. To rescue them if possible from the obscuring shadow of their collective reputation, to permit them once more to speak for themselves in their eighteenth century vernacular, is the purpose of this partial reprinting of their works. The record as they left it, very likely will not appeal to the taste of a far different age. We shall probably find their verse stilted and barren, and their robust prejudices hopelessly old-fashioned; but stilted and barren though their couplets may be, and extraordinary though their dogmatisms may seem to us, they throw a clear light on provincial New England in the acrid years of the seventeen-nineties, when America was angrily debating what path to follow in order to arrive at its predestined objective. The Hartford Wits may not deserve the high title of poets; they were smaller men than they esteemed each other and their generation rated them; but though they fell short of their ambitious goal, their works remain extraordinarily interesting documents of a critical period.

The title of the group sufficiently reveals their intellectual antecedents. That they alone amongst our early dabblers in verse succeeded in preëmpting the excellent name of Wits, suggests how late the spirit of eighteenth century English culture came to expression in America, and also how inadequately. That they were not alone in their efforts to shape American letters after the Augustan pattern, every student of our early verse knows. Others before them aspired to be Wits, and others after them. From Mather Byles to Robert Treat Paine the refinement of Pope and the trenchant severity of Churchill had been the admiration of American poetasters; but they alone achieved a measurable degree of success in domesticating the Wit ideals, and by their persistent labors in the field of satire they created for the first time in America what may be called a school of poetry. By the end of the century their reputation had spread well beyond the confines of New England, and when an ambitious collection of native verse was issued in New York in 1794, under the title of *The Columbian Muse*, the editor felt constrained to give up considerably more than half the total space to their work. Only Philadelphia could hope to enter into poetic rivalry with the Connecticut group. In the social and literary capital of America poetry was sedulously cultivated. Francis Hopkinson, an amiable dabbler in polite arts, had contributed a number of sprightly *jeux d'esprit;* young William Cliffton was preparing to dedicate his short life to verse; and Peter Porcupine—the brutally caustic William Cobbett—was achieving a lively notoriety as a purveyor of virulent couplets. But the culture of Philadelphia was smutched by the strife of partisan rivals. Young enthusiasts for the rights of man gathered there—Philip Freneau from New Jersey, and idealists from overseas—to throw their literary brickbats at the spokesmen of conservatism. There was wanting the solidarity of polite opinion that gave a sanction of authority to upper-class Yankee views, and no school of poetry arose to enshrine in clever couplets the culture of a homogeneous society.

This is what lends its chief significance to the work of the Hartford group. They embodied a conception of life and society that had taken form during nearly two hundred years of provincial experience; and they phrased that conception at the moment when vast changes were impending and the traditional New England was on the point of being caught in the grasp of forces that were to destroy what was most native in her life. The "Wits" were the last representatives of a literary mode that had slowly percolated through the crust of Puritan provincialism and imparted a certain sprightliness to a dour temper. They were the literary old guard of eighteenth century Toryism, the expiring gasp of a rationalistic age, given to criticism, suspicious of all emotion, contemptuous of idealistic programs. But though they aspired to follow the latest London modes, they could not wholly lay aside congenital prejudices, and they unconsciously gave to the imported fashion a homely domestic cut. If they were Wits they were Yankee Wits, and their manners were formed in Connecticut rather than at St. James's, at Yale College rather than Brooks Club. They aspired to unite culture with godliness, and this Puritan predilection for righteousness adds a characteristic native savor to their wit.

Although their writing was done at a time when the romantic revolution, soon to set all western civilization in ferment, was well under way in France, and had already entered America, there is in them no suggestion of sympathy for the new ideas. As good Calvinists and honest men they would hold no commerce with "French infidel philosophy." They stood stoutly by the customary and familiar. The age was visibly falling to decay before their eyes, yet they set themselves with the fury of dogmatic conviction to new-prop an order that had contented their fathers. They were the self-satisfied embodiment of the outworn. The nineteenth century was knocking at their door, but they would not open to it. And as they saw that century coming in the guise of revolution, exciting to unheard-of innovations in the fields of politics and economics and religion and letters; as they observed it sweeping triumphantly through Virginia, turmoiling the pugnacious society of Philadelphia, expressing itself in the rebellious work of Philip Freneau and Tom Paine and Matthew Carey, in Jacobin Clubs and Jeffersonian democracy, they set themselves seriously to the work of barring its progress in their own little world. They conveniently associated the economic unrest of post-war days—that gave birth to a strange progeny in Rhode Island and New Hampshire and Massachusetts—with the contamination of French atheism, charged all unrest to the account of democracy, and hastened to put it down in the name of law and righteousness. They hated new ways with the virtuous hatred of the well-to-do, and piously dreamed of a future America as like the past as one generation of oysters is like another.

I

There is a certain historical fitness in the fact that the Wits should have arisen in Connecticut and been the intellectual and spiritual children of Yale. For generations the snug little commonwealth had been the home of a tenacious conservatism, that clung to old ways and guarded the institutions of the fathers with pious zeal. In no other New England state did the ruling hierarchy maintain so glacial a grip on society. The Revolution of '76 had only ruffled the surface of Connecticut life; it left the social structure quite unchanged. The church retained its unquestioned control of the machinery of the commonwealth; and the church was dominated by a clerical aristocracy, hand in glove with a mercantile aristocracy. The Connecticut yeomanry was extraordinarily docile, content to follow its traditional leaders with implicit faith in their godliness. Those leaders would have been scarcely human if they had not come to regard authority as an inalienable prerogative of their caste, and office-holding as a natural right. To seek to turn a gentleman out of a place to which he had once been chosen, was reckoned by them wickedly Jacobinical. A small interlocking directorate controlled religion, business, and politics. Church, state, and trade were managed by the same little group to the common end of keeping all poachers off their preserves. If politics centered about the church it was because the church was the particular guardian of politics. In self-defense "her preachers were politicians and her politicians preachers," to quote a recent historian.[1] So narrowly oligarchical was the domination of this clerical-mercantile group of politicians, that a contemporary Republican described Connecticut as an "elective despotism or rather elective aristocracy"—a domination that was never seriously threatened till the revolution of 1818 finally unseated the old order. Other commonwealths might yield to the blandishments of the Jacobins, but so long as Timothy Dwight and Governor Trumbull lived Connecticut would keep to her ancient ways.

It was her aloofness more than anything else that held the little commonwealth back from the plunge into the maelstrom of nineteenth century change. Few immigrants came bringing different ideals; the yeomanry followed a familiar round of life; currents of thought that were stirring the pulpits of eastern Massachusetts—suggestions of Arianism that was to be the forerunner of a Unitarian movement destined to create a schism in the traditional church order—did not reach so far as New Haven, and the intellectual life of Connecticut was undisturbed by the inchoate liberalisms of pre-Revolutionary days. Year after year her brightest young men went up to Yale to be trained in the orthodox Calvinism, and departed thence to re-thresh the old straw in every steepled meeting-house in the commonwealth. Yale College was a very citadel of political and theological orthodoxy. It had been founded by devout Calvinists to offset the supposed defection of Harvard, and in the intervening years it had stood loyally to its purpose. No doubt Yale undergraduates were not always models of Calvinistic propriety—as Trumbull plainly suggests in *The Progress of Dulness*; certainly during the early days of the French Revolution many of them were polluted by French atheism;

[1] Purcell, *Connecticut in Transition*, p. 326.

but with the coming of Timothy Dwight to the presidency, all such uncleanness was swept away, and Yale dutifully turned to the pious work of preserving the commonwealth from all democratic innovation. The clergy who gathered for Commencement welcomed the young recruits to their ranks, impressing upon them the sacredness of the existing order with which their lives were to be linked, and dilating upon the social responsibility devolving on the holder of a Yale degree. If every Yale graduate were not a sound Calvinist and a sound Federalist it was no fault of a school that removed an instructor for espousing the Republican faith.

The daily round of life in Connecticut centered in the church to a degree that a later generation has difficulty in comprehending. Society was strait-laced in rigid dogma, and because that dogma was built about the core of total depravity, it imparted a peculiarly unfortunate bias to everyday thought. It is unnecessary here to discuss the familiar five points of Calvinism, but the intimate relations between those doctrines and the social and political faith of Connecticut require a measure of consideration. The Wits were stanch old-school Calvinists, and the robust prejudices that impart to their pronouncement a more than Johnsonian dogmatism, were the sour fruit of their religious faith. It is too often overlooked that historically and practically the doctrine of total depravity, in its larger implications, was quite as much social and political as theological; that it emerged originally as a by-product of social caste and carries in its face the mark of aristocracy; and that it has everywhere been pressed into the service of social inequality. Endowed with high theological sanction, pronounced by the church to be the inscrutable decree of God, it is perhaps the most pernicious doctrine that western civilization has ever given birth to. But pernicious as it is, carrying over into eternity the caste divisions of temporal orders, it has proved too convenient a doctrine to be lightly surrendered by those who find it useful. It wove itself through the entire fabric of social thought in old Connecticut. It provided an authoritative foundation for Connecticut Federalism. In the eyes of men like Timothy Dwight it sufficed to disprove the validity of all democratic aspiration. If the mass of men were outcasts from God—as the doctrine assumed—if they had no title or interest in the prerogatives of the elect, it was a presumption little short of blasphemous to assert that they were competent to manage the temporal affairs of society. Surely it was never intended by the divine wisdom that the sons of Adam should rule the children of God, that the powers of darkness should legislate for the lovers of light. In the background of Calvinistic thought the assumption persisted that the Saints are God's delegated policemen on whom devolves the responsibility of keeping order amongst the sinners. The politician seeking the votes of sinners would not, of course, put it so bluntly; but the doctrine was there implicitly, providing a high sanction for the major premises of New England Federalism. It was this translation into political terms of a decadent dogma that the democratic doctrine of natural rights ran full against in its slow progress through New England. It colored the thinking of the upper class, provided a useful sanction for their strict censorship of society, authorized their rigid monopoly of all political power. It is not easy to understand high Federalists like Jedidiah Morse, who taught the youth of New England in his *Geography* that the clergy was an autocratic balance against democracy, unless they are set against the background of such obsolete dogma.

A special and particular justification of the doctrine, in the opinion of New England conservatives, was provided in the disturbant spread of populistic heresies. The years following the peace of 'eighty-three were an unhappy period for a New England sadly confused by its Shays' Rebellion and its New Hampshire and Rhode Island agrarianism. A motley brood of war chickens were coming home to roost, and there was much unseemly clamor in the New England farmyard. Respectable fowls of the old breed resented the scrambling of newcomers for the best perches, and the nondescript loudly demanded what liberty meant if they were still to have no place to roost. In the opinion of honest gentlemen government was becoming mob-ridden and populistic legislatures were officially profaning the sacred principle that the political state should function in the interests of the well-to-do. Naturally they began to inquire into the causes of such untoward happenings, and took counsel with each other how best to prevent any such in the future. It was quickly agreed that democracy was the mother of the mischief abroad in the land, and that if the ancient virtues of New England were not to go down before the mob, gentlemen must reassert the authority of their traditional stewardship. On them rested the responsibility of saving society from anarchy.

It was from the passions let loose by the profound social readjustments then going forward, that New England Federalism was born, of which the Connecticut Wits were such stalwart exemplars. It was the political philosophy of the Puritan-Yankee, and its principles were derived from the dogmas of Calvinism and the needs of mercantilism. In its beginnings it was a reaction from agrarianism. It had first taken coherence from the menace of Shays' Rebellion, but it was enormously strengthened by the later spread of French Revolutionary doctrines. The appearance of Jacobinism in America put all respectable New England in a panic, and the virulence of dislike increased with the rise of the Democratic Societies. The doctrine of equalitarianism was a stench in the nostrils of all who loved the aristocratic ways of an earlier America, and they watched with growing concern the flocking to New England of old-world enthusiasts for liberty who threw in their lot with the disaffected amongst the native yeomanry. The Irish seem to have been the most offensive equalitarians. A New England gentleman, traveling in Pennsylvania in the 'nineties, wrote home: "I have seen many, very many, Irishmen, and with a few exceptions, they are . . . the most God-provoking Democrats on this side of Hell." [1] And in 1798 Harrison Gray Otis, the Feder-

---

[1] Quoted in Samuel Eliot Morison, *Harrison Gray Otis*, Vol. I, p. 107.

alist boss, wrote: "If some means are not adopted to prevent the indiscriminate admission of wild Irishmen & others to the right of suffrage, there will soon be an end to liberty & property." [1] To prevent, if possible, such an unhappy outcome, the upper classes of New England fell to drilling and organizing all the elements of conservatism for the purpose of a common defense. They wrote and spoke and preached, till the mind of respectable New England was saturated with prejudice. It was a golden age of propaganda. The democratic principle was converted into a bogy to frighten the simple. Such a hideous misshapen imp of darkness, such a vile hag of anarchy had never before been painted for the imagination of honest Yankees to shudder at; and if democracy seemed to them a wild and fearsome thing making ready to destroy their ancient social order, they only believed what the minister preached on the sabbath and the squire asserted on week-days. What headway could the plebeian democrat, very likely in debt, hope to make against the organized respectability of society! He was overwhelmed by a combined *odium theologicum et politicum*.

II

This well-bred composite of old prejudice and present interest, this close alliance of Calvinistic dogma and mercantile profits, provides the background against which the Connecticut Wits must be placed. They were stalwart Federalists of the common New England school, and of this dignified Federalism John Adams was the philosopher, Fisher Ames the orator and pamphleteer, and Timothy Pickering the practical politician. Meticulous in dress, careful to appear well in public, professing to be the special custodian of every public and private virtue, it presented to a credulous constituency the similitude of an angel of light warring against the ancient powers of darkness. It was as the sword of Gideon to smite the Philistines. But for the compre-

[1] *Ibid.*, Vol. i, p. 107.

hension of a more sophisticated generation it may be designated as the tie-wig school of American politics. The phrase sufficiently suggests its aristocratic antecedents. It was the party of the gentry. It was the last marshaling of the eighteenth century against the gathering forces of revolution, a stubborn attempt to bind changing conditions upon an earlier experience, a final effort to retain minority control of a society fast slipping from its grasp. Its affections were engaged to the past, to those static times when successive generations followed in the footsteps of the fathers, content to preserve what had hitherto existed. Aristocratic in taste, it was mercantile in its economic interests. Taking form before the rise of Lowell, industrialism changed the dominant economic interest of New England, it approved the dignified ways of legitimate trade, and disapproved the rising spirit of speculation.

The philosophy of this old-fashioned Federalism is an open book to whoever will take the trouble to turn a few pages of the yellow tracts. In part it derived from certain principles of Locke; in its major premises it was akin to English Whiggery; but its particular form was shaped by the traditional spirit of New England. As amplified in the solid works of John Adams it rested on a few broad principles, which, in his opinion, were as demonstrable as any theorem in Euclid. As a sound eighteenth century realist he discovered the basis of all politics in economics. Natural endowment, he was fond of pointing out, divides men into classes. Since every civilization rests upon exploitation, the strong and capable will rise to power on the backs of the weak, and those who have gained control of the economics of society will in the very nature of things rule society. The principle of aristocracy, hence, is implanted in the constitution of man, and to assume the principle of equality is to fly in the face of nature. From this universal fact of natural social classes arises the perennial problem of government, which is to secure order and justice in a society where few are friendly to their sway. In every society a potential class war for ever impends, and when customary restraints are loosed it breaks forth to find issue either in the anarchy of the mass or in the tyranny of the despot. Thus far Adams was translating Calvinistic dogma into political terms; under the mask of natural aristocracy and the incompetency of democracy, reappear the familiar doctrines of total depravity and the remnant of the Saints. But he was far too thoughtful a student of history and too sincerely concerned for political justice, to deduce from his premises conclusions wholly congenial to New England Federalism. He refused to narrow his philosophy to serve the ends of a particular class. That work fell to the ready hands of Fisher Ames, the idol of respectable New England, the complete embodiment of the prejudices of the tie-wig school. What particular twist Fisher Ames gave to the current philosophy, and from what sources he drew those asperities of conviction that edged his political views, are peculiarly suggestive to one who would understand the acrid dogmatisms of Theodore and Timothy Dwight or the acerbities of Dr. Lemuel Hopkins.

A caustic little gentleman suffering from an aggravated case of the political spleen, was this orator and pamphleteer who won such great renown among his fellow Yankees. Vivacious and intolerant, he nodded his tie-wig dogmatically and pronounced his opinions oracularly. A confirmed realist, he walked the streets of Boston a visible embodiment of a century that was passing. He relished his ample store of prejudices and prided himself on the skill with which he set them forth. If he was not the repository of all political wisdom that he believed himself to be, he could at least give a reason for the faith that was in him. His political philosophy, the sufficiency of which he never doubted, was an amalgam of Puritanism and economics, an ethical adaptation of the stake-in-society principle that conferred a special sanction on the rule of the squirarchy. In the primitive Calvinist-Yankee world, it must be remembered, such political theory as developed was shaped by the theocratic conception of stewardship, by which was meant an authoritative leadership reposing in the best and the wisest, serving the divine purpose and subject to the will of God as revealed in the Bible. Minister and magistrate, in consequence, professed to justify their acts, not by expediency or temporal interest, but by absolute ethical standards. The will of God was acknowledged to be the single source of law. Of that perfect law the minister was the expositor and the magistrate the executive. In the theocracy there was no place for the conception of democracy; the will of the majority was unrecognized; government was simplified to the narrow routine of adjudicating causes in accordance with the divine decrees. But unhappily the business of stewardship proved to be as tempting there as elsewhere. The interests of the steward too often confused themselves with God's, and as the Saints prospered they more and more confounded ethical and economic values, until the primitive doctrine of the stewardship slid over into the later doctrine of the stake-in-society. The sacred rights of property came to be the final objective of law and order, and government was looked upon as an agency to serve the interests of the dominant class.

Of this school of Puritan-Yankee theory Fisher Ames was a convinced disciple. Instinctively aristocratic, a lawyer with a narrow legalistic mind, he interpreted justice in terms of the common law of contract, and stewardship as the prerogative of the well-to-do to police society. The political state he regarded as the particular guardian of vested interests. "But the essence, and almost the quintessence, of good government is," he argued, "to protect property and its rights. When these are protected, there is scarcely any booty left for oppression to seize; the objects and motives to usurpation and tyranny are removed. By securing property, life and liberty can scarcely fail of being secured; where property is safe by rules and principles, there is liberty." [1] In every society, he believed, the persistent enemy of property are the propertyless. The major business of government becomes, therefore, the problem of keeping in due subjection to law and order the dangerous mass of the poor and vicious.

[1] *Phocion, Works,* p. 181.

That the poor in the main are vicious, and the vicious poor, he accepted as social axioms. Hence followed two major principles that he regarded as fundamental in any rational political theory: that government must be energetic to inspire fear in its subjects; that it must be strong to hold in subjection the unruly. The principle of coercive sovereignty he advocated as vehemently as Hamilton. In the doctrine of good will he put no faith. "Government does not subsist by making proselytes to sound reason, or by compromise and arbitration with its members; but by the power of the community compelling the obedience of individuals. If that is not done, who will seek its protection, or fear its vengeance?" [1]

Since in every society it is the improvident mass that is dangerous to the established order, the folly of the democratic principle seemed to him too patent to be worthy of serious consideration. All about him he discovered a selfish and licentious multitude unfriendly to justice, to that sober restraint and respect for rights necessary to a well-ordered society. To permit sovereign power to fall into such hands was to invite anarchy. The mortal disease of all democracies he discovered in their immorality. That the wicked will rule wickedly, seemed to him as plain as way to parish church. A democracy, he used to assert, sooner or later will make every people "thoroughly licentious and corrupt." "The known propensity of a democracy is to licentiousness, which the ambitious call, and the ignorant believe to be liberty." "There is universally a presumption in democracy that promises everything; and at the same time an imbecility that can accomplish nothing, not even preserve itself." [2] The sole security of society he discovered in the wisdom and firmness of the minority; and that minority, in the nature of things, must be the minority of the wealthy. The rich alone may permit themselves the luxury of disinterestedness. The propertied classes alone enjoy the leisure that is prerequisite to culture. Weighted with responsibility, they alone may be

[1] *Lucius Junius Brutus, Works*, p. 5.
[2] *Falkland, Works*, p. 151.

trusted to act as just stewards of society. To preserve New England, gravely threatened by demagogues like Daniel Shays—"bankrupts and sots, who have gambled or slept away their estates"—to prevent the devastating incursions of democracy, to assure the wise rule of a responsible minority, became therefore the master passion of Fisher Ames's life, to which he devoted himself with ever diminishing faith in the honesty of his fellow men. With all the intensity of his nature he hated Jefferson and Madison, "those apostles of the race-track and the cock-pit," and the French romantic philosophy they did so much to spread. But though black pessimism grew upon him in his later years, he discovered certain crumbs of comfort in his own virtue and the virtue of that Federalistic remnant that might even yet save Israel from the democratic despoilers. An unreconstructed Tory of a passing age, he was the most distinguished representative of the tie-wig school of political realism.

III

Of this virtuous remnant the Connecticut Wits were self-confessed exemplars. They were apostles of culture and patriotism to a people in grave danger of being seduced by strange gods. As they looked affectionately upon the pleasant little commonwealth of Connecticut, they feared for the future of this "model of free states." Agrarian dangers threatened from beyond the borders, and within matters were not going well. Her best sons were being drained off by the western frontier; her stagnant agriculture was proving inadequate to the economic needs of the people; a new capitalism was emerging with the development of banking and insurance; shipping and industrialism were making headway, and the towns were growing at the expense of the country. In short Connecticut was at the beginning of profound economic changes that in the next generation were to produce a political revolution. As the members of the little group contemplated these impending changes they were filled with concern. Their loyalties and their interests alike held them to the old order, so far as Connecticut was concerned, but their patriotism went out to the new venture in nationalism. Narrowly provincial in their local affections, they loved to envisage a glorious future for the emancipated states. A fervid patriotism runs through much of their work. The tremendous stir that came with the close of the Revolutionary War touched all the fields of polite culture, and summoned the Wits to activity. The duty of nationalism had been suddenly laid upon the conscience of thoughtful men. It was time for a free people to rid themselves of their colonial subservience to old-world culture. All things were being new-made, why not letters? To throw off the incubus of the past, and create a national literature, dedicated to the new America that was rising, seemed to many a patriotic duty. In this pressing work men wholly diverse in political sympathies joined heartily. The arch conservative, Noah Webster, devoted his life to differentiating the language of independent America from that of monarchical England; and Philip Freneau paused in his labors of berating the Federalists, to lament the intellectual subservience of America to old-world scholarship, as evidenced by its proneness to import British schoolmasters. The result was a premature attempt to write a declaration of intellectual independence, the youthful beginning of a long endeavor that needed more than a hundred years to accomplish.

Yet by a curious turn of the tide the work of emancipation was stopped almost before it was well begun. The extraordinary rise of French liberalism, with the resultant breakup of old orders, produced a panic amongst the cultivated classes of New England, and the imperialistic career of Napoleon threw them back into the arms of England. The earlier patriotism of revolution that was eager to make over all things, gave way to the patriotism of conservatism that desired nothing changed. The term "innovation" came to assume a sinister meaning in respectable ears. "A change, though for the better, is always to be deplored by the generation in which it is effected," asserted Fisher Ames. "Much is lost and more is hazarded." The disintegrating triumphs of political romanticism brought under a cloud the ideals of literary romanticism, and with the resurgence of the conservative spirit literature turned back to earlier models, with the consequent strengthening of the decadent Wit ideal. The romantic school discovered no followers in New England till the War of 1812 dissipated the dun twilight of the old and brought a new century to Boston. Between the years 1807 and 1812, marked by Bryant's *The Embargo* and *Lines to a Waterfowl*, occurred the great transition from the old century to the new, from the Wit ideal to the romantic.

The beginnings of the literary movement that produced the work of the Connecticut group, perhaps are to be found in the quickening interest in polite letters at Yale College in the late 'sixties. When Trumbull and Dwight became tutors there, they joined in the attempt then under way to revive a dead curriculum by the introduction of contemporary English literature, and they exemplified their creative interest by producing original work, Trumbull contributing *The Progress of Dulness* and Dwight *The Conquest of Canaan*. The literary fashion thus introduced was late Augustan, dominated by Goldsmith and Churchill, but supplemented by Pope and Thomson of an earlier generation. The work was consciously imitative. The immediate influence of Goldsmith and Denham on Dwight's *Greenfield Hill* is so evident as scarcely to need comment; *The Deserted Village* and *Cooper's Hill* suggested the theme and indicated the method of treatment. When they essayed greater originality, as became free poets of a republic, their work was likely to issue in a dubious exploitation of biblical themes or in an exuberant patriotism. *The Conquest of Canaan* and *The Vision of Columbus* are representative of the impulses that swayed the minds of the young Wits before the rise of domestic revolution threatened the permanence of the traditional Connecticut order.

But only a portion of the work of the "Wits," after all, was primarily literary. The times soon became too exigent for belletristic philandering, and with the demands of partisanship laid upon them they dedicated their pens to successive causes. The war first summoned them, then the contest with populism, then the cause of the federal union, and finally the acrimonious struggle against French romantic philosophies and the party of Jefferson. Their verse became increasingly militant, and the note of satire rose above the occasional bucolic strains. For the serious business of poetic warfare they sought inspiration from Churchill and the contemporary English satirists. The long party struggle between Whig and Tory in England, and the later contest between Toryism and Jacobinism, produced an abundant crop of scurrilous satire that debased the tone of English letters for half a century. Pope's mean and vindictive *Dunciad* and Butler's *Hudibras* —jaunty octosyllabics providing a brisk variation from the barbed pentameters—had shown that satire could be as useful to a gentleman as the small sword, and the literary dueling of rival partisans went on briskly. In this warfare of the English poetasters the American Wits found their weapons provided for them, and they hastened to follow the overseas example. They seized eagerly upon such works as the *Rolliad*, a contemporary English satire written by bright young politicians in defense of Fox and Sheridan, as suggestive models. They sharpened their quills to a needle point, dipped them in bitter ink, and pricked their opponents as mercilessly as English gentlemen were doing. It is not pleasant writing, much of it is ill done, it runs the scale from crude burlesque to downright blackguardry; but it suggests, as the soberer prose of the times does not, the raw nerves of a generation trying to stave off a rout. To ignore such a work as *The Anarchiad*, on the ground that it is very bad poetry, is to miss what is perhaps the most significant phase of their contribution to a generation perplexed by rival counselors.

The membership of the group was a bit elastic, additions and withdrawals changing the personnel as the years passed. The more important members were John Trumbull, Timothy Dwight, Joel Barlow, Lemuel Hopkins, David Humphreys, Richard Alsop, and Theodore Dwight. To these are frequently added the names of Dr. Elihu Hubbard Smith and Dr. Mason F. Cogswell, who were rather friends than active collaborators. Of the entire group Trumbull was perhaps the most gifted, Barlow the most original, and Timothy Dwight the most prolific. None to be sure loved the pruning knife, and none stinted the ready flow of his verse; yet the indefatigable Timothy managed to outrun the rest. They were all pretty much of an age. The oldest were Trumbull and Dr. Hopkins, both born in 1750; Timothy Dwight and Colonel Humphreys were two years younger; Barlow was born in 1754, Alsop in 1761, and Theodore Dwight, the baby of the group, was born in 1764 and survived till 1846. Collectively they were fairly representative of the oligarchical upper class of the provincial Connecticut society. Timothy Dwight, grandson of Jonathan Edwards, was a minister and president of Yale; Hopkins, Smith, and Cogswell were physicians of high standing, Trumbull and Theodore Dwight were lawyers, Barlow and Humphreys found their way into the diplomatic field, and Alsop was a merchant. They were all comfortably well off and several were wealthy. Alsop was one of the few millionaires of the time; Barlow acquired a fortune in France; and Humphreys late in life established a textile industry incorporated for half a million.

Although their literary work reveals little individual differentiation, they were men of notable ability and striking individuality, who would have made themselves felt in any community. The lesser members were quite as interesting as the major. The caustic tongue of Hopkins and the genial ways of Alsop were as individual as the distinguished manners of Colonel Humphreys, or the brilliant acerbity of Theodore Dwight. Perhaps the most attractive of the entire group was David Humphreys, son of a clergyman of Derby, Connecticut, and personal aide to Washington, whose Yankee provincialisms were worn away by much travel and familiar intercourse with distinguished men in Europe and America. That he was an unusually likable man, as well as capable, is suggested by his extraordinary advancement and the warm affection felt for him by those high in position, as well as by the plump face and easy tie-wig that appear in his portrait. Upwards of fourteen years he spent abroad. His friendships were many and his polished manners seem to have won all hearts. His love of country was great and constant, and his disinterested endeavors to further the well-being of America were widely recognized. He entered Yale in 1767, where he fell in with Trumbull and Dwight. In 1775 at the age of twenty-three he joined the army with the rank of captain. Three years later he was assigned to the staff of General Putnam with the rank of major, and in 1780 he joined Washington's staff with the rank of colonel. He is said to have distinguished himself at the siege of Yorktown and was voted a sword by Congress for gallantry; but as such rewards were commonly political, the distinction must not be taken too seriously. After the peace he went to Paris as Secretary to the Legation under Franklin and Adams, but returned to Hartford on the eve of the outbreak of Shays' Rebellion. He was appointed to the command of a regiment of Western Reserves—raised under authority of Congress to put down domestic disturbances; but on the suppression of the revolt he went to Mount Vernon and remained there for upwards of a year, acting as Washington's aide on the trip to New York where the new President took the oath of office. From 1791 to 1802 he was minister to Lisbon and Madrid, where through the skillful agency of Barlow he secured a treaty with the Barbary states for the release of American captives. In 1795 he married an Englishwoman of considerable fortune. He was elected a fellow of the Royal Society of London, was on intimate terms with the Duc de La Rochefoucauld-Liancourt in France, and when he returned to America soon after the accession of Jefferson, he was one of the distinguished men of his generation of Americans.

The Connecticut to which he returned in 1802 was in the midst of a far-reaching revolution that was silently transforming the traditional order of life. Banking, insurance, and shipping were going forward amazingly, but agriculture was stagnant, the domestic economy prevailed on the farms, there was no important staple for export, and industrialism was in its infancy. It was to a situation becoming acute that Humphreys brought his old-world observations, and the solution on which he settled assumed the double form of

improving agricultural methods and encouraging the production of a staple for manufacturing purposes. While at
Madrid he had interested himself in the quality of wool
grown by the Merino sheep. The Spanish jealously guarded
their flocks against export, but on his quitting his post he
was permitted, in lieu of the usual gift to departing ministers,
to ship one hundred head to his estate in Connecticut. He
at once engaged in the business of breeding, and set on foot
a movement to educate the Connecticut farmers in wool
growing. He established looms to weave a fine woolen cloth,
and when Madison took the oath of office in 1809 he was
dressed in a suit of domestic goods, the coat of which was
provided by Colonel Humphreys. Entering upon the work
as an experiment, he expanded the industry till in 1810
the Humphreysville Manufacturing Company was chartered,
with a capital stock of $500,000. But his major interest, as
was natural to an eighteenth century squire, lay in agriculture. He turned his farm into an experiment station and
in 1817 he founded the Connecticut Agricultural Society.

To further the cause in which he was embarked Humphreys frequently impressed his pen into service. While in
Europe he had often meditated on the beneficent effects of
sober habits of industry, and in particular how such industry
must assure an expanding well-being in America with its
vast potential resources. To inculcate this spirit he had
written several didactic poems—*On the Happiness of America,*
and *On the Future Glory of the United States of America;* but
the completest expression of the ideal to which his later
years were devoted is given in a poem *On the Industry of
the United States of America,* which provides an excellent sum-
mary of his social and economic views. As literature it is
scarcely notable, but as a document of the times it deserves
recalling. An honest and capable man was Colonel David
Humphreys—what we should call today a public-spirited
citizen, devoted to republican freedom and concerned for
the well-being of his fellow Americans. Although he was
one of the first Yankee industrialists to popularize the
philosophy of industrialism, he remained at heart a son of

that older world that honored agriculture above all other callings.[1]

Dr. Lemuel Hopkins, son of a Waterbury farmer, was the most picturesque member of the group, the most characteristically Yankee. Brought up at the plow tail, he received nevertheless an excellent education, and because of a hereditary predisposition to consumption turned to the medical profession. After serving his apprenticeship with a physician at Wallingford he entered upon his practice at Litchfield in 1776. During the Revolution he served for a short time as a volunteer, but soon returned to his lancet and medicine case. In 1784 he removed to Hartford to spend the remainder of his life there as physician and man of letters. In person he was tall, lean, stooping, rawboned, with coarse features and large brilliant eyes. His uncouth appearance and eccentricity of manner made him a striking figure, and his caustic wit made him a redoubtable antagonist. His memory was a marvel to his friends. "He could

---

[1] How greatly he was himself held in honor by his fellows appears from a contemporary *Epitaph* that exhales the sober dignity of the time:

> Oft to departed worth, benignant Heaven
> A power of working miracles has given;
> Insensate Matter's gloomy rest to break,
> Bid dust be eloquent, and marble speak.
> Then e'en this stone, by future patriots read,
> May bid the living emulate the dead:
> Him who in youth was arm'd for civil right
> And shar'd the dangers brav'd in freedom's fight.
> These sylvan plains, where first to life he sprung,
> His sword defended, and his numbers sung.
> In graver years the Statesman's toil he prov'd,
> And serv'd in foreign realms the land he lov'd.
> In age advanc'd, back to that land he bore
> The fleecy treasures of Theria's shore.
> Patron of arts, and guardian of the State;
> Friend to the poor, and favour'd by the great;
> To sum all titles to respect in one—
> Here Humphreys rests—belov'd of Washington!

quote verbatim," writes Kettell, "every writer, medical and literary, that he had ever read." As a physician he stood at the head of the Connecticut profession, both in reputation and in skill. He was one of the founders of the Medical Society of Connecticut, and as a frequent contributor to medical literature he exerted a wide influence on the current practice.

The eccentric Doctor seems to have been as honest as he was outspoken. He was uncompromising in his warfare on all quacks, both medical and political. For a time as a young man he was a disciple of French infidel philosophy, but he cured his mental indisposition by a severe biblical regimen, and having restored himself to the robust health of Calvinistic Christianity, he devoted himself to the work of curing others. He became in consequence a specialist in the treatment of the *Bacillus gallicus*. Kettell is authority for a story that reminds one of his *Epitaph on a Patient Killed by a Cancer Quack*. Calling one day with Dr. Cogswell on a patient in the last stages of consumption, he was shown a packet of "fever powders" reputed to be of marvelous curative potency, got from a well known local quack. "How administered?" the Doctor asked the nurse. "In molasses," she replied. Some molasses was brought and Hopkins took an entire paper of the powders, stirred it in a cup, and disregarding the protestations of the nurse, drank off the whole. Turning to Cogswell, he remarked: "I am going to Coventry today. If I die from this, write on my tombstone—'Here lies Hopkins killed by Grimes.'" A man who was willing to take a chance in order to demonstrate the quackery of a peripatetic dispenser of miraculous powders would have scant respect for any sort of humbug. For all political nostrums not listed in the Federalistic materia medica, he exhibited the same brusque contempt. He would temporize with what he regarded as quackery in government no more than in medicine, and when the Rhode Island legislature passed its paper money act in 1785, and six months later Shays' Rebellion broke out, and mobs were besieging the legislature of New Hampshire, he proposed to speak plainly to the good people of Connecticut on the follies of popular delusions. This would seem to have been the origin of *The Anarchiad*, the most celebrated political satire of the times. It sprang from the indignation of Dr. Hopkins, when, to quote from the poem,

> In visions fair, the scenes of fate unroll,
> And Massachusetts opens on my soul.
> There Chaos, Anarch old, asserts his sway,
> And mobs in myriads blacken all the way.

That Hopkins was chiefly responsible for *The Anarchiad* may be regarded as fairly certain, and that he contributed its most caustic portions may be accepted likewise. Kettell specifically attributed to him the portion entitled "A Plea for Union and the Constitution." The sardonic temper of the Doctor fitted him for virulent satire, and in this bitterest of the productions of the Wits the reins were on the neck of his muse. Some hand he had also in the writing of *The Echo*, but his chief contributions are believed to have taken the form of suggestions which Alsop put into verse. Other works in which he is supposed to have had a share were: *The Political Greenhouse*, done in collaboration with Alsop and Theodore Dwight—Hopkins' contributions being the passages on Tom Thumb and the arrival of Genet; *The Democratiad*, a personal and political satire written for the Philadelphia Jockey Club; and *The Guillotina, or a Democratic Dirge*, written for the *Hartford Courant* as a New Year's offering and printed January 1, 1796. Three other satires attributed to him are: *The Hypocrite's Hope, The Epitaph on a Patient Killed by a Cancer Quack*, and *Verses on General Ethan Allen*. That he had a knack at trenchant satire is sufficiently evident; and that he loved to impale a pretender with a poisoned epithet—that he could not resist the temptation to stick a pin in any bladder he met with, would argue that Dr. Lemuel Hopkins was a man who loved to speak his mind.

To recover the authentic lineaments of Richard Alsop from the faded records, is no easy task. The years have almost wholly obscured a fame that in his lifetime was as bright as a May day, with the poetic fields all abloom. A pleasant-mannered, agreeable gentleman, he seems to have been; with the exception of Trumbull perhaps the wittiest if not the cleverest of the group. He was born in Middletown, where his father, a prosperous merchant in New York, and for five years a member of the Continental Congress, had been born before him, and whither the latter removed upon the occupation of New York City by the British forces. He attended Yale for a time but did not take his degree, having been withdrawn by his father to be bred up in the mercantile business. This was the golden age of Connecticut shipping, and his ventures proved unusually successful. From the coastwise and West Indian traffic he amassed a great fortune. All his life he seems to have been a bookish man. To an excellent knowledge of the classics he added a generous acquaintance with English literature, and he even carried his studies into continental fields, French, Italian and Spanish, extending them so far as to embrace the Scandinavian literatures. A pronounced leaning towards the new gothic spirit that was undermining the Wit ideal in England, is revealed in his translations from *Ossian* and his fondness for the *Eddas*. Pale and exotic as such work might be, it sets him apart from the other members of the group, allying him with certain of the minor Philadelphia poets who followed the gothic fashion more closely. His genial temperament made him a general favorite, and his ample means afforded him abundant leisure. He was warm-hearted, simple and unaffected in manners. His lively imagination and playful humor made him an excellent companion; and his inexhaustible enthusiasm for poetic composition thrust him into every undertaking of the group. The collective reputation of the Wits seems to have owed much to the pen of Alsop. He died at Flatbush, Long Island, in 1815.

His writings have never been collected and much remains unprinted. He was distinctly an amateur in letters and turned to whatever theme caught his fancy. He was an incorrigible imitator of late eighteenth century English modes, and his most ambitious poem, *The Charm of Fancy*—a philosophical work in four cantos, only a fragment of which has been printed—is an echo of Akenside's *Pleasures of the Imagination*. Other ambitious attempts were a versification of Ossian, Habakkuk, and *The Twilight of the Gods*. Like every other poetaster of the times he lamented the death of the first President, his contribution taking the form of a *Monody on the Death of George Washington*. Later he translated from the Italian *The Natural and Civil History of Chili*, and just before his death he edited *The Captivity and Adventures of J. R. Jewett Among the Savages of Nootka Sound*. His most interesting work lay in the field of satire. In collaboration with Theodore Dwight he conceived *The Echo* and wrote considerable portions, in particular Number IX, Governor Hancock's Message on Stage Plays, and Number XX, Jefferson's Inaugural. The playful note of *The Echo*, that sets it sharply apart from the bitter *Anarchiad*, was attributed at the time to Alsop, and the genial burlesques of current provincialisms remain his most important contribution to the verse of New England. It was started to amuse the members of a club at Middletown, and was printed in the *American Mercury*. Cogswell, Smith, and Hopkins had a hand in its composition, but to Alsop and Dwight belongs the major credit.

In his own time Theodore Dwight, lawyer, editor, politician, and poetaster, was one of the most noted of the Wits; but the years have proved ungrateful, and his personality has become as dim as Alsop's. More deeply immersed in practical politics than any other member of the group, he was perhaps the most vehemently Federalistic—if shades may be discerned where all were dipped in the same strong dye. He was born at Northampton, Massachusetts, and took his degree at Yale. A cousin of Timothy Dwight, he studied law in the office of another kinsman, Judge Pierrepont Edwards, an eminent lawyer, high in the ruling aristocracy of Connecticut. From his tutor he seems to have learned little of that political liberalism that afterwards made Edwards the leader of the Connecticut Jeffersonians. He practiced his profession for a time at Hartford, later removing to New York to become a partner in the office of his cousin Aaron Burr; but dissenting from Burr's political opinions, he returned to Hartford. He served in Congress for a year, where he ventured into combat with John Randolph of Roanoke. In after years he devoted much time to newspaper work. In 1810 he founded *The Connecticut Mirror*, later removed to Albany to edit *The Daily Advertiser*, and in 1829 he went to New York City as editor of *The Daily Advertiser* of that place.

Better perhaps than any other member of the group he reveals the close interrelation in Connecticut of religion, politics, and business. He was a director of the Connecticut Bible Society—a religious political organization, the lay trustees of which, according to Purcell, were "Federalist bosses," and which was generally accounted by the opposition as being under clerical control. With his cousin Timothy he was a director of the Eagle Bank, a strong Federalist institution, and was bitterly opposed to the chartering of rival Republican banks. When the Phœnix Bank, a Republican-Episcopalian institution, applied to the legislature for a charter, he denounced it as "the child of intrigue and the mother of Discord." The new banking power was too useful to the ruling Congregational-Federalist party, to be suffered to pass into the hands of the disaffected. Politically Dwight seems to have been under the influence of Fisher Ames, Timothy Pickering, and Harrison Gray Otis. He served as secretary to the Hartford Convention, and later as its historian, publishing its *Journal* in 1833 with a defense of the movement. He was appealed to by Ames to introduce *The Boston Palladium*—the organ of high Federalism in Massachusetts—amongst "the clergy and good men" of Connecticut. He defended the preaching of politics in the pulpit as an excellent means of thwarting the democratic partisans who were seeking to "discredit the ministry, decry religion, and destroy public worship." Democracy was anathema to him, and he agreed with Otis that something must be done to stem the tide of old-world democrats who threatened to submerge the familiar landmarks of New England. Commenting on the spread of republicanism, he attributed to it the decay of religion and morality, and the impending break-up of family ties, exclaiming with somewhat extreme vivacity: "The outlaws of Europe, the fugitives from the pillory, and the gallows, have undertaken to assist our own abandoned citizens, in the pleasing work of destroying Connecticut . . . Can imagination paint anything more dreadful on this side of hell?"

Dwight is reputed to have been a brilliant debater, and his political writings are crisp and vigorous. His chief contributions to the work of the Wits are to be found in *The Echo* and *The Political Greenhouse*. The more biting pieces in the former are generally attributed to him. In the use of Hudibrastic verse he was probably the cleverest of the group if we except Trumbull; his sharp and bitter nature seeming to enjoy inflicting pin-pricks on his enemies. Of high personal integrity he permitted himself an occasional indulgence in humanitarianism, and like his cousin Timothy he was an outspoken opponent of slavery. Yet after all Theodore Dwight was not an important man in spite of his heritage of Edwards blood. The liberalism of his grandfather seems not to have descended to him, for he lived and died an acidulous upholder of the old order, the last of the tie-wig school of Federalists.

IV

Remain for brief comment the three members of the group whose reputations still exhibit some evidences of vitality, and whose work is most largely represented in the present edition. The lesser men have survived collectively, in those collaborations that comment pungently on the ways of the hour. Suggestive as such comments are to the historian, they do not rank high in a history of American *belles-lettres*, and the several individualities of the contributors are so merged that the critic finds difficulty in separating the whole into its parts. But Trumbull, Dwight, and Barlow may be accounted authentic men of letters, whose work is individual enough to be of some little importance in the development of our early literature. The striking variation of the Yankee character, as revealed in the scholarly Trumbull, the vigorously dogmatic Dwight, and the rebelliously energetic Barlow, is an interesting commentary on the fertility of that old New England in breeding men of diverse capacities.

There was the best of Yankee blood in the veins of John Trumbull. Among his kinsmen were the Reverend Benjamin Trumbull, historian of Connecticut, Governor Jonathan Trumbull—Washington's Brother Jonathan—and John Trumbull the painter. On his mother's side he was descended from the vigorous Solomon Stoddard, grandfather of Jonathan Edwards. His father was a scholarly minister, long a trustee of Yale College, at which school the son spent seven years as undergraduate and tutor. He was a precocious youth with a strong love of polite letters, and a praiseworthy desire to achieve literary distinction. Greek and Latin were the toys of his childhood and when he was seven years of age he passed the entrance examination to college. During the period of his tutorship he joined with Dwight and Joseph Howe in the work of overhauling the curriculum, supplementing Lilly's Grammar and Calvin with Pope and Churchill. Like other aspiring youths of the time he dabbled with Spectator papers, practiced his couplets, and eventually produced *The Progress of Dulness*, the cleverest bit of academic verse till then produced in America. At heart Trumbull was thoroughly academic, and nothing would have suited his temperament better than the life of a Yale professor; but the prospects seeming unfavorable, he began to mingle Blackstone with the poets in preparation for his future profession.

He was thus engaged during the middle years of the long dispute with England, the bitter wranglings of which seem not to have penetrated his quiet retreat. But in 1773 he resigned his tutorship to prepare himself further in the law. Removing to Boston he entered the office of John Adams, then rising to prominence as a spokesman of the popular party; and he took lodgings in the house of Caleb Cushing, Speaker of the Massachusetts Assembly. Placed thus at the storm center of provincial politics, he was soon infected with the common dissatisfaction with ministerial policies, and joined himself to the patriotic party. When Adams went to Philadelphia to sit in the Congress, Trumbull withdrew to Hartford, where he established himself. Before quitting Boston he published an *Elegy on the Times*, a political tract that seemed to Adams so useful to the cause that he marked the young poet for future service, and the year following he encouraged the writing of *M'Fingal*, the first part of which appeared in 1775. So great was the prestige that followed its appearance that Trumbull tinkered with it during the next seven years, publishing it finally in its completed form in 1782. The law seems to have been a jealous mistress then as now, and his dreams of further literary work were inadequately realized. He is believed to have had a hand in *The Anarchiad*, and he wrote some minor poems; but he soon drifted into politics, went on the bench, finally removed to Detroit in 1825, and died there at the home of his daughter in 1831, at the age of eighty-one. He had outlived his revolutionary generation, long outlived his literary ambitions, and was pretty much forgotten before he died. His collected works, published in 1820, proved a losing venture for the printer. America was turning romantic and few, it seems, cared to invest in two volumes of echoes.

Trumbull's reputation rests almost exclusively on *M'Fingal*. It was immensely popular in its time. More than thirty pirated editions were issued. It was broadcast by "newspapers, hawkers, pedlars, and petty chapmen," and it served its partisan purpose. The author was complimented by the Marquis de Chastellux on fulfilling all the conditions of burlesque poetry as approved since the days of Homer; but in spite of the indisputable cleverness of some of the lines, it is not a great work. In its final form it is spun out to extreme length, and pretty much swamped by the elaborate machinery on which the author visibly prided himself. Even in the thick of attack Trumbull did not forget his reading, but explains his allusions with meticulous care. He seems, indeed, rather more concerned about the laws of the mock epic than the threatened rights of America. The Scotch Tory hero is a figure so unlike the real Tory—the Olivers and Leonards and Hutchinsons, with their love of power and dignified display—that the caricature loses in effectiveness. Trumbull's patriotism was well bred and unmarked by fierce partisanship. His refined tastes ill fitted him for the turmoil of revolution. The ways of the radical were not lovely in his eyes; the Sons of Liberty with their tar and feather beds were too frequently rough fellows, and although they provided comic material to offset the blunderings of the Squire, they no doubt seemed to him little better than tools of demagogues. Very often this tousle-headed democracy behaved like a mob, and Trumbull in his tie-wig did not approve of mobs.

The more thoughtfully one reads *M'Fingal*, throwing upon it the light of the total career of its author, the more clearly one perceives that John Trumbull was not a rebellious soul, the stuff out of which revolutionaries are made. In the year 1773, while projecting some fresh adventures in the Spectator vein, "he congratulated himself on the fact 'that the ferment of politics' was, as he supposed, 'pretty much subsided,' and that at last the country was to enjoy a 'mild interval from the struggles of patriotism and self-interest, from noise and confusion, Wilkes and liberty.'" He had then no wish for embroilment in civil war. All his life he seems to have suffered from ill health, which probably sapped his militancy and lessened his pugnacity. From this settled mood came a certain detachment that suffered his partisanship to remain cooler than the passions of the time commonly allowed. He could permit himself the luxury of a laugh at the current absurdities; and it is this light-heartedness that made *M'Fingal* so immediately effective. The rollicking burlesque of the Tory argument, the telling *reductio ad absurdum* of their logic, must have tickled the ears of every Whig and provoked many a laugh in obscure chimney-seats. Laughter is the keenest of weapons, and Trumbull's gayety must have opened weak points in the Tory armor that were proof against Freneau's animosity. It was a rare note in those acrimonious times that produced the bitter invective of Jonathan Odell, and one likes Trumbull the better for minding his manners and engaging in the duel like a gentleman. After all this son of Yale had certain characteristics of the intellectual, and if his environment had been more favorable and the law had not claimed him, if he had enjoyed the ample leisure of Alsop, very likely he would have given a better account of the talents that were certainly his. He wrote with ease if not with finish, and he possessed the requisite qualities of a man of letters. A lovable man he seems to have been, but somewhat easy-going and indolent, too easily turned from his purpose; and in consequence his later life failed to realize the expectations of his early years.

Easy-going and lovable are certainly the last adjectives one would think of applying to the massive character of Timothy Dwight—a man armed at all points and walking amongst his fellows with magnificent confidence in his powers, a scholar who put his scythe in every field of knowledge and with flail and bellows separated the clean wheat from the tares, a mighty dialectician who annihilated Hume and Shaftesbury and Voltaire before breakfast and like Hotspur could say, "Fie upon this quiet life, I want work!" A tremendous figure indeed, a great preacher, an authoritative theologian, a distinguished educator—"every inch a college president"—a helpful counselor on any knotty point be it in law or politics or finance or literature or agriculture, a born leader of men, and by way of recreation an inditer of Hebraic epics and huge didactic poems and ample Connecticut pastorals, a confirmed traveler observing the ways of New England and adjoining states and preserving his observations in solid volumes for the enlightenment of others—here was a man to compel the admiration of his fellows and put his stamp upon his age. So vast was the reputation of Timothy Dwight and so many-sided, that after all these years one hesitates to question the superiority of his qualities or insinuate a doubt as to the fineness of this nugget of New England gold.

And yet the more curiously one considers the laborious life of the great President of Yale, the more insistent become one's doubts. It would seem that he impressed his fellow citizens by the completeness with which he measured up to every Connecticut ideal. He was a walking repository of the venerable *status quo*. His commanding presence and authoritative manner, his sonorous eloquence, his forwardness in defense of what few doubted, his vehement threshing of straw long since reduced to chaff, his prodigious labors, his abundant printing, seemed to his open-mouthed contemporaries the authentic seal of greatness. In his presence none had the temerity to deny it. Yet oddly enough that greatness has not survived the ravages of time. It has bated and dwindled sadly. Even Moses Coit Tyler, kindliest and most generous of critics, cannot take the great Timothy quite seriously. The figure would seem to have been blown to excessive dimensions by his admirers. He was certainly not so great as they esteemed him. He was very much smaller indeed, almost amusingly so. Scrutinize this father in Israel closely, remove from the scale the heavy weight of contemporary eulogy, and it appears that Timothy Dwight was not a real prophet, not an authentic voice at all, but only a sonorous echo; extraordinarily lifelike, to be sure, but only an echo. There was no sap of originality in him, no creative energy, but instead the sound of voices long silent, the chatter of a theology long since disintegrating, the authority of a hierarchy already falling into decay, the tongue in short of a dead past.

The intellectual inquisitiveness that gave birth to disintegrating tendencies in the mind of his grandfather Jonathan Edwards, and that made him such a revolutionary force in his time, was wholly lacking in the grandson. Timothy Dwight refused to follow the questioning intellect into unsurveyed fields. He would not meddle with change. His mind was closed as tight as his study windows in January. He read widely in the literature of rationalism, but he read only to refute. Now and then to be sure, certain liberal promptings visited him: he spoke out against slavery; he encouraged the higher education of women. But from such temptations to become a living voice he turned away to follow the main-traveled road of Connecticut prejudice. His eyes were fixed lovingly upon the past, and his fondest dreams for New England hovered about the ideal of a godly church-state which John Cotton had labored to establish and Increase Mather to preserve. Those capable theocrats of earlier days were his spiritual brothers. Two men could scarcely be more like than Timothy Dwight and Increase Mather; their careers ran in parallel lines; each of them was the unmitered pope of his generation, and each owed his extraordinary influence to the same sterling qualities. As ecclesiastical politicians they drew no line between religious and secular affairs, but were prompt with a hand in every affair of the commonwealth. They spoke and wrote with unquestioned authority. They regarded the minister as the responsible leader of society who must not suffer his flock to be led astray. The church was the guardian of morality and the state was its secular arm. The true faith must not be put in jeopardy by unfaith. To Timothy Dwight infidelity and republicanism went hand in hand, and to suffer the commonwealth to fall into the power of the godless meant an end to all religion and morality. To uphold the established order was for him, therefore, the first of Christian duties. A stalwart Federalist, he was a good hater of all Jacobins and a stout defender of the law and order for which he drew the plans and specifications. It was sometimes hinted that he was too much an aristocrat to feel the warmest sympathy for the unprosperous, and there seem to have been grounds for the suspicion. The unprosperous were likely to be republicans, and as he watched them being drawn off to the western frontier, he rejoiced that their voting power was no longer to be feared. Such restless spirits, he pointed out, "are impatient of the restraints of law, religion, and morality; grumble about the taxes, by which Rulers, Ministers, and Schoolmasters are supported . . . We have many troubles even now; but we should have more, if this body of foresters had remained at home."[1] If the disaffected did not like the

---

[1] *Travels*, Vol. ii, p. 458.

way the Congregational-Federalist party managed the good
state of Connecticut, it were a godsend if they should remove
beyond its boundaries.

But it is with the literary work of Timothy Dwight that
we are more immediately concerned, and in all his abundant
output, totaling fourteen volumes and perhaps as much
more in manuscript, the same solid qualities are revealed.
It is the occasional work of a man wanting humor, wit, play-
fulness, artistry, grace, lacking subtlety and suggestiveness,
but with a shrewd common sense, a great vigor, and a certain
grandiose imagination. A sonorous declaimer, he dearly
loved combat and the shock of marshaled argument. He was
always inviting majestic effects. In *The Conquest of Canaan*
he described so many thunderstorms that Trumbull suggested
he ought to furnish a lightning-rod with the poem. Such a
man could not move easily in narrow spaces. An epic was
none too slight to contain his swelling fancies or satisfy his
rhetoric; he walks with huge strides; he is prodigal of images;
one canto finished, other cantos clamor to emerge upon the
page. His ready versification, one often feels, runs like a
water pipe with the faucet off. There is never a pause to
pick or choose; his words flow in an unbroken stream from
his inkwell. Yet even in his amazing copiousness there is
vigor; a well-stocked mind is pouring out the gatherings of
years. When he pauses to give advice—as he was fond of
doing—his abundant sense is worth listening to. The homely
wisdom of his talk to the farmers in the sixth part of *Greenfield Hill* is not unlike Franklin. As a satirist he belongs to
the Churchill school; he is downright, abusive, often violent,
quite lacking the lightness of touch and easy gayety that
run so pleasantly through *M'Fingal*. His *Triumph of Infidelity* is good old-fashioned pulpit-thumping. The spirit of
toleration was withheld from him by his fairy godmother,
and he knows no other way of dealing with those who per-
sist in disagreement after their mistakes have been pointed
out, than the cudgel. In this tremendous poem he lays
about him vigorously. On Hume and Voltaire and Priestley,
and all the host of their followers, his blows fall smartly.

Bloody crowns ought to be plentiful, but—though the Doctor does not seem to know it—most of the blows fall on straw men and none proves to be mortal. On the whole one prefers him in the pastoral mood when he lays aside his ministerial gown, and *Greenfield Hill*, apart from *Travels in New England and New York*, justly remains his most attractive work. But even that is sadly in need of winnowing. A great college president Timothy Dwight is conceded to have been; he was worshiped by his admirers only this side idolatry; but a great thinker, a steadfast friend of truth in whatever garb it might appear, a generous kindly soul loving even publicans and sinners, regardful of others and forgetful of self, he assuredly was not. That he could ever have been looked upon as a great poet, is a fact to be wondered at.

That he should have long associated with the Hartford Wits and collaborated with them in defense of Connecticut Federalism, must have seemed to Joel Barlow in after years the choicest bit of comedy in his varied career. His subsequent adventures led him far from the strait path of Yale orthodoxy. In those ripe later years life had pretty well emptied him of all dogmatisms and taught him the virtue of catholic sympathies. He had become acquainted with diverse philosophies and had observed the ways of alien societies, and from such contacts the horizons of his mind had broadened and his character mellowed. It was a long road that he traveled from New Haven to his Washington *salon*. Born a Connecticut Yankee, he accepted in his youth all the Connecticut conventions, and graduated from Yale with as complete an assortment of respectable opinions as his classmate Noah Webster. An energetic capable fellow, he wanted to get on in life. He wanted to be rich and famous, and he tried many roads that promised to lead to that desirable goal—law, politics, journalism, poetry, psalmody, speculation. Wanting a job he volunteered soon after graduation as chaplain in the army. He had not prepared for the ministry and while preaching somewhat indifferently to ragged soldiers he dreamed of poetic fame, and devoted more time to his couplets than to pious meditation. His abilities discovering no more congenial field for their exercise than writing poetry, he was pretty much at a stand till chance sent him abroad as agent for one of the speculative land-companies that were rising like mushrooms in America. There he found his opportunity. In France, where he established his headquarters, he entered a world of thought vastly different from that of prim little Hartford. It was an extraordinarily stimulating experience into which he threw himself with zest. Eighteen years, from 1787 to 1805, he spent abroad on that first trip, and those years changed the provincial Yankee into one of the most cosmopolitan Americans of his generation. From a member of the Hartford Wits, ardent in defense of the traditional Connecticut order, he had become a citizen of the world, outspoken in defense of the rights of man.

It was this later Barlow, completely new-outfitted by French romantic tailors, that after years remember and that early friends could not forgive. In adopting the Jacobin mode and setting himself to the serious business of thinking, he invited the severe criticism of his former associates; yet nothing in his life was more creditable or marks him more definitely as an open-minded, intelligent man. He was as receptive to new ideas as Timothy Dwight was impervious. He plunged boldly into the maelstrom of speculation then boiling in Europe. He moved in the society of the intellectuals, inquired into the latest political and social theories, turned humanitarian, re-examined his Calvinistic theology in the light of current deism, and became one of the free democratic thinkers swarming in every European capital. He was equally at home in London and Paris, passing long periods of time in both cities. An active member of the Constitutional Society of London, he was intimate with Joseph Priestley, Horne Tooke, and Tom Paine, sympathized with every liberal movement and offered his pen to the cause of a freer England. His *Advice to the Privileged Orders* was eulogized by Fox on the floor of Commons, and the Pitt ministry was moved to suppress the work and proscribe the author. Thereupon Barlow went into hiding. There seems to have been considerable provocation for the government's action.

"It is safe to say," remarks his biographer, "that no political work of the day created so wide an interest or was so extensively read." With Paine and Barlow both loose in England there was need of the goverment looking to its fences. In 1793 he was made a citizen of France. His French career was not unlike Paine's, whom he resembled in many ways. He had much of the latter's genius for publicity and skill in propaganda, and his career was a great stimulus to radicals at home. He risked his life to serve the American prisoners in Africa and by his skill and address eventually freed them. In the meantime he had not neglected his private affairs. He made a fortune in the French funds, which he increased by able merchandising. He had come to his goal by distant roads, and on his return to America in 1805 he took up his abode at Washington, creating a delightful country seat on the outskirts of the capital where he maintained a *salon* for American liberals. Unlike Colonel Humphreys he felt no inclinations toward Connecticut; the old ties were broken past mending; the French Jacobin could not fit into the grooves of Hartford Federalism. Six years later he was impressed a second time into the diplomatic service, was sent to France on a difficult mission, followed Napoleon, then on the Russian campaign, was caught in the break-up of the grand army, suffered exposure, contracted pneumonia, and died in a village near Cracow in Poland—a fate which honest Federalists regarded as amply merited by his vicious principles.

The later reputation of Barlow has been far less than his services warranted or his solid merits deserved. His admirable prose writings have been forgotten and the *Columbiad* returns always to plague him. The common detraction of all Jacobins and republicans fell heavily on so conspicuous a head. "It is simply impossible," says his biographer, "for the historian of Federal proclivities and environment, to do justice to the great leaders of Republicanism in America." Barlow paid a heavy price for his intellectual independence. Thus John Adams, who had suffered many a sharp thrust from him, wrote to Washington, "Tom Paine is not a more worthless

fellow." Of the Yale dislike Barlow was well aware, for he
once confessed that he would have presented the school with
some needed chemical apparatus but he "supposed that,
coming from him, the college authorities would make a bonfire of them in the college yard." [1]   Yet it is hard for a later
generation to discover wherein lay the viciousness of his
principles. A warm-hearted humanitarian, he was concerned
always for the common well-being. The two major passions
of his life were freedom and education. During the last
years at Washington he was ardently promoting a plan for a
great national university at the seat of government, and had
he lived ten years longer his wide influence would probably
have accomplished it. His sins would seem to have been no
other than an open break with the Calvinism and Federalism
of the Connecticut oligarchy—somewhat slender grounds on
which to pillory him as an infidel and a scalawag.

The social foundation of Barlow's political philosophy is
lucidly presented in the *Advice to the Privileged Orders*, partly
reprinted in this edition; a work that deserves a place beside
Paine's *Rights of Man* as a great document of the times. It
does too much credit to American letters to be suffered to
lie buried with a dead partisanship. It is warm with the
humanitarian enthusiasm that was a common heritage from
the Physiocratic school of social thinkers. Two suggestive
ideas lie at the base of his thinking: the doctrine of the *res-
publica*, and the doctrine of social responsibility for individual
well-being. The former, given wide currency by the *Rights
of Man*, resulted from the imposition of social conscience on
abstract political theory, out of which was derived a new
conception of the duty and function of the political state—
that the state must become an agent of the whole rather than
the tool of a class, and that its true concern is the *public
thing*, safeguarding the social heritage as a common asset to
succeeding generations; the latter is a more specific inquiry
into the relation of the political state to the individual
citizen—its responsibility as the guardian of the social heri-

---

[1] Purcell, *Connecticut in Transition*, p. 27.

tage for the waste of individual lives through vice and incompetence, a waste that a rational social order would largely eradicate. Barlow flatly denies that the primary function of the state is the protection of property interests; its true end lies in the securing of justice. But justice without equal opportunity is a mockery; and equal opportunity is impossible unless the individual shall be equipped to live on an equal footing with his fellows. Hence the fine flower of political justice is discovered in education; in that generous provision for the young and the weak that shall equip them to become free members of the commonwealth. Like Paine's *Agrarian Justice*, the *Advice to the Privileged Orders* is an extraordinarily modern work, far more comprehensible today than when it was written. That the "State has no right to punish a man, to whom it has given no previous instruction," and that "She ought not only to instruct him in the artificial laws by which property is secured, but in the artificial industry by which it is obtained," are doctrines that seem far less preposterous to us than they seemed to Timothy Dwight. The President of Yale College was greatly troubled about Calvinistic sin; Joel Barlow was greatly troubled about social injustice; in that difference is measured the distance the latter had traveled in company with the French republicans.

A good French radical in economics and politics, Barlow was no innovator in polite literature. He pulled himself out of many Connecticut provincialisms but he stuck fast in the bog of provincial poetry. It has long been the fashion to make merry over *The Columbiad*, and there is only too patent a reason for it. To criticize it is a work of supererogation. The appeal of "the grand style" was too much for him. Some explanation doubtless is to be found in the fact that he was working over an earlier poem done in the days of an ebullient patriotism. It was a mistake to return to it, for the heroic note in the hands of a political pamphleteer must play havoc with it. What he now attempted, in the light of his European experience, was to embody in the narrative suitable political ideas, transforming *The Vision of Columbus* into an epic glorifying the great republican experiment. His purpose is set forth in the preface. The

real object of the poem is to inculcate the love of national liberty, and to discountenance the deleterious passion for violence and war; to show that on the basis of republican principle all good morals, as well as good government and hopes of permanent peace, must be founded; and to convince the student in political science, that the theoretical question of the future advancement of human society, till states as well as individuals arrive at universal civilization, is held in dispute and still unsettled only because we have had too little experience of organized liberty in the government of nations, to have well considered its effects.

Diverse politics incline to diverse literary judgments, and the critics are not yet done with Joel Barlow. If he was not a great man, he was at least capable, open-minded, with a sensitive social conscience—certainly the most interesting and original of the Connecticut Wits. Injustice has long been done him by overlooking his picturesque career and restricting his introduction to posterity to a few lines from *Hasty Pudding*. To make a mush of so honest a thinker, to ignore his contribution to republican America, is to impose too great a penalty upon his defection from Connecticut respectability. He suffered quite enough in his lifetime. In the thick of his revolutionary struggles his wife begged him "to go home and be respectable"; but it was not in the ardent nature of Joel Barlow to listen to such counsel of timidity. He was in too deep to go back, and so while Timothy Dwight was gathering laurels from every bush in Connecticut, this apostle of humanitarianism, this apostate from Calvinistic Federalism, was content to remain a byword and a shaking of the head in the villages of his native commonwealth. For all which perhaps, the Washington *salon* and the intimate association with Jefferson may have served as recompense. Better society could not be found even in Hartford.

VERNON LOUIS PARRINGTON

NOTE ON THE TEXTS

The several texts reproduced in the present edition have been taken from the following sources:

Alsop, Richard. From *American Poems*, edited by E. H. Smith, 1793.

Barlow, Joel. *The Columbiad*, from the edition of 1807; *Hasty Pudding*, mainly from the text given in Todd's *Life and Letters of Joel Barlow*, reprinted from the original manuscript; *The Conspiracy of Kings*, from the text in *The Columbian Muse*, 1794; *Advice to the Privileged Orders*, from the second (London) edition of 1796.

Dwight, Timothy. *The Conquest of Canaan*, from the edition of 1785; *Greenfield Hill*, from the edition of 1794; *The Triumph of Infidelity*, from the edition of 1797; the short poems, from the anthologies of Elihu H. Smith, Matthew Carey, and Charles W. Everest.

Hopkins, Lemuel. *Psalm CXXXVII*, from Duyckinck (given under the discussion of Barlow); *The Hypocrite's Hope* and *Epitaph*, from *The Columbian Muse*.

Humphreys, David. From his *Miscellaneous Works*, New York, 1804.

Trumbull, John. From the Hartford edition of 1820.

The Anarchiad. From the text given by Luther G. Riggs in the New Haven edition of 1861. (The original newspaper text has not been collated.)

The Echo. From the edition of 1807.

I acknowledge with pleasure my indebtedness to the librarians of Brown University, Harvard University, and the University of Chicago, for the courteous loan of rare volumes used in the preparation of the present edition of *The Connecticut Wits*; and to Mr. James E. Ernst of the University of Washington, who is largely responsible for the text and bibliography.

V. L. P.

Seattle, 16 July, 1925.

SELECTED READING LIST

Some comment on the Wits, usually rather stereotyped, is given in the several histories of American literature. The *Cambridge History of American Literature* includes a fairly satisfactory bibliography, but so scattered that it seems well to group the material in more convenient form, supplementing it with additional titles.

I. GENERAL

For the background of Connecticut in the later years of the eighteenth century, the excellent study by Richard J. Purcell, *Connecticut in Transition: 1775–1818*, Washington, American Historical Association, 1918, provides sufficient data.

King, Winnifred B. "The First American Satirists," *Conn. Mag.*, Vol. X (1906), p. 403.

Otis, William Bradley. *American Verse: 1625–1807.* 1900.

Patterson, Samuel White. *The Spirit of the American Revolution as Revealed in the Poetry of the Period.* Boston, n. d. (1915)

Sheldon, F. "Pleiades of Connecticut," *Atlantic Monthly*, Vol. XV (1865), p. 187.

Wright, R. W. "The Poets and Poetry of the Revolution," *Papers of the New Haven Colony Historical Society*, Vol. II.

II. SPECIAL

Dwight, Sereno E. and William Theodore. "Memoir of Timothy Dwight," *Theology Explained and Defended.* 1846.

Francis, Dr. *A Sketch of the Character of Theodore Dwight.* New York Historical Society. 1846.

Marble, Mrs. Annie Russell. *Heralds of American Literature.* University of Chicago. 1907.

Sprague, William B. *Life of Timothy Dwight.* Library of American Biography, Sparks, Second Series, Vol. IV. Boston, 1845.

—— "A Sketch of the Life of Timothy Dwight," *Annals of the American Pulpit*, Vol. II. 1859.

Todd, Charles Burr. *Life and Letters of Joel Barlow.* 1886.

Trumbull, James Hammond. *The Origin of M'Fingal*. Morrisiana, 1868.

Tyler, Moses Coit. *Three Men of Letters* (Dwight and Barlow). 1895.

III. ANTHOLOGIES

The American Museum or Repository of Ancient and Modern Fugitive Pieces. Matthew Carey, Philadelphia, 1787–1792.

The Columbian Muse. 1794. (Selections from Alsop, Hopkins, Humphreys, Dwight, Trumbull, Barlow.)

Duyckinck, Evert A. and George L. *Cyclopedia of American Literature*. Vol. I. Philadelphia, 1855.

Everest, Charles W. *The Poets of Connecticut*. 3 vols. 1873.

Griswold, Rufus W. *Poets and Poetry of America*. Philadelphia, 1842.

———— "Satirical, Dramatic and Other Poems of Public Affairs Written During the Revolution," *Curiosities of American Literature*. 1847.

Hagen, J. C. *Ballads of the Revolution*. 1866.

Kettell, S. *Specimens of American Poetry*. 3 vols. Boston, 1829.

McCarty, William. *Songs, Odes, and Other Poems on National Subjects*. 3 vols. 1842.

Moore, Frank. *Songs and Ballads of the American Revolution*. 1856.

Smith, Elihu Hubbard. *American Poems, Selected and Original*. Litchfield, n. d. (1793).

IV. RICHARD ALSOP (1751–1816)

The Conquest of Scandinavia. Unfinished. Published in part by E. H. Smith. Litchfield, 1793.

Versification of Ossian. A passage from the Fifth Book of Temora. Litchfield, 1793.

The Twilight of the Gods, or Destruction of the World. From the Edda. Runic poetry. Published by E. H. Smith. Litchfield, 1793.

A Poem: Sacred to the Memory of George Washington. Hartford, 1800.

The Enchanted Lake of the Fairy Morgana. 1808.

Captivity and Adventures of J. R. Jewett among the Savages of Nootka Sound. Edited by R. Alsop. 1815.

The Charms of Fancy: A Poem in Four Cantos. 1856.

Other works: *The Natural and Civil History of Chili*, from the Italian of Molina; *Hymn to Peace; Inscription for a Family Tomb*.

SELECTED READING LIST

V. JOEL BARLOW (1754–1812)

(Dates do not in all cases refer to the first edition.)

The Prospect of Peace. A political composition, delivered in Yale College, at the examination of the candidate for the degree of Bachelor of Arts, July 23, 1778. New Haven, 1778.

Elegy on the late Honorable Titus Hosmer, Esq. Hartford, 1780.

A Poem Spoken at Commencement of Yale College. Hartford, 1781.

Imitation of the Psalms of David, translated by Dr. Isaac Watts, corrected and enlarged by Joel Barlow. To which is added a collection of hymns. The whole applied to the state of the Christian Church and religion in general. Glasgow, 1786.

An Oration delivered at the North Church, Hartford, at the meeting of the Connecticut Society of Cincinnati, July 4, 1787, etc. Hartford, 1787.

The Vision of Columbus: A Poem in Nine Books. Hartford, 1787. London, 1787.

A Letter to the National Convention of France on the defence of the Constitution of 1791, and, the extent of the amendment which ought to be made. London, 1792.

Advice to the Privileged Orders in the several States of Europe. Resulting from the necessity and propriety of a general revolution in the principles of Governments. London, 1792, 1796.

The Conspiracy of Kings: A Poem Addressed to the Inhabitants of Europe from another Quarter of the Globe. London, 1792.

Preface and Notes to the fifth edition of Trumbull's *M'Fingal.* London, 1792.

The Hasty-Pudding: A Poem in Three Cantos. Written in Chambery, in Savoy, January, 1793. New York, 1796; Salem, 1799; Stockbridge, 1799.

A Letter Addressed to the People of Piedmont on the advantages of the French Revolution, and the necessity of adopting its principles in Italy. Translated from the French by the author. 1793.

Letters from Paris to the Citizens of the United States on the subject of the fallacy heretofore pursued by their Government relative to the commercial intercourse with England and France. London, 1800.

Memoir on Certain Principles of Public Maritime Law. Written for the French Government. London, 1800.

View on the Public Debt, Receipts and Expenditures of the United States. London, 1800.

Letter to Henry Gregoire, Count of Capri and Member of the Institute of France, in reply to his letter on the Columbiad. Washington, 1802.

The Columbiad: A Poem. Portrait and ten steel plates. Philadelphia, 1807. The same with index, royal 8vo. London, 1809.

The Excellency of the British Constitution, etc., consisting of certain extracts from the writings of Joel Barlow. London, n. d.

Other works: *Ruins of Empire*, translated from the French of Volney; *Propositions for a National Academy; Poem in commemoration of his wedding day*, January 26, 1793; "To My Wife"; Anniversary Poems, 1800, 1801, 1802 (in *Life and Letters of Joel Barlow*, by C. B. Todd, 1886); "To a Young Lady" (in *Life and Letters*); *Fame, Let thy Trumpet Sound.*

VI. THEODORE DWIGHT (1764–1846)

Ode to Conscience. Published by E. H. Smith, Litchfield, 1793.

Oration before the Connecticut Cincinnati, July 4, 1792.

Oration delivered at Hartford, July 4, 1798. (With the above.)

Oration delivered at New Haven, July 7, 1801, before the Society of Cincinnati. Hartford, 1801.

New Year's Verse. For the *Connecticut Mirror.* Before and during the War of 1812.

Sketches of the Scenery and Manners in the United States. 1829.

History of the Hartford Convention. Hartford, 1833.

The Northern Traveller, and Northern Tour, with the Routes to the Springs, Niagara, Quebec, and the Coal Mines of Pennsylvania; also Tour of New England. Fifth edition, 1834.

Character of Thomas Jefferson, as Exhibited in his own Writings. Boston, 1839.

History of Connecticut, from the first Settlement to the Present Time. 1841.

Outline of "Life and Writings" by Theodore Dwight. New York Historical Society. 1846.

Political Articles: As journalist and editor of the *Connecticut Courant* and the *Connecticut Mirror.*

VII. TIMOTHY DWIGHT (1752–1817)

Essays in imitation of *The Spectator.* In Boston and New Haven newspapers, 1769–1770.

History, Eloquence and Poetry of the Bible: A Master's Dissertation delivered at the Public Commencement at New Haven, 1772. New Haven, 1772.

America: or, a Poem on the Settlement of the British Colonies, addressed to the Friends of Freedom and their Country. By a Gentleman educated at Yale College. (Anonymous. Only known copy in Boston Public Library. Ascribed to Dwight by Griswold, but doubtful.) New Haven, n. d.

Columbia, Columbia. 1777–1778 (?).

Epistle to Colonel David Humphreys. Greenfield, 1785.

The Critics: A Fable. Written 1785; appeared in *The Gazette of the United States,* July 13, 1791.

The Conquest of Canaan: A Poem in Eleven Books. Hartford, 1785.

The Triumph of Infidelity: A Poem: 1788. (Printed in 1797 without name of author or place.)

Address of the Genius of Columbus: To the Members of the Continental Congress. 1788 (?).

A Hymn, sung at the Public Exhibition of the Scholars belonging to the Academy at Greenfield. 1788.

The Genuineness and Authenticity of the New Testament. 1793. Published as part of *Greenfield Hill.* 1794.

Greenfield Hill: A Poem in Seven Parts. 1794.

The Nature and Danger of the Infidel Philosophy, Exhibited in Two Discourses Addressed to the Candidates for the Baccalaureate in Yale College. New Haven, 1798.

The Duty of Americans at the Present Crisis, etc. New Haven, 1798.

Discourse on the character of George Washington, Esq. At the request of the citizens of New Haven . . . New Haven, 1800.

A Discourse on the Events of the Last Century, Delivered in the Brick Church in New Haven . . . New Haven, 1801.

The Psalms of David, Imitated in the Language of the New Testament, and Applied to the Christian Use and Worship. By I. Watts, D.D. A new Edition, etc. By Timothy Dwight . . . At the Request of the General Association of Connecticut. To the Psalms is added a collection of Hymns. Hartford, 1801.

Statistical Account of the City of New Haven. New Haven, 1811.

The Dignity and Excellence of the Gospel, delivered in New Haven, April 8, 1812. New York, 1812.

Sermon at Yale on Public Fast, July 23, 1812. New Haven, 1812.

Sermon delivered, Boston Sept. 16, 1813, before the American Board of Commissioners for Foreign Missions. Boston, 1813.

Decisions of Questions, discussed by the Senior Class in Yale College in 1813–1814. 1833.

Observations on the Language. Published in the Memoirs of the Connecticut Academy of Arts and Sciences, Vol. I, Part IV. New Haven, 1816.

Essay on Light. Published in the Memoirs of the Connecticut Academy of Arts and Sciences, Vol. I, Part IV. New Haven, 1816.

Theology Explained and Defended in a Course of 173 Sermons. In five volumes. Middletown, 1818; London, 1819. With memoir by his sons, Sereno E. Dwight and William Theodore Dwight. 1846.

Travels in New England and New York: 1796–1815. Four volumes. New Haven, 1821–1822; London, 1823.

Sermons. Two volumes. Edinburgh, 1828.

Other works: *The Trial of Faith; The Seasons Moralized; A Song; Message of Mordecai to Esther.*

VIII. LEMUEL HOPKINS (1750–1808)

Psalm CXXXVII. Said to have been written at the request of Barlow. 1785.

New Year's Verse for the Year 1794. 1795.

The Democratiad: A Poem in Retaliation for the Philadelphia Jockey Club. Philadelphia, 1795.

The Guillotina; or, a Democratic Dirge. A poem by the author of the Democratiad. New Year's poem for January 1, 1796. Philadelphia, n. d. (1796).

The Hypocrite's Hope.

Epitaph on a Patient Killed by a Cancer Quack.

Verses on General Ethan Allen.

IX. DAVID HUMPHREYS (1753–1818)

Miscellaneous Works. Portsmouth, 1790; New York, 1790; New York, 1804.

A Poem Addressed to the Armies of the United States of America. By a Gentleman of the Army. New Haven, 1780.

A Poem on the Happiness of America. Addressed to the Citizens of the United States. London, 1780; Hartford, 1780; New Haven, 1780; Albany, n. d.

The Glory of America; or, Peace Triumphant over War: A Poem. Philadelphia, 1783.

A Poem on Industry. Addressed to the Citizens of the United States of America. Philadelphia, 1783.

An Epistle to Dr. Dwight. 1784.

An Essay on the Life of the Honourable Major-General Israel Putnam. Addressed to the State Society of the Cincinnati in Connecticut, and published by their order. 1788.

An Oration on the Political Situation of the United States of America in the Year 1789. 1789.

Dissertation on the Breed of Spanish Sheep called Merino. 1802.

A Valedictory Address before the Connecticut Cincinnati, Hartford, July 4, 1804, at the dissolution of the Society. Boston, 1804.

Discourse on the Agriculture of the State of Connecticut and the means of making it more Beneficial to the State. New Haven, 1816.

X. JOHN TRUMBULL (1750–1831)

The Poetical Works. With Memoir of the Author. 2 vols. Hartford, 1820.

The Poetical Works. Reprinted from the 1820 edition by the Andiron Club of New York City, 1922.

Prospect of the Future Glory of America. Conclusion of an oration at the public commencement at Yale College, September 12, 1770.

An Elegy on the Death of Mr. Buckingham St. John, Tutor at Yale College, etc. New York, n. d. (1771?).

An Elegy: on the vanity of youthful Expectations. 1771.

Advice to Ladies of a Certain Age. 1771.

A Fable: the Owl and the Sparrow. 1772.

The Progress of Dulness: Part I. n. p. 1772. Exeter, 1794.

The Progress of Dulness: Part II. n. p. 1773.

The Progress of Dulness: Part III. New Haven, 1773.

The Prophecy of Balaam. 1773.

Ode to Sleep. 1773.

The Destruction of Babylon: an Imitation. 1774.

A Fable: To a Young Lady. 1774.

An Elegy on the Times. Boston, 1774; New Haven, 1775.

M'Fingal: A Modern Epic Poem. Canto I. Philadelphia, 1775. Includes what is now Cantos I and II, 1776, London, 1776.

M'Fingal: A Modern Epic Poem in Four Cantos. Hartford, 1782 (first complete edition); Boston, 1785; Philadelphia, 1791; London, 1792, 1793; New York, 1795; Boston, 1799; Baltimore, 1812; Augusta, 1813; Hallowell, 1813.

M'Fingal: An Epic Poem. With introduction by B. J. Lossing. 1860, 1864, 1881.

The Mischief of Legislative Caucuses exposed in an address to the people of Connecticut. Hartford, 1819.

XI. WORKS IN COLLABORATION

The Anarchiad: A Poem on the Restoration of Chaos and Substantial Night. Appeared in the *New Haven Gazette* and *Connecticut Magazine,* in a series of twelve papers during the years 1786–1787. By Barlow, Hopkins, Humphreys, and Trumbull. Collected and published by Luther G. Riggs, with introduction, New Haven, 1861.

The Echo, with Other Poems. A political, satirical poem in twenty numbers. By Alsop and Theodore Dwight, with the aid of Hopkins, Cogswell, and Smith. Appeared in the *American Mercury* in the years from 1791 to 1805. Collected and published, 1807.

The Political Greenhouse for the Year 1798. By Alsop, Theodore Dwight, and Hopkins. Hartford, 1799.

I

JOHN TRUMBULL (1750–1831)

THE PROGRESS OF DULNESS

PART I

OR THE ADVENTURES OF TOM BRAINLESS

"OUR TOM has grown a sturdy boy;
His progress fills my heart with joy;
A steady soul, that yields to rule,
And quite ingenious too, at school.
Our master says, (I'm sure he's right,)
There's not a lad in town so bright.
He'll cypher bravely, write and read,
And say his catechism and creed,
And scorns to hesitate or falter
In Primer, Spelling-book or Psalter.
Hard work indeed, he does not love it;
His genius is too much above it.
Give him a good substantial teacher,
I'll lay he'd make a special preacher.
I've loved good learning all my life;
We'll send the lad to college, wife."
     Thus sway'd by fond and sightless passion,
His parents hold a consultation;
If on their couch, or round their fire,
I need not tell, nor you enquire.
     The point's agreed; the boy well pleased,
From country cares and labor eased;
No more to rise by break of day
To drive home cows, or deal out hay;
To work no more in snow or hail,
And blow his fingers o'er the flail,
Or mid the toils of harvest sweat
Beneath the summer's sultry heat,
Serene, he bids the farm, good-bye,
And quits the plough without a sigh.

3

Propitious to their constant friend,
The powers of idleness attend.

   So to the priest in form he goes,
Prepared to study and to doze.
The parson, in his youth before,
Had run the same dull progress o'er;
His sole concern to see with care
His church and farm in good repair.
His skill in tongues, that once he knew,
Had bid him long, a last adieu;
Away his Latin rules had fled,
And Greek had vanish'd from his head.

   Then view our youth with grammar teazing,
Untaught in meaning, sense or reason;
Of knowledge e'er he gain his fill, he
Must diet long on husks of Lily,[1]
Drudge on for weary months in vain,
By mem'ry's strength, and dint of brain;
From thence to murd'ring Virgil's verse,
And construing Tully into farce,
Or lab'ring with his grave preceptor,
In Greek to blunder o'er a chapter.
The Latin Testament affords
The needed help of ready words;
At hand the Dictionary laid,
Gives up its page in frequent aid;
Hard by, the Lexicon and Grammar,
Those helps of mem'ry when they stammer;
The lesson's short; the priest contented;
His task to hear is sooner ended.
He lets him mind his own concerns,
Then tells his parents how he learns.

   Two years thus spent in gathering knowledge,
The lad sets forth t'unlade at college,
While down his sire and priest attend him,
To introduce and recommend him;

---

[1] Lily's was the only Latin Grammar then in use.

Or if detain'd, a letter's sent
Of much apocryphal content,
To set him forth, how dull soever,
As very learn'd and very clever;
A genius of the first emission,
With burning love for erudition;
So studious he'll outwatch the moon
And think the planets set too soon.
He had but little time to fit in;
Examination too must frighten.
Depend upon't he must do well,
He knows much more than he can tell;
Admit him, and in little space
He'll beat his rivals in the race;
His father's incomes are but small,
He comes now, if he come at all.

    So said, so done, at college now
He enters well, no matter how;
New scenes awhile his fancy please,
But all must yield to love of ease.
In the same round condemn'd each day,
To study, read, recite and pray;
To make his hours of business double—
He can't endure th' increasing trouble;
And finds at length, as times grow pressing,
All plagues are easier than his lesson.
With sleepy eyes and count'nance heavy,
With much excuse of *non paravi*,[1]
Much absence, *tardes* and *egresses*,
The college-evil on him seizes.
Then ev'ry book, which ought to please,
Stirs up the seeds of dire disease;
Greek spoils his eyes, the print's so fine,
Grown dim with study, or with wine;

[1] *Non paravi*, I have not prepared for recitation—an excuse commonly given; *tardes* and *egresses*, were terms used at college, for coming in late and going out before the conclusion of the service.

Of Tully's latin much afraid,
Each page, he calls the doctor's aid;
While geometry, with lines so crooked,
Sprains all his wits to overlook it.
His sickness puts on every name,
Its cause and uses still the same;
'Tis tooth-ache, cholic, gout or stone,
With phases various as the moon;
But though through all the body spread,
Still makes its cap'tal seat, the head.
In all diseases, 'tis expected,
The weakest parts be most infected.
    Kind head-ache hail! thou blest disease,
The friend of idleness and ease;
Who mid the still and dreary bound
Where college walls her sons surround,
In spite of fears, in justice' spite,
Assumest o'er laws dispensing right,
Sett'st from his task the blunderer free,
Excused by dulness and by thee.
The vot'ries bid a bold defiance
To all the calls and threats of science,
Slight learning human and divine,
And hear no prayers, and fear no fine.
    And yet how oft the studious gain,
The dulness of a letter'd brain;
Despising such low things the while,
As English grammar, phrase and style;
Despising ev'ry nicer art,
That aids the tongue, or mends the heart;
Read ancient authors o'er in vain,
Nor taste one beauty they contain;
Humbly on trust accept the sense,
But deal for words at vast expense;
Search well how every term must vary
From Lexicon to Dictionary;
And plodding on in one dull tone,
Gain ancient tongues and lose their own,

Bid every graceful charm defiance,
And woo the skeleton of science.
  Come ye, who finer arts despise,
And scoff at verse as heathen lies;
In all the pride of dulness rage
At Pope, or Milton's deathless page;
Or stung by truth's deep-searching line,
Rave ev'n at rhymes as low as mine;
Say ye, who boast the name of wise,
Wherein substantial learning lies.
Is it, superb in classic lore,
To speak what Homer spoke before,
To write the language Tully wrote,
The style, the cadence and the note?
Is there a charm in sounds of Greek,
No language else can learn to speak;
That cures distemper'd brains at once,
Like Pliny's rhymes for broken bones?
Is there a spirit found in Latin,
That must evap'rate in translating?
And say are sense and genius bound
To any vehicles of sound?
Can knowledge never reach the brains,
Unless convey'd in ancient strains?
While Homer sets before your eyes
Achilles' rage, Ulysses' lies,
Th' amours of Jove in masquerade,
And Mars entrapp'd by Phœbus' aid;
While Virgil sings, in verses grave,
His lovers meeting in a cave,
His ships turn'd nymphs, in pagan fables,
And how the Trojans eat their tables;
While half this learning but displays
The follies of the former days;
And for our linguists, fairly try them,
A tutor'd parrot might defy them.
  Go to the vulgar—'tis decreed,
There you must preach and write or plead;

Broach every curious Latin phrase
From Tully down to Lily's days:
All this your hearers have no share in,
Bate but their laughing and their staring.
Interpreters must pass between,
To let them know a word you mean.

    Yet could you reach that lofty tongue
Which Plato wrote and Homer sung;
Or ape the Latin verse and scanning,
Like Vida, Cowley or Buchanan;
Or bear ten phrase-books in your head;
Yet know, these languages are dead,
And nothing, e'er, by death, was seen
Improved in beauty, strength or mien,
Whether the sexton use his spade,
Or sorcerer wake the parted shade.
Think how would Tully stare or smile
At these wan spectres of his style,
Or Horace in his jovial way
Ask what these babblers mean to say.

    Let modern Logic next arise
With newborn light to glad your eyes,
Enthroned on high in Reason's chair,
Usurp her name, assume her air,
Give laws, to think with quaint precision,
And deal out loads of definition.

    Sense, in dull syllogisms confined,
Scorns these weak trammels of the mind,
Nor needs t'enquire by logic's leave
What to reject and what receive;
Throws all her trifling bulwarks down,
Expatiates free; while from her frown
Alike the dunce and pedant smart,
The fool of nature, or of art.

    On books of Rhetorick turn your hopes,
Unawed by figures or by tropes.
What silly rules in pomp appear!
What mighty nothings stun the ear!

Athroismos, Mesoteleuton,
Symploce and *Paregmenon!*
Thus, in such sounds high rumbling, run
The names of jingle and of pun;
Thus shall your pathos melt the heart,
And shame the Greek and Roman art.

Say then, where solid learning lies
And what the toil that makes us wise!
Is it by mathematic's aid
To count the worlds in light array'd,
To know each star, that lifts its eye,
To sparkle in the midnight sky?
Say ye, who draw the curious line
Between the useful, and the fine,
How little can this noble art
Its aid in human things impart,
Or give to life a cheerful ray,
And force our pains, and cares away.

Is it to know whate'er was done
Above the circle of the sun?
Is it to lift the active mind
Beyond the bounds by heaven assign'd;
And leave our little world at home,
Through realms of entity to roam;
Attempt the secrets dark to scan,
Eternal wisdom hid from man;
And make religion but the sign
In din of battle when to join?

Vain man, to madness still a prey,
Thy space a point, thy life a day,
A feeble worm, that aim'st to stride
In all the foppery of pride!
The glimmering lamp of reason's ray
Was given to guide the darksome way.
Why wilt thou spread thy insect wings,
And strive to reach sublimer things?
Thy doubts confess, thy blindness own,
Nor vex thy thoughts with scenes unknown.

Indulgent heaven to man below,
Hath all explain'd we need to know;
Hath clearly taught enough to prove
Content below, and bliss above.
Thy boastful wish how proud and vain,
While heaven forbids the vaunting strain!
For metaphysics rightly shown
But teach how little can be known:
Though quibbles still maintain their station,
Conjecture serves for demonstration,
Armies of pens draw forth to fight,
And * * * * and * * * * write.

Oh! might I live to see that day,
When sense shall point to youths their way;
Through every maze of science guide;
O'er education's laws preside;
The good retain, with just discerning
Explode the quackeries of learning;
Give ancient arts their real due,
Explain their faults, and beauties too;
Teach where to imitate, and mend,
And point their uses and their end.
Then bright philosophy would shine,
And ethics teach the laws divine;
Our youths might learn each nobler art,
That shews a passage to the heart;
From ancient languages well known
Transfuse new beauties to our own;
With taste and fancy well refin'd,
Where moral rapture warms the mind,
From schools dismiss'd, with lib'ral hand,
Spread useful learning o'er the land;
And bid the eastern world admire
Our rising worth, and bright'ning fire.

But while through fancy's realms we roam,
The main concern is left at home;
Return'd, our hero still we find
The same, as blundering, and as blind.

Four years at college dozed away
In sleep, and slothfulness and play,
Too dull for vice, with clearest conscience,
Charged with no fault but that of nonsense,
And nonsense long, with serious air,
Has wander'd unmolested there,
He passes trial, fair and free,
And takes in form his first degree.
  A scholar see him now commence
Without the aid of books or sense;
For passing college cures the brain,
Like mills to grind men young again.
The scholar-dress, that once array'd him,
The charm, *Admitto te ad gradum*,[1]
With touch of parchment can refine,
And make the veriest coxcomb shine,
Confer the gift of tongues at once,
And fill with sense the vacant dunce.
So kingly crowns contain quintessence
Of worship, dignity and presence;
Give learning, genius, virtue, worth,
Wit, valor, wisdom, and so forth;
Hide the bald pate, and cover o'er
The cap of folly worn before.
  Our hero's wit and learning now may
Be proved by token of diploma,
Of that diploma, which with speed
He learns to construe and to read;
And stalks abroad with conscious stride,
In all the airs of pedant pride,
With passport sign'd for wit and knowledge,
And current under seal of college.
  Few months now past, he sees with pain
His purse as empty as his brain;
His father leaves him then to fate,

---

[1] *Admitto te ad gradum*, I admit you to a degree; part of the words used in conferring the honours of college.

And throws him off, as useless weight;
But gives him good advice, to teach
A school at first, and then to preach.
 Thou reason'st well; it must be so;
For nothing else thy son can do.
As thieves of old, t'avoid the halter,
Took refuge in the holy altar;
Oft dulness flying from disgrace
Finds safety in that sacred place;
There boldly rears his head, or rests
Secure from ridicule or jests;
Where dreaded satire may not dare
Offend his wig's extremest hair;[1]
Where scripture sanctifies his strains,
And reverence hides the want of brains.
 Next see our youth at school appear,
Procured for forty pounds a year;
His ragged regiment round assemble,
Taught, not to read, but fear and tremble.
Before him, rods prepare his way,
Those dreaded antidotes to play.
Then throned aloft in elbow chair,
With solemn face and awful air,
He tries, with ease and unconcern,
To teach what ne'er himself could learn;
Gives law and punishment alone,
Judge, jury, bailiff, all in one;
Holds all good learning must depend
Upon his rod's extremest end,
Whose great electric virtue's such,
Each genius brightens at the touch;
With threats and blows, incitements pressing,
Drives on his lads to learn each lesson;
Thinks flogging cures all moral ills,
And breaks their heads to break their wills.

---

[1] A wig was then an essential part of the clerical dress. None appeared in the pulpit without it.

The year is done; he takes his leave;
The children smile; the parents grieve;
And seek again, their school to keep,
One just as good and just as cheap.
    Now to some priest, that's famed for teaching,
He goes to learn the art of preaching;
And settles down with earnest zeal
Sermons to study, and to steal.
Six months from all the world retires
To kindle up his cover'd fires;
Learns, with nice art, to make with ease
The scriptures speak whate'er he please;
With judgment, unperceived to quote
What Pool explain'd, or Henry wrote;
To give the gospel new editions,
Split doctrines into propositions,
Draw motives, uses, inferences,
And torture words in thousand senses;
Learn the grave style and goodly phrase,
Safe handed down from Cromwell's days,
And shun, with anxious care, the while,
The infection of a modern style;
Or on the wings of folly fly
Aloft in metaphysic sky;
The system of the world explain,
Till night and chaos come again;
Deride what old divines can say,
Point out to heaven a nearer way;
Explode all known establish'd rules,
Affirm our fathers all were fools;
The present age is growing wise,
But wisdom in her cradle lies;
Late, like Minerva, born and bred,
Not from a Jove's, but scribbler's head,
While thousand youths their homage lend her,
And nursing fathers rock and tend her.
    Round him much manuscript is spread,
Extracts from living works, and dead,

Themes, sermons, plans of controversy,
That hack and mangle without mercy,
And whence to glad the reader's eyes,
The future dialogue [1] shall rise.
  At length, matured the grand design,
He stalks abroad, a grave divine.
  Mean while, from every distant seat,
At stated time the clergy meet,
Our hero comes, his sermons reads,
Explains the doctrine of his creeds,
A license gains to preach and pray,
And makes his bow, and goes his way.
  What though his wits could ne'er dispense
One page of grammar, or of sense;
What though his learning be so slight,
He scarcely knows to spell or write;
What though his skull be cudgel-proof!
He's orthodox, and that's enough.
  Perhaps with genius we'd dispense;
But sure we look at least for sense.
  Ye fathers of our church attend
The serious counsels of a friend,
Whose utmost wish, in nobler ways,
Your sacred dignity to raise.
Though blunt the style, the truths set down
Ye can't deny—though some may frown.
  Yes, there are men, nor these a few,
The foes of virtue and of you;
Who, nurtured in the scorner's school,
Make vice their trade, and sin by rule;
Who deem it courage heav'n to brave,
And wit, to scoff at all that's grave;
Vent stolen jests, with strange grimaces,
From folly's book of common-places;
While mid the simple throng around

---

[1] Writing in dialogue was then a fashionable mode among the controversial divines.

Each kindred blockhead greets the sound,
And, like electric fire, at once,
The laugh is caught from dunce to dunce.
   The deist's scoffs ye may despise;
Within yourselves your danger lies;
For who would wish, neglecting rule,
To aid the trumphs of a fool?
From heaven at first your order came,
From heaven received its sacred name,
Indulged to man, to point the way,
That leads from darkness up to day.
Your highborn dignity attend,
And view your origin and end.
   While human souls are all your care,
By warnings, counsels, preaching, prayer,
In bands of christian friendship join'd,
Where pure affection warms the mind,
While each performs the pious race,
Nor dulness e'er usurps a place;
No vice shall brave your awful test,
Nor folly dare to broach the jest,
Each waiting eye shall humbly bend,
And reverence on your steps attend.
   But when each point of serious weight
Is torn with wrangling and debate,
When truth, mid rage of dire divisions,
Is left, to fight for definitions,
And fools assume your sacred place,
It threats your order with disgrace;
Bids genius from your seats withdraw,
And seek the pert, loquacious law;
Or deign in physic's paths to rank,
With every quack and mountebank;
Or in the ways of trade content,
Plod ledgers o'er of cent. per cent.
   While in your seats so sacred, whence
We look for piety and sense,
Pert dulness raves in school-boy style,

Your friends must blush, your foes will smile;
While men, who teach the glorious way,
Where heaven unfolds celestial day,
Assume the task sublime, to bring
The message of th' Eternal King,
Disgrace those honours they receive,
And want that sense, they aim to give.

   Now in the desk, with solemn air,
Our hero makes his audience stare;
Asserts with all dogmatic boldness,
Where impudence is yoked to dulness;
Reads o'er his notes with halting pace,
Mask'd in the stiffness of his face;
With gestures such as might become
Those statues once that spoke at Rome,
Or Livy's ox,[1] that to the state
Declared the oracles of fate,
In awkward tones, not said, nor sung,
Slow rumbling o'er the falt'ring tongue,
Two hours his drawling speech holds on,
And names it preaching, when he's done.

   With roving tired, he fixes down
For life, in some unsettled town.
People and priest full well agree,
For why—they know no more than he.
Vast tracts of unknown land he gains,
Better than those the moon contains;
There deals in preaching and in prayer,
And starves on sixty pounds a year,
And culls his texts, and tills his farms,
Does little good, and little harm;
On Sunday, in his best array,
Deals forth the dulness of the day,
And while above he spends his breath,
The yawning audience nod beneath.

   Thus glib-tongued Merc'ry in his hand

----

[1] *Bos locutus est. Liv. Histor.*

Stretch'd forth the sleep-compelling wand,
Each eye in endless doze to keep—
The God of speaking, and of sleep.

END OF PART FIRST

PART II

OR THE LIFE AND CHARACTER OF DICK HAIRBRAIN

'Twas in a town remote, the place
We leave the reader wise to guess,
(For readers wise can guess full well
What authors never meant to tell,)
There dwelt secure a country clown,
The wealthiest farmer of the town.
Though rich by villany and cheats,
He bought respect by frequent treats;
Gain'd offices by constant seeking,
'Squire, captain, deputy and deacon;
Great was his power, his pride as arrant;
One only son his heir apparent.
He thought the stripling's parts were quick,
And vow'd to make a man of Dick;
Bless'd the pert dunce, and praised his looks,
And put him early to his books.

More oaths than words Dick learn'd to speak
And studied knavery more than Greek;
Three years at school, as usual, spent
Then all equipp'd to college went,
And pleased in prospect, thus bestow'd
His meditations, as he rode.

"All hail, unvex'd with care and strife,
The bliss of academic life;
Where kind repose protracts the span,
While childhood ripens into man;

Where no hard parent's dreaded rage
Curbs the gay sports of youthful age;
Where no vile fear the genius awes
With grim severity of laws;
Where annual troops of bucks come down,
The flower of every neighb'ring town;
Where wealth and pride and riot wait,
And each choice spirit finds his mate.
   "Far from those walls, from pleasure's eye,
Let care and grief and labour fly,
The toil to gain the laurel prize,
That dims the anxious student's eyes,
The pedant air of learned looks,
And long fatigue of turning books.
Let poor dull rogues, with weary pains,
To college come to mend their brains,
And drudge four years, with grave concern
How they may wiser grow, and learn.
Is wealth of indolence afraid,
Or does wit need pedantic aid?
The man of wealth the world descries,
Without the help of learning wise;
The magic powers of gold, with ease,
Transform us to what shape we please,
Give knowledge bright and courage brave,
And sense, that nature never gave.
But nought avails the hoarded treasure;
In spending only lies the pleasure.
   "There vice shall lavish all her charms,
And rapture fold us in her arms,
Riot shall court the frolic soul,
And swearing crown the sparkling bowl;
While wit shall sport with vast applause,
And scorn the feeble tie of laws:
Our midnight joys no rule shall bound,
While games and dalliance revel round.
Such pleasures youthful years can know,
And schools there are, that such bestow.

"Those seats how blest for ease and sport,
Where wealth and idleness resort,[1]
Where free from censure and from shame,
They seek of learning but the name,
Their crimes of all degrees and sizes
Atoned by golden sacrifices;
Where kind instructors fix their price,
In just degrees, on every vice,
And fierce in zeal 'gainst wicked courses,
Demand repentance, of their purses;
Till sin, thus tax'd, produces clear,
A copious income every year,
And the fair schools, thus freed from scruples,
Thrive by the knavery of their pupils.

"Ev'n thus the Pope long since has made
Of human crimes a gainful trade;
Keeps ev'ry pleasing vice for sale,
For cash, by wholesale, or retail.
There, pay the prices and the fees,
Buy rapes, or lies, or what you please,
Then sin secure, with firm reliance,
And bid the ten commands defiance.

"And yet, alas, these happiest schools
Preserve a set of musty rules,
And in their wisest progress show
Perfection is not found below.
Even there, indulged, in humble station,
Learning resides by toleration;
No law forbids the youth to read;
For sense no tortures are decreed;
There study injures but the name,
And meets no punishment but shame."
Thus reas'ning, DICK goes forth to find

[1] There is a certain region on the western continent, situated within the northern temperate zone, where in some of the most notable and respectable schools, not only the indolence and dulness, but almost every crime, may by the rich be atoned for with pecuniary satisfaction. *Geographical Paradoxes.*

A college suited to his mind;
But bred in distant woods, the clown
Brings all his country airs to town;
The old address with awkward grace,
That bows with all-averted face;
The half-heard compliments, whose note
Is swallowed in the trembling throat;
The stiffen'd gait, the drawling tone,
By which his native place is known;
The blush, that looks, by vast degrees,
Too much like modesty to please;
The proud displays of awkward dress,
That all the country fop express,
The suit right gay, though much belated,
Whose fashion's superannuated;
The watch, depending far in state,
Whose iron chain might form a grate;
The silver buckle, dread to view,
O'ershad'wing all the clumsy shoe;
The white-gloved hand, that tries to peep
From ruffle, full five inches deep;
With fifty odd affairs beside,
The foppishness of country pride.

   Poor DICK! though first thy airs provoke
Th' obstreperous laugh and scornful joke,
Doom'd all the ridicule to stand,
While each gay dunce shall lend a hand;
Yet let not scorn dismay thy hope
To shine a witling and a fop.
Blest impudence the prize shall gain,
And bid thee sigh no more in vain.
Thy varied dress shall quickly show
At once the spendthrift and the beau.
With pert address and noisy tongue,
That scorns the fear of prating wrong,
'Mongst list'ning coxcombs shalt thou shine,
And every voice shall echo thine.
   How blest the brainless fop, whose praise

Is doom'd to grace these happy days,
When well-bred vice can genius teach,
And fame is placed in folly's reach,
Impertinence all tastes can hit,
And every rascal is a wit.
The lowest dunce, without despairing,
May learn the true sublime of swearing;
Learn the nice art of jests obscene,
While ladies wonder what they mean;
The heroism of brazen lungs,
The rhetoric of eternal tongues;
While whim usurps the name of spirit,
And impudence takes place of merit,
And every money'd clown and dunce
Commences gentleman at once.
  For now, by easy rules of trade,
Mechanic gentlemen are made!
From handicrafts of fashion born;
Those very arts so much their scorn.
To taylors half themselves they owe,
Who make the clothes, that make the beau.
  Lo! from the seats, where, fops to bless,
Learn'd artists fix the forms of dress,
And sit in consultation grave,
On folded skirt, or strait'ned sleeve,
The coxcomb trips with sprightly haste,
In all the flush of modern taste,
Oft turning, if the day be fair,
To view his shadow's graceful air;
Well pleased with eager eye runs o'er
The laced suit glitt'ring gay before; [1]
The ruffle, where from open'd vest
The rubied brooch adorns the breast;
The coat with length'ning waist behind,
Whose short skirts dangle in the wind;
The modish hat, whose breadth contains

[1] This passage alludes to the modes of dress then in fashion.

The measure of its owner's brains;
The stockings gay with various hues;
The little toe-encircling shoes;
The cane, on whose carv'd top is shown
An head, just emblem of his own;
While wrapp'd in self, with lofty stride,
His little heart elate with pride,
He struts in all the joys of show,
That taylors give, or beaux can know.

And who for beauty need repine,
That's sold at every barber's sign;
Nor lies in features or complexion,
But curls disposed in meet direction,
With strong pomatum's grateful odour,
And *quantum sufficit* of powder?
These charms can spread a sprightly grace,
O'er the dull eye and clumsy face;
While the trim dancing-master's art
Shall gestures, trips, and bows impart,
Give the gay piece its final touches,
And lend those airs, would lure a dutchess.

Thus shines the form, not aught behind,
The gifts that deck the coxcomb's mind;
Then hear the daring muse disclose
The sense and piety of beaux.

To grace his speech, let France bestow
A set of compliments for show.
Land of politeness! that affords
The treasure of new-fangled words,
And endless quantities disburses
Of bows and compliments and curses;
The soft address, with airs so sweet,
That cringes at the ladies' feet;
The pert, vivacious, play-house style,
That wakes the gay assembly's smile;
Jests that his brother beaux may hit,
And pass with young coquettes for wit,
And prized by fops of true discerning,

Outface the pedantry of learning.
Yet learning too shall lend its aid,
To fill the coxcomb's spongy head,
And studious oft he shall peruse
The labours of the modern muse.
From endless loads of novels gain
Soft, simp'ring tales of amorous pain,
With double meanings, neat and handy,
From Rochester and Tristram Shandy.[1]
The blund'ring aid of weak reviews,
That forge the fetters of the muse,
Shall give him airs of criticising
On faults of books, he ne'er set eyes on.
The magazines shall teach the fashion,
And common-place of conversation,
And where his knowledge fails, afford
The aid of many a sounding word.
    Then least religion he should need,
Of pious Hume he'll learn his creed,
By strongest demonstration shown,
Evince that nothing can be known;
Take arguments, unvex'd by doubt,
On Voltaire's trust, or go without;
'Gainst scripture rail in modern lore,
As thousand fools have rail'd before;
Or pleased a nicer art display
T'expound the doctrines all away,
Suit it to modern tastes and fashions
By various notes and emendations;
The rules the ten commands contain,
With new provisos well explain;
Prove all religion was but fashion,
Beneath the Jewish dispensation.
A ceremonial law, deep hooded
In types and figures long exploded;

[1] Sterne's Tristram Shandy was then in the zenith of its transitory
reputation.

Its stubborn fetters all unfit
For these free times of gospel light,
This rake's millenium, since the day
When sabbaths first were done away;
Since pandar-conscience holds the door,
And lewdness is a vice no more;
And shame, the worst of deadly friends,
On virtue, as its squire attends.

　Alike his poignant wit displays
The darkness of the former days,
When men the paths of duty sought,
And own'd what revelation taught;
Ere human reason grew so bright,
Men could see all things by its light,
And summon'd scripture to appear,
And stand before its bar severe,
To clear its page from charge of fiction,
And answer pleas of contradiction;
Ere miracles were held in scorn,
Or Bolingbroke, or Hume were born.

　And now the fop, with great energy,
Levels at priestcraft and the clergy,
At holy cant and godly prayers,
And bigot's hypocritic airs;
Musters each vet'ran jest to aid,
Calls piety the parson's trade;
Cries out 'tis shame, past all abiding,
The world should still be so priest-ridden;
Applauds free thought that scorns controul,
And gen'rous nobleness of soul,
That acts its pleasure good or evil,
And fears nor deity, nor devil.
These standing topics never fail
To prompt our little wits to rail,
With mimic droll'ry of grimace,
And pleased impertinence of face,
'Gainst virtue arm their feeble forces,
And sound the charge in peals of curses.

Blest be his ashes! under ground
If any particles be found,
Who friendly to the coxcomb race,
First taught those arts of commmon-place,
Those topics fine, on which the beau
May all his little wits bestow,
Secure the simple laugh to raise,
And gain the dunce's palm of praise.
For where's the theme that beaux could hit
With least similitude of wit,
Did not religion and the priest
Supply materials for the jest?
The poor in purse, with metals vile
For current coins, the world beguile;
The poor in brain, for genuine wit
Pass off a viler counterfeit;
While various thus their doom appears,
These lose their souls, and those their ears;
The want of fancy, whim supplies,
And native humour, mad caprice;
Loud noise for argument goes off,
For mirth polite, the ribald's scoff;
For sense, lewd droll'ries entertain us,
And wit is mimick'd by profaneness.

Thus 'twixt the taylor and the player,
And Hume, and Tristram, and Voltaire,
Complete in modern trim array'd,
The clockwork gentleman is made;
As thousand fops ere DICK have shown,
In airs, which DICK ere long shall own.

But not immediate from the clown,
He gains his zenith of renown;
Slow dawns the coxcomb's op'ning fray;
Rome was not finished in a day.
Perfection is the work of time;
Gradual he mounts the height sublime;
First shines abroad with bolder grace,
In suits of second-handed lace,

And learns by rote, like studious players,
The fop's infinity of airs;
Till merit, to full ripeness grown,
By constancy attains the crown.

   Now should our tale at large proceed,
Here might I tell, and you might read
At college next how DICK went on,
And prated much and studied none;
Yet shone with fair, unborrow'd ray,
And steer'd where nature led the way.
What though each academic science
Bade all his efforts bold defiance!
What though in algebra his station
Was negative in each equation;
Though in astronomy survey'd,
His constant course was retrograde;
O'er Newton's system though he sleeps
And finds his wits in dark eclipse!
His talents proved of highest price
At all the arts of cards and dice;
His genius turn'd, with greatest skill,
To whist, loo, cribbage and quadrille,
And taught, to every rival's shame,
Each nice distinction of the game.

   As noon-day sun, the case is plain,
Nature has nothing made in vain.
The blind mole cannot fly; 'tis found
His genius leads him underground.
The man that was not made to think,
Was born to game, and swear, and drink.
Let fops defiance bid to satire,
Mind Tully's rule, and follow nature.

   Yet here the muse, of DICK, must tell
He shone in active scenes as well;
The foremost place in riots held,
In all the gifts of noise excell'd,
His tongue, the bell, whose rattling din would
Summon the rake's nocturnal synod;

Swore with a grace that seem'd design'd
To emulate the infernal kind,
Nor only make their realms his due,
But learn, betimes, their language too;
And well expert in arts polite,
Drank wine by quarts to mend his sight,
For he that drinks till all things reel,
Sees double, and that's twice as well;
And ere its force confined his feet,
Led out his mob to scour the street;
Made all authority his may-game,
And strain'd his little wits to plague 'em.
Then, every crime atoned with ease,
Pro meritis,[1] received degrees;
And soon, as fortune chanced to fall,
His father died, and left him all.
Then, bent to gain all modern fashions,
He sail'd to visit foreign nations,
Resolved, by toil unaw'd, to import
The follies of the British court;
But in his course o'er looked whate'er
Was learned or valued, rich or rare.

As fire electric draws together
Each hair and straw and dust and feather,
The travell'd dunce collects betimes
The levities of other climes;
And when long toil has given success,
Returns his native land to bless,
A patriot fop, that struts by rules,
A Knight of all the shire of fools.

The praise of other learning lost,
To know the world is all his boast,
By conduct teach our country widgeons,
How coxcombs shine in other regions,
Display his travell'd airs and fashions,
And scoff at college educations.

[1] *For his merits*—the customary phrase in collegiate diplomas.

Whoe'er at college points his sneer,
Proves that himself learn'd nothing there,
And wisely makes his honest aim
To pay the mutual debt of shame.
    Meanwhile our hero's anxious care
Was all employed to please the fair;
With vows of love and airs polite,
Oft sighing at some lady's feet;
Pleased, while he thus in form address'd her,
With his own gracefulness of gesture,
And gaudy flattery, that displays
A studied elegance of phrase
So gay at balls the coxcomb shone,
He thought the female world his own.
By beauty's charms he ne'er was fired;
He flatter'd where the world admired.
Himself, so well he prized desert,
Possest his own unrivall'd heart;
Nor charms, nor chance, nor change could move
The firm foundations of his love;
His heart, so constant and so wise,
Pursued what sages old advise,
Bade others seek for fame or pelf;
His only study was himself.
    Yet DICK allow'd the fair, desert,
Nor wholly scorn'd them in his heart;
There was an end, as oft he said,
For which alone the sex were made,
Whereto, of nature's rules observant,
He strove to render them subservient;
And held the fair by inclination,
Were form'd exactly for their station,
That real virtue ne'er could find
Her lodging in a female mind;
Quoted from Pope, in phrase so smart,
That all the sex are 'rakes at heart,'
And praised Mahomet's sense, who holds
That women ne'er were born with souls.

Thus blest, our hero saw his name
Rank'd in the foremost lists of fame.
What though the learn'd, the good, the wise,
His light affected airs despise!
What though the fair of higher mind,
With brighter thought and sense refined,
Whose fancy rose on nobler wing,
Scorn'd the vain, gilt, gay, noisy thing!
Each light coquette spread forth her charms,
And lured the hero to her arms.
For beaux and light coquettes, by fate
Were each designed the other's mate,
By instinct love, for each may find
Its likeness in the other's mind.

Each gayer fop of modern days
Allow'd to Dick the foremost praise,
Borrow'd his style, his airs, grimace,
And aped his modish form of dress.
Even some, with sense endued, felt hopes
And warm ambition to be fops;
But men of sense, 'tis fix'd by fate,
Are coxcombs but of second rate.
The pert and lively dunce alone
Can steer the course that Dick has shown;
The lively dunce alone can climb
The summit, where he shines sublime.

But ah! how short the fairest name
Stands on the slippery steep of fame!
The noblest heights we're soonest giddy on;
The sun ne'er stays in his meridian;
The brightest stars must quickly set;
And Dick has deeply run in debt.
Not all his oaths can duns dismay,
Or deadly bailiffs fright away,
Not all his compliments can bail,
Or minuets dance him from the jail.
Law not the least respect can give
To the laced coat, or ruffled sleeve;

His splendid ornaments must fall,
And all is lost, for these were all.
   What then remains? in health's decline,
By lewdness, luxury, and wine,
Worn by disease, with purse too shallow,
To lead in fashions, or to follow,
The meteor's gaudy light is gone;
Lone age with hasty step comes on.
How pale the palsied fop appears,
Low shivering in the vale of years;
The ghost of all his former days,
When folly lent the ear of praise,
And beaux with pleased attention hung
On accents of his chatt'ring tongue.
Now all those days of pleasure o'er,
That chatt'ring tongue must prate no more.
From every place, that bless'd his hopes,
He's elbow'd out by younger fops.
Each pleasing thought unknown, that cheers,
The sadness of declining years,
In lonely age he sinks forlorn,
Of all, and even himself, the scorn.
   The coxcomb's course was gay and clever,
Would health and money last for ever,
Did conscience never break the charm,
Nor fear of future worlds alarm.
But oh, since youth and years decay,
And life's vain follies fleet away,
Since age has no respect for beaux,
And death the gaudy scene must close,
Happy the man, whose early bloom
Provides for endless years to come;
That learning seeks, whose useful gain
Repays the course of studious pain,
Whose fame the thankful age shall raise
And future times repeat its praise;
Attains that heart-felt peace of mind,
To all the will of heaven resign'd,

Which calms in youth, the blast of rage,
Adds sweetest hope to sinking age,
With valued use prolongs the breath,
And gives a placid smile to death.

END OF PART SECOND

PART III

OR THE ADVENTURES OF MISS HARRIET SIMPER

"COME hither, HARRIET, pretty Miss,
Come hither; give your aunt a kiss.
What, blushing? fye, hold up your head,
Full six years old and yet afraid!
With such a form, an air, a grace,
You're not ashamed to show your face!
Look like a lady—bold—my child!
Why ma'am, your HARRIET will be spoil'd.
What pity 'tis, a girl so sprightly
Should hang her head so unpolitely?
And sure there's nothing worth a rush in
That odd, unnatural trick of blushing;
It marks one ungenteelly bred,
And shows there's mischief in her head.
I've heard Dick Hairbrain prove from Paul,
Eve never blush'd before the fall.
'Tis said indeed, in latter days,
It gain'd our grandmothers some praise;
Perhaps it suited well enough
With hoop and farthingale and ruff;
But this politer generation
Holds ruffs and blushes out of fashion.
    "And what can mean that gown so odd?
You ought to dress her in the mode,
To teach her how to make a figure;
Or she'll be awkward when she's bigger,

And look as queer as Joan of Nokes,
And never rig like other folks;
Her clothes will trail, all fashion lost,
As if she hung them on a post,
And sit as awkwardly as Eve's
First pea-green petticoat of leaves.
   "And what can mean your simple whim here
To keep her poring on her primer?
'Tis quite enough for girls to know,
If she can read a billet-doux,
Or write a line you'd understand
Without a cypher of the hand.
Why need she learn to write, or spell?
A pothook scrawl is just as well;
Might rank her with the better sort,
For 'tis the reigning mode at court.
And why should girls be learn'd or wise?
Books only serve to spoil their eyes.
The studious eye but faintly twinkles,
And reading paves the way to wrinkles.
In vain may learning fill the head full;
'Tis beauty that's the one thing needful;
Beauty, our sex's sole pretence,
The best recipe for female sense,
The charm that turns all words to witty,
And makes the silliest speeches pretty.
Ev'n folly borrows killing graces
From ruby lips and roseate faces.
Give airs and beauty to your daughter,
And sense and wit will follow after."
   Thus round the infant Miss in state,
The council of the ladies meet,
And gay in modern style and fashion
Prescribe their rules of education.
The mother once herself a toast,
Prays for her child the self-same post;
The father hates the toil and pother,
And leaves his daughters to their mother;

From whom her faults, that never vary,
May come by right hereditary,
Follies be multiplied with quickness,
And whims keep up the family likeness.
   Ye parents, shall those forms so fair,
The graces might be proud to wear,
The charms those speaking eyes display,
Where passion sits in ev'ry ray,
Th' expressive glance, the air refined,
That sweet vivacity of mind,
Be doom'd for life to folly's sway,
By trifles lur'd, to fops a prey?
Say, can ye think that forms so fine
Were made for nothing but to shine,
With lips of rose and cheeks of cherry,
Outgo the works of statuary,
And gain a prize of show, as victors
O'er busts and effigies and pictures?
Can female sense no trophies raise,
Are dress and beauty all their praise,
And does no lover hope to find
An angel in his charmer's mind?
First from the dust our sex began,
But woman was refined from man;
Received again, with softer air,
The great Creator's forming care.
And shall it no attention claim
Their beauteous infant souls to frame?
Shall half your precepts tend the while
Fair nature's lovely work to spoil,
The native innocence deface,
The glowing blush, the modest grace,
On follies fix their young desire,
To trifles bid their souls aspire,
Fill their gay heads with whims of fashion,
And slight all other cultivation,
Let every useless, barren weed
Of foolish fancy run to seed.

And make their minds the receptacle
Of everything that's false and fickle;
Where gay caprice with wanton air,
And vanity keep constant fair,
Where ribbons, laces, patches, puffs,
Caps, jewels, ruffles, tippets, muffs,
With gaudy whims of vain parade,
Croud each apartment of the head;
Where stands, display'd with costly pains,
The toyshop of coquettish brains,
And high-crown'd caps hang out the sign,
And beaux as customers throng in;
Whence sense is banish'd in disgrace,
Where wisdom dares not show her face;
Where the light head and vacant brain
Spoil all the ideas they contain,
As th'air-pump kills in half a minute
Each living thing you put within it?
  It must be so; by ancient rule
The fair are nursed in folly's school,
And all their education done
Is none at all, or worse than none;
Whence still proceed in maid or wife,
The follies and the ills of life.
Learning is call'd our mental diet,
That serves the hungry mind to quiet,
That gives the genius fresh supplies,
Till souls grow up to common size:
But here, despising sense refined,
Gay trifles feed the youthful mind.
Chameleons thus, whose colours airy
As often as coquettes can vary,
Despise all dishes rich and rare,
And diet wholly on the air;
Think fogs blest eating, nothing finer,
And can on whirlwinds make a dinner;
And thronging all to feast together,
Fare daintily in blust'ring weather.

Here to the fair alone remain
Long years of action spent in vain;
Perhaps she learns (what can she less?)
The arts of dancing and of dress.
But dress and dancing are to women,
Their education's mint and cummin;
These lighter graces should be taught,
And weightier matters not forgot.
For there, where only these are shown,
The soul will fix on these alone.
Then most the fineries of dress,
Her thoughts, her wish and time possess;
She values only to be gay,
And works to rig herself for play;
Weaves scores of caps with diff'rent spires,
And all varieties of wires;
Gay ruffles varying just as flow'd
The tides and ebbings of the mode;
Bright flow'rs, and topknots waving high,
That float, like streamers in the sky;
Work'd catgut handkerchiefs, whose flaws
Display the neck, as well as gauze;
Or network aprons, somewhat thinnish,
That cost but six weeks time to finish,
And yet so neat, as you must own
You could not buy for half a crown.
Perhaps in youth (for country fashion
Prescribed that mode of education,)
She wastes long months in still more tawdry,
And useless labours of embroid'ry;
With toil weaves up for chairs together,
Six bottoms, quite as good as leather;
A set of curtains tapestry-work,
The figures frowning like the Turk;
A tentstitch picture, work of folly,
With portraits wrought of Dick and Dolly;
A coat of arms, that mark'd her house,
Three owls rampant, the crest a goose;

Or shows in waxwork goodman Adam,
And serpent gay, gallanting madam,
A woeful mimickry of Eden,
With fruit, that needs not be forbidden;
All useless works, that fill for beauties
Of time and sense their vast vacuities;
Of sense, which reading might bestow,
And time, whose worth they never know.

Now to some pop'lous city sent,
She comes back prouder than she went;
Few months in vain parades she spares,
Nor learns, but apes politer airs;
So formal acts, with such a set air,
That country manners far were better.
This springs from want of just discerning,
As pedantry from want of learning;
And proves this maxim true to sight,
The half-genteel are least polite.

Yet still that active spark, the mind
Employment constantly will find,
And when on trifles most 'tis bent,
Is always found most diligent;
For weighty works men show most sloth in,
But labour hard at doing nothing,
A trade, that needs no deep concern,
Or long apprenticeship to learn,
To which mankind at first apply
As naturally as to cry,
Till at the last their latest groan
Proclaims their idleness is done.
Good sense, like fruits, is rais'd by toil;
But follies sprout in every soil,
Nor culture, pains, nor planting need,
As moss and mushrooms have no seed.

Thus HARRIET, rising on the stage,
Learns all the arts, that please the age,
And studies well, as fits her station,
The trade and politics of fashion:

A judge of modes in silks and satins,
From tassels down to clogs and pattens;
A genius, that can calculate
When modes of dress are out of date,
Cast the nativity with ease
Of gowns, and sacks and negligees,
And tell, exact to half a minute,
What's out of fashion and what's in it;
And scanning all with curious eye,
Minutest faults in dresses spy;
(So in nice points of sight, a flea
Sees atoms better far than we;)
A patriot too, she greatly labours,
To spread her arts among her neighbors,
Holds correspondences to learn
What facts the female world concern,
To gain authentic state-reports
Of varied modes in distant courts,
The present state and swift decays
Of tuckers, handkerchiefs, and stays,
The colour'd silk that beauty wraps,
And all the rise and fall of caps.
Then shines, a pattern to the fair,
Of mien, address and modish air,
Of every new, affected grace,
That plays the eye, or decks the face,
The artful smile, that beauty warms,
And all the hypocrisy of charms.
  On Sunday, see the haughty maid
In all the glare of dress array'd,
Deck'd in her most fantastic gown,
Because a stranger's come to town.
Heedless at church she spends the day,
For homelier folks may serve to pray,
And for devotion those may go,
Who can have nothing else to do.
Beauties at church must spend their care in
Far other work, than pious hearing;

They've beaux to conquer, belles to rival;
To make them serious were uncivil.
For, like the preacher, they each Sunday
Must do their whole week's work in one day.

   As though they meant to take by blows
Th' opposing galleries of beaux,[1]
To church the female squadron move,
All arm'd with weapons used in love.
Like coloured ensigns gay and fair,
High caps rise floating in the air;
Bright silk its varied radiance flings,
And streamers wave in kissing-strings;
Each bears th' artill'ry of her charms,
Like training bands at viewing arms.

   So once, in fear of Indian beating,
Our grandsires bore their guns to meeting,
Each man equipp'd on Sunday morn,
With psalm-book, shot and powder-horn;
And look'd in form, as all must grant,
Like th' ancient, true church militant;
Or fierce, like modern deep divines,
Who fight with quills, like porcupines.

   Or let us turn the style and see
Our belles assembled o'er their tea;
Where folly sweetens ev'ry theme,
And scandal serves for sugar'd cream.
   "And did you hear the news? (they cry)
The court wear caps full three feet high,
Built gay with wire, and at the end on't,
Red tassels streaming like a pendant.
Well sure, it must be vastly pretty;
'Tis all the fashion in the city.
And were you at the ball last night?
Well, Chloe look'd like any fright;
Her day is over for a toast;

[1] Young people of different sexes used then to sit in the opposite galleries.

She'd now do best to act a ghost.
You saw our Fanny; envy must own
She figures, since she came from Boston.
Good company improves one's air—
I think the troops were station'd there.
Poor Cœlia ventured to the place;
The small-pox quite has spoil'd her face,
A sad affair, we all confest:
But providence knows what is best.
Poor Dolly, too, that writ the letter
Of love to Dick; but Dick knew better;
A secret that; you'll not disclose it;
There's not a person living knows it.
Sylvia shone out, no peacock finer;
I wonder what the fops see in her.
Perhaps 'tis true what Harry maintains,
She mends on intimate acquaintance."

  Hail British lands! to whom belongs
Unbounded privilege of tongues,
Blest gift of freedom, prized as rare
By all, but dearest to the fair;
From grandmothers of loud renown,
Thro' long succession handed down,
Thence with affection kind and hearty,
Bequeath'd unlessen'd to poster'ty!
And all ye powers of slander, hail,
Who teach to censure and to rail!
By you, kind aids to prying eyes,
Minutest faults the fair one spies,
And specks in rival toasts can mind,
Which no one else could ever find;
By shrewdest hints and doubtful guesses,
Tears reputations all in pieces;
Points out what smiles to sin advance,
Finds assignations in a glance;
And shews how rival toasts (you'll think)
Break all commandments with a wink.

So priests [1] drive poets to the lurch
By fulminations of the church,
Mark in our title-page our crimes,
Find heresies in double rhymes,
Charge tropes with damnable opinion,
And prove a metaphor, Arminian,
Peep for our doctrines, as at windows,
And pick out creeds of innuendoes.

And now the conversation sporting
From scandal turns to trying fortune.
Their future luck the fair foresee
In dreams, in cards, but most in tea.
Each finds in love some future trophy
In settlings left of tea, or coffee;
There fate displays its book, she believes,
And lovers swim in form of tea-leaves;
Where oblong stalks she takes for beaux,
And squares of leaves for billet-doux;
Gay balls in parboil'd fragments rise,
And specks for kisses greet her eyes.

So Roman augurs wont to pry
In victim's hearts for prophecy,
Sought from the future world advices,
By lights and lungs of sacrifices,
And read with eyes more sharp than wizards'
The book of fate in pigeon's gizzards;
Could tell what chief would be survivor,
From aspects of an ox's liver,
And cast what luck would fall in fights,
By trine and quartile of its lights.

Yet that we fairly may proceed,
We own that ladies sometimes read,
And grieve, that reading is confin'd

[1] On the appearance of the first part of this poem, some of the clergy, who supposed themselves the objects of satire, raised a clamor against the author, as the calumniator of the sacred order, and undertook, from certain passages in it, to prove that he was an infidel, or what they viewed as equally heretical, an Arminian.

To books that poison all the mind;
Novels and plays, (where shines display'd
A world that nature never made,)
Which swell their hopes with airy fancies,
And amorous follies of romances;
Inspire with dreams the witless maiden
On flowery vales and fields Arcadian,
And constant hearts no chance can sever,
And mortal loves, that last for ever.

For while she reads romance, the fair one
Fails not to think herself the heroine;
For every glance, or smile, or grace,
She finds resemblance in her face,
Expects the world to fall before her,
And every fop she meets adore her.
Thus HARRIET reads, and reading really
Believes herself a young Pamela,
The high-wrought whim, the tender strain
Elate her mind and turn her brain:
Before her glass, with smiling grace,
She views the wonders of her face;
There stands in admiration moveless,
And hopes a Grandison, or Lovelace.[1]

Then shines she forth, and round her hovers,
The powder'd swarm of bowing lovers;
By flames of love attracted thither,
Fops, scholars, dunces, cits, together.
No lamp exposed in nightly skies,
E'er gather'd such a swarm of flies;
Or flame in tube electric draws
Such thronging multitudes of straws.
(For I shall still take similes
From fire electric when I please.)[2]

[1] Richardson's novels were then in high request. Young misses were enraptured with the love-scenes, and beaux admired the character of Lovelace.

[2] Certain small critics had triumphed on discovering, that the writer had several times drawn his similes from the phenomena of electricity.

With vast confusion swells the sound,
When all the coxcombs flutter round.
What undulation wide of bows!
What gentle oaths and am'rous vows!
What double entendres all so smart!
What sighs hot-piping from the heart!
What jealous leers! what angry brawls
To gain the lady's hand at balls!
What billet-doux, brimful of flame!
Acrostics lined with HARRIET's name!
What compliments, o'er-strained with telling
Sad lies of Venus and of Helen!
What wits half-crack'd with commonplaces
On angels, goddesses and graces!
On fires of love what witty puns!
What similes of stars and suns!
What cringing, dancing, ogling, sighing,
What languishing for love, and dying!
  For lovers of all things that breathe
Are most exposed to sudden death,
And many a swain much famed in rhymes
Hath died some hundred thousand times;
Yet though love oft their breath may stifle,
'Tis sung it hurts them but a trifle;
The swain revives by equal wonder,
As snakes will join when cut asunder,
And often murder'd still survives;
No cat hath half so many lives.
  While round the fair, the coxcombs throng
With oaths, cards, billet-doux, and song,
She spread her charms, and wish'd to gain
The heart of every simple swain;
To all with gay, alluring air,
She hid in smiles the fatal snare,
For sure that snare must fatal prove,
Where falsehood wears the form of love;
Full oft with pleasing transport hung
On accents of each flattering tongue,

And found a pleasure most sincere
From each erect, attentive ear;
For pride was her's, that oft with ease
Despised the man she wished to please.
She loved the chace, but scorn'd the prey,
And fish'd for hearts to throw away;
Joy'd at the tale of piercing darts,
And tort'ring flames and pining hearts,
And pleased perused the billet-doux,
That said, "I die for love of you;"
Found conquest in each gallant's sighs
And blest the murders of her eyes.

So doctors live but by the dead,
And pray for plagues, as daily bread;
Thank providence for colds and fevers,
And hold consumptions special favors;
And think diseases kindly made,
As blest materials of their trade.

'Twould weary all the pow'rs of verse
Their amorous speeches to rehearse,
Their compliments, whose vain parade
Turns Venus to a kitchen-maid;
With high pretence of love and honour,
They vent their folly all upon her,
(Ev'n as the scripture precept saith,
More shall be given to him that hath;)
Tell her how wondrous fair they deem her,
How handsome all the world esteem her;
And while they flatter and adore,
She contradicts to call for more.

"And did they say I was so handsome?
My looks—I'm sure no one can fancy 'em.
'Tis true we're all as we were framed,
And none have right to be ashamed;
But as for beauty—all can tell
I never fancied I look'd well;
I were a fright, had I a grain less.
You're only joking, Mr. Brainless."

Yet beauty still maintain'd her sway,
And bade the proudest hearts obey;
Ev'n sense her glances could beguile,
And vanquish'd wisdom with a smile;
While merit bow'd and found no arms,
To oppose the conquests of her charms,
Caught all those bashful fears, that place
The mask of folly on the face,
That awe, that robs our airs of ease,
And blunders, when it hopes to please;
For men of sense will always prove
The most forlorn of fools in love.
The fair esteem'd, admired, 'tis true,
And praised—'tis all coquettes can do.

And when deserving lovers came,
Believed her smiles and own'd their flame,
Her bosom thrill'd, with joy affected
T' increase the list, she had rejected;
While pleased to see her arts prevail,
To each she told the self-same tale.
She wish'd in truth they ne'er had seen her,
And feign'd what grief it oft had giv'n her,
And sad, of tender-hearted make,
Grieved they were ruin'd for her sake.
'Twas true, she own'd on recollection,
She'd shown them proofs of kind affection:
But they mistook her whole intent,
For friendship was the thing she meant.
She wonder'd how their hearts could move 'em
So strangely as to think she'd love 'em;
She thought her purity above
The low and sensual flames of love;
And yet they made such sad ado,
She wish'd she could have loved them too.
She pitied them, and as a friend
She prized them more than all mankind,
And begg'd them not their hearts to vex,
Or hang themselves, or break their necks,

Told them 'twould make her life uneasy,
If they should run forlorn, or crazy;
Objects of love she could not deem 'em;
But did most marv'lously esteem 'em.

For 'tis esteem, coquettes dispense
Tow'rd learning, genius, worth and sense,
Sincere affection, truth refined,
And all the merit of the mind.

But love's the passion they experience
For gold, and dress, and gay appearance.

For ah! what magic charms and graces
Are found in golden suits of laces!
What going forth of hearts and souls
Tow'rd glare of gilded button-holes!
What lady's heart can stand its ground
'Gainst hats with glittering edging bound?
While vests and shoes and hose conspire,
And gloves and ruffles fan the fire,
And broadcloths, cut by taylor's arts,
Spread fatal nets for female hearts.

And oh, what charms more potent shine,
Drawn from the dark Peruvian mine!
What spells and talismans of Venus
Are found in dollars, crowns and guineas!
In purse of gold, a single stiver
Beats all the darts in Cupid's quiver.
What heart so constant, but must veer,
When drawn by thousand pounds a year!
How many fair ones ev'ry day
To houses fine have fall'n a prey,
Been forced on stores of goods to fix,
Or carried off in coach and six!
For Cœlia, merit found no dart;
Five thousand sterling broke her heart,
So witches, hunters say, confound 'em,
For silver bullets only wound 'em.

But now the time was come, our fair
Should all the plagues of passion share,

And after ev'ry heart she'd won,
By sad disaster lose her own.
So true the ancient proverb sayeth,
'Edge-tools are dang'rous things to play with';
The fisher, ev'ry gudgeon hooking,
May chance himself to catch a ducking;
The child that plays with fire, in pain
Will burn its fingers now and then;
And from the dutchess to the laundress,
Coquettes are seldom salamanders.

   For lo! Dick Hairbrain heaves in sight,
From foreign climes returning bright;
He danced, he sung to admiration,
He swore to gen'ral acceptation,
In airs and dress so great his merit,
He shone—no lady's eyes could bear it.
Poor HARRIET saw; her heart was stouter;
She gather'd all her smiles about her;
Hoped by her eyes to gain the laurels,
And charm him down, as snakes do squirrels.
So prized his love and wish'd to win it,
That all her hopes were center'd in it;
And took such pains his heart to move,
Herself fell desp'rately in love;
Though great her skill in am'rous tricks,
She could not hope to equal Dick's;
Her fate she ventured on his trial,
And lost her birthright of denial.

   And here her brightest hopes miscarry;
For Dick was too gallant to marry.
He own'd she'd charms for those who need 'em,
But he, be sure, was all for freedom;
So, left in hopeless flames to burn,
Gay Dick esteem'd her in her turn.
In love, a lady once given over
Is never fated to recover,
Doom'd to indulge her troubled fancies,
And feed her passion by romances;

And always amorous, always changing,
From coxcomb still to coxcomb ranging,
Finds in her heart a void, which still
Succeeding beaux can never fill:
As shadows vary o'er a glass,
Each holds in turn the vacant place;
She doats upon her earliest pain,
And following thousands loves in vain.

Poor HARRIET now hath had her day;
No more the beaux confess her sway;
New beauties push her from the stage;
She trembles at th' approach of age,
And starts to view the alter'd face,
That wrinkles at her in her glass:
So Satan, in the monk's tradition,
Fear'd, when he met his apparition.

At length her name each coxcomb cancels
From standing lists of toasts and angels;
And slighted where she shone before,
A grace and goddess now no more,
Despised by all, and doom'd to meet
Her lovers at her rival's feet,
She flies assemblies, shuns the ball,
And cries out, vanity, on all;
Affects to scorn the tinsel-shows
Of glittering belles and gaudy beaux;
Nor longer hopes to hide by dress
The tracks of age upon her face.
Now careless grown of airs polite,
Her noonday nightcap meets the sight;
Her hair uncomb'd collects together,
With ornaments of many a feather;
Her stays for easiness thrown by,
Her rumpled handkerchief awry,
A careless figure half undress'd,
(The reader's wits may guess the rest;)
All points of dress and neatness carried,
As though she'd been a twelvemonth married;

She spends her breath, as years prevail,
At this sad wicked world to rail,
To slander all her sex *impromptu*,
And wonder what the times will come to.

   Tom Brainless, at the close of last year,
Had been six years a rev'rend Pastor,
And now resolved, to smooth his life,
To seek the blessing of a wife.
His brethren saw his amorous temper,
And recommended fair Miss Simper,
Who fond, they heard, of sacred truth,
Had left her levities of youth,
Grown fit for ministerial union,
And grave, as Christian's wife in Bunyan.

   On this he rigg'd him in his best,
And got his old grey wig new dress'd,
Fix'd on his suit of sable stuffs,
And brush'd the powder from his cuffs,
With black silk stockings, yet in being,
The same he took his first degree in;
Procured a horse of breed from Europe,
And learn'd to mount him by the stirrup,
And set forth fierce to court the maid;
His white-hair'd Deacon went for aid;
And on the right, in solemn mode,
The Reverend Mr. Brainless rode.
Thus grave, the courtly pair advance,
Like knight and squire in famed romance.
The priest then bow'd in sober gesture,
And all in scripture terms address'd her;
He'd found, for reasons amply known,
It was not good to be alone,
And thought his duty led to trying
The great command of multiplying;
So with submission, by her leave,
He'd come to look him out an Eve,
And hoped, in pilgrimage of life,
To find an helpmate in a wife,

A wife discreet and fair withal,
To make amends for Adam's fall.
    In short, the bargain finish'd soon
A reverend Doctor made them one.
    And now the joyful people rouse all
To celebrate their priest's espousal;
And first, by kind agreement set,
In case their priest a wife could get,
The parish vote him five pounds clear,
T' increase his salary every year.
Then swift the tag-rag gentry come
To welcome Madam Brainless home;
Wish their good Parson joy; with pride
In order round salute the bride;
At home, at visits and at meetings,
To Madam all allow precedence;
Greet her at church with rev'rence due,
And next the pulpit fix her pew.

END OF PART THIRD

M'FINGAL

CANTO I

THE TOWN-MEETING, A. M.

When Yankies,* skill'd in martial rule,
First † put the British troops to school;
Instructed them in warlike trade,
And new manœuvres of parade,
The true war-dance of Yankee reels,
And *manual exercise* of heels;
Made them give up, like saints complete,
The arm of flesh, and trust the feet,
And work, like Christians undissembling,
Salvation out, by fear and trembling;
Taught Percy fashionable races,
And modern modes of Chevy-Chases: ‡
From Boston, in his best array,
Great 'Squire M'Fingal took his way,
And graced with ensigns of renown,
Steer'd homeward to his native town.

His high descent our heralds trace
From Ossian's § famed Fingalian race:
For though their name some part may lack,
Old Fingal spelt it with a Mac;

---

* *Yankies,*—a term formerly of derision, but now merely of distinction, given to the people of the four eastern states. *Lond. Edit.*
[The notes in *M'Fingal* are Trumbull's.]

† At the battle of Lexington. . . .

‡ Lord Percy commanded the party, that was first opposed to the Americans at Lexington. This allusion to the family renown of Chevy-Chase arose from the precipitate manner of his Lordship's quitting the field of battle, and returning to Boston. *Lond. Edit.*

§ . . . The complete name of Ossian, according to the Scottish nomenclature, will be Ossian M'Fingal.

Which great M'Pherson, with submission,
We hope will add the next edition.
   His fathers flourish'd in the Highlands
Of Scotia's fog-benighted islands;
Whence gain'd our 'Squire two gifts by right,
Rebellion, and the Second-sight.
Of these, the first, in ancient days,
Had gain'd the noblest palm of praise,
'Gainst kings stood forth and many a crown'd head
With terror of its might confounded;
Till rose a king with potent charm
His foes by meekness to disarm,
Whom every Scot and Jacobite
Strait fell in love with at first sight;
Whose gracious speech with aid of pensions,
Hush'd down all murmurs of dissensions,
And with the sound of potent metal
Brought all their buzzing swarms to settle;
Who rain'd his ministerial manna,
Till loud Sedition sung hosanna;
The grave Lords-Bishops and the Kirk
United in the public work;
Rebellion, from the northern regions,
With Bute and Mansfield swore allegiance;
All hands combin'd to raze, as nuisance,
Of church and state the Constitutions,
Pull down the empire, on whose ruins
They meant to edify their new ones;
Enslave th' Amer'can wildernesses,
And rend the provinces in pieces.
With these our 'Squire, among the valiant'st,
Employ'd his time, and tools and talents,
And found this new rebellion pleasing
As his old king-destroying treason.
   Nor less avail'd his optic sleight,
And Scottish gift of second-sight.*

* . . . Consult the profound Johnson, in his Tour to the Hebrides.

No ancient sybil, famed in rhyme,
Saw deeper in the womb of time;
No block in old Dodona's grove
Could ever more orac'lar prove.
Nor only saw he all that could be,
But much that never was, nor would be;
Whereby all prophets far outwent he,
Though former days produced a plenty:
For any man with half an eye
What stands before him can espy;
But optics sharp it needs, I ween,
To see what is not to be seen.
As in the days of ancient fame,
Prophets and poets were the same,
And all the praise that poets gain
Is for the tales they forge and feign:
So gain'd our 'Squire his fame by seeing
Such things, as never would have being;
Whence he for oracles was grown
The very tripod * of his town.
Gazettes no sooner rose a lie in,
But strait he fell to prophesying;
Made dreadful slaughter in his course,
O'erthrew provincials, foot and horse,
Brought armies o'er, by sudden pressings,
Of Hanoverians, Swiss and Hessians,
Feasted with blood his Scottish clan,
And hang'd all rebels to a man,
Divided their estates and pelf,
And took a goodly share himself.
All this with spirit energetic,
He did by second-sight prophetic.
   Thus stored with intellectual riches,
Skill'd was our 'Squire in making speeches;
Where strength of brains united centers

* The tripod was a sacred three-legged stool, from which the ancient priests uttered their oracles.

With strength of lungs surpassing Stentor's.*
But as some muskets so contrive it,
As oft to miss the mark they drive at,
And though well aim'd at duck or plover,
Bear wide, and kick their owners over:
So fared our 'Squire, whose reas'ning toil
Would often on himself recoil,
And so much injured more his side,
The stronger arguments he applied;
As old war-elephants, dismay'd,
Trod down the troops they came to aid,
And hurt their own side more in battle,
Than less and ordinary cattle.
Yet at Town-meetings every chief
Pinn'd faith on great M'FINGAL's sleeve;
Which when he lifted, all by rote
Raised sympathetic hands to vote.

The Town, our hero's scene of action,
Had long been torn by feuds of faction,
And as each party's strength prevails,
It turn'd up different, heads or tails;
With constant rattling, in a trice,
Show'd various sides, as oft as dice.
As that famed weaver, wife t' Ulysses,†
By night her day's-work pick'd in pieces,
And though she stoutly did bestir her,
Its finishing was ne'er the nearer:
So did this town with ardent zeal
Weave cobwebs for the public weal,
Which when completed, or before,
A second vote in pieces tore.
They met, made speeches full long-winded,
Resolv'd, protested and rescinded;
Addresses sign'd; then chose committees

* Stentor, the loud-voic'd herald in Homer.
† Homer's Odyssey.

To stop all drinking of Bohea teas, *
With winds of doctrine veer'd about,
And turn'd all whig committees out.
Meanwhile our Hero, as their head,
In pomp the tory faction led,
Still following, as the 'Squire should please,
Successive on, like files of geese.
    And now the town was summon'd, greeting,
To grand parading of Town-meeting;
A show, that strangers might appal,
As Rome's grave senate did the Gaul.
High o'er the rout, on pulpit stairs,†
Mid den of thieves in house of prayers,
(That house, which loth a rule to break
Serv'd heaven, but one day in the week,
Open the rest for all supplies
Of news, and politics, and lies;)
Stood forth the Constable; and bore
His staff, like Merc'ry's wand of yore,
Waved potent round, the peace to keep,
As that laid dead men's souls to sleep.
Above and near th' hermetic staff,
The Moderator's ‡ upper half
In grandeur o'er the cushion bow'd,
Like Sol half seen behind a cloud.
Beneath stood voters of all colours,
Whigs, Tories, orators and brawlers;
With every tongue in either faction

*. . . The committees referred to, were called Committees of
Correspondence: part of their business was to enforce the execution
of the voluntary [non-consumption] regulations made by the people
in the several towns.

  † In country towns in New England, the town-meeting is generally
held in the church, or meeting-house.

  ‡ Moderator is the name given to the chairman or speaker of a
town-meeting. He is here seated in the pulpit.

Prepared like minute-men* for action;
Where truth and falsehood, wrong and right,
Drew all their legions forth to fight.
With equal uproar scarcely rave
Opposing winds in Æolus' cave;
Such dialogues with earnest face
Held never Balaam with his ass.

With daring zeal and courage blest,
Honorius first the crowd addres'd.
When now our 'Squire, returning late,
Arrived to aid the grand debate;
With strange, sour faces sate him down,
While thus the orator went on.
—"For ages blest thus Britain rose,
The terror of encircling foes;
Her heroes ruled the bloody plain,
Her conq'ring standard awed the main.
The different palms her triumph grace
Of arms in war, of arts in peace.
Unharrass'd by maternal care,
Each rising province flourish'd fair;
Whose various wealth, with liberal hand,
By far o'erpaid the parent land.†
But though so bright her sun might shine,
'Twas quickly hasting to decline,
With feeble ray, too weak t' assuage
The damps, that chill the eve of age.

"For states, like men, are doom'd as well
Th' imfirmities of age to feel,
And from their different forms of empire,
Are seiz'd with every deep distemper.
Some states high fevers have made head in,

* Minute-men were that part of the militia of our country . . .
prepared to march at a minute's warning wherever the public safety
required.

† Before the revolution, the colonies ever stiled Britain their
mother-country, themselves her children, and England their home.

Which nought could cure but copious bleeding;
While others have grown dull and dozy,
Or fix'd in helpless idiocy;
Or turn'd demoniacs to belabour
Each peaceful habitant and neighbour;
Or vex'd with hypochondriac fits,
Have broke their strength, and lost their wits.
Thus now while hoary years prevail,
Good mother Britain seem'd to fail;
Her back bent, crippled with the weight
Of age, and debts, and cares of state.
For debts she owed, and those so large,
As twice her wealth could ne'er discharge,
And now 'twas thought, so high they'd grown,
She'd come upon the parish soon.
Her arms, of nations once the dread,
She scarce could lift above her head;
Her deafen'd ears, 'twas all their hope,
The final trump perhaps might ope;
So long they'd been, in stupid mood,
Shut to the hearing of all good.
Grim death had put her in his scroll
Down on the execution-roll;
And Gallic crows, as she grew weaker,
Began to whet their beaks to pick her.
  "And now her powers decaying fast,
Her grand climact'ric had she pass'd,
And just like all old women else,
Fell in the vapors much by spells.
Strange whimsies on her fancy struck,
And gave her brain a dismal shock;
Her memory fails, her judgment ends;
She quite forgot her nearest friends,
Lost all her former sense and knowledge,
And fitted fast for Bedlam-college.
Of all the powers she once retain'd,
Conceit and pride alone remain'd.
As Eve, when falling, was so modest

To fancy she should grow a goddess; *
As madmen, straw who long have slept on,
Style themselves Jupiter and Neptune:
So Britain in her airs so flighty,
Now took a whim to be Almighty; †
Urg'd on to desperate heights of frenzy,
Affirm'd her own Omnipotency;
Would rather ruin all her race,
Than yield supremacy, an ace;
Assumed all rights divine, as grown
The church's head, like good Pope Joan; ‡
Swore all the world should bow and skip,
At her almighty goodyship;
Anath'matized each unbeliever,
And vow'd to live and rule for ever.
Her servants humour'd every whim,
And own'd at once her power supreme;
Her follies nursed in all their stages,
For sake of liveries and wages;
In Stephen's Chapel § then in state too
Set up her golden calf to pray to;
Proclaim'd its power and right divine,
And call'd for worship at its shrine;
And for poor heretics to burn us,
Bade North ¶ prepare his fiery furnace;
Struck bargains with the Romish churches,

---

* So says Milton.

† See the Act declaring her right to bind the colonies *in all cases whatsoever.* See also Blackstone's remarks, in his Commentaries, on the *Omnipotence* of the British Parliament.

‡ Whether there actually was a woman, who assumed the dress of a monk, and was finally elected Pope, has occasioned violent disputes among the ecclesiastical historians. To them we must leave it—since the world have not the benefit, as in the case of the Chevalier D'Eon, of the report of any legal trial for ascertaining her sex, before any Lord Mansfield of that age.

§ The parliament-house is called St. Stephen's Chapel.

¶ Her Prime Minister of State at that period.

Infallibility to purchase;
Set wide for Popery the door,*
Made friends with Babel's scarlet whore,
Till both the matrons join'd in clan;
No sisters made a better span.
   "What wonder then, ere this was over,
That she should make her children suffer?
She first without pretence or reason,
Claim'd right whate'er we had to seize on;
And with determin'd resolution
To put her claims in execution,
Sent fire and sword, and call'd it Lenity;
Starv'd us, and christen'd it Humanity.
For she, her case grown desperater,
Mistook the plainest things in nature;
Had lost all use of eyes or wits,
Took slavery for the bill of rights;
Trembled at whigs and deem'd them foes,
And stopp'd at loyalty her nose;
Styled her own children, brats and catiffs,
And knew us not from th' Indian natives.
   "What though with supplicating prayer,
We begg'd our lives and goods she'd spare;
Not vainer vows with sillier call
Elijah's prophets raised to Baal;
A worshipp'd stock of god or goddess
Had better heard and understood us.
So once Egyptians at the Nile
Ador'd their guardian crocodile,
Who heard them first with kindest ear,
And ate them to reward their prayer;
And could he talk, as kings can do,
Had made as gracious speeches too.
   "Thus, spite of prayers, her schemes pursuing,
She still went on to work our ruin;

---

* Alluding to the Act of parliament, establishing the Papal worship and religion in Canada.

Annull'd our charters of releases,
And tore our title-deeds in pieces;
Then sign'd her warrants of ejection,
And gallows rais'd to stretch our necks on:
And on these errands sent in rage
Her bailiff, and her hangman, Gage;
And at his heels, like dogs to bait us,
Dispatch'd her *Posse Comitatus*.
  "No state e'er chose a fitter person
To carry such a silly farce on.
As heathen gods in ancient days
Receiv'd at second hand their praise,
Stood imaged forth in stones and stocks,
And deified in barber's blocks:
So Gage* was chose to represent
Th' omnipotence of Parliament.
As antient heroes gain'd by shifts,
From gods, as poets tell, their gifts;
Our General, as his actions show,
Gain'd like assistance from below,
By satan graced with full supplies
From all his magazine of lies.
Yet could his practice ne'er impart
The wit to tell a lie with art.
Those lies alone are formidable
Where artful truth is mix'd with fable.
But Gage has bungled oft so vilely,
No soul would credit lies so silly,
Outwent all faith, and stretch'd beyond
Credulity's extremest end:
Whence plain it seems, though satan once
O'erlook'd with scorn each brainless dunce,
And blundering brutes in Eden shunning,

---

* General Gage, commander in Chief of the king's troops in North America, was in 1773 appointed Governor and Vice-Admiral of Massachusetts; in the room of Hutchinson, who had been the most active agent of the Minister in fomenting the disputes which brought on the war. *Lond. Edit.*

Chose out the serpent for his cunning;
Of late he is not half so nice,
Nor picks out aids because they're wise:
For had he stood upon perfection,
His present friends had lost th' election,
And fared as hard, in this proceeding,
As owls and asses did in Eden.

"Yet fools are often dangerous enemies;
As meanest reptiles are most venomous:
Nor e'er could Gage, by craft or prowess,
Have done a whit more mischief to us;
Since he began th' unnat'ral war,
The work his masters sent him for.

"And are there in this freeborn land
Among ourselves a venal band;
A dastard race, who long have sold
Their souls and consciences for gold;
Who wish to stab their country's vitals,
Could they enjoy surviving titles;
With pride behold our mischiefs brewing,
Insult and triumph in our ruin?
Priests, who, if satan should sit down
To make a bible of his own,
Would gladly, for the sake of mitres,
Turn his inspired and sacred writers;
Lawyers, who, should he wish to prove
His claim to his old seat above,
Would, if his cause he'd give them fees in,
Bring writs of *Entry sur disseisin*,
Plead for him boldly at the session,
And hope to put him in possession;
Merchants who, for his friendly aid
Would make him partner in their trade,
Hang out their signs in goodly show,
Inscribed with, *Beelzebub & Co.*;
And judges, who would list his pages,
For proper liveries and wages;
And who as humbly cringe and bow

To all his mortal servants now?
There are; and shame, with pointing gestures,
Marks out th' Addressers * and Protesters;
Whom following down the stream of fate,
Contempts ineffable await;
And public infamy forlorn,
Dread hate and everlasting scorn."
  As thus he spake, our 'Squire M'FINGAL
Gave to his partisans a signal.
Not quicker roll'd the waves to land,
When Moses waved his potent wand,
Nor with more uproar, than the Tories
Set up a general rout in chorus;
Laugh'd, hiss'd, hem'd, murmur'd, groan'd and jeer'd;
Honorius now could scarce be heard.
Our Muse, amid th' increasing roar,
Could not distinguish one word more;
Though she sate by, in firm record
To take in short hand every word,
As ancient Muses wont; to whom
Old bards for depositions come;
Who must have writ them; for how else
Could they each speech verbatim tell 's?
And though some readers of romances
Are apt to strain their tortured fancies,
And doubt (when lovers all alone
Their sad soliloquies do groan,
Grieve many a page, with no one near 'em,
And nought, but rocks and groves, to hear 'em)
What sprite infernal could have tattled,
And told the authors all they prattled;
Whence some weak minds have made objection
That what they scribbled must be fiction:

* The Addressers were those who addressed General Gage with expressions of gratitude and attachment, on his arrival with a fleet and army to subdue the country: the Protesters, those who published protests against the measures of the first Congress, and the resolves of the people in town-meetings and conventions.

'Tis false; for while the lover spoke,
The Muse was by with table-book,
And least some blunder should ensue,
Echo stood clerk, and kept the cue.
And though the speech ben't worth a groat,
It can't be call'd the author's fault;
But error merely of the prater,
Who should have talk'd to th' purpose better:
Which full excuse, my critic brothers,
May help me out as well as others;
And 'tis design'd, though here it lurk,
To serve as Preface to this work.
So let it be—for now our 'Squire
No longer could contain his ire,
And rising 'midst applauding Tories,
Thus vented wrath upon Honorius.

    Quoth he, " 'Tis wondrous what strange stuff
Your Whigs-heads are compounded of;
Which force of logic cannot pierce,
Nor syllogistic *carte and tierce*,
Nor weight of scripture or of reason
Suffice to make the least impression.
Not heeding what ye rais'd contest on,
Ye prate, and beg, or steal the question;
And when your boasted arguings fail,
Strait leave all reas'ning off, to rail.

    "Have not our High-church Clergy* made it
Appear from Scriptures, which ye credit,
That right divine from heaven was lent
To kings, that is, the Parliament,
Their subjects to oppress and teaze,
And serve the devil when they please?
Did not they write, and pray, and preach,
And torture all the parts of speech,

---

* The absurd doctrines of passive obedience, non-resistance, and
the divine right of Kings, were inculcated with great vehemence at
this period.

About rebellion make a pother,
From one end of the land to th' other?
And yet gain'd fewer proselyte Whigs,
Than old St. Anth'ny 'mongst the pigs; *
And changed not half so many vicious,
As Austin when he preach'd to fishes,
Who throng'd to hear, the legend tells,
Were edified, and wagg'd their tails:
But scarce you'd prove it, if you tried,
That e'er one Whig was edified.
Have ye not heard from Parson Walter †
Much dire presage of many a halter?
What warnings had ye of your duty,
From our old rev'rend Sam. Auchmuty; †
From priests of all degrees and metres,
T' our fag-end man, poor Parson Peters? ‡
Have not our Cooper and our Seabury
Sung hymns, like Barak and old Deborah;
Proved all intrigues to set you free
Rebellion 'gainst *the Pow'rs that be;*
Brought over many a scripture text,
That used to wink at rebel sects,
Coax'd wayward ones to favor regents,
And paraphrased them to obedience;
Proved every king, ev'n those confest
Horns of the Apocalyptic beast,
And sprouting from its noddles seven,
Ordain'd, as Bishops are, by heaven;

* The stories of St. Anthony and his pig, and of St. Austin's preaching to the fishes, are told in the Popish Legends.

† High-church clergymen, one at Boston, one at New York.

‡ Peters, a Tory clergyman of Connecticut, who after rendering himself generally detestable, absconded from the contempt, rather than the vengeance of his fellow-citizens, and went to England, where he published a libel, which he called, A History of that Colony; Cooper, a writer of the same stamp, President of the College at New York, Poet, Punster and Satyrist; Seabury, a clergyman of the same Province.

(For reasons similar, as we're told
That Tophet was ordain'd of old)
By this lay-ordination valid,
Becomes all sanctified and hallow'd,
Takes patent out as heaven has sign'd it,
And starts up strait, the Lord's Anointed?
As extreme unction, which can cleanse
Each penitent from deadly sins;
Make them run glib, when oiled by priest,
The heav'nly road, like wheels new greased;
Serve them, like shoe-ball, for defences,
'Gainst wear and tear of consciences:
So king's anointment clears betimes,
Like fuller's earth, all spots of crimes,
For future knaveries gives commissions,
Like Papists sinning under license.
For heaven ordain'd the origin,
Divines declare,* of pain and sin,
Prove such great good they both have done us,
Kind mercy 'twas they came upon us;
For without sin and pain and folly,
Man ne'er was blest, nor wise, nor holy:
And we should thank the Lord 'tis so,
As authors grave wrote long ago.
Now heav'n its issues never brings
Without the means, and these are kings;
And he who blames when they announce ills,
Would counteract th' eternal counsels.
As when the Jews, a murm'ring race,
By constant grumblings fell from grace,
Heav'n taught them first to know their distance,
By famine, slavery and Philistines;
When these could no repentance bring,
In wrath it sent them last a king:
So nineteen, 'tis believ'd, in twenty
Of modern kings for plagues are sent you;

* See the modern Metaphysical Divinity.

Nor can your cavillers pretend
But that they answer well their end.
'Tis yours to yield to their command,
As rods in Providence's hand;
For when it means to send you pain,
You toss your foreheads up in vain;
Your way is, hush'd in peace, to bear it,
And make necessity a merit.
Hence sure perdition must await
The man, who rises 'gainst the State,
Who meets at once the damning sentence,
Without one loophole for repentance;
Even though he gain the Royal See,
And rank among *the Powers that be*.
For hell is theirs, the scripture shows,
Who e'er *the Powers that be* oppose;
And all those Powers (I'm clear that 'tis so)
Are damn'd for ever, *ex officio*.
    "Thus far our Clergy; but 'tis true
We lack'd not earthly reas'ners too.
Had I the Poet's* brazen lungs,
As soundboard to his hundred tongues,
I could not half the scribblers muster,
That swarm'd round Rivington† in cluster;
Assemblies, Councilmen, forsooth,
Brush, Cowper, Wilkins, Chandler, Booth:
Yet all their arguments and sapience
You did not value at three halfpence.
Did not our Massachusettensis ‡
For your conviction strain his senses;

* Virgil.
† Rivington, printer of the Royal Gazette in New York—The Legislature of that Province were opposed to the measures of the country.
‡ A course of Essays under that signature was published in Boston, in the latter part of 1774 and beginning of 1775. It was the last combined effort of Tory wit and argument to write down the Revolution.

Scrawl every moment he could spare
From cards and barbers and the fair;
Show, clear as sun in noonday heavens,
You did not feel a single grievance;
Demonstrate all your opposition
Sprung from the eggs * of foul Sedition;
Swear he had seen the nest she laid in,
And knew how long she had been sitting;
Could tell exact what strength of heat is
Required to hatch out her Committees;
What shapes they take, and how much longer's
The time before they grow t' a Congress?
He white-wash'd Hutchinson, and varnish'd
Our Gage, who'd got a little tarnish'd;
Made them new masks, in time no doubt,
For Hutchinson's was quite worn out:
Yet while he muddled all his head,
You did not heed a word he said.

　　"Did not our grave Judge Sewall † hit
The summit of newspaper wit;
Fill every leaf of every paper
Of Mills & Hicks, and mother Draper; ‡
Draw proclamations, works of toil,
In true sublime of scarecrow style,
Write farces too 'gainst sons of freedom,
All for your good, and none would read 'em;
Denounce damnation on their frenzy,
Who died in Whig-impenitency;
Affirm that heav'n would lend us aid,
As all our Tory writers said;

* "Committees of correspondence are the foulest and most venomous serpent, that ever issued from the eggs of Sedition," etc. *Massachusettensis.* . . .

† Judge of Admiralty and Attorney General of Massachusetts, Gage's chief adviser and proclamation-maker, author of a farce, called "The American roused," and of a multitude of news-paper essays.

‡ Printers of ministerial gazettes in Boston.

And calculate so well its kindness,
He told the moment when it joined us?
" 'Twas then belike," Honorius cried,
"When you the public fast defied,
Refused to heaven to raise a prayer,
Because you'd no connections there;
And since with reverent hearts and faces,
To Governors you'd paid addresses,
In them, who made you Tories, seeing
You lived and moved and had your being,
Your humble vows you would not breathe
To powers, you'd no acquaintance with.
"As for your fasts," replied our 'Squire,
"What circumstance could fasts require?
We kept them not, but 'twas no crime,
We held them merely loss of time.
For what advantage firm and lasting,
Pray, did you ever get by fasting,
Or what the gain, that can arise
From vows and offerings to the skies?
Will heaven reward with posts and fees,
Or send us tea,* as consignees,
Give pensions, salaries, places, bribes,
Or chuse us judges, clerks or scribes?
Has it commissions in its gift,
Or cash to serve us at a lift?
Are acts of parliament there made,
To carry on the placeman's trade,
Or has it pass'd a single bill
To let us plunder whom we will?
    "And look our list of placemen all over;
Did heaven appoint our chief Judge Oliver,†
Fill that high bench with ignoramus,

---

* Alluding to the famous cargo of tea, which was destroyed in
Boston harbour, the consignees of which were the tools of the British
ministry.

† Peter Oliver Esq. without legal science or professional education,
was appointed Chief Judge of the Supreme Court in Massachusetts.

Or has it councils by mandamus? *
Who made that wit of water-gruel
A judge of admiralty, Sewall?
And were they not mere earthly struggles,
That raised up Murray, say, and Ruggles?
Did heaven send down, our pains to medicine,
That old simplicity of Edson,
Or by election pick out from us
That Marshfield blunderer, Nat. Ray Thomas;
Or had it any hand in serving
A Loring, Pepperell, Browne or Irving?
   "Yet we've some saints, the very thing,
To pit against the best you'll bring;
For can the strongest fancy paint,
Than Hutchinson, a greater saint?
Was there a parson used to pray,
At times more regular, twice a day;
As folks exact have dinners got,
Whether they've appetites or not?
Was there a zealot more alarming
'Gainst public vice to hold forth sermon,
Or fix'd at church, whose inward motion
Roll'd up his eyes with more devotion?
What puritan could ever pray
In godlier tone, than Treasurer Gray,
Or at town-meetings speechifying,
Could utter more melodious whine,
And shut his eyes, and vent his moan,
Like owl afflicted in the sun;
Who once sent home, his canting rival,
Lord Dartmouth's self, might outbedrivel.
   "Have you forgot," Honorious cried,

---

* The Council of that Province had ever, by its charter, been elective. The charter was declared void, and the King appointed them by writ of *mandamus*. The persons, named in this paragraph, were some of the most conspicuous of the new members.

"How your prime saint the truth* defied,
Affirm'd he never wrote a line
Your charter'd rights to undermine,
When his own letters then were by,
Which proved his message all a lie?
How many promises he seal'd
To get th' oppressive acts repeal'd,
Yet once arrived on England's shore,
Set on the Premier to pass more?
But these are no defects, we grant,
In a right loyal Tory saint,
Whose godlike virtues must with ease
Atone for venial crimes, like these:
Or ye perhaps in scripture spy
A new commandment, "Thou shalt lie;"
If this be so (as who can tell?)
There's no one sure ye keep so well."

    Quoth he, "For lies and promise-breaking,
Ye need not be in such a taking:
For lying is, we know and teach,
The highest privilege of speech;
The universal Magna Charta,
To which all human race is party,
Whence children first, as David says,
Lay claim to 't in their earliest days;
The only stratagem in war,
Our generals have occasion for;
The only freedom of the press,
Our politicians need in peace.

* Hutchinson, while Governor of the Province, in his letters to the
ministry declared the necessity, in order to maintain government,
of *destroying the Charter, abridging* what he termed *English Liberties,*
making the Judges dependent only on the crown, and erecting a
nobility in America. Doctor Franklin, then provincial Agent at the
British Court, obtained a number of the originals, and transmitted
them to Boston. In 1773. . . Hutchinson's letters were . . . published in Boston, to the utter confusion of all his pretensions, political
and religious.

Thank heaven, your shot have miss'd their aim,
For lying is no sin nor shame.
　"As men last wills may change again,
Tho' drawn, 'In name of God, Amen;'
Be sure they must have clearly more
O'er promises as great a power,
Which, made in haste, with small inspection,
So much the more will need correction;
And when they've, careless, spoke or penn'd 'em,
Have right to look them o'er and mend 'em;
Revise their vows, or change the text,
By way of codicil annex'd;
Strike out a promise, that was base,
And put a better in its place.
　"So Gage of late agreed, you know,
To let the Boston people go;
Yet when he saw 'gainst troops that braved him,
They were the only guards that saved him,
Kept off that satan of a Putnam*
From breaking in to maul and mutton him;
He'd too much wit, such leagues t' observe,
And shut them in again, to starve.
　"So Moses writes, when female Jews
Made oaths and vows unfit for use,
Their parents then might set them free
From that conscientious tyranny:
And shall men feel that spir'tual bondage
For ever, when they grow beyond age?
Shall vows but bind the stout and strong,
And let go women weak and young,

* General Putnam took the command of the provincial troops, and
blockaded Boston, immediately after the battle of Lexington. Gage,
while his army were in possession of that place, promised to permit
the inhabitants to retire into the country, on condition of surrendering up their arms; but after their compliance, he refused to perform
his engagement—hoping that the Americans would not attempt to
bombard the town, or enter it by storm, while they must endanger
the lives of so many thousands of their fellow-citizens.

As nets enclose the larger crew,
And let the smaller fry creep through?
Besides, the Whigs have all been set on,
The Tories to affright and threaten,
Till Gage amidst his trembling fits,
Has hardly kept him in his wits;
And though he speak with fraud and finesse,
'Tis said beneath *duress per minas.*
For we're in peril of our souls
From your vile feathers, tar and poles;
And vows extorted are not binding
In law, and so not worth the minding.
For we have in this hurly-burly
Sent off our consciences on furlow;
Thrown our religion o'er in form,
Our ship to lighten in the storm.
Nor need we blush your Whigs before;
Had we no virtue, you've no more.

   "Yet black with sins, would spoil a mitre,
Rail ye at faults by ten tints whiter?
And, stuff'd with choler atrabilious,
Insult us here for pecadilloes?
While all your vices run so high
That mercy scarce could find supply:
And should you offer to repent,
You'd need more fasting days than Lent,
More groans than haunted church-yard vallies,
And more confessions than broad-alleys.*
I'll show you all at fitter time,
Th' extent and greatness of your crime,
And here demonstrate to your face,
Your want of virtue, as of grace,
Evinced from topics old and recent:
But thus much must suffice at present.

* Alluding to church discipline, where a person is obliged to stand
in the ile of the church, called in New-England the *broad-alley*, name
the offence he has committed, and ask pardon of his brethren.

To th' after portion of the day,
I leave what more remains to say;
When, I've good hope, you'll all appear,
More fitted and prepared to hear,
And grieved for all your vile demeanour:
But now 'tis time t' adjourn for dinner."

END OF CANTO FIRST

CANTO II

THE TOWN-MEETING, P. M.

THE Sun, who never stops to dine,
Two hours had pass'd the mid-way line,
And driving at his usual rate,
Lash'd on his downward car of state.
And now expired the short vacation,
And dinner o'er in epic fashion,
While all the crew, beneath the trees,
Eat pocket-pies, or bread and cheese,
(Nor shall we, like old Homer, care
To versify their bill of fare)
Each active party, feasted well,
Throng'd in, like sheep, at sound of bell;
With equal spirit took their places,
And meeting oped with three *Oh Yesses:*
When first, the daring Whigs t'oppose,
Again the great M'FINGAL rose,
Stretch'd magisterial arm amain,
And thus resumed th' accusing strain.
   "Ye Whigs attend, and hear affrighted
The crimes whereof ye stand indicted;
The sins and follies past all compass,
That prove you guilty, or *non compos.*
I leave the verdict to your senses,
And jury of your consciences;

Which though they're neither good nor true,
Must yet convict you and your crew.
  "Ungrateful sons! a factious band,
That rise against your parent land!
Ye viper race, that burst in strife
The genial womb that gave you life,
Tear with sharp fangs and forked tongue
The indulgent bowels whence ye sprung;
And scorn the debt and obligation,
You justly owe the British nation,
Which, since you cannot pay, your crew
Affect to swear was never due.
  "Did not the deeds of England's * primate
First drive your fathers to this climate,
Whom jails and fines and every ill
Forced to their good against their will?
Ye owe to their obliging temper
The peopling your new-fangled empire,
While every British act and canon
Stood forth your *causa sine qua non.*
Who'd seen, except for these restraints,
Your witches, quakers, whigs and saints,
Or heard of Mather's† famed *Magnalia,*
If Charles and Laud had chanced to fail you?
Did they not send your charters o'er,
And give you lands you own'd before,
Permit you all to spill your blood,
And drive out heathens where you could;
On these mild terms, that, conquest won,
The realm you gain'd should be their own?
And when of late attack'd by those,

* The persecutions of the English church under Archbishop Laud
. . . *Lond. Edit.*

† See in Mather's Magnalia, a history of the miracles, which occurred in the first settlement of New-England; see also his "Wonders
of the invisible World," for a full and true account of the witchcraft
at Salem.

Whom her connection made your foes,*
Did they not then, distress'd by war,
Send generals to your help from far,
Whose aid you own'd, in terms less haughty,
And thankfully o'er paid your quota?
Say, at what period did they grudge
To send you Governor or Judge,
With all their Missionary† crew,
To teach you law and gospel too?
They brought all felons in the nation
To help you on in population;
Proposed their Bishops to surrender,
And made their Priests a legal tender,
Who only asked, in surplice clad,
The simple tithe of all you had:
And now, to keep all knaves in awe,
Have sent their troops t' establish law,
And with gunpowder, fire and ball,
Reform your people, one and all.
Yet when their insolence and pride
Have angered all the world beside;
When fear and want at once invade,
Can you refuse to lend them aid,
And rather risk your heads in fight,
Than gratefully throw in your mite?
Can they for debts make satisfaction,
Should they dispose their realm at auction,
And sell off Britain's goods and land all

* The war of 1755, between the English and the French, was doubt-less excited by causes foreign to the interests of those Colonies, which now form the United States. They however paid more than their proportion of the expense, and a balance was repaid them by the British Government after the war. *Lond. Edit. . . .*

† These Missionaries were Clergymen, ordained by the Bishop of London, and settled in America. Those in the northern colonies were generally attached to the royal cause.—*Lond. Edit.*

Great efforts were also made to send us Bishops, to rule the New England churches; but this was prevented by the revolution.

To France and Spain, by inch of candle?
Shall good King George, with want oppress'd,
Insert his name in bankrupt list,
And shut up shop, like failing merchant,
That fears the bailiffs should make search in 't;
With poverty shall princes strive,
And nobles lack whereon to live?
Have they not rack'd their whole inventions
To feed their brats on posts and pensions;
Made their Scotch friends with taxes groan,
And pick'd poor Ireland to the bone:
Yet have on hand, as well deserving,
Ten thousand bastards,* left for starving?
And can you now, with conscience clear,
Refuse them an asylum here,
And not maintain, in manner fitting,
These geniune sons of mother Britain?
  "T' evade these crimes of blackest grain
You prate of liberty in vain,
And strive to hide your vile designs
In terms abstruse, like school-divines.
  "Your boasted patriotism is scarce,
And country's love is but a farce:
For after all the proofs you bring,
We Tories know there's no such thing.
Hath not Dalrymple† show'd in print,
And Johnson too, there's nothing in 't;
Produced you demonstration ample,
From others and their own example,
That self is still, in either faction,
The only principle of action;

* A great proportion of the old English peerage consists of the left-handed progeny of their Kings. In this business, Charles the second was the last hero.
  † This writer undertook to demonstrate, that all the celebrated British patriots [Hampden, Sidney, Admiral Russell, and others] were pensioners, in the pay of France. His proof is derived from the letters of the French embassadors. . . .

The loadstone, whose attracting tether
Keeps the politic world together:
And spite of all your double dealing,
We all are sure 'tis so, from feeling.
　"Who heeds your babbling of transmitting
Freedom to brats of your begetting,
Or will proceed, as tho' there were a tie,
And obligation to posterity?
We get them, bear them, breed and nurse.
What has posterity done for us,
That we, least they their rights should lose,
Should trust our necks to gripe of noose?
　"And who believes you will not run?
Ye're cowards, every mother's son;
And if you offer to deny,
We've witnesses to prove it by.
Attend th' opinion first, as referee,
Of your old general, stout Sir Jeffery; *
Who swore that with five thousand foot
He'd rout you all, and in pursuit
Run thro' the land, as easily
As camel thro' a needle's eye?
Did not the mighty Colonel Grant
Against your courage pour his rant,
Affirm your universal failure
In every principle of valour,
And swear no scamperers e'er could match you,
So swift, a bullet scarce could catch you?
And will you not confess, in this
A judge most competent he is;
Well skill'd on running to decide,
As what himself has often tried?
'Twould not methinks be labor lost,
If you'd sit down and count the cost,
And ere you call your Yankies out,

* Sir Jeffery Amherst, Grant and other officers, who had served
in America, were so ignorant, silly or malicious, as to make such
assertions in parliament.

First think what work you've set about.
Have you not roused, his force to try on,
That grim old beast, the British Lion;
And know you not, that at a sup
He's large enough to eat you up?
Have you survey'd his jaws beneath,
Drawn inventories of his teeth,
Or have you weighed, in even balance,
His strength and magnitude of talons?
His roar would change your boasts to fear,
As easily, as sour* small beer;
And make your feet from dreadful fray,
By native instinct run away.
Britain, depend on 't, will take on her
T' assert her dignity and honor,
And ere she'd lose your share of pelf,
Destroy your country, and herself.
For has not North declared they fight
To gain substantial rev'nue by 't,
Denied he'd ever deign to treat,
Till on your knees and at his feet?
And feel you not a trifling ague
From Van's " *Delenda est Carthago?* " †
For this now Britain has projected,
Think you she has not means t' effect it?
Has she not set at work all engines
To spirit up the native Indians,
Send on your backs the tawney band,
With each an hatchet in his hand,
T' amuse themselves with scalping knives,
And butcher children and your wives;
And paid them for your scalps at sale

---

* It is asserted that the roar of a lion will turn small beer sour.

† *Carthage must be annihilated.* There actually existed a little time before the war, a member of parliament of the name of *Van*, who in a speech there applied this famous threat of Cato to America, and particularly to Boston, as the place to begin the work of destruction.

More then your heads would fetch by tale;
That she might boast again with vanity,
Her English national humanity?
For now in its primeval sense
This term, *humanity*, comprehends
All things of which, on this side hell,
The *human mind* is capable;
And thus 'tis well, by writers sage,
Applied to Britain and to Gage.
On this brave work to raise allies,
She sent her duplicate of Guys,
To drive at different parts at once on,
Her stout Guy Carlton and Guy Johnson; *
To each of whom, to send again you,
Old Guy of Warwick were a ninny,
Though the dun cow he fell'd in war,
These kill cows are his betters far.
    "And has she not essay'd her notes
To rouse your slaves to cut your throats;
Sent o'er ambassadors with guineas,
To bribe your blacks in Carolinas?
And has not Gage, her missionary,
Turn'd many an Afric to a Tory;
Made the New-England Bishop's see grow,
By many a new-converted negro?
As friends to government, when he
Your slaves at Boston late set free,
Enlisted them in black parade,
Emboss'd with regimental red;
While flared the epaulette, like flambeau,
On Captain Cuff and Ensign Sambo:
And were they not accounted then
Among his very bravest men?
And when such means she stoops to take,
Think you she is not wide awake?

* A half-breed son of the famous Sir William, who influenced and
led some of their tribes against us during the war.

As the good man of old in Job
Own'd wondrous allies through the globe,
Had brought the stones* along the street
To ratify a cov'nant meet,
And every beast, from lice to lions,
To join in leagues of strict alliance:
Has she not cringed, in spite of pride,
For like assistance, far and wide,
Till all this formidable league rose
Of Indians, British troops and Negroes?
And can you break these triple bands
By all your workmanship of hands?

"Sir," quoth Honorious, "we presume
You guess from past feats what's to come,
And from the mighty deeds of Gage
Foretell how fierce the war he'll wage.
You doubtless recollected here
The annals of his first great year:
While, wearying out the Tories' patience,
He spent his breath in proclamations;
While all his mighty noise and vapour
Was used in wrangling upon paper,
And boasted military fits
Closed in the straining of his wits;
While troops, in Boston commons placed,
Laid nought, but quires of paper, waste;
While strokes alternate stunn'd the nation,
Protest, Address and Proclamation,
And speech met speech, fib clash'd with fib,
And Gage still answer'd, squib for squib.

"Though this not all his time was lost on;
He fortified the town of Boston,
Built breastworks, that might lend assistance

* The stones and all the elements with thee
  Shall ratify a strict confederacy,
  Wild beasts their savage temper shall forget,
  And for a firm alliance with thee treat, etc.
                    Blackmore's paraphrase of Job.

To keep the patriots at a distance;
For howsoe'er the rogues might scoff,
He liked them best the farthest off;
Works of important use to aid
His courage, when he felt afraid,
And whence right off, in manful station,
He'd boldly pop his proclamation.
Our hearts must in our bosoms freeze,
At such heroic deeds as these."

    "Vain," said the 'Squire, "you'll find to sneer
At Gage's first triumphant year;
For Providence, disposed to teaze us,
Can use what instruments it pleases.
To pay a tax, at Peter's wish,
His chief cashier was once a fish;
An ass, in Balaam's sad disaster,
Turn'd orator and saved his master;
A goose, placed sentry on his station,
Preserved old Rome from desolation;
An English bishop's* cur of late
Disclosed rebellions 'gainst the state;
So frogs croak'd Pharaoh to repentance,
And lice delay'd the fatal sentence:
And heaven can ruin you at pleasure,
By Gage, as soon as by a Cæsar.
Yet did our hero in these days
Pick up some laurel wreaths of praise.
And as the statuary of Seville
Made his crackt saint an exc'llent devil;
So though our war small triumph brings,
We gained great fame in other things.

    "Did not our troops show great discerning,
And skill your various arts in learning?
Outwent they not each native noodle

    * See Atterbury's trial.

By far, in playing Yankee-doodle,*
Which as 'twas your New-England tune,
'Twas marvellous they took so soon?
And ere the year was fully through,
Did they not learn to foot it too,†
And such a dance, as ne'er was known,
For twenty miles on end lead down?
Did they not lay their heads together,
And gain your art to tar and feather,‡
When Colonel Nesbitt, thro' the town,
In triumph bore the country-clown?
Oh what a glorious work to sing
The veteran troops of Britain's king,
Adventuring for th' heroic laurel
With bag of feathers and tar-barrel!

* This was a native air of New-England, and was often played in derision by the British troops, particularly on their march to Lexington. Afterwards the captive army of Burgoyne was obliged to march to this tune, in the ceremony of piling their arms at Saratoga. *Lond. Edit.*

† At the battle of Lexington.

‡ In the beginning of 1775, to bring forward an occasion for a more serious quarrel, than had yet taken place between the people and the army, Lieutenant Colonel Nesbitt laid the following plan. The country people being in the habit of purchasing arms, he directed a soldier to sell one of them an old rusty musket. The soldier soon found a purchaser, a man who brought vegetables to market, who paid him three dollars for it. Scarcely had the man departed from the soldier when he was seized by Nesbitt and conveyed to the guard-house, where he was confined all night. Early the next morning they stripped him entirely naked, covered him with warm tar, then with feathers, placed him on a cart, conducted him to the north end of town, then back to the south end, as far as Liberty-Tree; where the people began to collect in vast numbers, and the military, fearing for their own safety, dismissed the man, and made a retreat to the barracks.

The party consisted of about thirty grenadiers of the 47th regiment, with fixed bayonets, twenty drums and fifes playing the Rogue's March, headed by Nesbitt with a drawn sword. *Lond. Edit.*

To paint the cart where culprits ride,
And Nesbitt marching at its side,
Great executioner and proud,
Like hangman high on Holborn road;
And o'er the slow-drawn rumbling car,
The waving ensigns of the war!
As when a triumph Rome decreed
For great Caligula's valiant deed,
Who had subdued the British seas,
By gath'ring cockles from their base;
In pompous car the conq'ror bore
His captive scallops from the shore,
Ovations gain'd his crabs for fetching,
And mighty feats of oyster-catching:
'Gainst Yankies thus the war begun,
They tarr'd, and triumph'd over, one;
And fought and boasted through the season,
With force as great and equal reason.

  "Yet thus though skill'd in vict'ry's toils,
They boast, not unexpert, in wiles.
For gained they not an equal fame in
The arts of secrecy and scheming;
In stratagem show'd wondrous force,
And modernized the Trojan horse,
Play'd o'er again the tricks Ulyssean,
In their famed Salem expedition?
For as that horse, the poets tell ye,
Bore Grecian armies in its belly,
Till their full reckoning run, with joy
Shrewd Sinon midwived them in Troy:
So in one ship was Leslie bold
Cramm'd with three hundred men in hold,
Equipp'd for enterprize and sail,
Like Jonas stow'd in womb of whale.
To Marblehead in depth of night
The cautious vessel wing'd her flight.
And now the sabbath's silent day
Call'd all your Yankies off to pray;

Safe from each prying jealous neighbour,
The scheme and vessel fell in labor.
Forth from its hollow womb pour'd hast'ly
The Myrmidons of Colonel Leslie.
Not thicker o'er the blacken'd strand,
The frogs detachment,* rush'd to land,
Furious by onset and surprize
To storm th' entrenchment of the mice.
Through Salem straight, without delay,
The bold battalion took its way,
March'd o'er a bridge,† in open sight
Of several Yankies armed for fight;
Then without loss of time or men,
Veer'd round for Boston back again,
And found so well their projects thrive,
That every soul got home alive.
    "Thus Gage's arms did fortune bless
With triumph, safety and success.
But mercy is without dispute
His first and darling attribute;
So great, it far outwent and conquer'd
His military skill at Concord.
There, when the war he chose to wage,
Shone the benevolence of Gage;
Sent troops to that ill-omen'd place,
On errands mere of special grace;
And all the work, he chose them for,

* See Homer's Battle of the Frogs and Mice.
† . . . This expedition was to seize some provincial artillery and
stores, placed at a short distance from Salem. . . . When he came
to a small river, Leslie found the bridge taken up, the stores removed,
and the people . . . rapidly collecting in his front, as well as rear.
He then opened a parley, and promised that if they would lay down
the bridge and suffer him to march over it, he would immediately
return from whence he came, without doing harm to any person or
thing. The treaty was concluded; Leslie . . . performed every
article on his part, with the greatest honor and safety.

Was to *prevent a civil war;* *
For which kind purpose he projected
The only certain way t' effect it,
To seize your powder, shot and arms,
And all your means of doing harms;
As prudent folks take knives away,
Lest children cut themselves at play.
And yet, when this was all his scheme,
The war you still will charge on him;
And tho' he oft has swore and said it,
Stick close to facts, and give no credit.
Think you, he wish'd you'd brave and beard him?
Why, 'twas the very thing, that scared him.
He'd rather you should all have run,
Than staid to fire a single gun.
So, for the civil war you lament,
Faith, you yourselves must take the blame in't;
For had you then, as he intended,
Given up your arms, it must have ended:
Since that's no war, each mortal knows,
Where one side only gives the blows,†
And t'other bears them; on reflection
The most we call it is correction.
Nor could the contest have gone higher,
If you had ne'er returned the fire:
But when you shot, and not before,
It then commenced a civil war.
Else Gage, to end this controversy,
Had but corrected you in mercy;
Whom mother Britain, old and wise,
Sent o'er, the colonies to chastise;
Command obedience on their peril
Of ministerial whip and ferule;
And since they ne'er must come of age,

* This Gage solemnly declared in a letter to Governor Trumbull
of Connecticut, soon after the expedition. The correspondence was
immediately published.

† Si rixa est, ubi tu pulsas, ego vapulo tantum.—*Juvenal.* . . .

M'FINGAL

Govern'd and tutor'd them by Gage.
Still more, that mercy was their errand,
The army's conduct makes apparent.
What though at Lexington you can say,
They kill'd a few, they did not fancy;
At Concord then with manful popping,
Discharged a round, the ball to open;
Yet when they saw your rebel rout
Determined still to brave it out,
Did they not show their love of peace,
Their wish that discord straight might cease;
Demonstrate, and by proofs uncommon,
Their orders were to injure no man? *
For did not every regular† run,
As soon as e'er you fired a gun;
Take the first shot you sent them, greeting,
As meant their signal for retreating;
And fearful, if they staid for sport,
You might by accident be hurt,
Convey themselves with speed away
Full twenty miles in half a day;
Race till their legs were grown so weary,
They scarce sufficed their weight to carry?
Whence Gage extols, from general hearsay,
The great activity of Lord Percy; ‡
Whose brave example led them on,
And spirited the troops to run;
Who now may boast, at royal levees,
A Yankee-chace worth forty Chevys.
   "Yet you, as vile as they were kind,
Pursued, like tygers, still behind;

---

* This was another assertion by Gage, in his letter mentioned in the former note.

† . . . The term, *Regulars*, was applied to the British troops, to distinguish them from the Provincials. . . .

‡ "Too much praise cannot be given to Lord Percy for his remarkable *activity* through the whole day."
        Gage's account of the Lexington battle.

Fired on them at your will, and shut
The town, as though you'd starve them out;
And with parade preposterous* hedged,
Affect to hold them there besieged:
Though Gage, whom proclamations call
Your Gov'nor and Vice-Admiral,
Whose power gubernatorial still
Extends as far as Bunker's hill,
Whose admiralty reaches, clever,
Near half a mile up Mistic river,
Whose naval force yet keeps the seas,
Can run away whene 'er he'd please.
Nay, stern with rage grim Putnam boiling
Plunder'd both Hogg and Noddle Island; †
Scared troops of Tories into town,
Burn'd all their hay and houses down,
And menaced Gage, unless he'd flee,
To drive him headlong to the sea;
As once, to faithless Jews a sign,
The De'el, turn'd hog-reeve, did the swine.
  "But now your triumphs all are o'er;
For see from Britain's angry shore,
With deadly hosts of valor join
Her Howe, her Clinton and Burgoyne!
As comets thro' th' affrighted skies
Pour baleful ruin as they rise;
As Ætna with infernal roar
In conflagration sweeps the shore;
Or as Abijah White,‡ when sent

---

* "And with a preposterous parade of military arrangement, they affect to hold the army besieged."
                    Gage's last grand proclamation.
† Two islands in the harbour of Boston.
‡ He was representative of Marshfield, and was employed to carry to Boston their famous town-resolves, censuring the Whigs and reprobating the destruction of the Tea. He armed himself in as ridiculous military array, as a second Hudibras, pretending he was afraid he should be robbed of them.

Our Marshfield friends to represent,
Himself while dread array involves,
Commissions, pistols, swords, resolves,
In awful pomp descending down
Bore terror on the factious town:
Not with less glory and affright,
Parade these generals forth to fight.
No more each British colonel runs
From whizzing beetles, as air-guns;
Thinks horn-bugs bullets, or thro' fears
Muskitoes takes for musketeers; *
Nor scapes, as if you'd gain'd supplies,
From Beelzebub's whole host of flies.
No bug these warlike hearts appalls;
They better know the sound of balls.
I hear the din of battle bray;
The trump of horror marks its way.
I see afar the sack of cities,
The gallows strung with Whig-committees;
Your moderates triced, like vermin,
And gate-posts graced with heads of chairmen;
Your Congress for wave-off'rings hanging,
And ladders thronged with priests haranguing.
What pillories glad the Tories' eyes
With patriot ears for sacrifice!
What whipping-posts your chosen race
Admit successive in embrace,
While each bears off his sins, alack!

---

* Absurd as this may appear, it was a fact. Some British officers, soon after Gage's arrival in Boston, walking on Beacon-Hill after sunset, were affrighted by noises in the air (supposed to be the flying of bugs and beetles) which they took to be the sound of bullets. They left the hill with great precipitation, spread the alarm in their encampment, and wrote terrible accounts to England of being shot at with air-guns; as appears by their letters, extracts from which were soon after published in the London papers. Indeed, for some time they seriously believed, that the Americans were possessed of a kind of magic white powder, which exploded and killed without report.

Like Bunyan's pilgrim, on his back! *
Where then, when Tories scarce get clear,
Shall Whigs and Congresses appear?
What rocks and mountains will you call
To wrap you over with their fall,
And save your heads, in these sad weathers,
From fire and sword, and tar and feathers?
For lo! with British troops tar-bright,
Again our Nesbitt heaves in sight;
He comes, he comes, your lines to storm,
And rig your troops in uniform.†
To meet such heroes will ye brag,
With fury arm'd and feather-bag,
Who wield their missile pitch and tar
With engines new in British war?

  "Lo! where our mighty navy brings
Destruction on her canvass wings,‡
While through the deep the British thunder
Shall sound th' alarm, to rob and plunder!
As Phœbus first, so Homer speaks,
When he march'd out t' attack the Greeks,
'Gainst mules sent forth his arrows fatal,
And slew th' auxiliaries, their cattle:
So where our ships § shall stretch the keel,
What vanquish'd oxen shall they steal!
What heroes, rising from the deep,
Invade your marshall'd hosts of sheep;
Disperse whole troops of horse, and pressing,
Make cows surrender at discretion;
Attack your hens, like Alexanders,

---

  * Bunyan represents his pilgrim, as setting forth burdened with a
very heavy pack, containing all his sins, original and actual.
  † The want of uniform dresses in the American army was a constant
theme of ridicule with the British, at the beginning of the war.
    ‡ Where'er our navy spreads her canvas wings,
       Honor to thee and peace to all she brings.   *Waller.*
  § The British navy was at first employed in plundering our sea-
coasts, to obtain fresh provisions.

And regiments rout of geese and ganders;
Or where united arms combine,
Lead captive many a herd of swine!
Then rush in dreadful fury down
To fire on every seaport town;
Display their glory and their wits,
Fright helpless children into fits;
And stoutly, from the unequal fray,
Make many a woman run away.

  "And can ye doubt, whene 'er we please,
Our chiefs shall boast such deeds as these?
Have we not chiefs transcending far
The old famed *thunderbolts of war;* *
Beyond the brave knight-errant fighters,
Stiled swords of death, by novel-writers;
Nor in romancing ages e'er rose
So terrible a tier of heroes.
From Gage what sounds alarm the waves!
How loud a blunderbuss is Graves! †
How Newport dreads the blustering sallies,
That thunder from our popgun, Wallace,
While noise in formidable strains,
Spouts from his thimble-full of brains!
I see you sink in awed surprise!
I see our Tory brethren rise!
And as the sect'ries Sandemanian,
Our friends, describe their hoped millennium; ‡
Boast how the world in every region
At once shall own their true religion,
For heaven shall knock, with vengeance dread,
All unbelievers on the head;
And then their church, the meek in spirit,

        * . . . duo fulmina belli,
        Scipiadas.   *Virgil.*
  † Graves was the admiral; Wallace, Captain of a frigate stationed
before Newport.
  ‡ The year 1793 was the period they fixed upon, for this event to
take place.

The earth, as promised, shall inherit
From the dead wicked, as heirs male,
Or next remainder-men in tail:
Such ruin shall the Whigs oppress;
Such spoils our Tory friends shall bless;
While Confiscation at command
Shall stalk in terror through the land,
Shall give all whig-estates away,
And call our brethren into play.

   "And can you pause, or scruple more?
These things are near you, at the door.
Behold! for though to reasoning blind,
Signs of the times you still might mind,
And view impending fate, as plain
As you'd foretell a shower of rain.

   "Hath not heaven warn'd you what must ensue,
And providence declared against you?
Hung forth the dire portents of war
By fires and beacons in the air; *
Alarm'd old women all around
With fearful noises under ground,
While earth, for many a hundred leagues,
Groan'd with her dismal load of Whigs?
Was there a meteor, far and wide,
But muster'd on the Tory side;
A star malign, that has not bent
Its aspects for the parliament,
Foreboding your defeat and misery,
As once they fought against old Sisera?
Was there a cloud, that spread the skies,
But bore our armies of allies,

---

* Stories of prodigies were at that time industriously propagated
by the Tories in various parts of New England, and with some success in alarming and intimidating the superstitious. In fact, about
the commencement of the war, a large meteor passed through our
atmosphere, and the Aurora borealis appeared more frequently, and
assumed more singular appearances, than usual. These materials
were sufficient for a beginning; nonsense easily supplied the rest.

While dreadful hosts of flame stood forth
In baleful streamers from the north?
Which plainly show'd what part they join'd;
For North's the minister, ye mind;
Whence oft your quibblers in gazettes
On *Northern blasts* have strain'd their wits;
And think you not, the clouds know how
To make the pun, as well [as] you?
Did there arise an apparition,
But grinn'd forth ruin to sedition;
A death-watch, but has join'd our leagues,
And click'd destruction to the Whigs?
Heard ye not, when the wind was fair,
At night our prophets in the air,
Who, loud, like admiralty libel,
Read awful chapters from the Bible,
And war and death and plague denounced,
And told you how you'd soon be trounced?
I see, to join our conq'ring side,
Heaven, earth and hell at once allied;
See from your overthrow and end,
The Tory paradise ascend,
Like that new world, which claims its station,
Beyond the final conflagration.
I see the day, that lots your share,
In utter darkness and despair;
The day of joy, when North, our lord,
His faithful fav'rites shall reward.
No Tory then shall set before him
Small wish of 'Squire and Justice Quorum;
But to his mistaken eyes
See lordships, posts and pensions rise.
    "Awake to gladness then, ye Tories!
Th' unbounded prospect lies before us.
The power, display'd in Gage's banners,
Shall cut their fertile lands to manors;
And o'er our happy conquer'd ground,
Dispense estates and titles round.

Behold! the world shall stare at new setts
Of home-made Earls* in Massachusetts;
Admire, array'd in ducal tassels,
Your Ol'vers, Hutchinsons and Vassals;
See join'd in ministerial work
His Grace of Albany, and York.
What lordships from each carved estate,
On our New-York Assembly wait!
What title Jauncys, Gales and Billops; †
Lord Brush, Lord Wilkins and Lord Philips!
In wide-sleeved pomp of godly guise,
What solemn rows of Bishops rise!
Aloft a Cardinal's hat is spread
O'er punster Cooper's reverend head.
In Vardell, that poetic zealot,‡
I view a lawn-bedizen'd Prelate;
While mitres fall, as 'tis their duty,
On heads of Chandler and Auchmuty!
Knights, Viscounts, Barons, shall ye meet,
As thick as pebbles in the street;
E'en I perhaps (heaven speed my claim!)
Shall fix a *Sir* before my name.
For titles all our foreheads ache,
For what blest changes can they make!
Place Reverence, Grace and Excellence,
Where neither claim'd the least pretence;
Transform by patent's magic words
Men, likest devils, into Lords;
Whence commoners, to Peers translated,

* See Hutchinson's and Oliver's letters.
† Members of the ministerial majority in the Legislature of New York.
‡ Cooper, President of King's College in New York, was a notorious punster; Vardell, author of some poetical satires on the sons of liberty in New York; Chandler and Auchmuty, high-church and tory writers of the clerical order.

Are justly said to be *created*.*
Now where commissioners you saw,
Shall boards of nobles deal you law;
Long-robed comptrollers judge your rights,
And tide-waiters start up in knights.
While Whigs subdued, in slavish awe,
Our wood shall hew, our water draw,
And bless the mildness, when past hope,
That saved their necks from noose of rope.
For since our leaders have decreed,
Their blacks, who join us, shall be freed,
To hang the conquer'd whigs, we all see,
Would prove but weak, and thriftless policy,
Except their Chiefs: the vulgar knaves
Will do more good, preserved for slaves."

" 'Tis well," Honorious cried; "your scheme
Has painted out a pretty dream.
We can't confute your second-sight;
We shall be slaves and you a knight.
These things must come, but I divine,
They'll come not in your day, nor mine.

"But, oh my friends, my brethren, hear;
And turn for once th' attentive ear.
Ye see how prompt to aid our woes
The tender mercies of our foes;
Ye see with what unvaried rancour
Still for our blood their minions hanker;
Nor aught can sate their mad ambition,
From us, but death, or worse, submission.
Shall these then riot in our spoil,
Reap the glad harvest of our toil,
Rise from their country's ruins proud,
And roll their chariot-wheels in blood?
See Gage, with inauspicious star,
Has oped the gates of civil war,

* "To create a Peer" is the English technical phrase, . . . thus
Adam *was formed of the dust of the ground.* Gen. II, 7.

When streams of gore, from freemen slain,
Encrimson'd Concord's fatal plain;
Whose warning voice, with awful sound,
Still cries, like Abel's from the ground;
And heaven, attentive to its call,
Shall doom the proud oppressor's fall.
   "Rise then, ere ruin swift surprize,
To victory, to vengeance, rise.
Hark, how the distant din alarms;
The echoing trumpet breathes, to arms.
From provinces remote, afar,
The sons of glory rouse to war.
'Tis Freedom calls! the raptured sound
The Apalachian hills rebound.
The Georgian * coasts her voice shall hear,
And start from lethargies of fear.
From the parch'd zone, with glowing ray
Where pours the sun intenser day,
To shores where icy waters roll,
And tremble to the glimm'ring pole,
Inspired by freedom's heavenly charms,
United nations wake to arms.
The star of conquest lights their way,
And guides their vengeance on their prey.
Yes, though tyrannic force oppose,
Still shall they triumph o'er their foes;
Till heaven the happy land shall bless
With safety, liberty and peace.
   "And ye, whose souls of dastard mould
Start at the bravery of the bold;
To love your country who pretend,
Yet want all spirit to defend;
Who feel your fancies so prolific,
Engend'ring visions whims terrific,
O'errun with horrors of coercion,
Fire, blood and thunder in reversion;

* The province of Georgia had not then joined the union.

King's standards, pill'ries, confiscations,
And Gage's scare-crow proclamations;
Who scarce could rouse, if caught in fray,
Presence of mind to run away;
See nought but halters rise to view,
In all your dreams, and deem them true;
And while these phantoms haunt your brains,
Bow down your willing necks to chains.
Heavens! are ye sons of sires so great,
Immortal in the fields of fate,
Who braved all deaths, by land or sea,
Who bled, who conquer'd to be free?
Hence cowards souls, the worst disgrace
Of our forefathers' valiant race;
Hie homeward from the glorious field,
There turn the wheel, the distaff wield;
Act what ye are, nor dare to stain
The warrior's arms with touch profane;
There beg your more heroic wives
To guard your own, your children's, lives;
Beneath their aprons seek a screen,
Nor dare to mingle more with men."
    As thus he spake, the Tories' anger
Could now restrain itself no longer;
Who tried before by many a freak, or
Insulting noise, to stop the speaker;
Swung th' un-oil'd hinge of each pew-door,
Their feet kept shuffling on the floor;
Made their disapprobation known
By many a murmur, hum and groan,
That to his speech supplied the place
Of counterpart in thorough bass.
Thus bagpipes, while the tune they breathe,
Still drone and grumble underneath;
And thus the famed Demosthenes*

---

* . . . Which party made the most noise, history does not inform us.

Harangued the rumbling of the seas,
Held forth with elocution grave,
To audience loud of wind and wave;
And had a stiller congregation,
Than Tories are, to hear th' oration.
The uproar now grew high and louder,
As nearer thund'rings of a cloud are,
And every soul with heart and voice
Supplied his quota of the noise.
Each listening ear was set on torture,
Each Tory bellowing, "Order, Order;"
And some, with tongue not low or weak,
Were clam'ring fast, for leave to speak;
The Moderator, with great vi'lence,
The cushion thump'd with, "Silence, Silence!"
The Constable to every prater
Bawl'd out, "Pray hear the moderator;"
Some call'd the vote, and some in turn
Were screaming high, "Adjourn, Adjourn."
Not Chaos heard such jars and clashes,
When all the el'ments fought for places.
The storm each moment fiercer grew;
His sword the great M'FINGAL drew,
Prepared in either chance to share,
To keep the peace, or aid the war.
Nor lack'd they each poetic being,
Whom bards alone are skill'd in seeing;
Plumed Victory stood perch'd on high,
Upon the pulpit-canopy,
To join, as is her custom tried,
Like Indians, on the strongest side;
The Destinies, with shears and distaff,
Drew near their threads of life to twist off;
The Furies 'gan to feast on blows,
And broken head, and bloody nose:
When on a sudden from without
Arose a loud terrific shout;
And straight the people all at once heard

Of tongues an universal concert;
Like Aesop's times, as fable runs,
When every creature talk'd at once,
Or like the variegated gabble,
That crazed the carpenters of Babel.
Each party soon forsook the quarrel,
And let the other go on parol,
Eager to know what fearful matter
Had conjured up such general clatter;
And left the church in thin array,
As though it had been lecture-day.*
Our 'Squire M'FINGAL straitway beckon'd
The Constable to stand his second;
And sallied forth with aspect fierce
The crowd assembled to disperse.

    The Moderator, out of view,
Beneath the desk had lain perdue;
Peep'd up his head to view the fray,
Beheld the wranglers run away,
And left alone, with solemn face
Adjourn'd them without time or place.

END OF CANTO SECOND

CANTO III

THE LIBERTY POLE

Now warm with ministerial ire,
Fierce sallied forth our loyal 'Squire,
And on his striding steps attends

---

* In the New England churches, previous to the administration of the sacrament, religious service was performed, and a sermon preached, on some day in the week preceding. These sermons were styled *Lectures*, and the day called *Lecture-day*. But usually these meetings were very thinly attended, like the *Wall-lectures* in the English Universities, in which to supply an audience, they depend on the proverb, that *Walls have ears. See V. Knox's Essays No.* 77.

His desperate clan of Tory friends.
When sudden met his wrathful eye
A pole ascending through the sky,
Which numerous throngs of whiggish race
Were raising in the market place.
Not higher school-boy's kites aspire,
Or royal mast, or country spire;
Like spears at Brobdignagian tilting,
Or Satan's walking-staff in Milton.
And on its top, the flag unfurl'd
Waved triumph o'er the gazing world,
Inscribed with inconsistent types
Of *Liberty* and *thirteen stripes*.*
Beneath, the crowd without delay
The dedication-rites essay,
And gladly pay, in antient fashion,
The ceremonies of libation;
While briskly to each patriot lip
Walks eager round the inspiring flip: †
Delicious draught! whose powers inherit
The quintessence of public spirit;
Which whoso tastes, perceives his mind
To nobler politics refined;
Or roused to martial controversy,
As from transforming cups of Circe;
Or warm'd with Homer's nectar'd liquor,
That fill'd the veins of gods with ichor.
At hand for new supplies in store,
The tavern opes its friendly door,
Whence to and fro the waiters run,
Like bucket-men at fires in town.
Then with three shouts that tore the sky,
'Tis consecrate to Liberty.
To guard it from th' attacks of Tories,

* The American flag. It would doubtless be wrong to imagine
that the stripes bear any allusion to the slave trade.

† Flip, a liquor composed of beer, rum and sugar; the common
treat at that time in the country towns of New England.

A grand Committee cull'd of four is;
Who foremost on the patriot spot,
Had brought the flip, and paid the shot.
   By this, M'FINGAL with his train
Advanced upon th' adjacent plain,
And full with loyalty possest,
Pour'd forth the zeal, that fired his breast.
   "What mad-brain'd rebel gave commission,
To raise this May-pole of sedition?
Like Babel, rear'd by bawling throngs,
With like confusion too of tongues,
To point at heaven and summon down
The thunders of the British crown?
Say, will this paltry Pole secure
Your forfeit heads from Gage's power?
Attack'd by heroes brave and crafty,
Is this to stand your ark of safety;
Or driven by Scottish laird and laddie,
Think ye to rest beneath its shadow?
When bombs, like fiery serpents, fly,
And balls rush hissing through the sky,
Will this vile Pole, devote to freedom,
Save like the Jewish pole in Edom;
Or like the brazen snake of Moses,
Cure your crackt skulls and batter'd noses?
   "Ye dupes to every factious rogue
And tavern-prating demagogue,
Whose tongue but rings, with sound more full,
On th' empty drumhead of his scull;
Behold you not what noisy fools
Use you, worse simpletons, for tools?
For Liberty, in your own by-sense,
Is but for crimes a patent license,
To break of law th' Egyptian yoke,
And throw the world in common stock;
Reduce all grievances and ills
To Magna Charta of your wills;
Establish cheats and frauds and nonsense,

Framed to the model of your conscience;
Cry justice down, as out of fashion,
And fix its scale of depreciation; *
Defy all creditors to trouble ye,
And keep new years of Jewish jubilee;
Drive judges out, † like Aaron's calves,
By jurisdiction of white staves,
And make the bar and bench and steeple
Submit t' our Sovereign Lord, The People;
By plunder rise to power and glory,
And brand all property, as Tory;
Expose all wears to lawful seizures
By mobbers or monopolizers;
Break heads and windows and the peace,
For your own interest and increase;
Dispute and pray and fight and groan
For public good, and mean your own;
Prevent the law by fierce attacks
From quitting scores upon your backs;
Lay your old dread, the gallows, low,
And seize the stocks, your ancient foe,
And turn them to convenient engines
To wreak your patriotic vengeance;
While all, your rights who understand,
Confess them in their owner's hand;
And when by clamours and confusions,
Your freedom's grown a public nuisance,
Cry "Liberty," with powerful yearning,
As he does "Fire!" whose house is burning;
Though he already has much more
Than he can find occasion for.

* Alluding to the depreciation of the Continental paper money.
Congress finally ascertained the course of its declension at different
periods, by what was called, A Scale of Depreciation.

† On the commencement of the war, the courts of justice were
everywhere shut up. In some instances, the judges were forced to
retire, by the people, who assembled in multitudes, armed with
white staves.

While every clown, that tills the plains,
Though bankrupt in estate and brains,
By this new light transform'd to traitor,
Forsakes his plough to turn dictator,
Starts an haranguing chief of Whigs,
And drags you by the ears, like pigs.
All bluster, arm'd with factious licence,
New-born at once to politicians.
Each leather-apron'd dunce, grown wise,
Presents his forward face t' advise,
And tatter'd legislators meet,
From every workshop through the street.
His goose the tailor finds new use in,
To patch and turn the Constitution;
The blacksmith comes with sledge and grate
To iron-bind the wheels of state;
The quack forbears his patients' souse,
To purge the Council and the House;
The tinker quits his moulds and doxies,
To cast assembly-men and proxies.
From dunghills deep of blackest hue,
Your dirt-bred patriots spring to view,
To wealth and power and honors rise,
Like new-wing'd maggots changed to flies,
And fluttering round in high parade,
Strut in the robe, or gay cockade.
See Arnold quits, for ways more certain,
His bankrupt-perj'ries for his fortune,
Brews rum no longer in his store,
Jockey and skipper now no more,
Forsakes his warehouses and docks,
And writs of slander for the pox; *

* Arnold's perjuries at the time of his pretended bankruptcy, which
was the first rise of his fortune; and his curious lawsuit against a
brother skipper, who had charged him with having caught the above-
mentioned disease, by his connection with a certain African princess
in the West-Indies, were among the early promises of his future
greatness, and honors.

And cleansed by patriotism from shame,
Grows General of the foremost name.
For in this ferment of the stream
The dregs have work'd up to the brim,
And by the rule of topsy-turvies,
The scum stands foaming on the surface.
You've caused your pyramid t' ascend,
And set it on the little end.
Like Hudibras, your empire's made,
Whose crupper had o'ertopped his head.
You've pushed and turn'd the whole world up-
Side down, and got yourselves at top,
While all the great ones of your state
Are crush'd beneath the popular weight;
Nor can you boast, this present hour,
The shadow of the former power.
For what's your Congress* or its end?
A power, t' advise and recommend;
To call forth troops, adjust your quotas—
And yet no soul is bound to notice;
To pawn your faith to th' utmost limit,
But cannot bind you to redeem it;
And when in want no more in them lies,
Than begging from your State-Assemblies;
Can utter oracles of dread,
Like friar Bacon's brazen head,
But when a faction dares dispute 'em,
Has ne'er an arm to execute 'em:
As tho' you chose supreme dictators,
And put them under conservators.
You've but pursued the self-same way
With Shakespeare's Trinc'lo† in the play;

* . . . the principal defects of the first federal constitution of
the United States: all which have been since removed in the new
Constitution, established in the year 1789. So that the prophecy
below, *You'll ne'er have sense enough to mend it*, must be ranked among
the other sage blunders of his second-sighted hero. *Lond. Edit.*
  † This political plan of Trinculo in the Tempest. . . .

"You shall be Viceroys here, 'tis true,
"But we'll be Viceroys over you."
What wild confusion hence must ensue?
Tho' common danger yet cements you:
So some wreck'd vessel, all in shatters,
Is held up by surrounding waters,
But stranded, when the pressure ceases,
Falls by its rottenness to pieces.
And fall it must! if wars were ended,
You'll ne'er have sense enough to mend it:
But creeping on, by low intrigues,
Like vermin of a thousand legs,*
'Twill find as short a life assign'd,
As all things else of reptile kind.
Your Commonwealth's a common harlot,
The property of every varlet;
Which now in taste, and full employ,
All sorts admire, as all enjoy:
But soon a batter'd strumpet grown,
You'll curse and drum her out of town.
Such is the government you chose;
For this you bade the world be foes;
For this, so mark'd for dissolution,
You scorn the British Constitution,
That constitution form'd by sages,
The wonder of all modern ages;
Which owns no failure in reality,
Except corruption and venality;
And merely proves the adage just,
That best things spoil'd corrupt to worst:
So man supreme in earthly station,
And mighty lord of this creation,
When once his corse is dead as herring,
Becomes the most offensive carrion,
And sooner breeds the plague, 'tis found,
Than all beasts rotting on the ground.
Yet with republics to dismay us,

*Millepedes.

You've call'd up Anarchy from chaos,
With all the followers of her school,
Uproar and Rage and wild Misrule:
For whom this rout of Whigs distracted,
And ravings dire of every crack'd head;
These new-cast legislative engines
Of County-meetings and Conventions;
Committees vile of correspondence,
And mobs, whose tricks have almost undone 's:
While reason fails to check your course,
And Loyalty's kick'd out of doors,
And Folly, like inviting landlord,
Hoists on your poles her royal standard;
While the king's friends, in doleful dumps,
Have worn their courage to the stumps,
And leaving George in sad disaster,
Most sinfully deny their master.
What furies raged when you, in sea,
In shape of Indians, drown'd the tea; *
When your gay sparks, fatigued to watch it,
Assumed the moggison and hatchet,
With wampum'd blankets hid their laces,
And like their sweethearts, primed† their faces:
While not a red-coat dared oppose,
And scarce a Tory show'd his nose;
While Hutchinson,‡ for sure retreat,
Manœuvred to his country seat,

---

* The cargo of tea sent to Boston, after being guarded for twenty nights, by voluntary parties of the Whigs, to prevent its being clandestinely brought ashore, was thrown into the sea, by a party of about two hundred young men, dressed, armed and painted like Indians; but many a ruffled shirt and laced vest appeared under their blankets.

† *Primed*, i. e. painted.

‡ When the leading Whigs in Boston found it impossible to procure the Tea to be sent back, they secretly resolved on its destruction, and prepared all the necessary means. To cover the design, a meeting of the people of the whole County was convened on the day appointed.

And thence affrighted, in the suds,
Stole off bareheaded through the woods.
   "Have you not roused your mobs to join,
And make Mandamus-men resign,
Call'd forth each duffil-drest curmudgeon,
With dirty trowsers and white bludgeon,
Forced all our Councils through the land,
To yield their necks at your command;
While paleness marks their late disgraces,
Through all their rueful length of faces?
   "Have you not caused as woeful work
In our good city of New-York,
When all the rabble, well cockaded,
In triumph through the streets paraded,
And mobb'd the Tories, scared their spouses,
And ransack'd all the custom-houses; *
Made such a tumult, bluster, jarring,
That mid the clash of tempests warring,
Smith's† weather-cock, in veers forlorn,
Could hardly tell which way to turn?
Burn'd effigies in higher powers,
Contrived in planetary hours;
As witches with clay-images
Destroy or torture whom they please:
Till fired with rage, th' ungrateful club
Spared not your best friend, Beelzebub,
O'erlooked his favors, and forgot

. . . Hutchinson was alarmed at the meeting, and retired privately in the morning, to his country seat at Milton. Whether from mistake or design, information was sent to him, that the mob was coming to pull down his house. He escaped in the utmost haste across the fields. The story of the day was, that the alarm was given, at the time, when he sate half shaved under the hands of his barber.

* The custom-house was broken open at New York, and all the public monies seized.

† William Smith, an eminent Lawyer in New York. He at first opposed the claims of Britain, but after wavering some time, at last joined our enemy. He has since been Chief Justice in Canada.

The reverence due his cloven foot,
And in the selfsame furnace frying,
Stew'd him, and North and Bute and Tryon? *
Did you not, in as vile and shallow way,
Fright our poor Philadelphian, Galloway,
Your Congress, when the loyal ribald
Belied, berated and bescribbled?
What ropes† and halters did you send,
Terrific emblems of his end,
Till, least he'd hang in more than effigy,
Fled in a fog the trembling refugee?
Now rising in progression fatal,
Have you not ventured to give battle?
When Treason chaced our heroes troubled,
With rusty gun,‡ and leathern doublet;
Turn'd all stone-walls and groves and bushes,
To batteries arm'd with blunderbusses;
And with deep wounds, that fate portend,
Gaul'd many a Briton's latter end;
Drove them to Boston, as in jail,
Confined without mainprize or bail.
Were not these deeds enough betimes,
To heap the measure of your crimes:

* Tryon was Governor of New York and a British General during
the war. He had the glory of destroying the towns of Fairfield and
Norwalk. Burnings in effigy were frequently the amusements of the
mob at that period, and in imitation of the former custom of the
English in burning annually the Pope, the Devil and the Pretender,
Beelzebub, with his usual figure and accoutrements, was always
joined in the conflagration with the other obnoxious characters.

† Galloway began by being a flaming patriot: but being disgusted
at his own want of influence, and the greater popularity of others,
he turned Tory, wrote against the measures of Congress and absconded. Just before his escape, a trunk was put on board a vessel
in the Delaware, to be delivered to Joseph Galloway, Esquire. On
opening it, he found it contained only, as Shakespeare says,
          "A halter gratis, and leave to hang himself."
‡ At the battle of Lexington.

But in this loyal town and dwelling,
You raise these ensigns of rebellion?
'Tis done! fair Mercy shuts her door;
And Vengeance now shall sleep no more.
Rise then, my friends, in terror rise,
And sweep this scandal from the skies.
You'll see their Dagon, though well jointed,
Will shrink before the Lord's anointed; *
And like old Jericho's proud wall,
Before our ram's horns prostrate fall."

    This said, our 'Squire yet undismay'd,
Call'd forth the Constable to aid,
And bade him read, in nearer station,
The Riot-act and Proclamation.
He swift, advancing to the ring,
Began, "Our Sovereign Lord, the King"—
When thousand clam'rous tongues he hears,
And clubs and stones assail his ears.
To fly was vain; to fight was idle;
By foes encompass'd in the middle,
His hope, in stratagems, he found,
And fell right craftily to ground;
Then crept to seek an hiding place,
'Twas all he could, beneath a brace;
Where soon the conq'ring crew espied him,
And where he lurk'd, they caught and tied him.

    At once with resolution fatal,
Both Whigs and Tories rush'd to battle.
Instead of weapons, either band
Seized on such arms as came to hand.
And as famed Ovid† paints th' adventures
Of wrangling Lapithæ and Centaurs,
Who at their feast, by Bacchus led,
Threw bottles at each other's head;

  * The Tory clergy always stiled the King, the Lord's Anointed.
The language of Cromwell's and Charles' days was yet frequent in
New England.
  † See Ovid's Metamorphoses, book 12th.

And these arms failing in their scuffles,
Attack'd with andirons, tongs and shovels:
So clubs and billets, staves and stones
Met fierce, encountering every sconce,
And cover'd o'er with knobs and pains
Each void receptacle for brains;
Their clamours rend the skies around,
The hills rebellow to the sound;
And many a groan increas'd the din
From batter'd nose and broken shin.
M'Fingal, rising at the word,
Drew forth his old militia-sword;
Thrice cried "King George," as erst in distress,
Knights of romance invoked a mistress:
And brandishing the blade in air,
Struck terror through th' opposing war.
The Whigs, unsafe within the wind
Of such commotion, shrunk behind.
With whirling steel around address'd,
Fierce through their thickest throng he press'd,
(Who roll'd on either side in arch,
Like Red Sea waves in Israel's march)
And like a meteor rushing through,
Struck on their Pole a vengeful blow.
Around, the Whigs, of clubs and stones
Discharged whole vollies, in platoons,
That o'er in whistling fury fly;
But not a foe dares venture nigh.
And now perhaps with glory crown'd
Our 'Squire had fell'd the pole to ground,
Had not some Pow'r, a whig at heart,
Descended down and took their part; *
(Whether 'twere Pallas, Mars or Iris,
'Tis scarce worth while to make inquiries)
Who at the nick of time alarming,
Assumed the solemn form of Chairman,

* . . . The single combats of Paris and Menelaus in Homer,
Aeneas and the Turnus in Virgil, and Michael and Satan in Milton.

Address'd a Whig, in every scene
The stoutest wrestler on the green,
And pointed where the spade was found,
Late used to set their pole in ground,
And urged, with equal arms and might,
To dare our 'Squire to single fight.
The Whig thus arm'd, untaught to yield,
Advanced tremendous to the field:
Nor did M'FINGAL shun the foe,
But stood to brave the desp'rate blow;
While all the party gazed, suspended
To see the deadly combat ended;
And Jove* in equal balance weigh'd
The sword against the brandish'd spade,
He weigh'd; but lighter than a dream,
The sword flew up, and kick'd the beam.
Our 'Squire on tiptoe rising fair
Lifts high a noble stroke in air,
Which hung not, but like dreadful engines,
Descended on his foe in vengeance.
But ah! in danger, with dishonor
The sword perfidious fails its owner;
That sword, which oft had stood its ground,
By huge trainbands encircled round;
And on the bench, with blade right loyal,
Had won the day at many a trial,†
Of stones and clubs had braved th' alarms,
Shrunk from these new Vulcanian arms.‡

* Jupiter ipse duas aequato examine lances
  Sustinet & fata imponit diversa duorum,
  Quem damnet labor, etc.   *Aeneid*, 12.
† It was the fashion in New England at that time, for judges to
wear swords on the bench.
‡— Postquam arma Dei ad Vulcania ventum est,
  Mortalis mucro, glacies ceu futilis, ictu
  Dissiluit; fulva resplendent fragmina arena. *Virgil.*
                              The sword
  Was given him temper'd so, that neither keen

The spade so temper'd from the sledge,
Nor keen nor solid harm'd its edge,
Now met it, from his arm of might,
Descending with steep force to smite;
The blade snapp'd short—and from his hand,
With rust embrown'd the glittering sand.
Swift turn'd M'FINGAL at the view,
And call'd to aid th' attendant crew,
In vain; the Tories all had run,
When scarce the fight was well begun;
Their setting wigs he saw decreas'd
Far in th' horizon tow'rd the west.
Amazed he view'd the shameful sight,
And saw no refuge, but in flight:
But age unwieldy check'd his pace,
Though fear had wing'd his flying race;
For not a trifling prize at stake;
No less than great M'FINGAL's back.*
With legs and arms he work'd his course,
Like rider that outgoes his horse,
And labor's hard to get away, as
Old Satan† struggling on through chaos;
'Till looking back, he spied in rear
The spade-arm'd chief advanced too near:
Then stopp'd and seized a stone, that lay
An ancient landmark near the way;
Nor shall we as old bards have done,
Affirm it weigh'd an hundred ton; ‡
But such a stone, as at a shift
A modern might suffice to lift,
Since men, to credit their enigmas,

Nor solid might resist that edge; it met
The sword of Satan with steep force to smite
Descending and in half cut sheer. *Milton*
* . . . nec enim levia aut ludicra petuntur
Praemia, sed Turni de vita et sanguine certant. *Virgil.*
† In Milton.
‡ This thought is taken from Juvenal, Satire 15.

Are dwindled down to dwarfs and pigmies,
And giants exiled with their cronies
To Brobdignags and Patagonias.
But while our Hero turn'd him round,
And tugg'd to raise it from the ground,
The fatal spade discharged a blow
Tremendous on his rear below:
His bent knee fail'd, * and void of strength
Stretch'd on the ground his manly length.

Like ancient oak o'erturn'd, he lay,
Or tower to tempests fall'n a prey,
Or mountain sunk with all his pines,
Or flow'r the plow to dust consigns,
And more things else—but all men know 'em,
If slightly versed in epic poem.

At once the crew, at this dread crisis,
Fall on, and bind him, ere he rises;
And with loud shouts and joyful soul,
Conduct him prisoner to the pole.

When now the mob in lucky hour
Had got their en'mies in their power,
They first proceed, by grave command,
To take the Constable in hand.

Then from the pole's sublimest top
The active crew let down the rope,
At once its other end in haste bind,
And make it fast upon his waistband;
Till like the earth, as stretch'd on tenter,
He hung self-balanced on his centre.†
Then upwards, all hands hoisting sail,
They swung him, like a keg of ale,
Till to the pinnacle in height
He vaulted, like balloon or kite.

* Genua labant . . . incidit ictus,
   Ingens ad terram duplicato poplite Turnus. *Virgil.*
† And earth self-balanced on her centre hung. *Milton.*

As Socrates* of old at first did
To aid philosophy get hoisted,
And found his thoughts flow strangely clear,
Swung in a basket in mid air:
Our culprit thus, in purer sky,
With like advantage raised his eye,
And looking forth in prospect wide,
His Tory errors clearly spied,
And from his elevated station,
With bawling voice began addressing.

"Good Gentlemen and friends and kin,
For heaven's sake hear, if not for mine!
I here renounce the Pope, the Turks,
The King, the Devil and all their works;
And will, set me but once at ease,
Turn Whig, or Christian, what you please;
And always mind your rules so justly,
Should I live long as old Methus'lah,
I'll never join in British rage,
Nor help Lord North, nor Gen'ral Gage;
Nor lift my gun in future fights,
Nor take away your Charter-rights;
Nor overcome your new-raised levies,
Destroy your towns, nor burn your navies;
Nor cut your poles down while I've breath,
Though raised more thick than hatchel-teeth:
But leave King George and all his elves
To do their conq'ring work themselves."

This said, they lower'd him down in state,
Spread at all points, like falling cat;
But took a vote first on the question,
That they'd accept this full confession,
And to their fellowship and favor,
Restore him on his good behaviour.

Not so our 'Squire submits to rule,
But stood, heroic as a mule.

* In Aristophanes' Comedy of the Clouds, Socrates is represented
as hoisted in a basket to aid contemplation.

"You'll find it all in vain, quoth he,
To play your rebel tricks on me.
All punishments, the world can render,
Serve only to provoke th' offender;
The will gains strength from treatment horrid
As hides grow harder when they're curried.
No man e'er felt the halter draw,
With good opinion of the law;
Or held in method orthodox
His love of justice, in the stocks;
Or fail'd to lose by sheriff's shears
At once his loyalty and ears.
Have you made Murray* look less big,
Or smoked old Williams* to a Whig?
Did our mobb'd Ol'ver† quit his station,
Or heed his vows of resignation?
Has Rivington,‡ in dread of stripes,
Ceased lying since you stole his types?
And can you think my faith will alter,
By tarring, whipping or the halter?
I'll stand the worst; for recompense
I trust King George and Providence.
And when with conquest gain'd I come,
Array'd in law and terror home,
Ye'll rue this inauspicious morn,
And curse the day, when ye were born,
In Job's high style of imprecations,
With all his plagues, without his patience."

* Members of the Mandamus Council in Massachusetts. The operation of smoking Tories was thus performed. The victim was confined in a close room before a large fire of green wood, and a cover applied to the top of the chimney.

† Thomas Oliver, Esq. Lieut. Governor of Massachusetts. He was surrounded at his seat in the country and intimidated by the mob into the signing of his resignation.

‡ Rivington was a tory Printer in New York. Just before the commencement of the war, a party from New Haven attacked his press, and carried off, or destroyed the types.

Meanwhile, beside the pole, the guard
A Bench of Justice had prepared,*
Where sitting round in awful sort
The grand Committee hold their Court;
While all the crew, in silent awe,
Wait from their lips the lore of law.
Few moments with deliberation
They hold the solemn consultation;
When soon in judgment all agree,
And Clerk proclaims the dread decree;
"That 'Squire M'FINGAL having grown
The vilest Tory in the town,
And now in full examination
Convicted by his own confession,
Finding no tokens of repentance,
This Court proceeds to render sentence:
That first the Mob a slip-knot single
Tie round the neck of said M'FINGAL,
And in due form do tar him next,
And feather, as the law directs;
Then through the town attendant ride him
In cart with Constable beside him,
And having held him up to shame,
Bring to the pole, from whence he came."
Forthwith the crowd proceed to deck
With halter'd noose M'FINGAL's neck,
While he in peril of his soul
Stood tied half-hanging to the pole;
Then lifting high the ponderous jar,
Pour'd o'er his head the smoking tar.
With less profusion once was spread
Oil on the Jewish monarch's head,
That down his beard and vestments ran,
And cover'd all his outward man.

---

* An imitation of legal forms was universally practiced by the
mobs in New England, in the trial and condemnation of Tories. This
marks a curious trait of national character.

As when (so Claudian* sings) the Gods
And earth-born Giants fell at odds,
The stout Enceladus in malice
Tore mountains up to throw at Pallas;
And while he held them o'er his head,
The river, from their fountains fed,
Pour'd down his back its copious tide,
And wore its channels in his hide:
So from the high-raised urn the torrents
Spread down his back their various currents;
His flowing wig, as next the brim,
First met and drank the sable stream;
Adown his visage stern and grave
Roll'd and adhered the viscid wave;
With arms depending as he stood,
Each cuff capacious holds the flood;
From nose and chin's remotest end,
The tarry icicles descend;
Till all o'erspread, with colors gay,
He glitter'd to the western ray,
Like sleet-bound trees in wintry skies,
Or Lapland idol carved in ice.
And now the feather-bag display'd
Is waved in triumph o'er his head,
And clouds him o'er with feathers missive,
And down, upon the tar, adhesive:
Not Maia's† son, with wings for ears,
Such plumage round his visage wears;
Nor Milton's six-wing'd‡ angel gathers
Such superfluity of feathers.
Now all complete appears our 'Squire,
Like Gorgon or Chimæra dire;
Nor more could boast on Plato's§ plan

* Claudian's Gigantomachia.
† Mercury, described by the Poets with wings on his head and feet.
‡ And angel wing'd—six wings he wore— *Milton*.
§ Alluding to Plato's famous definition of Man, *Animal bipes implume*—a two-legged animal without feathers.

To rank among the race of man,
Or prove his claim to human nature,
As a two-legg'd unfeather'd creature.
  Then on the fatal cart, in state
They raised our grand Duumvirate.
And as at Rome* a like committee,
Who found an owl within their city,
With solemn rites and grave processions,
At every shrine perform'd lustrations;
And least infection might take place
From such grim fowl with feather'd face,
All Rome attends him through the street
In triumph to his country seat:
With like devotion all the choir
Paraded round our awful 'Squire;
In front the martial music comes
Of horns and fiddles, fifes and drums,
With jingling sound of carriage bells,
And treble creak of rusted wheels.
Behind, the croud, in lengthen'd row
With proud procession, closed the show.
And at fit periods every throat
Combined in universal shout;
And hail'd great Liberty in chorus,
Or bawl'd ' confusion to the Tories.'
Not louder storm the welkin braves
From clamors of conflicting waves;
Less dire in Lybian wilds the noise
When rav'ning lions lift their voice;
Of triumphs at town-meetings made,
On passing votes to regulate trade. †
  Thus having borne them round the town,
Last at the pole they set them down;

* Livy's History.
  † Such votes were frequently passed at town-meetings, with the
view to prevent the augmentation of prices, and stop the depreciation
of the paper money.

And to the tavern take their way
To end in mirth the festal day.
   And now the Mob, dispersed and gone,
Left 'Squire and Constable alone.
The Constable with rueful face
Lean'd sad and solemn o'er a brace;
And fast beside him, cheek by jowl,
Stuck 'Squire M'FINGAL 'gainst the pole,
Glued by the tar t' his rear applied,
Like barnacle on vessel's side.
But though his body lack'd physician,
His spirit was in worse condition.
He found his fears of whips and ropes
By many a drachm outweigh'd his hopes.
As men in jail without mainprize
View every thing with other eyes,
And all goes wrong in church and state,
Seen through perspective of the grate:
So now M'FINGAL's Second-sight
Beheld all things in gloomier light;
His visual nerve, well purged with tar,
Saw all the coming scenes of war.
As his prophetic soul grew stronger,
He found he could hold in no longer.
First from the pole, as fierce he shook,
His wig from pitchy durance broke,
His mouth unglued, his feathers flutter'd,
His tarr'd skirts crack'd, and thus he utter'd.
   "Ah, Mr. Constable, in vain
We strive 'gainst wind and tide and rain!
Behold my doom! this feathery omen
Portends what dismal times are coming.
Now future scenes, before my eyes,
And second-sighted forms arise.
I hear a voice, * that calls away,
And cries, 'The Whigs will win the day.'

    * I hear a voice, you cannot hear,
      That says, I must not stay—   *Tickell's Ballad.*

My beck'ning Genius gives command,
And bids me fly the fatal land;
Where changing name and constitution,
Rebellion turns to Revolution,
While Loyalty, oppress'd, in tears,
Stands trembling for its neck and ears.

"Go, summon all our brethren, greeting,
To muster at our usual meeting;
There my prophetic voice shall warn 'em,
Of all things future that concern 'em.
And scenes disclose on which, my friend,
Their conduct and their lives depend.
There I—but first 'tis more of use,
From this vile pole to set me loose;
Then go with cautious steps and steady,
While I steer home and make all ready.

END OF CANTO THIRD

CANTO IV

THE VISION

Now Night came down, and rose full soon
That patroness of rogues, the Moon;
Beneath whose kind protecting ray,
Wolves, brute and human, prowl for prey.
The honest world all snored in chorus,
While owls and ghosts and thieves and Tories,
Whom erst the mid-day sun had awed,
Crept from their lurking holes abroad.
On cautious hinges, slow and stiller,
Wide oped the great M'FINGAL's cellar, *
Where safe from prying eyes, in cluster,
The Tory Pandemonium muster.

* Secret meetings of the Tories, in cellars and other lurking places, were frequent during the revolutionary war.

Their chiefs all sitting round descried are,
On kegs of ale and seats of cider; *
When first M'FINGAL, dimly seen,
Rose solemn from the turnip-bin. †
Nor yet his form had wholly lost
Th' original brightness it could boast, ‡
Nor less appear'd than Justice Quorum,
In feather'd majesty before 'em.
Adown his tar-streak'd visage, clear
Fell glistening fast th' indignant tear,
And thus his voice, in mournful wise,
Pursued the prologue of his sighs.

"Brethren and friends, the glorious band
Of loyalty in rebel land!
It was not thus you've seen me sitting,
Return'd in triumph from town-meeting;
When blust'ring Whigs were put to stand,
And votes obey'd my guiding hand,
And new commissions pleased my eyes;
Blest days, but ah, no more to rise!
Alas, against my better light,
And optics sure of second-sight,§
My stubborn soul, in error strong,
Had faith in Hutchinson too long.
See what brave trophies still we bring
From all our battles for the king;

* Panditur interea domus omnipotentis Olympi,
Conciliumque vocat Divum pater atq; hominum Rex
Sideream in sedem. *Virgil.*

† In most of the country cellars in New England, a *bin* is raised at one corner, about four feet high, to hold turnips and other vegetables. M'Fingal uses it here as a desk for a speaker.

‡ . . . His form had not yet lost
All its original brightness, nor appear'd
Less than archangel ruin'd. *Milton.*

§ The second-sight of the Highlanders furnishes poetry with a new kind of machinery. Walter Scott has since made use of it with great advantage, in several of his poems.

And yet these plagues, now past before us,
Are but our entering wedge of sorrows!
    "I see, in glooms tempestuous, stand
The cloud impending o'er the land;
That cloud, which still beyond their hopes
Serves all our orators with tropes;
Which, though from our own vapors fed,
Shall point its thunders on our head!
I see the Mob, beflipp'd at taverns,
Hunt us, like wolves, through wilds and caverns!
What dungeons open on our fears!
What horsewhips whistle round our ears!
Tar, yet in embryo in the pine,
Shall run on Tories' backs to shine;
Trees, rooted fair in groves of sallows,
Are growing for our future gallows;
And geese unhatch'd, when pluck'd in fray,
Shall rue the feathering of that day.*
    "For me, before that fatal time,
I mean to fly th' accursed clime,
And follow omens, which of late
Have warn'd me of impending fate.
    "For late in visions of the night
The gallows stood before my sight;
I saw its ladder heaved on end;
I saw the deadly rope descend,
And in its noose, that wavering swang,
Friend Malcolm† hung, or seem'd to hang.
How changed‡ from him, who bold as lion,

        * The child shall rue, that is unborn,
          The hunting of that day. *Chevy-chase.*
    † Malcolm was a Scotchman, Aid to Governor Tryon in his expedi-
tion against the Regulators, as they called themselves, in North
Carolina. He was afterwards an under-officer of the Customs in
Boston, where becoming obnoxious, he was tarred, feathered and
half-hanged by the mob, about the year 1774.
        ‡ . . . quantum mutatus ab illo
          Hectore, qui rediit spoiliis indutus. *Virg.*

Stood Aid-de-camp to Gen'ral Tryon,
Made rebels vanish once, like witches,
And saved his life, but dropp'd* his breeches.
I scarce had made a fearful bow,
And trembling asked him, "How d'ye do;"
When lifting up his eyes so wide,
His eyes alone, his hands were tied;
With feeble voice, as spirits use,
Now almost choak'd by gripe of noose;

"Ah, fly my friend, he cried, escape,
And keep yourself from this sad scrape;
Enough you've talked and writ and plann'd;
The Whigs have got the upper hand.
Could mortal† arm our fears have ended,
This arm (and shook it) had defended.
Wait not till things grow desperater,
For hanging is no laughing matter.
Adventure then no longer stay;
But call your friends and haste away.

"For lo, through deepest glooms of night,
I come to aid thy second-sight,
Disclose the plagues that round us wait,
And scan the dark decrees of fate.

"Ascend this ladder, whence unfurl'd

* This adventure was thus reported among the anecdotes of the day. When Governor Tryon marched with his militia, to suppress the insurgents in the western counties of North Carolina, and found them, drawn up in array to oppose him, Malcolm was sent with a flag to propose terms, and demand the surrender of their arms. Before the conclusion of the parley, Tryon's militia began to fire on the Regulators. The fire was immediately returned. Malcolm started to escape to his party; and by the violence of his pedestrian exertion (as Shakespeare says)

"His points being broken, down fell his hose;" and he displayed the novel spectacle of a man running the gauntlet *sans culottes*, betwixt two armies engaged in action, and presenting an unusual mark to his enemy.

† . . . *Si Pergama dextra*
  Defendi possent, etiam hac defensa fuissent. Virg.

The curtain opes of t'other world;
For here new worlds their scenes unfold,
Seen from this backdoor* of the old.
As when Æneas risk'd his life,
Like Orpheus vent'ring for his wife,
And bore in show his mortal carcase
Through realms of Erebus and Orcus,
Then in the happy fields Elysian,
Saw all his embryon sons in vision;
As shown by great Archangel, Michael,
Old Adam † saw the world's whole sequel,
And from the mount's extended space,
The rising fortunes of his race:
So from this stage shalt thou behold
The war its coming scenes unfold,
Raised by my arm to meet thine eye;
My Adam, thou; thine angel, I.

But first my pow'r, for visions bright,
Must cleanse from clouds thy mental sight,
Remove the dim suffusions spread,
Which bribes and salaries there have bred;
And from the well of Brute infuse
Three genuine drops of Highland dews,
To purge, like euphrasy‡ and rue,
Thine eyes, for much thou hast to view.

Now freed from Tory darkness, raise
Thy head and spy the coming days.
For lo, before our second-sight,
The Continent ascends in light.
From north to south, what gath'ring swarms
Increase the pride of rebel arms!
Through every State our legions brave
Speed gallant marches to the grave,
Of battling Whigs the frequent prize,
While rebel trophies stain the skies.

* Leaving the old, both worlds at once they view,
   Who stand upon the threshold of the new. *Waller.*

† Milton—Paradise Lost, Book 11.   ‡ Milton.

Behold o'er northern realms afar
Extend the kindling flames of war!
See famed St. John's and Montreal
Doom'd by Montgomery's arm to fall!
Where Hudson with majestic sway
Through hills disparted plows his way,
Fate spreads on Bemus' heights alarms,
And pours destruction on our arms;
There Bennington's ensanguined plain,
And Stony-Point, the prize of Wayne.
Behold near Del'ware's icy roar,
Where morning dawns on Trenton's shore,
While Hessians spread their Christmas feasts,
Rush rude these uninvited guests;
Nor aught avails the captured crew
Their martial whiskers' grisly hue!
On Princeton plains our heroes yield,
And spread in flight the vanquish'd field;
While fear to Mawhood's* heels puts on
Wings, wide as worn by Maia's son.
Behold the Pennsylvanian shore
Enriched with streams of British gore;
Where many a veteran chief in bed
Of honor rests his slumb'ring head,†
And in soft vales, in land of foes,
Their wearied virtue finds repose!
See plund'ring Dunmore's‡ negro band
Fly headlong from Virginia's strand;
And far on southern hills our cousins,
The Scotch M'Donalds, fall by dozens;

* Col. Mawhood gained great reputation among the British, by escaping with about two hundred men from the battle at Princeton.
　　　† . . . Have ye chos'n this place,
　　　　After the toils of battle, to repose
　　　　Your wearied virtue; for the ease ye find
　　　　To slumber here, as in the vales of heaven? *Milton*
‡ Lord Dunmore was Governor of Virginia at the commencement of the war. He fled with all the slaves and plunder he could collect.

Or where King's Mountain lifts its head,
Our ruin'd bands in triumph led!
Behold, o'er Tarlton's blustring train
Defeat extends the captive chain!
Afar near Eutaw's fatal springs,
Lo, rebel Vict'ry spreads her wings!
Through all the land, in varied chace,
We hunt the rainbow of success,
In vain! their Chief, superior still,
Eludes our force with Fabian skill;
Or swift descending by surprize,
Like Prussia's eagle, sweeps the prize.
　　"I look'd; nor yet, oppress'd with fears,
Gave credit to my eyes or ears;
But held the sights an empty dream,
On Berkley's * immaterial scheme;
And pond'ring sad with troubled breast,
At length my rising doubts express'd.
'Ah, whither thus, by rebels smitten,
Is fled th' omnipotence of Britain;
Or fail'd its usual guard to keep,
Absent from home or fast asleep?
Did not, retired to bowers Elysian,
Great Mars leave with her his commission,
And Neptune erst, in treaty free,
Give up dominion o'er the sea?
Else where's the faith of famed orations, †
Address, debate and proclamations,
Or courtly sermon, laureate ode,
And ballads on the wat'ry God; ‡

* Berkley, an English philosopher, who refining on Locke's ideal system, denied the existence of matter.

† In this stile, the British orators and poets talk and write of themselves.

‡ Alluding to an English ballad, much sung and famous at that time, in which Neptune (called the *Watry God*) with great deference surrenders his trident to King George, and acknowledges him, as monarch and ruler of the ocean.

With whose high strains great George enriches
His eloquence of gracious speeches?
Not faithful to our Highland eyes,
These deadly forms of vision rise.
Some whig-inspiring rebel sprite
Now palms delusion on our sight.
I'd scarcely trust a tale so vain,
Should revelation prompt the strain;
Or Ossian's ghost the scenes rehearse
In all the melody of Erse.'"*
   "Too long," quoth Malcolm, "from confusion,
You've dwelt already in delusion;
As sceptics, of all fools the chief,
Hold faith in creeds of unbelief.
I come to draw thy veil aside
Of error, prejudice and pride.
Fools love deception, but the wise
Prefer sad truths to pleasing lies.
For know, those hopes can ne'er succeed,
That trust on Britain's breaking reed.
For weak'ning long from bad to worse,
By cureless atrophy of purse,
She feels at length with trembling heart,
Her foes have found her mortal part.
As famed Achilles, dipp'd by Thetis
In Styx, as sung in antient ditties,
Grew all case-harden'd o'er, like steel,
Invulnerable, save his heel;
And laugh'd at swords and spears and squibs,
And all diseases, but the kibes;
Yet met at last his deadly wound,
By Paris' arrow nail'd to ground:
So Britain's boasted strength deserts
In these her empire's utmost skirts,
Removed beyond her fierce impressions,
And atmosphere of omnipresence;

  * Erse, the ancient Scottish language. . . .

Nor to this shore's remoter ends
Her dwarf-omnipotence extends.
Hence in this turn of things so strange,
'Tis time our principles to change;
For vain that boasted faith, that gathers
No perquisite, but tar and feathers;
No pay, but stripes from whiggish malice,
And no promotion but the gallows.
I've long enough stood firm and steady,
Half-hang'd for loyalty already,
And could I save my neck and pelf,
I'd turn a flaming whig myself.
But since, obnoxious here to fate,
This saving wisdom comes too late,
Our noblest hopes already crost,
Our sal'ries gone, our titles lost,
Doom'd to worse suff'rings from the mob,
Than Satan's surg'ries used on Job;
What hope remains, but now with sleight
What's left of us to save by flight?
    'Now raise thine eyes, for visions true
Again ascending wait thy view.'
    "I look'd; and clad in early light,
The spires of Boston met my sight;
The morn o'er eastern hills afar
Illumed the varied scenes of war;
Great Howe* had sweetly in the lap
Of Loring taken out his nap;
When all th' encircling hills around
With instantaneous breastworks crown'd,†

* The sun had long since, in the lap
    Of Thetis, taken out his nap. *Butler*.

† The heights of Dorchester overlook the south part of Boston
and command the passage of the harbor. By an unexpected movement, Washington took possession and erected works on them in a
single night. Putnam placed a number of barrels in front, filled with
sand, to be rolled down on the British columns, in case they should
attempt to scale the eminence. Howe after sundry manœuvres was

With pointed thunders met his sight,
Like magic, rear'd the former night.
Each summit, far as eye commands,
Shone, peopled with rebellious bands.
Aloft their tow'ring heroes rise,
As Titans erst assail'd the skies; *
Leagued in superior force to prove
The sceptred hand of British Jove.
Mounds piled on hills ascended fair
With batt'ries placed in middle air,
That hurl'd their fiery bolts amain,
In thunder on the trembling plain.
I saw, along the prostrate strand
Our baffled generals quit the land,
Eager, as frighted mermaids, flee
T' our boasted element, the sea,
And tow'rd their town of refuge fly,
Like convict Jews condemn'd to die.
Then to the north I turn'd my eyes,
Where Saratoga's heights arise,
And saw our chosen vet'ran band
Descend in terror o'er the land;
T' oppose this fury of alarms,
Saw all New-England wake to arms,
And every Yankee, full of mettle,
Swarm forth, like bees at sound of kettle.
Not Rome, when Tarquin raped Lucretia,
Saw wilder must'ring of militia.
Through all the woods and plains of fight,
What mortal battles pain'd my sight,

discouraged from the attempt, and as Boston was no longer tenable, made a truce with Washington, evacuated the place, and sailed with his troops to Halifax.

* The Titans are described by the old poets, as giants, sons of the earth, who made an insurrection against Jupiter. They heaped mountains upon mountains, in order to scale the Gibraltar of the pagan Olympus; but were foiled by the thunders of Jove and the arrows of Apollo. See *Hesiod, etc.*

While British corses strew'd the shore,
And Hudson tinged his streams with gore.
What tongue can tell the dismal day,
Or paint the parti-color'd fray,
When yeomen left their fields afar
To plow the crimson plains of war;
When zeal to swords transform'd their shares,
And turn'd their pruning hooks to spears,
Changed tailor's geese to guns and ball,
And stretch'd to pikes the cobbler's awl;
While hunters, fierce like mighty Nimrod,
Made on our troops a furious inroad,
And levelling squint on barrel round,
Brought our beau-officers to ground;
While sunburnt wigs, in high command,
Rush daring on our frighted band,
And ancient beards* and hoary hair,
Like meteors, stream in troubled air;
While rifle-frocks drove Gen'rals cap'ring,
And Red-coats† shrunk from leathern apron,
And epaulette and gorget run
From whinyard brown and rusty gun.
With locks unshorn not Samson more
Made useless all the show of war,
Nor fought with ass's jaw for rarity
With more success, or singularity.
I saw our vet'ran thousands yield,
And pile their muskets on the field,
And peasant guards, in rueful plight,
March off our captured bands from fight;
While every rebel fife in play
To Yankee-doodle tuned its lay,
And like the music of the spheres,
Mellifluous sooth'd their vanquish'd ears."

* Loose his beard and hoary hair
  Stream'd like a meteor to the troubled air. *Gray.*

  † An American cant name for the British troops, taken from the
color of their uniform.

"Alas, I cried, what baleful star
Sheds fatal influence on the war?
And who that chosen Chief of fame,
That heads this grand parade of shame?"
   "There see how fate, great Malcolm cried,
Strikes with its bolts the tow'ers of pride!
Behold that martial Macaroni,
Compound of Phœbus and Bellona,
Equipp'd alike for feast or fray,
With warlike sword and singsong lay,
Where equal wit and valour join!
This, this is he—the famed Burgoyne!
Who pawn'd his honor or commission,
To coax the patriots to submission,
By songs and balls secure allegiance,
And dance the ladies to obedience.*
Oft his Camp-Muses he'll parade
At Boston in the grand blockade;
And well inspired with punch of arrack,
Hold converse sweet in tent or barrack,
Aroused to more poetic passion,
Both by his theme and situation.
For genius works more strong and clear
When close confined, like bottled beer.
So Prior's† wit gain'd matchless power
By inspiration of the Tower;
And Raleigh, once to prison hurl'd,
Wrote the whole hist'ry of the world;
So Wilkes grew, while in jail he lay,
More patriotic every day,
But found his zeal, when not confined,
Soon sink below the freezing point,

* Such were Burgoyne's declarations, when he was setting out to command in America. This pleasant mode of warfare not meeting with the expected success at Boston, he appears to have changed his plan in his northern expedition. . . .

† Prior wrote his Alma, the best of his works, while in confinement in the Tower of London.

And public spirit, once so fair,
Evaporate in open air.
But thou, great favorite of Venus,
By no such luck shalt cramp thy genius;
Thy friendly stars, till wars shall cease,
Shall ward th' ill fortune of release,
And hold thee fast in bonds not feeble,
In good condition still to scribble.
Such merit fate shall shield from firing,
Bomb, carcase, langridge and cold iron,
Nor trust thy doubly-laurell'd head,
To rude assaults of flying lead.
Hence thou, from Yankee troops retreating,
For pure good fortune shalt be beaten,
Not taken oft, released or rescued,
Pass for small change, like simple Prescott; *
But captured then, as fates befall,
Shall stand thy fortune, once for all.
Then raise thy daring thoughts sublime,
And dip thy conq'ring pen in rhyme,
And changing war for puns and jokes,
Write new Blockades and Maids of Oaks." †

    This said, he turn'd and saw the tale
Had dyed my trembling cheeks with pale; ‡
Then pitying in a milder vein,
Pursued the visionary strain;
    "Too much perhaps hath pain'd your view,

---

  * General Prescott was taken and exchanged several times during the war.

  † The *Maid of Oaks* is a farce by Burgoyne. . . . During the winter in which the British troops were shut up in Boston, they amused themselves with the acting of a new farce, called *The Blockade of Boston;* the humor of which consisted in burlesquing the Yankee phrases, unmilitary dress, and awkward appearance of the new American levies, by whom they were besieged. . . . This play was generally ascribed to the pen of Burgoyne. . . . he has since written the comedy of *The Heiress.* . . .

  ‡ . . . . dyed her cheeks with pale. *Milton*

From vic'tries of the Rebel crew.
Now see the deeds, not small or scanty,
Of British valour and humanity;
And learn from this heroic sight,
How England's sons and friends can fight,
In what dread scenes their courage grows,
And how they conquer all their foes."
    I look'd, and saw in wintry skies
Our spacious prison-walls arise,
Where Britons, all their captives taming,
Plied them with scourging, cold and famine,
By noxious food and plagues contagious
Reduced to life's last, fainting stages.
Amid the dead, that crowd the scene,
The moving skeletons were seen.
Aloft the haughty Loring * stood,
And thrived, like Vampire, on their blood,
And counting all his gains arising,
Dealt daily rations out, of poison.
At hand our troops, in vaunting strain,
Insulted all their wants and pain,
And turn'd upon the dying tribe
The bitter taunt and scornful gibe;
The British captains, chiefs of might,
Exulting in the joyous sight,
On foes disarm'd, with courage daring,
Exhausted all their tropes of swearing.
Distain'd around with rebel blood,
Like Milton's Lazar† house it stood,

---

* Loring was a refugee from Boston, made commissary of prisoners
by General Howe. The consummate cruelties, practised on the
American prisoners under his administration, almost exceed the ordinary powers of human invention. The conduct of the Turks in put-
ing all prisoners to death is certainly much more rational and humane,
than that of the British army for the first three years of the American
war, or till after the capture of Burgoyne. *London Edit.*
                                    † . . . a place
    Before his eyes appear'd, sad, noisom, dark,

Where grim Despair presided Nurse,
And Death was Regent of the house.
   Amazed I cried, "Is this the way
That British valor wins the day?"
More had I said in strains unwelcome,
Till interrupted thus by Malcolm.
   "Blame not, said he, but learn the reason
Of this new mode of conq'ring treason.
'Tis but a wise, politic plan
To root out all the rebel clan;
For surely treason ne'er can thrive
Where not a soul is left alive;
A scheme all other chiefs to surpass,
And do th' effectual work to purpose.
Know, War itself is nothing further
Than th' art and mystery of Murther;
He, who most methods has essay'd,
Is the best Gen'ral of the trade,
And stands Death's plenipotentiary
To conquer, poison, starve and bury.
This Howe well knew and thus began;
(Despising Carlton's* coaxing plan,
To keep his pris'ners well and merry,
And deal them food, like commissary,
And by parol or ransom vain,
Dismiss them all to fight again)
Hence his first captives, with great spirit
He tied up, for his troops to fire at,†

   A Lazar house it seem'd. . . . Despair
   Tended the sick, busiest from couch to couch,
   And over them triumphant Death his dart
   Shook, but delay'd to strike. . . . *Milton*

* Sir Guy Carlton, afterwards Lord Dorchester, was Governor of
Canada, at the time of our unfortunate attack on Quebec by the
forces under Montgomery. He treated his American prisoners on
principles of humanity, and formed the only exception to the cruelty
and folly of the British commanders.

† This was done openly and without censure, in many instances, by
the troops under Howe's command, on his first conquest of Long Island.

And hoped they'd learn on foes thus taken,
To aim at rebels without shaking.
Then deep in stratagem, he plann'd,
The sure destruction of the land;
Turn'd famine, torture and despair
To useful enginry of war;
Sent forth the small-pox,* and the greater,
To thin the land of every traitor;
Spread desolation o'er their head,
And plagues in providence's stead;
Perform'd with equal skill and beauty
Th' avenging Angel's tour of duty:
Then bade these prison-walls arise,
Like temple tow'ring to the skies,
Where British Clemency renown'd
Might fix her seat on hallow'd ground,
(That Virtue, as each herald saith,
Of whole blood kin to Punic Faith)
Where all her godlike pow'rs unveiling,
She finds a grateful shrine to dwell in:
And at this altar for her honor,
Chose this High-priest to wait upon her,
Who with just rites, in ancient guise,
Offers the human sacrifice.
Here every day, her vot'ries tell,
She more devours, than th' idol Bel;
And thirsts more rav'nously for gore,
Than any worshipp'd Power before.
That ancient heathen godhead, Moloch,
Oft stay'd his stomach with a bullock;
And if his morning rage you'd check first,
One child suffic'd him for a breakfast:
But British clemency with zeal
Devours her hundreds at a meal;
Right well by nat'ralists defined

---

* Great pains was taken by emissaries from New York, to communicate the small-pox through the country. It became necessary to counteract the attempt by a general inoculation of the inhabitants.

A being of carniv'rous kind:
So erst Gargantua* pleased his palate,
And eat six pilgrims up in sallad.
Not blest with maw less ceremonious
The wide-mouth'd whale, that swallow'd Jonas;
Like earthquake gapes, to death devote,
That open sepulchre, her throat;
The grave or barren womb you'd stuff,
And sooner bring to cry, enough;
Or fatten up to fair condition
The lean-flesh'd kine of Pharaoh's vision.

Behold her temple, where it stands
Erect, by famed Britannic hands.
'Tis the Black-hole of Indian structure,
New-built in English architecture,
On plan, 'tis said, contrived and wrote
By Clive, before he cut his throat;
Who, ere he took himself in hand,
Was her high-priest in nabob-land:
And when with conq'ring triumph crown'd,
He'd well enslaved the nation round,
With tender British heart, the Chief,
Since slavery's worse than loss of life,
Bade desolation circle far,
And famine end the work of war;
And loosed their chains, and for their merits,
Dismiss'd them free to worlds of spirits.
Whence they with choral hymns of praise,
Return'd to sooth his latter days,†
And hov'ring round his restless bed,
Spread nightly visions o'er his head.

Now turn thine eyes to nobler sights,

* See Rabelais' History of the Giant Gargantua.

† Clive in the latter years of his life, conceived himself haunted by the Ghosts of those persons, who were the victims of his humanity in the East-Indies. It is presumed that he showed them the vote of Parliament, returning thanks for his services.

And mark the prowess of our fights.
Behold, like whelps of Britain's lion,
Our warriors, Clinton, Vaughan, and Tryon,
March forth with patriotic joy
To ravish, plunder, burn, destroy,
Great Gen'rals, foremost in their nation,
The journeymen of Desolation!
Like Samson's foxes, each assails,
Let loose with firebrands in their tails,
And spreads destruction more forlorn,
Than they among Philistine corn.
And see in flames their triumphs rise,
Illuming all the nether skies,
O'er-streaming, like a new Aurora,
The western hemisphere with glory!
What towns, in ashes laid, confess
These heroes' prowess and success!
What blacken'd walls and burning fanes,
For trophies spread the ruin'd plains!
What females, caught in evil hour,
By force submit to British power;
Or plunder'd negroes in disaster
Confess King George their lord and master!
What crimson corses strew their way,
What smoking carnage dims the day!
Along the shore, for sure reduction,
They wield the besom of destruction.
Great Homer likens, in his Ilias,
To dogstar bright the fierce Achilles;
But ne'er beheld in red procession
Three dogstars rise in constellation
Nor saw, in glooms of evening misty,
Such signs of fiery triplicity,
Which, far beyond the comet's tail,
Portend destruction where they sail.
Oh, had Great-Britain's warlike shore
Produced but ten such heroes more,
They'd spared the pains, and held the station

Of this world's final conflagration;
Which when its time comes, at a stand,
Would find its work all done t' its hand!
    Yet though gay hopes our eyes may bless,
Malignant fate forbids success;
Like morning dreams our conquest flies,
Dispersed before the dawn arise."
    Here Malcolm paused; when pond'ring long
Grief thus gave utt'rance to my tongue.
"Where shrink in fear our friends dismay'd,
And where the Tories' promised aid?
Can none, amid these fierce alarms,
Assist the power of royal arms?"
"In vain, he cried, our King depends
On promised aid of Tory friends.
When our own efforts want success,
Friends ever fail, as fears increase.
As leaves, in blooming verdure wove,
In warmth of summer clothe the grove,
But when autumnal frosts arise,
Leave bare their trunks to wintry skies:
So, while your power can aid their ends,
You ne'er can need ten thousand friends;
But once in want, by foes dismay'd,
May advertize them, stol'n or stray'd.
Thus ere Great-Britain's force grew slack,
She gain'd that aid she did not lack;
But now in dread, imploring pity,
All hear unmoved her dol'rous ditty;
Allegiance wand'ring turns astray,
And Faith grows dim for lack of pay.
In vain she tries, by new inventions,
Fear, falsehood, flatt'ry, threats and pensions;
Or sends Commiss'ners with credentials
Of promises and penitentials.
As, for his fare o'er Styx of old,
The Trojan stole the bough of gold.
And least grim Cerb'rus should make head,

Stuff'd both his fobs with ginger-bread: *
Behold, at Britain's utmost shifts,
Comes Johnstone† loaded with like gifts,
To venture through the whiggish tribe,
To cuddle, wheedle, coax and bribe;
And call, to aid his desp'rate mission,
His petticoated politician,
While Venus, joined to act the farce,
Strolls forth embassadress for Mars.
In vain he strives, for while he lingers,
These mastiffs bite his off'ring fingers;
Nor buys for George and realms infernal
One spaniel, but the mongrel, Arnold.

" ' Twere vain to paint, in vision'd show,
The mighty nothings done by Howe;
What towns he takes in mortal fray,
As stations whence to run away;
What triumphs gain'd in conflict warm,
No aid to us, to them no harm;
For still th' event alike is fatal,
Whate'er success attend the battle,
Whether he vict'ry gain or lose it,
Who ne'er had skill enough to use it.
And better 'twere, at their expense,
T' have drubb'd him into common sense,
And waked, by bastings on his rear,

---

* . . . medicatam frugibus offam. *Virgil*.

† In the year 1778, after the capture of Burgoyne, our good Government passed an act, repealing all acts of which the Americans complained, provided they would rescind their declaration of Independence, and continue to be our colonies. The ministry then sent over three Commissioners, Mr. Johnstone, Mr. Eden, and a certain Lord. These Commissioners began their operations and finished them, by attempting to bribe individuals among the members of the States, and of the army. This bait appears to have caught nobody but Arnold. The *petticoated politician*, here mentioned, was a woman of Philadelphia, through whose agency they offered a bribe to Joseph Reed, Governor of Pennsylvania. *Lond. Edit.*

Th' activity, though but of fear.
By slow advance his arms prevail,
Like emblematic march of snail,
That, be Millenium nigh or far,
'Twould long before him end the war.
From York to Philadelphian ground,
He sweeps the pompous flourish round,
Wheel'd circ'lar by eccentric stars,
Like racing boys at prison-bars,
Who take th' opposing crew in whole,
By running round the adverse goal;
Works wide the traverse of his course,
Like ship t' evade the tempest's force;
Like mill-horse circling in his race,
Advances not a single pace,
And leaves no trophies of reduction,
Save that of cankerworms, destruction.
Thus having long both countries curst,
He quits them as he found them first,
Steers home disgraced, of little worth,
To join Burgoyne and rail at North.
   "Now raise thine eyes and view with pleasure,
The triumphs of his famed successor."
   "I look'd, and now by magic lore
Faint rose to view the Jersey shore:
But dimly seen in gloom array'd,
For night had pour'd her sable shade,
And every star, with glimm'rings pale,
Was muffled deep in ev'ning veil.
Scarce visible, in dusky night
Advancing red-coats rose in sight;
The length'ning train in gleaming rows
Stole silent from their slumb'ring foes;
No trembling soldier dared to speak,
And not a wheel presumed to creak.
My looks my new surprise confess'd,
Till by great Malcolm thus address'd.
"Spend not thy wits in vain researches;

'Tis one of Clinton's moonlight marches.
From Philadelphia now retreating
To save his baffled troops a beating,
With hasty strides he flies in vain,
His rear attack'd on Monmouth plain.
With various chance the dread affray
Holds in suspense till close of day,
When his tired bands, o'ermatched in fight,
Are rescued by descending night.
He forms his camp, with great parade,
While evening spreads the world in shade,
Then still, like some endanger'd spark,
Steals off on tiptoe in the dark:
Yet writes his king in boasting tone
How grand he march'd by light of moon. *
I see him, but thou canst not; proud
He leads in front the trembling crowd,
And wisely knows, as danger's near,
'Twill fall much heaviest on his rear.
Go on, great Gen'ral, nor regard
The scoffs of every scribbling bard;
Who sings how gods, that fearful night,
Aided by miracle your flight,
As once they used, in Homer's day,
To help weak heroes run away;
Tells how the hours, at this sad trial,
Went back, as erst on Ahaz' dial,
While British Joshua stay'd the moon
On Monmouth plains for Ajalon.
Heed not their sneers or gibes so arch,
Because she set before your march.
A small mistake! your meaning right;
You take her influence for her light:
Her influence which shall be your guide,

* General Clinton's official dispatches, giving an account of his marching from Monmouth by moonlight, furnished a subject of much pleasantry in America; where it was known that the moon had set two hours before the march began. *Lond. Edit.*

And o'er your Gen'ralship preside.
Hence still shall teem your empty skull
With vict'ries, when the moon's at full,
Which by transition passing strange
Wane to defeats before the change.
Still shall you steer, on land or ocean,
By like eccentric lunar motion;
Eclips'd in many a fatal crisis,
And dimm'd when Washington arises.
 "And see how Fate, herself turn'd traitor,
Inverts the ancient course of nature;
And changes manners, tempers, climes,
To suit the genius of the times!
See, Bourbon forms a gen'rous plan,
New guardian of the rights of man,
And prompt in firm alliance joins
To aid the Rebels' proud designs!
Behold from realms of eastern day
His sails* innum'rous shape their way,
In warlike line the billows sweep,
And roll the thunders of the deep!
See, low in equinoctial skies,
The western islands fall their prize;
See British flags, o'ermatch'd in might,
Put all their faith in instant flight,
Or broken squadrons, from th' affray,
Drag slow their wounded hulks away!
Behold his Chiefs, in daring setts,
D'Estaignes, De Grasses and Fayettes,
Spread through our camps their dread alarms,
And swell the fear of rebel arms!
Yet ere our glories sink in night,
A gleam of hope shall strike your sight;

* In 1779, the French king sent a powerful fleet to the West-Indies which was very successful in the conquest of St. Vincents and Grenada, the defeat of Admiral Biron in a naval engagement, and the capture of a British ship of the line and several frigates, on the American coast.

As lamps, that fail of oil and fire,
Collect one glimm'ring to expire.
  "For lo, where southern shores extend,
Behold our gather'd hosts descend,
Where Charleston views, with varying beams
Her turrets gild th' encircling streams!
There by superior force compell'd,
Behold their gallant Lincoln* yield;
Nor aught the wreaths avail him now,
Pluck'd from Burgoyne's imperious brow,
See, furious from the vanguish'd strand,
Cornwallis leads his mighty band;
The southern realms and Georgian shore
Submit and own the victor's power;
Lo! sunk before his wasting way,
The Carolinas fall his prey!
See, shrinking from his conq'ring eye,
The Rebel legions fall or fly;
And with'ring in these torrid skies,
The northern laurel fades and dies! †
With rapid force he leads his train
To fair Virginia's cultured plain,
Triumphant eyes the travell'd zone,
And boasts the southern realm his own.
  "Nor yet this hero's glories bright
Blaze only in the fields of fight.
Not Howe's humanity more deserving
In gifts of hanging and of starving;
Not Arnold plunders more tobacco,

---

* General Lincoln was second in command in the army of General Gates, during the campaign of 1777, which ended in the capture of General Burgoyne. He afterwards commanded the army in South Carolina, and was taken prisoner with the garrison of Charleston in 1780. *Lond. Edit.*

† This refers to the fortune of General Gates, who after having conquered Burgoyne in the North, was defeated by Cornwallis in the South. *Lond. Edit.*

Or steals more negroes for Jamaica; *
Scarce Rodney's self, among th' Eustatians,
Insults so well the laws of nations;
Ev'n Tryon's fame grows dim, and mourning
He yields the civic crown of burning.
I see, with pleasure and surprise,
New triumph sparkling in your eyes;
But view, where now renew'd in might,
Again the Rebels dare the fight."
"I look'd, and far in southern skies
Saw Greene, their second hope, arise,
And with his small, but gallant, band,
Invade the Carolinian land.
As winds, in stormy circles whirl'd,
Rush billowy o'er the darken'd world,
And where their wasting fury roves
Successive sweep th' astonish'd groves:
Thus where he pours the rapid fight,
Our boasted conquests sink in night,
And far o'er all the extended field
Our forts resign, our armies yield,
Till now, regain'd the vanquish'd land,
He lifts his standard on the strand.
    "Again to fair Virginia's coast
I turn'd and view'd the British host,
Where Chesapeak's wide waters lave
Her shores and join th' Atlantic wave.
There famed Cornwallis tow'ring rose,
And scorn'd secure his distant foes;
His bands the haughty rampart raise,
And bid the Royal standard blaze.
When lo, where ocean's bounds extend,

---

* Arnold, in the year 1781, having been converted to our cause,
commanded a detachment of our army in Virginia; where he plundered many cargoes of negroes and tobacco, and sent them to Jamaica
for his own account. How far Lord Rodney may have excelled him
in this kind of heroic achievements, time perhaps will never discover.
Lond. Edit.

Behold the Gallic sails ascend,
With fav'ring breezes stem their way,
And crowd with ships the spacious bay.
Lo! Washington, from northern shores,
O'er many a region wheels his force,
And Rochambeau, with legions bright,
Descends in terror to the fight.
Not swifter cleaves his rapid way
The eagle, cow'ring o'er his prey;
Or knights in famed romance, that fly
On fairy pinions through the sky.
Amazed, the Briton's startled pride
Sees ruin wake on every side,
And all his troops, to fate consign'd,
By instantaneous stroke, Burgoyned.*
Not Cadmus view'd with more surprise,
From earth embattled armies rise,
Who from the dragon's teeth beheld
Men starting fierce with spear and shield! †
I saw, with looks downcast and grave,
The Chief emerging from his cave,
Where chased, like fox, in mighty round,
His hunters earth'd him first in ground; ‡
And doom'd by fate to rebel sway,
Yield all his captured host a prey.
There while I view'd the vanquish'd town,
Thus with a sigh, my friend went on."

"Behold'st thou not that band forlorn,
Like slaves in Roman triumphs borne,
Their faces length'ning with their fears,
And cheeks distain'd with streams of tears;
Like *dramatis personæ* sage,

---

* To *Burgoyne an army* was during the war, a favorite phrase in America, to express a complete capture.

† See Ovid's Metamorphoses.

‡ Alluding to the fact of Cornwallis' taking up his residence in a kind of Cave, made bomb-proof, during the siege of York Town.

Equipp'd to act on Tyburn's stage.
Lo, these are they, who lured by follies,
Left all, and follow'd great Cornwallis,
Expectant of the promised glories,
And new Millennial reign of Tories!
Alas! in vain, all doubts forgetting,
They tried th' omnipotence of Britain;
But found her arm, once strong and brave,
So shorten'd now, she cannot save.
Not more aghast, departed souls
Who risk'd their fate on Popish bulls,
And find St. Peter, at the wicket,
Refuse to countersign their ticket,
When driven to purgatory back,
With each his pardon in his pack;
Than Tories, must'ring at their stations,
On faith of royal proclamations.
As Pagan chiefs at every crisis,
Confirm'd their leagues by sacrifices,
And herds of beasts, to all their deities,
Oblations fell, at close of treaties:
Cornwallis thus, in ancient fashion,
Concludes his grand capitulation; *
And heedless of their screams or suff'rings,
Gives up the Tories for sin-off'rings.
See where, relieved from sad embargo,
Steer off consign'd a recreant cargo;
Like old scape-goats to roam in pain,
Marked like their great forerunner, Cain.
The rest now doom'd by British leagues
To vengeance of resentful Whigs,
Hold doubtful lives on tenure ill
Of tenancy at Rebel-will,
While hov'ring o'er their forfeit persons,

---

* All the favor, which Cornwallis, on his surrender, stipulated for
the Tories who had joined him, was a single frigate free from search,
to convey away a few of the most obnoxious.

The gallows waits his just reversions.
   "Thou too, M'FINGAL, ere that day,
Shalt taste the terrors of th' affray.
See, o'er thee hangs in angry skies,
Where Whiggish Constellations rise,
And while plebeian signs ascend,
Their mob-inspiring aspects bend,
That baleful Star, whose horrid hair*
Shakes forth the plagues of down and tar!
I see the pole, that rears on high
Its flag terrific through the sky;
The mob beneath prepared t' attack,
And tar predestined for thy back.
Ah quit, my friend, this dang'rous home,
Nor wait the darker scenes to come.
For know, that fate's auspicious door,
Once shut to flight, is oped no more;
Nor wears its hinge, by changing stations,
Like Mercy's door in Proclamations.†

   "But lest thou pause, or doubt to fly,
To stranger visions turn thine eye.
Each cloud, that dimm'd thy mental ray,
And all the mortal mists decay.
See, more than human pow'rs befriend,
And lo! their hostile forms ascend.‡
There tow'ring o'er the extended strand,
The Genius§ of this western land,
For vengeance arm'd, his sword assumes,

---

      * . . . From his horrid hair
        Shakes pestilence and war. *Milton.*

  † *The door of mercy is now open,* and *the door of mercy will be shut,* were phrases so often used in the proclamations of the British Generals in America, that our Poet seems to fear, that the hinge of that door will be quite worn out. *Lond. Edit.*

      ‡ Apparent dirae facies, inimicaq; Trojae
        Numina magna deum. *Virgil.*

  § Generally drawn in symbolical paintings, in the dress of a native, with his head ornamented with a high plume of feathers.

Or stands, like Tories, dress'd in plumes!
See, o'er yon Council-seat, with pride
How Freedom spreads her banners wide!
There Patriotism, with torch address'd
To fire with zeal each daring breast;
While all the Virtues in their train,
Escaped with pleasure o'er the main,
Desert their ancient British station,
Possess'd with rage of emigration.
Honor, his bus'ness at a stand,
For fear of starving quits their land;
And Justice, long disgraced at Court, had
By Mansfield's sentence been transported.
Vict'ry and Fame attend their way,
Though Britain wish their longer stay;
Care not what George or North would be at,
Nor heed their writs of *Ne exeat;*
But fired with love of colonizing,
Quit the fall'n empire for the rising."

"I look'd, and saw, with horror smitten,
These hostile pow'rs averse to Britain.

"When lo, an awful spectre rose,
With languid paleness on his brows;
Wan dropsies swell'd his form beneath,
And iced his bloated cheeks with death;
His tatter'd robes exposed him bare
To every blast of ruder air;
On two weak crutches propp'd he stood,
That bent at every step he trod;
Gilt titles graced their sides so slender,
One, "Regulation," t'other, "Tender;"
His breastplate graved, with various dates,
"The Faith of all th' United States;"*
Before him went his funeral pall,
His grave stood, dug to wait his fall.

---

* On all the emissions of Continental Bills of credit, Congress
pledged for their punctual redemption, *The Faith of the United States.*

"I started, and aghast I cried,
"What means this spectre at their side?
What danger from a pow'r so vain,
Or union with that splendid train?"
    "Alas, great Malcolm cried, experience
Might teach you not to trust appearance.
Here stands, as dress'd by fell Bellona,
The ghost of Continental Money! *
Of Dame Necessity descended,
With whom Credulity engender'd:
Though born with constitution frail,
And feeble strength, that soon must fail,
Yet strangely vers'd in magic lore,
And gifted with transforming power.
His skill the wealth Peruvian joins,
With diamonds of Brazilian mines.
As erst Jove fell, by subtile wiles,
On Danae's† apron through the tiles,
In show'rs of gold; his potent wand
Shall shed like show'rs o'er all the land.

* The description here given of the Continental paper-money is
not more remarkable, as a splendid example of the sublime burlesque,
than as a faithful picture of that financial operation. Though this
money was counterfeited by waggon loads in the British garrisons,
and sent into circulation in the country, yet none of the consequences
followed, which were expected from this manoeuvre. The paper
money carried on the war for five years; when it gave place to other
measures, which the circumstances of the country rendered practica-
ble, and went peaceably to rest, as here described by the Author. . . .
The "weak crutches," called *Regulation and Tender,* by which this
Spectre is supported, allude to the different acts of the State legislatures, made with the design of maintaining the credit of the Continental paper. Some of these acts regulated the prices of commodi-
ties, others made this paper a legal tender in payment. *Lond. Edit.*

† The ancient poets say, that Jupiter having fallen in love with
Danae, who was imprisoned and guarded in a brazen tower, succeeded in transforming himself into a shower of gold, and falling
through the roof into her lap. Persea, quem pluvio Danae conceperat
auro. *Ovid Metam. Lib.* 4.

Less great the wondrous art was reckon'd
Of tallies cast by Charles the second,
Or Law's famed Mississippi schemes,
Or all the wealth of South-Sea dreams.
For he, of all the world alone
Owns the long-sought Philos'pher's stone,
Restores the fabulous times to view,
And proves the tale of Midas* true.
O'er heaps of rags he waves his wand;
All turn to gold at his command,
Provide for present wants and future,
Raise armies, victual, clothe, accoutre,
Adjourn our conquests by essoin,
Check Howe's advance, and take Burgoyne;
Then makes all days of payment vain,
And turns all back to rags again.
In vain great Howe† shall play his part
To ape and counterfeit his art;
In vain shall Clinton,† more belated,
A conj'rer turn to imitate it.
With like ill luck and pow'rs as narrow,
They'll fare, like sorcerers of old Pharaoh;
Who, though the art they understood
Of turning rivers into blood,
And caused their frogs and snakes t' exist,
That with some merit croak'd and hiss'd,
Yet ne'er by every quaint device
Could frame the true Mosaic lice.
He for the Whigs his arts shall try,
Their first, and long their sole, ally;

* Midas, says the fable, had the gift of turning every thing he touched to gold.

† Vast quantities of counterfeit bills, in imitation of the American currency, were struck and sent into the country from New York and Long Island, while those Generals commanded the British army, with the hope of aiding the depreciation of the Continental money . . . a mode of warfare which they esteemed very honorable against *Rebels*.

A Patriot firm, while breath he draws,
He'll perish in his Country's cause,
And when his magic labors cease,
Lie buried in eternal peace.

   Now view the scenes, in future hours,
That wait the famed European powers.
See, where yon chalky cliffs arise,
The hills of Britain strike your eyes;
Its small extension long supplied
By full immensity of pride;
So small, that had it found a station
In this new world, at first creation,
Or doom'd by justice, been betimes
Transported* over for its crimes.
We'd find full room for't in lake Erie, or
That larger water-pond, Superior,†
Where North at margin taking stand,
Would scarce be able to spy land.‡

* Transportation to the colonies for felony is a common punishment by the English laws: but that the whole British Island should
be transported seems an idea extravagantly poetical.

† Lake Superior is more than 2200 miles in circumference; an
extent sufficient to warrant the assertion of the poet, that the inhabitants of Britain, in the supposed situation, would not be able to spy
the surrounding shores of the lake.

‡ This has been a most unlucky couplet. The poem, completed
by the addition of the two last Cantos, was first published in America
in the year 1782. Some years after, the whole was reprinted in London. In that interval, Lord North was so unhappy, as to lose his
sight. And the British reviewers of that day, with their wonted
sagacity, imagined that these lines were intended as an insult upon
him for that misfortune; thinking, as we may presume, that M'Fingal
foresaw the future blindness of his Lordship, by the aid of his second-
sight. Their abuse of the author, as wanting candor and common
sense, need not be repeated. In a subsequent copy of the poem, he
struck out the name of Lord North and inserted that of King George
. . . and lo, in a few years more, the king also was afflicted with
blindness. To prevent all further mishaps, the lines are now restored
to their original form. *See the London Edition of* 1792.

See, dwindling from her height amain,
What piles of ruin spread the plain;
With mould'ring hulks her ports are fill'd,
And brambles clothe the lonely field!
See, on her cliffs her Genius lies,
His handerchief at both his eyes,
With many a deep-drawn sigh and groan,
To mourn her ruin, and his own!
While joyous Holland, France and Spain
With conq'ring navies awe the main;
And Russian banners wide unfurl'd
Spread commerce round the eastern world.
  And see, (sight hateful and tormenting!)
This Rebel Empire, proud and vaunting,
From anarchy shall change her crasis,
And fix her pow'r on firmer basis;
To glory, wealth and fame ascend,
Her commerce wake, her realms extend;
Where now the panther guards his den,
Her desert forests swarm with men;
Gay cities, tow'rs and columns rise,
And dazzling temples meet the skies;
Her pines, descending to the main,
In triumph spread the wat'ry plain,
Ride inland seas with fav'ring gales,
And crowd her ports with whitening sails:
Till to the skirts of western day,
The peopled regions own her sway."
  Thus far M'FINGAL told his tale,
When startling shouts his ears assail;
And strait the Constable, their sentry,
Aghast rush'd headlong down the entry,
And with wild outcry, like magician,
Dispersed the residue of vision.
For now the Whigs the news had found
Of Tories must'ring under ground,
And with rude bangs and loud uproar,

'Gan thunder* furious at the door.
The lights put out, each tory calls,
To cover him on cellar walls,
Creeps in each box, or bin, or tub,
To hide him from the rage of mob,
Or lurks, where cabbage-heads in row
Adorn'd the sides with verdant show.
M'FINGAL deem'd it vain to stay,
And risk his bones in second fray:
But chose a grand retreat from foes,
In literal sense, *beneath their nose.*†
The window then, which none else knew,
He softly open'd, and crept through,
And crawling slow in deadly fear,
By movements wise made good his rear.
Then scorning all the fame of martyr,
For Boston took his swift departure,
Nor look'd back on the fatal spot,
More than the family of Lot.
Not North in more distress'd condition,
Out-voted first by opposition;
Not good King George, when our dire phantom
Of Independence came to haunt him,‡
Which hov'ring round by night and day,
Not all his conj'rers e'er could lay.
His friends, assembled for his sake,
He wisely left in pawn, at stake,
To tarring, feath'ring, kicks and drubs
Of furious, disappointed mobs,
Or with their forfeit heads to pay

* . . . either tropic now
'Gan thunder. *Milton—Paradise Regained.*
† This, during the American war, was a fashionable phrase with the
British. No officer, who had a lucky escape, failed of stating in his
report, that he made a grand retreat *under the very Nose of the enemy.*
‡ On the Declaration of Independence, the ministerial speakers
in Parliament amused themselves by calling it, the *phantom of In-
dependence.* The wit was echoed by all their Newspapers.

For him, their leader,* crept away.
So when wise Noah summon'd greeting,
All animals to gen'ral meeting,
From every side the members went,
All kinds of beasts to represent;
Each, from the flood, took care t' embark,
And save his carcase in the ark:
But as it fares in state and church,
Left his constituents in the lurch.

* As the flight of Mahomet to Mecca fixes the Æra of Mussulman computation; so the flight of M'Fingal to Boston forms the grand catastrophe of this immortal work. So sublime a denouement, as the French critics term it, never appeared before in Epic Poetry, except that of the Hero turning Papist, in the Henriade of Voltaire.

TIMOTHY DWIGHT
(1752–1817)

NOTE ON "THE CONQUEST OF CANAAN"

THIS ambitious work with its "eleven dreadful books of conventional rhymed pentameters," was announced by Dwight as the first epic poem to appear in America. It is a free handling of the familiar biblical narrative, rearranged, distorted and swollen with declamation, that gives point to the English poet Cowper's comment that "he who would learn by what steps the Israelites became possessed of the promised land, must still seek his information in the Bible." To increase the popularity of the work and inculcate patriotism, Dwight scattered through the text numerous allusions to events and personalities of the American Revolution. That the conquest of Canaan under Joshua is intended to suggest the revolutionary struggle under Washington, is sufficiently obvious. An interesting contemporary criticism of the work will be found in Cowper, *Works*, edited by Southey, Vol. IV, pp. 355–58.

THE CONQUEST OF CANAAN

BOOK VIII

ARGUMENT

Morning. Joshua joins Irad. Jobab's character, and challenge. Irad accepts it, and kills Jobab. Battle. Irad kills Samlah, and engages Jabin. His death. Judah routed with great slaughter. Death of Uzal, and Shelumiel. Caleb, with a large division, marches out, rallies Judah, and renews the battle. Irad's death throws the whole army into confusion. Joshua inspirits them, and makes great havoc of the enemy. Zimri's exploits. He kills the king of the Hittites and routs them. Joshua kills the king of Shimron, and routs the centre. Jabin, perceiving the other divisions of the army defeated, orders a retreat, which is performed with regularity. Joshua's lamentation over Irad. Scene of Selima's distress at the sight of his corpse. Evening

O'ER misty hills the day-star led the morn,
And streaming light in heaven began to burn;
Wide scenes of woe the boundless blaze display'd,
Where the steel triumph'd, and the deluge spread.
On wasted plains unnumber'd corses lay,
And smokes far scatter'd climb'd upon the day,
Still clouded flames o'er eastern mountains rise,
And Ai's broad ruins sadden all the skies.
    When lo! in glimmering arms, and black array,
Like storms low-hovering in th' etherial way,
Far round the north a gloomy cloud ascends,
Its horror deepens, and its breadth extends.
Compact and firm, as mov'd by one great soul,
A front immense, the widening squadrons roll;
Thick shoot the spears; the trembling helmets beam,
And waving bucklers cast a moony gleam.

As the dire comet, swift through ether driven,
In solemn silence climbs the western heaven;
His sanguine hair, portending fearful wars,
Streams down the midnight sky, and blots the stars;
Pale death and terror light the dusky gloom,
And quivering nations read their sudden doom.
So in the flaming van great Joshua rose,
And shot red glories on the wondering foes.
At his command the trumpet sounded nigh,
Aerial ensigns dancing in the sky;
Near and more near, they trac'd a dreadful way,
Join'd Irad's host, and stretch'd in long array.
　　From Hazor's ranks that now before the wood,
In three embattled squares, refulgent stood,
Great Jobab strode. In Madon's realms he reign'd:
Red was his eye, his brow with blood distain'd;
A beam his spear; his vast, expanded shield
Shot a bright morning o'er the crimson field;
His head sublime a mighty helmet crown'd;
His quivering plumes with sable horror frown'd;
Six cubits from the earth, he rais'd his frame;
His wish was battle, and his life was fame.
　　Proud was his father; prouder was the son:
Nought mov'd his pride; the tear, nor piercing groan:
Unmatch'd his force, he claim'd a matchless fame,
And every combat deck'd his brightening name.
Princes, his captiv'd slaves, before him bow'd,
Stalk'd in his train, and round his chariot rode;
While their fair partners, first in triumph led,
Held the rich cup, or grac'd the brutal bed.
Oft had surrounding realms his aid requir'd,
Ere Zimri's hand Ai's hapless turrets fir'd;
But still their prayers, and still their gifts were vain,
Till Joshua's glory rous'd his fierce disdain.
Else had no proffer mov'd his haughty mind,
That deem'd himself the champion of mankind,
When the joint wishes of the various band
To nobler Jabin gave the first command.

But Joshua's triumphs fill'd his anguish'd ear;
Fir'd at the sound, he snatch'd the deathful spear,
Resolv'd at once to prove the hero's might,
And claim, alone, the wreaths of single fight.
'Twas he, when Irad rais'd his dreadful voice,
And inmost Hazor trembled at the noise,
When prudent Jabin urg'd a nightly storm,
Ere the Youth's voice the slumbering camp should arm:
Bade his vast squadrons in the wood delay,
Nor lift a spear, till morn should lead the day.
Shall this brave host th' unmanly path pursue,
Fight ambush'd foes, and basely creep from view?
Shall Jobab, like the thief, to conquest steal,
And bravery call, what coward minds can feel?

   And now, from Jabin the proud chief demands,
To lead, as first in place, the central bands.
He, coolly wise, resigns the shadowy name,
And, pleas'd with substance, boasts a nobler fame.

   Forth from the host, in steely pomp, he strode,
And 'twixt th' embattled lines sublimely stood.
His towering stride, vast height, and awful arms
Chill'd all his foes, and scatter'd wide alarms:
When thus the chief—Ye sons of Israel know
The dauntless challenge of no common foe.
If in your host three heroes can be found,
(Be Joshua one) to tempt this dangerous ground,
Here shall they learn what strength informs the brave,
And find no God can shield them from the grave.

   Stung with the insult cast upon his God,
To the great Leader Irad nimbly strode,
And thus—Shall yonder heathen's haughty cry
Dare Israel's host, and Israel's God defy?
Let me this boaster whelm in instant shame,
Avenge my nation's cause, my Maker's name.

   Exalted Youth! the smiling Chief replied,
This elder arm shall crop his towering pride.
Scarce in thy breast has manhood fix'd her seat;
Blot not thy bloom, nor urge untimely fate.

Brave as thou art, his strength must win the fight,
And Israel's glory sink in endless night.
    Think not, he cried, of Irad's tender age,
Nor heed the mockery of yon heathen's rage.
This hand, though young, shall boast a conquering day;
Blind is wild rage, and pride an easy prey.
Here too shall Joshua's potent prayers be given,
And the bless'd aid, that Virtue hopes from Heaven.
Should Irad perish, none the wound shall know;
Should Joshua fall, our race is whelm'd in woe:
Heaven gave his chosen to thy guardian care,
To rule in peace, to save in dangerous war;
On thee alone our fates suspended lie,
With thee we flourish, and with thee we die.
    Oh best of youths! provoke not hasty doom,
Nor rush impetuous to an early tomb.
I lov'd thy sire, the good, the just, the brave—
And shall this voice consign thee to the grave?
Swift thy name ripens into matchless praise;
My son, my chosen, still prolong thy days.
In future fields thy arm shall brighter shine;
Thine be the glory, but the danger mine.
    Ah grant my wish! th' impatient Youth replies,
While two full tears stand glistening in his eyes—
This arm, unhurt, shall bid the monster bleed;
Angels will guard my course, and Heaven succeed.
My spear, when night her latest darkness spread,
Had sunk him breathless in the field of dead;
But some kind spirit sav'd his life, till morn
Should grace the fight, and Irad's name adorn.
Aid me, oh aid me, Hezron's every friend!
Your voice, your wishes, must the Leader bend.
    Won by his earnest cries, the generous Chief
Forc'd his consent; but could not hide his grief.
A sigh steals silent from his bleeding breast,
As his slow tongue permits the sad request.
    Wrapp'd in bright arms, while smiles his joy reveal'd,
The Youth stalk'd fearless, o'er the horrid field;

The host, with rapture, view'd his lofty stride,
The leap alert, the port of conscious pride;
But each grave chief, by long experience wise,
With faltering accent, to his comrade cries—
I fear, I fear, lest, on the bloody sand,
The bold Youth perish, by yon monster's hand.
What bravery can, fair Irad will perform,
But can the opening floweret meet the storm?
Ah, that such sweetness, such etherial fire
Should fall, the victim of a heathen's ire!
Thy votary's course, all-gracious Heaven, survey!
Let some kind angel hover round his way!

   Now near the scene bold Irad urg'd his course,
Where Jobab triumph'd in resistless force;
When the huge warrior, swell'd with angry pride,
With bended brow, and voice contemptuous, cried—
Art thou the champion of thy vaunting race?
Shall this poor victory Jobab's falchion grace?
Go, call great Joshua, long to war inur'd,
Whose arm hath toils, whose skill hath hosts endur'd,
With him, ten chiefs; this hand shall crush them all;
Shame stains the steel, that bids a stripling fall;
Retire, ere vengeance on thy helmet light;
Fly to yon troop, and save thy life by flight.

   His haughty foe the Youth undaunted heard;
Vain, empty threats his bosom never fear'd;
O'er the vast form he turn'd his smiling eyes,
And saw unmov'd the livid vengeance rise.
Then, with a rosy blush of conscious worth,
Calm from his tongue his manly voice broke forth—
Do threats like these become a hero's voice?
Can courage find a vent in empty noise?
To every brave man give the well-earn'd praise,
Nor think on scoffs a bright renown to raise;
True bravery claims a noble generous fame;
But the base wretch from vaunts expects his name.
Let shame, let truth, those coward words recall;
Thou seek'st my life; I glory in thy fall.

To me thy pride, to me thy threats are vain;
Heaven sees alone whose arm the prize shall gain.
And know, where e'er may light his angry rod,
I fear no boaster that defies my GOD.

　Now shield to shield, and lance to lance, they stand;
With taunts imperious shout the heathen band;
While hopeless Israel heaven with prayer assails,
And grateful incense fills the rising gales.
Stung by the just reproof, with whizzing sound
The giant plung'd his javelin in the ground:
For passion, ever blind, impell'd his arm,
Steer'd a wild course, and sav'd the youth from harm;
He, calm and fearless, with a pleas'd surprise,
Survey'd its curious form and mighty size;
Then 'gainst his foe, with sure, unerring eye
Drove the swift lance, and lodg'd it in his thigh.
Enrag'd, the warrior saw his bubbling gore,
Writh'd with keen anguish, and the javelin tore.
The flesh pursued; a copious, sable stream
Pour'd from the wound, and stain'd the steely gleam;
Then high in air he shook his sunlike shield,
And wav'd his falchion o'er th' astonish'd field.
With matchless force the vengeful weapon fell;
The wary hero nimbly shunn'd the steel;
And while his foe with foaming fury cried,
Oft pierc'd his arm, and wounded oft his side.
Wild, and more wild, the giant's strokes resound,
Glance from the shield, and plough the cleaving ground;
Till, gathering all his strength for one vast blow,
Dark as a storm, he rushes on his foe;
Lightly the hero springs; the monster falls,
Like sudden ruins of a turret's walls;
Full on his neck descends the gladsome blade,
And from the trunk disparts the grisly head.

　Loud shouts of joy, from Israel's thousands driven,
Burst o'er the plain, and shook the walls of heaven:
Amaz'd the heathens saw their champion lost,
And a wide, sullen groan was heard from all the host.

Alert, bold Irad seiz'd the giant's shield,
His sword, his spear, and bore them thro' the field;
At Joshua's feet, with self-approving smiles,
He cast the grandeur of the glittering spoils;
The hoary warriors gather'd round his way,
And gazed and wonder'd at the curious prey;
Then bless'd the chief, with transport in their eyes,
And own'd th' assistance of auspicious Skies;
While youths unhappy rais'd less ardent prayers,
And wish'd the deed, and wish'd the glory, theirs.

Led by soft impulse tow'rd th' imbattled train,
Rov'd sad Selima down the spacious plain.
Afar she stood, and cast an anxious eye,
And strove in vain her favourite to descry.
At once, with distant din, the shouts ascend,
And painful fears her tender bosom rend;
Slow tow'rd the camp her lingering steps inclin'd;
But oft the fair one cast a look behind.

Now the long thunders of the clarion sound,
Reclaim'd from hills, and plains, and groves around,
O'er the dire field the rushing squadrons driven,
Extend their shady files, and blacken heaven:
High in the central front great Joshua stands,
And shoots wide terror thro' th' astonish'd bands;
Mid eastern thousands Zimri towers along,
And Irad shines before the western throng.

Unfurl'd, the sudden banners stream afar,
And, wrapp'd in thunder, joins the dreadful war;
Wide roll the volumes of the dust around,
And clouds on clouds envelope all the ground.
As floods, increas'd by long-descending rains,
Pour a brown deluge o'er the wintery plains,
Loud from a thousand hills, the torrents join,
Where azure bonds the river's course confine;
The maddening ice, in boundless ruin driven,
Bursts, like the thunders of a falling heaven;
The white rocks foam; the gloomy blasts arise,
Toss the wild stream, and roar along the skies.

So clos'd the squadrons of th' unnumber'd foes;
So stormy shouts and hollow groans arose.
  Long in an even ballance hung th' affray,
Nor those would loose, nor these could gain, the day.
'Till Irad's rapid path, like heaven's red fire,
Shot through the ranks, and bade the foe retire;
With joy, their chief surrounding warriors view,
And troops on troops the generous course pursue.
  At distance small, proud Samlah's glittering car,
Whirl'd by white coursers, tempts the grisly war;
O'er all the plain, with piercing sound, arise
His stern injunctions, and his conquering cries.
With shouts bold Irad darts along the field,
Now bright in arms, and now in dust conceal'd,
From rank to rank the well-known chief pursues,
And oft his flashing steel in blood imbrues.
Vain, impious wretch, he cried, thy nimble flight,
And vain, the covert of surrounding might.
Once hast thou fled the swift-pursuing spear,
But fled'st in vain, for vengeance finds thee here.
Learn from this hand what fate betides the knave,
Who yields, unmov'd, a brother to the grave.
If now thy feet escape the righteous doom,
Let Heaven protect thee to a peaceful tomb!
  In dread amaze astonish'd Samlah stood;
From his pale face retir'd the freezing blood;
His wild eye star'd; all bristling rose his hair;
Quick from his quivering hand the useless spear
Dropp'd; his teeth rattled, and the falling reins
At random trembled on the coursers' manes;
Behind he gaz'd, and found no path to fly;
For aid he panted, but no aid was nigh.
Deep in his back was lodg'd the fatal steel;
His breathless form, before the rolling wheel,
Plung'd headlong; mournful rung a pitying groan,
So fair, so mild, his beauteous aspect shone;
Even Irad, touch'd by Adnor's kind request,
Felt soft emotions stealing through his breast.

Then swift he wheel'd the lightening of his sword;
Behind him, Judah's host like torrents pour'd;
Shrill rose the tumult of the fields around,
Trembled through heaven and wav'd along the ground:
With souls undaunted, both the hosts contend;
Spears fill the air, and shouts the concave rend.
    Far distant, Joshua moves his awful form,
Swells the confusion, and directs the storm.
Beyond him, Zimri, swift as rapid fire,
Darts through the fight, and bids the foe expire.
A mingled horror clouds the dreadful plain;
Here rush the fighting, and there fall the slain.
    Now the mid sun had finish'd half his course,
When Irad raging with resistless force,
And far before him breathing wide dismay,
On Jabin's chariot drove his rapid way.
Brave youths around him throng'd the crimson fight,
Eyed the bless'd chief, and smil'd a fierce delight;
From every sword increasing vengeance fell,
And Death sate hovering o'er the sanguine steel.
Thron'd in proud state, the savage Monarch rode;
Like two red stars his wrathful eye-balls glow'd;
Hoarse from his voice a dreadful thunder came,
And his bright armour flash'd a sudden flame.
Two steeds, bedropp'd with gore, and pale to view,
Emblems of death, his smoking chariot drew.
Cheer'd by his hand, the coursers swiftly sprang;
Beat by their hoofs, the brazen bucklers rang;
Tow'rd Irad's path the heathen wing'd his way,
And, boding conquest, snuff'd the fancied prey.
    Unmov'd, th' angelic Youth, with wearied hands
Pav'd his red path, and drove the circling bands—
Stay, lovely hero! stay; thy course forbear;
Enough that sword has rul'd the glorious war—
Ah stay, till Israel's sons thy steps surround;
Return, return, and be with glory crown'd!
    Great Jabin stood, and o'er the bloody field
Rais'd the broad terrors of his flaming shield:

His grimy brow, all blacken'd o'er with dust,
Frown'd like a storm, and froze the trembling host;
Near beautious Irad stream'd the sounding ear,
And opening squadrons yield the dreadful war.
  The foaming Chief, serene the Youth beheld,
And rear'd his javelin o'er the purple field;
Shrill sung the lance along the dusty sky,
Bor'd the strong shield, and pierc'd the Monarch's thigh,
Enrag'd, to earth the haughty Warrior sprang;
His red eyes flam'd; his arms descending rang;
With lofty action, each his hand upraised;
The falchions flash'd; aghast the squadrons gaz'd;
Two generous youths between them nimbly broke,
And bow'd their lives beneath the fatal stroke.
Their lovely heads (their helmets cleft in twain)
Dyed the keen swords, and spouted on the plain.
More fierce the Monarch's disappointed ire
Glow'd in his face, and blaz'd with gloomy fire.
In Irad, innocence serenely mild,
And beauty's sweetness with soft splendor smil'd;
Round his fair forehead beams of bravery play,
Nor stain'd with rage, nor mingled with dismay.
  Again in ether rose the dreadful steel;
Again it lighten'd, and again it fell;
The Heathen's, ringing, leap'd from Irad's shield;
The Youth's in fragments, treacherous, strew'd the field.
Held by a chief, swift-leaping from the band,
A second falchion touch'd his reaching hand,
When—loveliest Youth! why did thy buckler's bound
Shield but thy breast? why not thy form surround?
Where stood thy friends? was no kind hero near,
To guard thy life, and stay Selima's tear?—
From some base arm unseen, in covert flung,
Through his white side a coward javelin sung,
He fell—a groan sad-murmur'd round the host,
Their joy, their glory, and their leader lost.
  Forth from the train a youth impatient sprung,
Spread his fond arms, and round the hero clung,

With soft endearments stay'd the fleeting breath,
And wish'd to save him from the hand of death.
But Jabin's sword, driven through his friendly side,
Stain'd his white armour with a spotless tide:
In kind imbrace their heaving bosoms lay,
And all life's blooming beauty died away.
Through fields of air, their social spirits join'd
Wing'd their light way, nor lost a look behind;
While two bright forms, on rosy pinions borne,
Sail'd round their path, and op'd the gates of morn.

   Mid countless warriors Irad's limbs were spread,
Even there distinguish'd from the vulgar dead.
Fair as the spring, and bright as rising day,
His snowy bosom open'd as he lay;
From the deep wound a little stream of blood
In silence fell, and on the javelin glow'd.
Grim Jabin, frowning o'er his hapless head,
Deep in his bosom plung'd the cruel blade;
Foes, even in death, his vengeance ne'er forgave,
But hail'd their doom, insatiate as the grave;
No worth, no bravery could his rage disarm,
Nor smiling love could melt, nor angel-beauty charm.

   With dreadful sound, he rais'd his voice on high,
Froze the pale bands, and thunder'd thro' the sky—
Haste, warriors, haste; your conquering arms display;
Here gasps their leader, to the dogs a prey.
See the slaves fly; ere evening's dusky hour,
The beasts shall rend them, and the hawks devour.
Receive, illustrious Oran! here receive
The poor, the sole reward, thy prince can give.
This victim first; a nation soon shall come
To pay due honours at thy sacred tomb,
Wide streams of gore in rich libations flow,
And shades unnumber'd wait thy call below.
Here, dastards, here the worthless carcase yield,
Nor wait the vengeance of a future field.
To day this raptur'd hand your camp shall burn,
And sires, and wives, and sons to mingled ashes turn.

Thus spoke the haughty Chief: with flashing eyes,
To fiercer fight inspir'd the warriors rise;
Clouds after clouds in gloomy pomp ascend,
And stormy clamours troubled ether rend.
The thickening tempest Judah's host survey'd,
And wedg'd their volumes in the dusty shade;
Man lock'd with man, and helm with helm combin'd,
And sword with sword in glimmering order join'd,
A long dread front, impervious, hides the fields,
Cloth'd with the grandeur of a thousand shields.

First, in the flaming van to vengeance rose
Bold Irad's train, and dar'd their ardent foes.
Their young, brave minds immortal fame inspires;
Each glowing thought the patriot's virtue fires;
Serene they smil'd to see the ruin nigh;
In death they triumph'd, but they fear'd to fly.

O'er the dark deep, as some tall wave impends;
Its white foam hisses, and its point ascends;
'Gainst hoary rocks the bursting ruins roar,
Shake all the main, and echo round the shore,
So Jabin's car with gloomy terror flew,
And crush'd the ranks that near him rashly drew;
Roll'd in one mighty mass, the heathen force,
The swift-wing'd chariot, and the foaming horse,
O'er all the lovely band resistless fly,
And countless warriors round their Irad die.
Thus, on the stream's fair bank in beauty rise
Young, towering trees, and feel indulgent skies;
In spring's mild beam their lovely boughs aspire,
Wave o'er the flowers, and call the plumy choir:
At once the floods descend, the torrents roar;
The trees lie withering on the wasted shore.

All firmly brave, imbrown'd with dust and blood
'Gainst the rude tempest Judah's veterans stood;
Fix'd, even to death, their nation to defend,
With stout, stiff strength, the stubborn ranks contend;
To fate undaunted many a hero springs,
The shouts redouble, and the concave rings

Full in the front brave Uzal moveless stood,
His falchion reeking with incessant blood;
Fight, warriors, fight, or fall—he said, nor more;
But wheel'd his arm, and stepp'd in floods of gore;
Above his feet the purple torrents ran,
And high before him man was pil'd on man.
So thick the swords around his helmet hung,
That sword clave sword; aloud his armour rung;
Panting he stood; in floods the sweat distill'd;
Nor moves the Hero, nor the squadrons yield.
   From his bright car, that rattling pour'd along,
With shouts, and threatnings, Jabin fir'd the throng;
Man leap'd o'er man: from every side they rush'd;
Bold warriors fell, by other warriors crush'd;
'Till, hurl'd by Jabin's hand, a javelin flew,
Pierc'd Uzal's heart, and life's fair current drew,
Pleas'd, the great hero gave his parting breath;
My nation own'd my life, and now demands my death.
   Thus hung with wounds, a prey to savage steel,
In Princeton's fields the gallant Mercer fell.
When first his native realm her sons decreed,
In slavery's chains, with want and woe to bleed,
Check'd, through his bosom fond remembrance ran,
The cause of freedom was the cause of man.
In that fair cause he bar'd his manly breast,
The friend, the hope, the champion, of th' oppress'd,
From height to height on glory's pinions rose,
Bless'd by his friends, and prais'd by generous foes;
Swift flew the shaft; the eagle ceas'd to rise,
And mourning millions trac'd him down the skies.
   He fell; the throng, that press'd against his shield,
Plung'd in one heap, and spread along the field;
Bucklers on bucklers rang; steel clash'd on steel;
Their own swords gash'd them, wounding as they fell.
In one broad ruin lay the mingled crowd,
And cries, and hollow groans were heard aloud.
So some tall prop, that bears extended walls,
Mouldering, gives way; the mossy structure falls,

The long beams thundering echo round the skies.
Earth shakes beneath, and clouds of dust arise.
Thus sunk the warriors, some to rise no more,
Some, nimbly bounding, bath'd their spears in gore.
　　Now haughty Jabin lifts a louder cry,
The tall hills echo, and the fields reply.
Fly, dastards, fly; death haunts your impious way;
Your proud name sinks; your squadrons swift decay;
Where now's the chief, that led your hosts abroad?
Your far-fam'd bravery, and fictitious GOD?
Call the dread Power, that cleft th' Egyptian wave,
To mourn your fate, and ope your heads a grave.
Pour on, my heroes, while yon friendly light
Shines in the heaven, and joys to view the fight.
He spoke, and onward wing'd his dreadful form;
Hazor behind him, like an evening storm,
That rides on gloomy blasts above the hills,
And wakes the thunder of the mountain rills,
Roll'd blackening. Israel's sons in sad dismay.
Bent tow'rd the camp their slow, unwilling way.
　　Enrag'd Shelumiel rais'd his angry voice,
But rais'd in vain; no hero heeds the noise:
Hoarse with shrill cries, and wild with deep despair,
He rush'd resistless on the thickest war,
From Jabin's lance a grateful exit found,
Sunk in his arms, and stiffen'd on the ground.
　　Far from the fight, despoil'd of helm and shield,
Slept beauteous Irad on the mournful field;
Deaf to the groans, and careless of the cries;
His hair soft-whistling o'er his half-shut eyes.
On either side his lifeless arms were spread,
And blood ran round him from the countless dead.
Even there, two warriors, rushing o'er the plain,
O'er crimson torrents, and o'er piles of slain,
Stopp'd, when the lovely form arose to sight,
Survey'd his charms, and wish'd no more the fight.
　　Ah, hapless Youth! cried one, with tender voice,
The Gods' fair offspring, form'd for milder joys!

A face like thine the gentlest thoughts must move,
The gaze of Beauty, and the song of Love.
Sleep on, fair hero! for thy corse must lie
Bare to the fury of a stormy sky.
Thus he. His friend, by softer passions warm'd,
By grief afflicted, and by beauty charm'd,
Cries sadly—No; for when my steps return,
This bleeding breast thy early fate shall mourn;
The melting song declare thy hapless doom,
And my own hand erect thy head a tomb.

    But now, outspread o'er all the northern plain,
In sable grandeur roll'd a countless train,
With trembling spears, with waving bucklers, bright,
And the quick gleams of interrupted light.

    When Joshua strode the heathen host to dare,
To guard the camp was prudent Caleb's care.
He, coolly wise, had summon'd all the train,
Dispos'd in ranks, and guided o'er the plain,
All arm'd for war, at distance meet to stay,
And wait the changes of the dreadful day.
In even scale while dubious combat hung,
And far in southern fields the tumult rung,
Silent, they listen'd to the blended cry,
And heard faint shouts in distant murmurs die.

    But now th' approaching clarion's dreadful sound
Denounces flight, and shakes the banner'd ground;
From clouded plains increasing thunders rise,
And drifted volumes roll along the skies.
At once the chief commands; th' unnumber'd throng,
Like gathering tempests, darkly pour'd along:
High on the winds, unfurl'd in purple pride,
Th' imperial standard cast the view aside;
A hero there sublimely seem'd to stand,
To point the conquest, and the flight command;
In arms of burnish'd gold the warrior shone,
And wav'd and brighten'd in the falling sun.

    Swift tow'rd the fight approach'd th' impatient throng,
And wider pour'd the thickening dust along:

Loud, and more loud, victorious clamours grow,
And, more distinguish'd, breathe the sounds of woe;
Pale Judah's sons a yielding fight maintain,
And many a face looks backward o'er the plain,
When Caleb's mighty voice, in thunder driven,
Starts all the host, and rends the clouded heaven.
What dismal scenes, enrag'd the hero cries—
Convulse this heart, and pierce these bleeding eyes!
Shall Judah's race, my brethren and my boast,
Flee, vanquish'd, driven, before a heathen host?
Can men, can warriors own so black a part,
The best of chiefs, your Joshua to desert?
Say with what pangs will Heaven the wretches try,
That know no honour, and that feel no tie?
On yon bright plain, the conquering Chief behold,
Troops wing'd before him, cars tumultuous roll'd,
With Heaven's imperial sword the fight commands,
And drives fierce ruin o'er decreasing bands!
Say, shall the Man, who fights, who bleeds for all,
See your base flight, and perish in your fall?
The Chief, as angels kind, as angels true,
Sink in the doom, he warded long from you?
Fly then; but know, a few short furlongs past,
Yon camp wild flames, and savage swords shall waste;
Besmear'd with streaming blood, your parents lie,
And, dash'd on stones, your gasping infants die;
Your wives, betray'd by such base culprits, feel
Abuse, more dreadful than the griding steel?
No arm, no sword the falling nation save,
But this dire evening ope our common grave.
Can these dread scenes even dastards fail to arm?
Spring from the trance, and burst the sleepy charm;
Rise, rise like men; with shame, with vengeance burn;
Wipe foul disgrace, and swift to fight return.
And ye brave chiefs, that never knew to yield,
Or turn a backward foot from glory's field,
But, led by me, the van's bright honours claim,
Smile at fair death, and shrink from torturing shame;

Lift high th' avenging sword, from pity free,
And cleave the wretch that basely dares to flee.
　He spoke: the sound their manly bosoms fir'd,
Wheel'd their long ranks, and every arm inspir'd;
Even cowards now to generous combat arm'd,
And fainting heroes with new vengeance warm'd:
Fierce Hazor's sons with equal fury driven,
Like one wide cloud, that shades the skirts of even,
Rush'd dark and dreadful: ranks, by ranks impell'd,
Felt the keen lance, and heap'd the streaming field.
Pois'd in a dire suspense, the combat hung;
Swords clash'd, mail rattled, striking bucklers rung;
Here his bold ranks great Caleb's arm inspir'd;
There Jabin's mighty hand his warriors fir'd:
No more the foaming steeds could trace their way,
So thick the squadrons wedg'd their black array:
Loud tumults roar, the clouded heavens resound,
And deep convulsions heave the labouring ground.
　Meantime, great Joshua, lightening o'er the plain,
Hedg'd his dire path with heaps of ghastly slain;
Back roll'd the squadrons; death's encircling shade
Involv'd his course, and hover'd o'er his head.
At once a quivering voice fair Irad nam'd,
Announc'd his ruin, and the flight proclaim'd;
From ranks to trembling ranks, the mournful sound
Wak'd a sad groan, and breath'd a gloom around,
With livid paleness clouded every face,
Congeal'd each vein, and stopp'd the growing chace.
On the far camp they turn'd a frequent view;
Their fainting falchions scarce the fight renew;
Throng'd in a blackening storm, the foe descends;
Swift drive the chariots; far the dust extends:
With smiles, bold heathens hail commencing flight;
Their lances shower; their eye-balls flash delight.
Loud as old ocean beats the rocky shore,
Loud as the storm's deep-bursting thunders roar,
Vast shouts uprolling rend th' etherial round,
Trembles all heaven, and shakes the gory ground.

Amaz'd, the Hero saw the wild despair;
Nor knew the cause, 'till Irad fill'd the air;
Irad, re-echoing with a fearful noise,
Pal'd the blank face, and froze the faltering voice.
Loud o'er the bellowing shouts resounds his cry—
My sons, my heroes, whither will ye fly?
Will ye pursue the camp? desert the slain?
And leave your Irad on the bloody plain?
Alas! you fly to more tremendous fates;
There ruin seeks you, and base death awaits;
There, in sad horror, will your eyes behold
Flames round your camp, your wives, your children roll'd:
Let vengeance rouse, let Israel's name inspire,
Let danger steel you, and let Irad fire,
Turn, turn, this instant seals your final doom;
You gain the day, or fall without a tomb.
He said, and wav'd his broad, ensanguin'd shield;
Turn, warriors, turn, resounds along the field;
A new-born bravery fires the meanest soul:
Thick spears protend; ranks lengthening onward roll:
Less loud fierce whirlwinds through the valley pour:
Less loud broad flames the spiry town devour,
When, wing'd by blasts, red conflagrations rise,
Blaze in the cloud-capp'd towers, and scorch the skies.
Black drifts of dust smoke through the vast profound;
Shouts hoarsely rage, and hollow groans resound.
As, when through ether's fields dark storms are driven,
The swift-wing'd flame, descending, kindles heaven,
Scath'd by the dreadful stream, the huge pines fall,
And bursting glory wraps the smoking ball;
O'er the tall mountains rolls the voice of GOD
The plains all tremble, and the forests nod:
So swift, so bright, the rushing hero pour'd;
With every stroke his sword a life devour'd;
Full on his foes he bore resistless storm,
Pale squadrons opening to his angry form;
His shield blaz'd horror, and his lofty hand
Fell, with swift ruin, on the lessening band;

Gash'd by his hand, the coursers burst their reins,
And hurl'd their riders on the bloody plains;
Gash'd by his hand, the prostrate riders die;
Crack the round wheels, the splendid trappings fly.
   Meantime, far eastward Asher crouds the war,
Nor heeds the terrors of the rattling car.
Swift as on wings of fire a meteor driven,
Mounts o'er the hills, and sweeps the nightly heaven,
When the pale wanderer, lost in devious ways,
With bristling hair, starts at the sudden blaze,
Rush'd rapid Zimri through the parting host;
Mark'd by his eye the hapless foe was lost;
O'er quivering ranks his sword incessant hung;
Loud in their ears his voice funereal rung
Death's hideous peal; hard-following on the sound
Sunk the last stroke, and corses cloath'd the ground.
   Now while the Hittites fled the dire alarm,
Their haughty king withstood th' invading arm.
Shrill rose the thunders of his piercing cry,
Lost in deaf ears, and echoing through the sky;
With swifter steps, his warriors urg'd their flight,
And dark behind them rush'd pursuing night.
Fierce on the king's bright car, with rapid force,
Resistless Zimri drove his dreadful course;
The dauntless monarch cast his mighty spear,
That sung, and trembled through th' enlighten'd air;
Full on brave Zimri's helm the polish'd steel
Clash'd harmless, and to earth, rebounding, fell.
Regardless of the shock, the nimble chief
Sprang to the car; no sword could lend relief;
Caught by his arm, the heathen beat the ground;
Wide on his bosom sunk the fatal wound;
The greedy blade, deep-plunging, gash'd his side,
And down his buckler pour'd a bubbling tide.
   Wing'd with fierce ardour, Zimri mounts the car,
And calls his heroes to the crimson war.—
Rush on to conquest, every generous band,
Lo the bless'd triumphs of this happy hand!

Here, through his side the sword indignant thrust,
Their furious leader, gasping, bites the dust.—
Fly, miscreants, fly, and let your lives remain
To grace the falchions of a future plain.
From dovelike foes what warrior hopes a name?
So cheap the purchase, victory scarce is fame.—
Thus, loud and taunting, rose the hero's cry;
Swift rush his bands; the heathen swifter fly:
High in the chariot, in dread pomp reveal'd,
His gloomy hand the firey steeds impell'd;
In dusty clouds the hosts are snatch'd from sight,
And Death, and Zimri, darken o'er the flight.

While thus brave Asher trod the conquering plain,
And drove wild ruin on the heathen train,
In the dire centre, to resistless war
Proud Shimron's monarch urg'd the thundering car.
In early youth, he saw fierce Jabin's hand
Seize his fair crown, and rule his fertile land;
Then to the victor's court a captive brought,
In arms was train'd, in arts politic taught,
Won by soft wiles, his throne of Jabin held,
And bade his realm imperial tributes yield.
There, fir'd to glory by the monarch's voice,
He mock'd his pattern, and obey'd his choice,
And hop'd from conduct, form'd by rules so just,
Alone to reign, when Jabin slept in dust.

Full on his lofty breast the flashing shield
Gleam'd a bright terror through the clouded field:
As when the Sun, o'er scorch'd Peruvia's plain,
Disease, and Death, and Horror in his train,
Unveils his crimson face, distain'd with blood,
Burns the brown hills, and sickens every flood.
Loud rang the hero's voice; his lances flew,
And every lance the foremost warrior slew.
On him great Joshua glanc'd a darkening eye,
And rush'd impetuous, with a deathful cry:
His sword, swift-circling, hew'd his dismal way,
Fell'd ranks at once, and broke the deep array.

Amaz'd, the heathen cast a look behind,
And thus in doubt, explor'd his mighty mind.—
Shall I resisting dare that arm of death,
And reach his heart, or nobly yield my breath;
Or with some distant band the foe engage
Where bravery fails, and turn the battle's rage?
This arm, this spear may spill his hated life;
And O what wreaths shall crown the happy strife!
What bright rewards shall Jabin's hand bestow!
What matchless honours round my temples flow?
I claim the contest—hence base flight and shame—
To fight is glory, and to die is fame.

He spoke; while Ruin, riding thro' the plain,
Burst o'er his ranks, and mark'd her path with slain;
On Joshua's helm she sate; tremendous hung
His arm on high, his voice like thunder rung:
Near the bright car he wheel'd his streaming blade,
And dust around him cast a night-like shade.
Full on his buckler clash'd the heathen's spear,
Pierc'd the thick plates, and flash'd behind in air;
Grazing his side, it cut the folded garb,
And drops of crimson stain'd the polish'd barb.
With joy, the king his faithful javelin view'd,
Leap'd from his car, and with his sword pursued.
Then Joshua's hand uprear'd his falchion high,
Its flames bright-circling in the dusky sky;
First his foe's arm dropp'd on the bloody field;
The second stroke divides his glittering shield;
Full on his throat the fierce avenging blade
Sinks; the freed spirit flits to midnight shade.

"Pour on to glory"—rung the Leader's voice,
The trembling host shrunk backward at the noise;
Sad Shimron's sons beheld their monarch dead,
Rais'd one deep howl, and, wing'd with horror, fled.
Throng'd in a gloomy storm, their head-long foes
Round the dire flight with lifted falchions rose;
Broad streams of blood o'er-ran the scenes of death,
And sullen groans proclaim'd the parting breath,

As boiling Etna rolls a flood of fire
Down her rough rocks; and plains, and towns expire,
Lick'd by the flames, exhaling rivers rise,
And crumbling groves smoke upward to the skies,
Swift pours the blazing deluge on the shore,
The scorch'd main foams, the hissing billows roar:
So fierce and dreadful, flew the victor host,
In night involv'd, in dusty volumes lost.
Squadrons thick-strown were scatter'd o'er the fields,
And helms, and swords, and spears, and sanguine shields.
  Huge piles of slaughter gathering round his course,
On Shimron Joshua wing'd his mighty force.
Like two red flames his vivid eye-balls glow,
And shoot fierce lightenings on th' astonish'd foe;
Before, expanded, his meteorous shield
Blaz'd a broad ruin thro' the stormy field;
Round the wild war his flashing terrors fly;
Cars burst before him;—steeds, and heroes die.
So rush'd an angel down the midnight gloom,
When Egypt's first-born sunk in one broad tomb;
High in dark clouds th' avenging Vision hung,
His path, like distant thunder, hoarsely rung;
Flames shot before him, whirlwinds roll'd around,
Bow'd the tall hills, and heav'd the trembling ground.
Not with less terror blaz'd the Leader on;
'Twas ruin all and one unbounded groan;
None look'd behind, none turn'd a hearkening ear;
Nor hills, nor streams impede the full career:
High o'er the ragged rocks they nimbly bound,
Dash thro' the floods, and scower the level ground:
First in the tumult, Youth impels his flight;
Springs o'er the field, and scapes pursuing night:
Pale Age with quivering limbs, and slow-drawn pace,
Feels the keen sword, and sinks beneath the chace.
  Far distant, Zimri, like a sweeping storm,
Grim in the chariot rais'd his gloomy form;
Still on the hindmost fell his fateful sword;
Earth shook, air trembled, heaven with thunder roar'd;

Oft, from the car descending to the plain,
He stream'd, like lightening, o'er the ghastly slain,
Then swiftly rose, and on the heathens sped,
His wheels dark-rolling o'er th' unnumber'd dead.
  Meantime, with all the rage of combat fir'd,
While throngs of warriors round his steps expir'd;
While now, first disobedient to his call,
The balanc'd victory doubted where to fall:
While Caleb's arm with youthful vigor warm'd,
Sham'd Judah's thousands and their vengeance arm'd;
From rank to rank impatient Jabin flew,
Drove these with threats, and those with praises drew.
  But now the eastern plain loud thunders rend;
The shrill cars rattle; hoarser cries ascend;
Progressive clouds, in thickening volumes driven,
Roll tow'rd the south, and shade the dusty heaven.
From the tall car the Chief survey'd the field,
And every circling scene at once beheld,
Even the far wood, with sudden flashes bright,
And the dire omens of tumultuous flight.
Around the war he cast a searching view,
Saw the day lost, and all its evils knew;
Deep from his inmost soul burst forth a sigh,
And momentary sadness gloom'd his eye.
But soon his brow resum'd a cheerful grace,
And living ardour fir'd his artful face.
Full well the monarch knew that fears begun,
From breast to breast, like glancing lightenings, run;
That one rank fled instructs a host to fly,
And cowards' eyes teach heroes' hearts to die—
Then, ere his friends the dire event divine,
Or Judah's sons their kindred victors join,
A wise retreat his mighty mind ordain'd,
And thus the rage of war his voice restrain'd.
Hear, all ye chiefs, brave Hazor's bands that guide,
Your nation's pillars, and your monarch's pride.
Your matchless deeds this raptur'd eye has told,
And fame's bright hand to distant years enroll'd.

But see, o'er western hills the sun's low fire
Cuts short the day, and bids the host retire.
Firm be your ranks, man fast inlock'd with man,
The rear led onward, fix'd the generous van;
At once let chief with chief inspir'd combine,
And 'gainst the foe extend th' embattled line;
Brace firm the shield; the moveless spear protend;
Join hand and heart, and every rank defend.
Your prince behold; when Hazor claims the strife,
My wounds are transport, and a toy my life.
    The hero spoke: as by one soul inspir'd,
Swift to their well-known posts the chiefs retir'd;
At once, by banners rang'd, to brave the storm,
Firm, dreadful lines th' experienc'd squadrons form.
Dire o'er the van-guard, shield with shield combin'd,
Spear lock'd with spear, th' undaunted leaders join'd;
'Gainst Judah's host, with ridgy terrors bright,
Rose a long wall, and flash'd a fearful light.
O'er the tremendous scene the Monarch's car
Pour'd death around, and rul'd the grisly war:
Fierce on the foe, where'er their steps pursue,
From rank to rank the mighty warrior flew;
Hearts form'd of stubborn steel his deeds appall;
The distant tremble, and the nearer fall;
Till Caleb's voice commands the chace to stay,
And yields his foes an unmolested way.
    Then, still and slow, while Judah's host admir'd,
In gloomy strength the sullen storm retir'd.
So, when in heaven propitious breezes rise,
And on the deep the nimble vessel flies,
Shagg'd with brown shades, that o'er the billows lower,
In grim, dark pomp recedes the clifted shore;
Less seen, and less, the awful scenes decay,
And lost in blue confusion fade away.
    With gore all hideous, and with dust imbrown'd,
In the dire front terrific Jabin frown'd;
His lifted arm prepar'd the fatal blow,
And menac'd vengeance to th' approaching foe.—

So, forward driven by earth's convulsive pangs,
The tall, hoar cliff in dubious terror hangs;
High pois'd in dread suspense, its hovering brow
Lowers swift destruction on the world below:
Amaz'd, the swain, while sudden fears appall
Starts, as the tottering ruin seems to fall.
Enjoy, he cried, imperious foes, enjoy
The fancied triumph, combat shall destroy:
But know, ye boasters, soon this arm shall tear
The short-liv'd crown, your haughty temples wear;
Soon your vain chiefs, your nation want a name,
And all your glories sink in endless shame.

But now, sublime in crimson triumph borne,
The sacred standard mock'd th' etherial morn;
Wide on the winds its waving splendors flow'd,
And call'd the warriors from the distant wood.
Behind great Joshua, Hazor's sons to dare,
Pour the bold thousands to the western war,
Beyond Ai's walls, the lessening heathen train
In well-form'd squadrons cross the distant plain;
Part still in sight their shady files extend;
Part fill the wood, and part the hills ascend;
To cease from toil the prudent Chief commands,
And balmy quiet sooths the wearied bands.

Half lost in mountain groves, the sun's broad ray
Shower'd a full splendor round his evening way;
Slow Joshua strode the lovely Youth to find;
Th' unwilling bands more slowly mov'd behind.
Soon as the matchless form arose to view,
O'er their sad faces shone the sorrowing dew;
Silent they stood. To speak the Leader tried,
But the choak'd accents on his palate died.
His bleeding bosom beat with inward pains,
And leaden languors ran along his veins.

Ah, best and bravest of thy race! he said,
And gently rais'd the pale, reclining head—
Lost are thy matchless charms, thy glory gone—
Gone is the glory which thy hand hath won.

In vain on thee thy nation cast her eyes;
In vain with joy beheld thy light arise;
In vain she wish'd thy sceptre to obey;
Vain were her wishes; vain the destin'd sway.
Oh! Irad, loveliest Irad, nature's pride!
Would Heaven, myself for thee, for thee had died!
Nor more; the thoughts lay struggling in his breast;
But tears, expressive tears forbade the rest.
Borne by six chiefs, in silence, o'er the plain,
Fair Irad mov'd before the mournful train;
Great Joshua's arm sustain'd his sword, and shield;
Th' afflicted thousands lengthening thro' the field.
When, crown'd with flowers, the maidens at her side,
With gentle steps advanc'd great Caleb's pride.
Her snowy hand, inspir'd by restless love,
Of the lone wild-rose two rich wreaths inwove;
Fresh in her hand the flowers rejoice to bloom,
And round the fair one shed the mild perfume.
O'er all the train her active glances rov'd;
She gaz'd, and gazing, miss'd the Youth she lov'd;
Some dire mischance her boding heart divin'd,
And thronging terrors fill'd her anxious mind.
As near the host her quickening footsteps drew,
The breathless hero met her trembling view;
From her chill'd hand the headlong roses fell,
And life's gay beauty bade her cheeks farewell;
O'er her fair face unmeaning paleness sate,
And, sunk to earth, she felt no hapless fate.
  With anguish Caleb saw her fading charms,
And caught the favourite in his hastening arms.
Reviv'd with piercing voice, that froze his soul,
She forc'd the big, round tear unwish'd to roll;
By all his love, besought him soon to lead
Where cruel friendship snatch'd his lovely dead.
In vain the chief his anguish strove to hide,
Sighs rent his breast, and chill'd the vital tide.
  To Joshua then, whose heart beside her mourn'd,
With gaze of keen distress, the charmer turn'd.—

Oh, generous Chief, to misery ever kind,—
Thou lov'st my sire—support his sinking mind!
Thy friendly wish delights to lessen woe—
See how his tears for fallen Irad flow!
He claims thy friendship—generous hero, see,
Lost to himself, his fondness bleeds for me.—
To view the hapless Youth, distress'd he fears,
Would wound my soul, and force too copious tears.
But lead, oh lead me, where the Youth is borne!
Calm is my heart, now will my bosom mourn—
So cold that heart, it yields no pitying sigh—
And see no tear bedews this marbled eye.

   She said, and look'd resistless; soft reclin'd
On Joshua's arm, she forc'd his melting mind.
Pressing her hand, he trac'd a gentle way,
Where breathless Irad, lost in slumbers lay.
From the pale face his chilling hand withdrew
The decent veil, and gave the Youth to view.
Fix'd o'er the form, with solemn gaze she hung,
And strong, deep sighs burst o'er her frozen tongue.
On Joshua then she cast a wishful look;
Wild was her tearless eye, and rolling spoke
Anguish unutterable. Thrice she tried
To vent her woes, and thrice her efforts died.
At length, in accents of estatic grief,
Her voice bewilder'd, gave her heart relief.

   Is this the doom we dread?—is this to die?
To sleep?—to feel no more?—to close the eye?—
Slight is the change—how vain the childish fear,
That trembles, and recoils, when death is near?
I too, methinks, would share the peaceful doom,
And seek a calm repose in Irad's tomb.
This breath I know, this useless breath must fail,
These eyes be darken'd, and this face grow pale—
But thou art pale, oh Youth! thy lot I crave,
And every grief shall vanish in the grave.

   She ceas'd, the tender chief without delay,
Soft pressing, kindly forc'd her steps away.

Slow tow'rd the camp, with solemn pace, thy drew;
The corse moves on; the mournful bands pursue.
Pale Uzal follows, virtuous now no more;
And brave Shelumiel, black with clotted gore.
Unnumber'd tears their hapless fate bewail,
And voice to voice resounds the dreadful tale.
But Irad, matchless Irad, call'd in vain,
Breathes wide a solemn sadness round the plain:
Unhappy, to their tents the host retir'd,
And gradual; o'er the mountains day expir'd.

GREENFIELD HILL

DWIGHT intended the poem to be an answer to those European critics who asserted that America afforded no adequate themes or impressive settings for native poetry. From the hilltop on which his home was situated, he gazes over the countryside. In Part I he sweeps in the main features of the landscape and rises to the conception of the social felicity of its inhabitants. Into this framework he fits certain historical episodes—the burning of Fairfield, the destruction of the Pequods—and then proceeds to moral instruction in "The Clergyman's Advice to the Villagers" and "The Farmer's Advice to the Villagers." The poem ends, as many eighteenth century poems were likely to end, with "The Vision, or Prospect of the Future Happiness of America." The plan of the work is taken from Denham's *Cooper's Hill*, but in the several parts he consciously imitated different English poets, such as Thomson, Goldsmith, Beattie, Gay, and Pope.

PART I

THE PROSPECT

ARGUMENT

Spring. General Prospect. View of the Inland Country. Of the beauty of Vegetation at the time of Harvest. Of the happy state of the Inhabitants. Men esteemed in New-England according to their personal qualities. State of New England. Connecticut. State of Society in Europe contrasted to that of New-England. People of New-England exhorted not to copy the Government, Manners, etc., of other nations. Remembrance of the late Councils and Armies of the United States. Prospect of the Country between Greenfield Hill and the Sound. Description of the

*Sound.   Retrospect of the troubles occasioned by the British
Marauding Parties.   Wish for perpetual Peace.   Beauty
of the Scenes of Nature.   Happiness of a Clergyman in the
Country.   Address to the Clergy.*

FROM southern isles, on winds of gentlest wing,
Sprinkled with morning dew, and rob'd in green,
Life in her eye, and music in her voice,
Lo Spring returns, and wakes the world to joy!
Forth creep the smiling herbs; expand the flowers;
New-loos'd, and bursting from their icy bonds,
The streams fresh-warble, and through every mead
Convey reviving verdure; every bough,
Full-blown and lovely, teems with sweets and songs;
And hills, and plains, and pastures feel the prime.

    As round me here I gaze, what prospects rise?
Etherial! matchless! such as Albion's sons,
Could Albion's isle an equal prospect boast,
In all the harmony of numerous song,
Had tun'd to rapture, and o'er Cooper's hill,
And Windsor's beauteous forest, high uprais'd,
And sent on fame's light wing to every clime.
Far inland, blended groves, and azure hills,
Skirting the broad horizon, lift their pride.
Beyond, a little chasm to view unfolds
Cerulean mountains, verging high on Heaven,
In misty grandeur. Stretch'd in nearer view,
Unnumber'd farms salute the cheerful eye;
Contracted there to little gardens; here outspread
Spacious, with pastures, fields, and meadows rich;
Where the young wheat its glowing green displays,
Or the dark soil bespeaks the recent plough,
Or flocks and herds along the lawn disport.

    Fair is the landscape; but a fairer still
Shall soon inchant the soul—when harvest full
Waves wide its bending wealth. Delightful task!
To trace along the rich, enamell'd ground,

The sweetly varied hues; from India's corn,
Whose black'ning verdure bodes a bounteous crop,
Through lighter grass, and lighter still the flax,
The paler oats, the yellowish barley, wheat
In golden glow, and rye in brighter gold.
These soon the sight shall bless. Now other scenes
The heart dilate, where round, in rural pride
The village spreads its tidy, snug retreats,
That speak the industry of every hand.

How bless'd the sight of such a numerous train
In such small limits, tasting every good
Of competence, of independence, peace,
And liberty unmingled; every house
On its own ground, and every happy swain
Beholding no superior, but the laws,
And such as virtue, knowledge, useful life,
And zeal, exerted for the public good,
Have rais'd above the throng. For here, in truth,
Not in pretence, man is esteem'd as man.
Not here how rich, of what peculiar blood,
Or office high; but of what genuine worth,
What talents bright and useful, what good deeds,
What piety to God, what love to man,
The question is. To this an answer fair
The general heart secures. Full many a rich,
Vile knave, full many a blockhead, proud
Of ancient blood, these eyes have seen float down
Life's dirty kennel, trampled in the mud,
Stepp'd o'er unheeded, or push'd rudely on;
While Merit, rising from her humble skiff
To barks of nobler, and still nobler size,
Sail'd down the expanding stream, in triumph gay,
By every ship saluted.

                              Hail, O hail
My much-lov'd native land! New Albion hail!
The happiest realm, that, round his circling course,

The all-searching sun beholds. What though the breath
Of Zembla's winter shuts thy lucid streams,
And hardens into brass thy generous soil;
Though, with one white, and cheerless robe, thy hills,
Invested, rise a long and joyless waste;
Leafless the grove, and dumb the lonely spray,
And every pasture mute; What though with clear
And fervid blaze, thy summer rolls his car,
And drives the languid herd, and fainting flock
To seek the shrouding umbrage of the dale;
While Man, relax'd and feeble, anxious waits
The dewy eve, to slake his thirsty frame:
What though thy surface, rocky, rough, and rude,
Scoop'd into vales, or heav'd in lofty hills,
Or cloud-embosom'd mountains, dares the plough,
And threatens toil intense to every swain:
What though foul Calumny, with voice malign,
Thy generous sons, with every virtue grac'd,
Accus'd of every crime, and still rolls down
The kennell'd stream of impudent abuse:
Yet to high HEAVEN my ardent praises rise,
That in thy lightsome vales he gave me birth,
All-gracious, and allows me still to live.

   Cold is thy clime, but every western blast
Brings health, and life, and vigour on his wings;
Innerves the steely frame, and firms the soul
With strength and hardihood; wakes each bold
And manly purpose; bears above the ills,
That stretch, upon the rack, the languid heart
Of summer's maiden sons, in pleasure's lap,
Dandled to dull repose. Exertion strong
Marks their whole life. Mountains before them sink
To mole-hills; oceans bar their course in vain.
Thro' the keen wintry wind they breast their way,
Or summer's fiercest flame. Dread dangers rouse
Their hearts to pleasing conflict; toils and woes,
Quicken their ardour: while, in milder climes,

Their peers effeminate they see, with scorn
On lazy plains, dissolv'd in putrid sloth,
And struggling hard for being. Thy rough soil
Tempts hardy labour, with his sturdy team,
To turn, with sinewy hand, the stony glebe,
And call forth every comfort from the mould,
Unpromising, but kind. Thy houses, barns,
Thy granaries, and thy cellars, hence are stor'd
With all the sweets of life: while, thro thy realm,
A native beggar rarely pains the sight.

Thy summer glows with heat; but choicest fruits
Hence purple in the sun: hence sparkling flowers
Gem the rich landscape; double harvests hence
Load the full fields: pale Famine scowls aloof,
And Plenty wantons round thy varied year.

Rough is thy surface; but each landscape bright,
With all of beauty, all of grandeur dress'd,
Of mountains, hills, and sweetly winding vales,
Of forests, groves, and lawns, and meadows green,
And waters, varied by the plastic hand,
Through all their fairy splendour, ceaseless charms,
Poetic eyes. Springs bubbling round the year,
Gay-wand'ring brooks, wells at the surface full,
Yield life, and health, and joy, to every house,
And every vivid field. Rivers, with foamy course,
Pour o'er the ragged cliff the white cascade,
And roll unnumber'd mills; or, like the Nile,
Fatten the beauteous interval; or bear
The sails of commerce through the laughing groves.

With wisdom, virtue, and the generous love
Of learning, fraught, and freedom's living flame,
Electric, unextinguishable, fir'd,
Our Sires established, in thy cheerful bounds,
The noblest institutions, man has seen,
Since time his reign began. In little farms

They measur'd all thy realms, to every child
In equal shares descending; no entail
The first-born lifting into bloated pomp,
Tainting with lust, and sloth, and pride, and rage,
The world around him: all the race beside,
Like brood of ostrich, left for chance to rear,
And every foot to trample. Reason's sway
Elective, founded on the rock of truth,
Wisdom their guide, and equal good their end,
They built with strength, that mocks the battering storm,
And spurns the mining flood; and every right
Dispens'd alike to all. Beneath their eye,
And forming hand, in every hamlet, rose
The nurturing school; in every village, smil'd
The heav'n-inviting church, and every town
A world within itself, with order, peace,
And harmony, adjusted all its weal.

    Hence every swain, free, happy, his own lord,
With useful knowledge fraught, of business, laws,
Morals, religion, life, unaw'd by man,
And doing all, but ill, his heart can wish,
Looks round, and finds strange happiness his own;
And sees that happiness on laws depend.
On this heav'n-laid foundation rests thy sway;
On knowledge to discern, and sense to feel,
That free-born rule is life's perennial spring
Of real good. On this alone it rests.
For, could thy sons a full conviction feel,
That government was noxious, without arms,
Without intrigues, without a civil broil,
As torrents sweep the sand-built structure down,
A vote would wipe it's every trace away.
Hence too each breast is steel'd for bold defence;
For each has much to lose. Chosen by all,
The messenger of peace, by all belov'd,
Spreads, hence, the truth and virtue, he commends.
Hence manners mild, and sweet, their peaceful sway

Widely extend. Refinement of the heart
Illumes the general mass. Even those rude hills,
Those deep embow'ring woods, in other lands
Prowl'd round by savages, the same soft scenes,
Mild manners, order, virtue, peace, disclose;
The howling forest polish'd as the plain.

From earliest years, the same enlightened soul
Founded bright schools of science. Here the mind
Learn'd to expand its wing, and stretch its flight
Through truth's broad fields. Divines, and lawyers, hence,
Physicians, statesmen, all with wisdom fraught,
And learning, suited to the use of life,
And minds, by business, sharpen'd into sense,
Sagacious of the duty, and the weal,
Of man, spring numberless; and knowledge hence
Pours its salubrious streams, through all the spheres
Of human life. Its bounds, and generous scope,
Hence Education opens, spreading far
Through the bold yeomanry, that fill thy climes,
Views more expanded, generous, just, refin'd,
Than other nations know. In other lands,
The mass of man, scarce rais'd above the brutes,
Drags dull the horsemill round of sluggish life:
Nought known, beyond their daily toil; all else
By ignorance' dark curtain hid from sight.
Here, glorious contrast! every mind, inspir'd
With active inquisition, restless wings
Its flight to every flower, and, settling, drinks
Largely the sweets of knowledge.

                              Candour, say,
Is this a state of life, thy honest tongue
Could blacken? These a race of men, thy page
Could hand to infamy? The shameful task
Thy foes at first began, and still thy foes,
Laborious, weave the web of lies. 'Tis hence
The generous traveller round him looks, amazed,
And wonders at our unexpected bliss.

But chief, Connecticut! on thy fair breast
These splendours glow. A rich improvement smiles
Around thy lovely borders; in thy fields
And all that in thy fields delighted dwell.
Here that pure, golden mean, so oft of yore
By sages wish'd, and prais'd, by Agur's voice
Implor'd, while God th' approving sanction gave
Of wisdom infinite; that golden mean,
Shines unalloy'd; and here the extended good,
That mean alone secures, is ceaseless found.

Oh, would some faithful, wise, laborious mind,
Develop all thy springs of bliss to man;
Soon would politic visions fleet away,
Before awakening truth! Utopias then,
Ancient and new, high fraught with fairy good,
Would catch no more the heart. Philosophy
Would bow to common-sense; and man, from facts,
And real life, politic wisdom learn.

Ah then, thou favour'd land, thyself revere!
Look not to Europe, for examples just
Of order, manners, customs, doctrines, laws,
Of happiness, or virtue. Cast around
The eye of searching reason, and declare
What Europe proffers, but a patchwork sway;
The garment Gothic, worn to fritter'd shreds,
And eked from every loom of following times.
Such as the sway, the system shows entire,
Of silly pomp, and meanness train'd t' adore;
Of wealth enormous, and enormous want;
Of lazy sinecures, and suffering toil;
Of grey-beard systems, and meteorous dreams;
Of lordly churches, and dissention fierce,
Rites farsical, and phrenzied unbelief.
See thick and fell her lowering gibbets stand,
And gibbets still employ'd! while, through thy realms,
The rare-seen felon startles every mind

And fills each mouth with news. Behold her jails
Countless, and stow'd with wretches of all kinds!
Her brothels, circling, with their tainted walls,
Unnumber'd female outcasts, shorne from life,
Peace, penitence, and hope; and down, down plung'd
In vice' unbottom'd gulph! Ye demons, rise,
Rise, and look upward, from your dread abode;
And, if you've tears to shed, distil them here!
See too, in countless herds, the mistress vile,
Even to the teeth of matron sanctity,
Lift up her shameless bronze, and elbow out
The pure, the chaste, the lovely angel-form
Of female excellence! while leachers rank, and
Bloated, call aloud on vengeance' worms,
To seize their prey, on this side of the grave.
See the foul theatre, with Upaz steams,
Impoisoning half mankind! See every heart
And head from dunghills up to thrones, moon'd high
With fashion, frippery, falling humbly down
To a new head-dress; barbers, milliners,
Taylors, and mantua-makers, forming gods,
Their fellow-millions worship! See the world
All set to sale; truth, friendship, public trust,
A nation's weal, religion, scripture, oaths,
Struck off by inch of candle! Mark the mien,
Out-changing the Cameleon; pleasing all,
And all deceiving! Mark the snaky tongue,
Now lightly vibrating, now hissing death!
See war, from year to year, from age to age,
Unceasing, open on mankind the gates
Of devastation; earth wet-deep with blood,
And pav'd with corpses; cities whelm'd in flames;
And fathers, brothers, husbands, sons, and friends,
In millions hurried to th' untimely tomb;
To gain a wigwam, built on Nootka Sound,
Or Falkland's fruitful isles; or to secure
That rare soap-bubble, blown by children wise,
Floated in air, and ting'd with colours fine,

Pursu'd by thousands, and with rapture nam'd
National honour. But what powers suffice
To tell the sands, that form the endless beach,
Or drops, that fill the immeasurable deep.

   Say then, ah say, would'st thou for these exchange
Thy sacred institutions? thy mild laws?
Thy pure religion? morals uncorrupt?
Thy plain and honest manners? order, peace,
And general weal? Think whence this weal arose.
From the same springs it still shall ceaseless rise.
Preserve the fountains sweet, and sweetest streams
Shall still flow from them. Change, but change alone,
By wise improvement of thy blessings rare;
And copy not from others. Shun the lures
Of Europe. Cherish still, watch, hold,
And hold through every trial, every snare,
All that is thine. Amend, refine, complete;
But still the glorious stamina retain.
Still, as of yore, in church, and state, elect
The virtuous, and the wise; men tried, and prov'd,
Of steady virtue, all thy weal to guide;
And HEAVEN shall bless thee, with a parent's hand.

   When round I turn my raptur'd eyes, with joy
O'erflowing, and thy wonderous bliss survey,
I love to think of those, by whom that bliss
Was purchas'd; those firm councils, that brave band,
Who nobly jeoparded their lives, their all,
And cross'd temptation's whirlpool, to secure,
For us, and ours, this rich estate of good.
Ye souls illustrious, who, in danger's field,
Instinct with patriot fire, each terror brav'd;
And fix'd as these firm hills, the shock withstood
Of war's convulsing earthquake, unappall'd,
Whilst on your labours gaz'd, with reverent eyes,
The pleas'd and wondering world; let every good,
Life knows, let peace, esteem, domestic bliss,
Approving conscience, and a grateful land,

Glory through every age, and Heaven at last,
To crown the splendid scene, your toils reward.

Heavens, what a matchless group of beauties rare
Southward expands! where, crown'd with yon tall oak,
Round-hill the circling land and sea o'erlooks;
Or, smoothly sloping, Grover's beauteous rise,
Spreads its green sides, and lifts its single tree,
Glad mark for seamen; or, with ruder face,
Orchards, and fields, and groves, and houses rare,
And scatter'd cedars, Mill-hill meets the eye;
Or where, beyond, with every beauty clad,
More distant heights in vernal pride ascend.
On either side, a long, continued range,
In all the charms of rural nature dress'd,
Slopes gently to the main. Ere Tryon sunk
To infamy unfathom'd, thro' yon groves,
Once glister'd Norwalk's white-ascending spires,
And soon, if HEAVEN permit, shall shine again.
Here, sky-encircled, Stratford's churches beam;
And Stratfield's turrets greet the roving eye.
In clear, full view, with every varied charm,
That forms the finish'd landscape, blending soft
In matchless union, Fairfield and Green's Farms,
Give lustre to the day. Here crown'd with pines
And skirting groves, with creeks and havens fair
Embellish'd, fed with many a beauteous stream,
Prince of the waves, and ocean's favorite child,
Far westward fading in confusion blue,
And eastward stretch'd beyond the human ken,
And mingled with the sky, there Longa's Sound
Glorious expands. All hail! of waters first
In beauties of all kinds; in prospects rich
Of bays, and arms, and groves, and little streams,
Inchanting capes and isles, and rivers broad,
That yield eternal tribute to thy wave!
In use supreme: fish of all kinds, all tastes,
Scaly or shell'd, with floating nations fill

Thy spacious realms; while, o'er thy lucid waves,
Unceasing Commerce wings her countless sails.
Safe in thy arms, the treasure moves along,
While, beat by Longa's coast, old ocean roars
Distant, but roars in vain. O'er all thy bounds,
What varied beauties, changing with the sun,
Or night's more lovely queen, here splendid glow.
Oft, on thy eastern wave, the orb of light
Refulgent rising, kindles wide a field
Of mimic day, slow sailing to the west,
And fading with the eve; and oft, through clouds,
Painting their dark skirts on the glassy plain,
The strong, pervading lustre marks th' expanse,
With streaks of glowing silver, or with spots
Of burnish'd gold; while clouds, of every hue,
Their purple shed, their amber, yellow, grey,
Along the faithful mirror. Oft, at eve,
Thron'd in the eastern sky, th' ascending moon,
Distain'd with blood, sits awful o'er the wave,
And, from the dim dark waters, troubled calls
Her dreary image, trembling on the deep,
And boding every horror. Round yon isles,
Where every Triton, every Nereid, borne
From eastern climes, would find perpetual home,
Were Grecian fables true, what charms intrance
The fascinated eye! where, half withdrawn
Behind yon vivid slope, like blushing maids,
They leave the raptur'd gaze. And O how fair
Bright Longa spreads her terminating shore,
Commix'd with whit'ning cliffs, with groves obscure,
Farms shrunk to garden-beds, and forests fallen
To little orchards, slow-ascending hills,
And dusky vales, and plains! These the pleas'd eye
Relieve, engage, delight; with one unchang'd,
Unbounded ocean, wearied, and displeas'd.

Yet scarce six suns are pass'd, since these wide bounds,
So still so lovely now, were wanton'd o'er

By sails of British foes, with thunders dread
Announcing desolation to each field,
Each town, and hamlet; in the sheltering night
Wafting base throngs of plunderers to our coast,
The bed of peace invading; herds and flocks
Purloining from the swain; and oft the house
Of innocence and peace, in cruel flames
With fell revenge, encircling. Now, afar
With shame retir'd, his bands no more, no more
(And oh may HEAVEN the fond prediction seal)
Shall hostile bands, from earth's extended bounds,
Th' infernal talk [sic] resume. Henceforth, through time,
To peace devoted, 'till millenian suns
Call forth returning Eden, arts of peace
Shall triumph here. Speed, oh speed, ye days
Of bliss divine! when all-involving HEAVEN,
The mystery finish'd, come the second birth
Of this sin-ruin'd, this apostate world,
And clos'd the final scene of wild misrule,
All climes shall clothe again with life, and joy,
With peace, and purity; and deathless spring
Again commence her bright, etherial reign.

  O who can paint, like Nature? who can boast
Such scenes, as here inchant the lingering eye?
Still to thy hand, great parent of the year!
I turn obsequious; still to all thy works
Of beauty, grandeur, novelty, and power,
Of motion, light, and life, my beating heart
Plays unison; and, with harmonious thrill,
Inhales such joys, as Avarice never knew.

  Ah! knew he but his happiness, of men
Not the least happy he, who, free from broils,
And base ambition, vain and bust'ling pomp,
Amid a friendly cure, and competence,
Tastes the pure pleasures of parochial life.
What though no crowd of clients, at his gate,

To falsehood, and injustice, bribe his tongue,
And flatter into guilt; what though no bright,
And gilded propects lure ambition on
To legislative pride, or chair of state;
What though no golden dreams entice his mind
To burrow, with the mole, in dirt, and mire;
What though no splendid villa, Eden'd round
With gardens of enchantment, walks of state,
And all the grandeur of superfluous wealth,
Invite the passenger to stay his steed,
And ask the liveried foot-boy, "who dwells here?"
What though no swarms, around his sumptuous board,
Of soothing flatterers, humming in the shine
Of opulence, and honey, from its flowers,
Devouring, 'till their time arrives to sting,
Inflate his mind; his virtues, round the year,
Repeating, and his faults, with microscope
Inverted, lessen, 'till they steal from sight:
Yet, from the dire temptations, these present,
His state is free; temptations, few can stem;
Temptations, by whose sweeping torrent hurl'd
Down the dire steep of guilt, unceasing fall,
Sad victims, thousands of the brightest minds,
That time's dark reign adorn; minds, to whose grasp
Heaven seems most freely offer'd; to man's eye,
Most hopeful candidates for angels' joys.

His lot, that wealth, and power, and pride forbids,
Forbids him to become the tool of fraud,
Injustice, misery, ruin; saves his soul
From all the needless labours, griefs, and cares,
That avarice, and ambition, agonize;
From those cold nerves of wealth, that, palsied, feel
No anguish, but its own; and ceaseless lead
To thousand meanesses, as gain allures.

Though oft compell'd to meet the gross attack
Of shameless ridicule, and towering pride,

Sufficient good is his; good, real, pure,
With guilt unmingled. Rarely forc'd from home,
Around his board, his wife and children smile;
Communion sweetest, nature here can give,
Each fond endearment, office of delight,
With love and duty blending. Such the joy,
My bosom oft has known. His, too, the talk,
To rear the infant plants, that bud around;
To ope their little minds to truth's pure light;
To take them by the hand, and lead them on,
In that straight, narrow road, where virtue walks;
To guard them from a vain, deceiving world;
And point their course to realms of promis'd life.

His too th' esteem of those, who weekly hear
His words of truth divine; unnumber'd acts
Of real love attesting, to his eye,
Their filial tenderness. Where'er he walks,
The friendly welcome and inviting smile
Wait on his steps, and breathe a kindred joy.

Oft too in friendliest Association join'd,
He greets his brethren, with a flowing heart,
Flowing with virtue; all rejoic'd to meet,
And all reluctant parting; every aim,
Benevolent, aiding with purpose kind;
While, season'd with unblemish'd cheerfulness,
Far distant from the tainted mirth of vice,
Their hearts disclose each contemplation sweet
Of things divine; and blend in friendship pure,
Friendship sublim'd by piety and love.

All virtue's friends are his: the good, the just,
The pious, to his house their visits pay,
And converse high hold of the true, the fair,
The wonderful, the moral, the divine;
Of saints, and prophets, patterns bright of truth,
Lent to a world of sin, to teach mankind,

How virtue, in that world, can live, and shine;
Of learning's varied realms; of Nature's works;
And that bless'd book, which gilds man's darksome way,
With light from heaven; of bless'd Messiah's throne
And kingdom; prophesies divine fulfill'd,
And prophesies more glorious, yet to come,
In renovated days; of that bright world,
And all the happy trains, which that bright world
Inhabit, whither virtue's sons are gone:
While GOD the whole inspires, adorns, exalts,
The source, the end, the substance, and the soul.

This too the task, the bless'd, the useful task,
T' invigour order, justice, law, and rule;
Peace to extend, and bid contention cease;
To teach the words of life; to lead mankind
Back from the wild of guilt, and brink of woe,
To virtue's house and family; faith, hope,
And joy, t' inspire; to warm the soul,
With love of GOD, and man; to cheer the sad,
To fix the doubting, rouse the languid heart;
The wandering to restore; to spread with down,
The thorny bed of death; console the poor,
Departing mind, and aid its lingering wing.

To him, her choicest pages Truth expands,
Unceasing, where the soul-intrancing scenes,
Poetic fiction boasts, are real all:
Where beauty, novelty, and grandeur, wear
Superior charms, and moral worlds unfold
Sublimities, transporting and divine.

Not all the scenes, Philosophy can boast,
Tho' them with nobler truths he ceaseless blends,
Compare with these. They, as they sound the mind,
Still leave it; more inform'd, but not more wise.
These wiser, nobler, better, make the man.

Thus every happy mean of solid good
His life, his studies, and profession yield.
With motives hourly new, each rolling day,
Allures, through wisdom's path, and truth's fair field,
His feet to yonder skies. Before him heaven
Shines bright, the scope sublime of all his prayers,
The meed of every sorrow, pain, and toil.

Then, O ye happy few! whom GOD allows
To stand his messengers, in this bad world,
And call mankind to virtue, weep no more,
Though pains and toils betide you: for what life,
On earth, from pains and toils was ever free?
When Wealth and Pride around you gaily spread
Their vain and transient splendour, envy not.
How oft (let virtue weep!) is this their all?
For you, in sunny prospect, daily spring
Joys, which nor Pride can taste, nor Wealth can boast;
That, planted here, beyond the wintery grave
Revive and grow with every vernal bloom.

Hail these, oh hail! and be't enough for you,
To 'scape a world unclean; a life to lead
Of usefulness, and truth; a Prince to Serve,
Who suffers no sincere and humble toil
To miss a rich reward; In Death's dark vale,
To meet unbosom'd light; beyond the grave
To rise triumphant, freed from every stain,
And cloth'd with every beauty; in the sky
Stars to outshine; and, round th' eternal year,
With saints, with angels, and with CHRIST, to reign.

END OF FIRST PART

PART II

THE FLOURISHING VILLAGE

THE ARGUMENT

View of the Village invested with the pleasing appearances of Spring—Recollection of the Winter—Pleasures of Winter—Of Nature and humble life—March—Original subject resumed—Freedom of the Villages from manorial evils—Address to Competence, reciting its pleasures, charitable effects, virtues attendant upon it, and its utility to the public—Contrasted by European artificial society—Further effects of Competence on Society, particularly in improving the People at large—African appears—State of Negro Slavery in Connecticut—Effects of Slavery on the African, from his childhood through life—Slavery generally characterized—West-Indian Slavery—True cause of the calamities of the West-Indies—Church—Effects of the Sabbath—Academic School—School-master—House of Sloth—Female Worthy—Inferior Schools—Female Visit—What is not, and what is, a social female visit—Pleasure of living in an improving state of society, contrasted by the dullness of stagnated society—Emigrations to the Western Country—Conclusion.

FAIR Verna! loveliest village of the west;
Of every joy, and every charm, possess'd;
How pleas'd amid thy varied walks I rove,
Sweet, cheerful walks of innocence, and love,
And o'er thy smiling prospects cast my eyes,
And see the seats of peace, and pleasure, rise,
And hear the voice of Industry resound,
And mark the smile of Competence, around!
Hail, happy village! O'er thy cheerful lawns,
With earliest beauty, spring delighted dawns;
The northward sun begins his vernal smile;
The spring-bird carols o'er the cressy rill:

The shower, that patters in the ruffled stream,
The ploughboy's voice, that chides the lingering team,
The bee, industrious, with his busy song,
The woodman's axe, the distant groves among,
The waggon, rattling down the rugged steep,
The light wind, lulling every care to sleep,
All these, with mingled music, from below,
Deceive intruding sorrow, as I go.

How pleas'd, fond Recollection, with a smile,
Surveys the varied round of wintery toil!
How pleas'd, amid the flowers, that scent the plain,
Recalls the vanish'd frost, and sleeted rain;
The chilling damp, the ice-endangering street,
And treacherous earth that slump'd beneath the feet.

Yet even stern winter's glooms could joy inspire:
Then social circles grac'd the nutwood fire;
The axe resounded, at the sunny door;
The swain, industrious, trimm'd his flaxen store;
Or thresh'd, with vigorous flail, the bounding wheat,
His poultry round him pilfering for their meat;
Or slid his firewood on the creaking snow;
Or bore his produce to the main below;
Or o'er his rich returns exulting laugh'd;
Or pledg'd the healthful orchard's sparkling draught:
While, on his board, for friends and neighbours spread,
The turkey smok'd, his busy housewife fed;
And Hospitality look'd smiling round,
And leisure told his tale, with gleeful sound.

Then too, the rough road hid beneath the sleigh,
The distant friend despis'd a length of way,
And join'd the warm embrace, and mingling smile,
And told of all his bliss, and all his toil;
And, many a month elaps'd, was pleas'd to view
How well the household far'd, the children grew;
While tales of sympathy deceiv'd the hour,
And sleep, amus'd, resign'd his wonted power.

Yes! let the proud despise, the rich deride,
These humble joys, to Competence allied:
To me, they bloom, all fragrant to my heart,
Nor ask the pomp of wealth, nor gloss of art.
And as a bird, in prison long confin'd,
Springs from his open'd cage, and mounts the wind,
Thro' fields of flowers, and fragrance, gaily flies,
Or re-assumes his birth-right, in the skies:
Unprison'd thus from artificial joys,
Where pomp fatigues, and fussful fashion cloys,
The soul, reviving, loves to wander free
Thro' native scenes of sweet simplicity;
Thro' Peace' low vale, where Pleasure lingers long,
And every songster tunes his sweetest song,
And Zephyr hastes, to breathe his first perfume,
And Autumn stays, to drop his latest bloom:
'Till grown mature, and gathering strength to roam,
She lifts her lengthen'd wings, and seeks her home.

But now the wintery glooms are vanish'd all;
The lingering drift behind the shady wall;
The dark-brown spots, that patch'd the snowy field;
The surly frost, that every bud conceal'd;
The russet veil, the way with slime o'erspread,
And all the saddening scenes of March are fled.

Sweet-smiling village! loveliest of the hills!
How green thy groves! How pure thy glassy rills!
With what new joy, I walk thy verdant streets!
How often pause, to breathe thy gale of sweets;
To mark thy well-built walls! thy budding fields!
And every charm, that rural nature yields;
And every joy, to Competence allied,
And every good, that Virtue gains from Pride!

No griping landlord here alarms the door,
To halve, for rent, the poor man's little store.
No haughty owner drives the humble swain

To some far refuge from his dread domain;
Nor wastes, upon his robe of useless pride,
The wealth, which shivering thousands want beside;
Nor in one palace sinks a hundred cots;
Nor in one manor drowns a thousand lots;
Nor, on one table, spread for death and pain,
Devours what would a village well sustain.

O Competence, thou bless'd by Heaven's decree,
How well exchang'd is empty pride for thee!
Oft to thy cot my feet delighted turn,
To meet thy cheerful smile, at peep of morn;
To join thy toils, that bid the earth look gay;
To mark thy sports, that hail the eve of May;
To see thy ruddy children, at thy board,
And share thy temperate meal, and frugal hoard;
And every joy, by winning prattlers giv'n,
And every earnest of a future Heaven.

There the poor wanderer finds a table spread,
The fireside welcome, and the peaceful bed.
The needy neighbour, oft by wealth denied,
There finds the little aids of life supplied;
The horse, that bears to mill the hard-earn'd grain;
The day's work given, to reap the ripen'd plain;
The useful team, to house the precious food,
And all the offices of real good.

There too, divine Religion is a guest,
And all the Virtues join the daily feast.
Kind Hospitality attends the door,
To welcome in the stranger and the poor;
Sweet Chastity, still blushing as she goes;
And Patience smiling at her train of woes;
And meek-eyed Innocence, and Truth refin'd,
And Fortitude, of bold, but gentle mind.

Thou pay'st the tax, the rich man will not pay;
Thou feed'st the poor, the rich man drives away.

Thy sons, for freedom, hazard limbs, and life,
While pride applauds, but shuns the manly strife:
Thou prop'st religion's cause, the world around,
And shew'st thy faith in works, and not in sound.

Say, child of passion! while, with idiot stare,
Thou seest proud grandeur wheel her sunny car;
While kings, and nobles, roll bespangled by,
And the tall palace lessens in the sky;
Say, while with pomp thy giddy brain runs round,
What joys, like these, in splendour can be found?
Ah, yonder turn thy wealth-inchanted eyes,
Where that poor, friendless wretch expiring lies!
Hear his sad partner shriek, beside his bed,
And call down curses on her landlord's head,
Who drove, from yon small cot, her household sweet,
To pine with want, and perish in the street.
See the pale tradesman toil, the livelong day,
To deck imperious lords, who never pay!
Who waste, at dice, their boundless breadth of soil,
But grudge the scanty meed of honest toil.
See hounds and horses riot on the store,
By HEAVEN created for the hapless poor!
See half a realm one tyrant scarce sustain,
While meagre thousands round him glean the plain!
See, for his mistress' robe, a village sold,
Whose matrons shrink from nakedness and cold!
See too the Farmer prowl around the shed,
To rob the starving household of their bread;
And seize, with cruel fangs, the helpless swain,
While wives, and daughters, plead, and weep, in vain;
Or yield to infamy themselves, to save
Their sire from prison, famine, and the grave.

There too foul luxury taints the putrid mind,
And slavery there imbrutes the reasoning kind:
There humble worth, in damps of deep despair,
Is bound by poverty's eternal bar:

No motives bright the ethereal aim impart,
Nor one fair ray of hope allures the heart.

But, O sweet Competence! how chang'd the scene,
Where thy soft footsteps lightly print the green!
Where Freedom walks erect, with manly port,
And all the blessings to his side resort,
In every hamlet, Learning builds her schools,
And beggars' children gain her arts, and rules;
And mild Simplicity o'er manners reigns,
And blameless morals Purity sustains.

From thee the rich enjoyments round me spring,
Where every farmer reigns a little king;
Where all to comfort, none to danger, rise;
Where pride finds few, but nature all supplies;
Where peace and sweet civility are seen,
And meek good-neighbourhood endears the green.
Here every class (if classes those we call,
Where one extended class embraces all,
All mingling, as the rainbow's beauty blends,
Unknown where every hue begins or ends)
Each following each, with uninvidious strife,
Wears every feature of improving life.
Each gains from other comeliness of dress,
And learns, with gentle mien to win and bless,
With welcome mild the stranger to receive,
And with plain, pleasing decency to live;
Refinement hence even humblest life improves;
Not the loose fair, that form and frippery loves;
But she, whose mansion is the gentle mind,
Is thought, and action, virtuously refin'd.
Hence, wives and husbands act a lovelier part,
More just the conduct, and more kind the heart;
Hence brother, sister, parent, child, and friend,
The harmony of life more sweetly blend;
Hence labour brightens every rural scene;
Hence cheerful plenty lives along the green;

Still Prudence eyes her hoard, with watchful care,
And robes of thrift and neatness, all things wear.

But hark! what voice so gaily fills the wind?
Of care oblivious, whose that laughing mind?
'Tis yon poor black, who ceases now his song,
And whistling, drives the cumbrous wain along.
He never, dragg'd, with groans, the galling chain;
Nor hung, suspended, on th' infernal crane;
No dim, white spots deform his face, or hand,
Memorials hellish of the marking brand!
No seams of pincers, scars of scalding oil;
No waste of famine, and no wear of toil.
But kindly fed, and clad, and treated, he
Slides on, thro' life, with more than common glee.
For here mild manners good to all impart,
And stamp with infamy th' unfeeling heart;
Here law, from vengeful rage, the slave defends,
And here the gospel peace on earth extends.

He toils, 'tis true; but shares his master's toil;
With him, he feeds the herd, and trims the soil;
Helps to sustain the house, with clothes, and food,
And takes his portion of the common good;
Lost liberty his sole, peculiar ill,
And fix'd submission to another's will.
Ill, ah, how great! without that cheering sun,
The world is chang'd to one wide, frigid zone;
The mind, a chill'd exotic, cannot grow,
Nor leaf with vigour, nor with promise blow;
Pale, sickly, shrunk, it strives in vain to rise,
Scarce lives, while living, and untimely dies.

See fresh to life the Afric infant spring,
And plume its powers, and spread its little wing!
Firm is its frame, and vigorous is its mind,
Too young to think, and yet to misery blind.
But soon he sees himself to slavery born;
Soon meets the voice of power, the eye of scorn;

Sighs for the blessings of his peers, in vain;
Condition'd as a brute, tho' form'd a man.
Around he casts his fond, instinctive eyes,
And sees no good, to fill his wishes, rise:
(No motive warms, with animating beam,
Nor praise, nor property, nor kind esteem,
Bless'd independence, on his native ground,
Nor sweet equality with those around;)
Himself, and his, another's shrinks to find,
Levell'd below the lot of human kind.
Thus, shut from honour's paths, he turns to shame,
And filches the small good, he cannot claim.
To sour, and stupid, sinks his active mind;
Finds joys in drink, he cannot elsewhere find;
Rule disobeys; of half his labour cheats;
In some safe cot, the pilfer'd turkey eats;
Rides hard, by night, the steed, his art purloins;
Serene from conscience' bar himself essoins;
Sees from himself his sole redress must flow,
And makes revenge the balsam of his woe.

Thus slavery's blast bids sense and virtue die;
Thus lower'd to dust the sons of Afric lie.
Hence sages grave, to lunar systems given,
Shall ask, why two-legg'd brutes were made by HEAVEN;
HOME seek, what pair first peopled Afric's vales,
And nice MONBODDO calculate their tails.

O thou chief curse, since curses here began;
First guilt, first woe, first infamy of man;
Thou spot of hell, deep smirch'd on human kind,
The uncur'd gangrene of the reasoning mind;
Alike in church, in state, and household all,
Supreme memorial of the world's dread fall;
O slavery! laurel of the Infernal mind,
Proud Satan's triumph over lost mankind!

See the fell Spirit mount his sooty car!
While Hell's black trump proclaims the finish'd war;

Her choicest fiends his wheels exulting draw,
And scream the fall of GOD's most holy law.
In dread procession see the pomp begin,
Sad pomp of woe, of madness, and of sin!
Grav'd on the chariot, all earth's ages rolls,
And all her climes, and realms, to either pole.
Fierce in the flash of arms, see Europe spread!
Her jails, and gibbets, fleets, and hosts, display'd!
Awe-struck, see silken Asia silent bow!
And feeble Afric writhe in blood below!
Before, peace, freedom, virtue, bliss, move on,
The spoils, the treasures, of a world undone;
Behind, earth's bedlam millions clank the chain,
Hymn their disgrace, and celebrate their pain;
Kings, nobles, priests, dread senate! lead the van,
And shout "Te-Deum!" o'er defeated man.

　　Oft, wing'd by thought, I seek those Indian isles,
Where endless spring, with endless summer smiles,
Where fruits of gold untir'd Vertumnus pours,
And Flora dances o'er undying flowers.
There, as I walk thro' fields, as Eden gay,
And breathe the incense of immortal May,
Ceaseless I hear the smacking whip resound;
Hark! that shrill scream! that groan of death-bed sound!
See those throng'd wretches pant along the plain,
Tug the hard hoe, and sigh in hopeless pain!
Yon mother, loaded with her sucking child,
Her rags with frequent spots of blood defil'd,
Drags slowly fainting on; the fiend is nigh;
Rings the shrill cowskin; roars the tyger-cry;
In pangs, th' unfriended suppliant crawls along,
And shrieks the prayer of agonizing wrong.

　　Why glows yon oven with a sevenfold fire?
Crisp'd in the flames, behold a man expire!
Lo! by that vampyre's hand, yon infant dies,
Its brains dash'd out, beneath its father's eyes.

Why shrinks yon slave, with horror, from his meat?
Heavens! 'tis his flesh, the wretch is whipp'd to eat.
Why streams the life-blood from that female's **throat?**
She sprinkled gravy on a guest's new coat!

. . . . .

Why croud those quivering blacks yon dock around?
Those screams announce; that cowskin's shrilling sound.
See, that poor victim hanging from the crane,
While loaded weights his limbs to torture strain;
At each keen stoke, far spouts the bursting gore,
And shrieks, and dying groans, fill all the shore.
Around, in throngs, his brother-victims wait,
And feel, in every stroke, their coming fate;
While each, with palsied hands, and shuddering fears,
The cause, the rule, and price, of torment bears.

Hark, hark, from morn to night, the realm around,
The cracking whip, keen taunt, and shriek, resound!
O'ercast are all the splendors of the spring;
Sweets court in vain; in vain the warblers sing;
Illusions all! 'tis Tartarus round me spreads
His dismal screams, and melancholy shades.
The damned, sure, here clank th' eternal chain,
And waste with grief, or agonize with pain.
A Tartarus new! inversion strange of hell!
Guilt wreaks the vengeance, and the guiltless feel.
The heart, not form'd of flint, here all things rend;
Each fair a fury, and each man a fiend;
From childhood, train'd to every baleful ill,
And their first sport, to torture, and to kill.

Ask not, why earthquakes rock that fateful land;
Fires waste the city; ocean whelms the strand;
Why the fierce whirlwind, with electric sway,
Springs from the storm, and fastens on his prey,
Shakes heaven, rends earth, upheaves the cumbrous wave,

And with destruction's besom fills the grave:
Why dark disease roams swift her nightly round,
Knocks at each door, and wakes the gasping sound.

Ask, shuddering ask, why, earth-embosom'd sleep
The unbroken fountains of the angry deep:
Why, bound, and furnac'd, by the globe's strong frame,
In sullen quiet, waits the final flame:
Why surge not, o'er yon isles its spouting fires,
'Till all their living world in dust expires.
Crimes sound their ruin's moral cause aloud,
And all heaven, sighing, rings with cries of brother's blood.

Beside yon church, that beams a modest ray,
With tidy neatness reputably gay,
When, mild and fair, as Eden's seventh-day light,
In silver silence, shines the Sabbath bright,
In neat attire, the village household come,
And learn the path-way to the eternal home.
Hail solemn ordinance! worthy of the SKIES;
When thousand richest blessings daily rise;
Peace, order, cleanliness, and manners sweet,
A sober mind, to rule submission meet,
Enlarging knowledge, life from guilt refin'd,
And love to God, and friendship to mankind.
In the clear splendour of thy vernal morn,
New-quicken'd man to light, and life, is born;
The desert of the mind with virtue blooms;
Its flowers unfold, its fruits exhale perfumes;
Proud guilt dissolves, beneath the searching ray,
And low debasement, trembling, creeps away;
Vice bites the dust; foul Error seeks her den;
And God, descending, dwells anew with men.
Where yonder humbler spire salutes the eye,
Its vane slow turning in the liquid sky,
Where, in light gambols, healthy striplings sport,
Ambitious learning builds her outer court;
A grave preceptor, there, her usher stands,

And rules, without a rod, her little bands.
Some half-grown sprigs of learning grac'd his brow:
Little he knew, though much he wish'd to know,
Inchanted hung o'er Virgil's honey'd lay,
And smiled, to see desipient Horace play;
Glean'd scraps of Greek; and, curious, trac'd afar,
Through Pope's clear glass, the bright Maeonian star.
Yet oft his students at his wisdom star'd,
For many a student to his side repair'd,
Surpriz'd, they heard him Dilworth's knots untie,
And tell, what lands beyond the Atlantic lie.

Many his faults; his virtues small, and few;
Some little good he did, or strove to do;
Laborious still, he taught the early mind,
And urg'd to manners meek, and thoughts refin'd;
Truth he impress'd, and every virtue prais'd;
While infant eyes, in wondering silence, gaz'd;
The worth of time would, day by day, unfold,
And tell them, every hour was made of gold.
Brown Industry he lov'd; and oft declar'd
How hardly Sloth, in life's sad evening, far'd;
Through grave examples, with sage meaning, ran,
Whist was each form, and thus the tale began.

"Beside yon lonely tree, whose branches bare
Rise white, and murmur to the passing air,
There, where the twining briars the yard enclose,
The house of Sloth stands hush'd in long repose."

"In a late round of solitary care,
My feet instinct to rove, they knew not where,
I thither came. With yellow blossoms gay,
The tall rank weed begirt the tangled way:
Curious to view, I forc'd a path between,
And climb'd the broken stile, and gaz'd the scene."

"O'er an old well, the curb half-fallen spread,
Whose boards, end-loose, a mournful creaking made;

Poiz'd on a leaning post, and ill-sustained,
In ruin sad, a mouldering sweep remain'd;
Useless, the crooked pole still dangling hung,
And, tied with thrumbs, a broken bucket swung."

"A half-made wall around the garden lay,
Mended, in gaps, with brushwood in decay.
No culture through the woven briars was seen,
Save a few sickly plants of faded green:
The starv'd potato hung its blasted seeds,
And fennel struggled to o'ertop the weeds.
There gaz'd a ragged sheep, with wild surprise,
And two lean geese upturn'd their slanting eyes."

"The cottage gap'd, with many a dismal yawn,
Where, rent to burn, the covering boards were gone;
Or, by one nail, where others endwise hung,
The sky look'd thro', and winds portentous rung.
In waves, the yielding roof appear'd to run,
And half the chimney-top was fallen down."

"The ancient cellar-door, of structure rude,
With tatter'd garments calk'd, half open stood.
There, as I peep'd, I saw the ruin'd bin;
The sills were broke; the wall had crumbled in;
A few, long-emptied casks lay mouldering round,
And wasted ashes sprinkled o'er the ground;
While, a sad sharer in the household ill,
A half-starv'd rat crawl'd out, and bade farewell."

"One window dim, a loop-hole to the sight,
Shed round the room a pale, penurious light;
Here rags gay-colour'd eked the broken glass;
There panes of wood supplied the vacant space."

"As, pondering deep, I gaz'd, with gritty roar,
The hinges creak'd, and open stood the door.
Two little boys, half-naked from the waist,

With staring wonder, ey'd me, as I pass'd.
The smile of Pity blended with her tear—
Ah me! how rarely Comfort visits here!"

"On a lean hammoc, once with feathers fill'd,
His limbs by dirty tatters ill conceal'd,
Tho' now the sun had rounded half the day,
Stretch'd at full length, the lounger snoring lay:
While his sad wife, beside her dresser stood,
And wash'd her hungry household's meagre food,
His aged sire, whose beard, and flowing hair,
Wav'd silvery, o'er his antiquated chair,
Rose from his seat; and, as he watch'd my eye,
Deep from his bosom heav'd a mournful sigh—
"Stranger, he cried, once better days I knew;"
And, trembling, shed the venerable dew.
I wish'd a kind reply; but wish'd in vain;
No words came timely to relieve my pain:
To the poor parent, and her infants dear,
Two mites I gave, besprinkled with a tear;
And, fix'd again to see the wretched shed,
Withdrew in silence, clos'd the door, and fled."

"Yet, this so lazy man I've often seen
Hurrying, and bustling, round the busy green;
The loudest prater, in a blacksmith's shop;
The wisest statesman, o'er a drunken cup;
(His sharp-bon'd horse, the street that nightly fed,
Tied, many an hour, in yonder tavern-shed)
In every gambling, racing match, abroad:
But a rare hearer, in the house of God."

"Such, such, my children, is the dismal cot,
Where drowsy Sloth receives her wretched lot:
But O how different is the charming cell,
Where Industry and Virtue love to dwell!"

"Beyond that hillock, topp'd with scatter'd trees,
That meet, with freshest green, the hastening breeze,

There, where the glassy brook reflects the day,
Nor weeds, nor sedges, choke its crystal way,
Where budding willows feel the earliest spring,
And wonted red-breasts safely nest, and sing,
A female Worthy lives; and all the poor
Can point the way to her sequester'd door."

"She, unseduc'd by dress and idle shew,
The forms, and rules, of fashion never knew;
Nor glittering in the ball, her form display'd;
Nor yet can tell a diamond, from a spade.
Far other objects claim'd her steady care;
The morning chapter, and the nightly prayer;
The frequent visit to the poor man's shed;
The wakeful nursing, at the sick man's bed;
Each day, to rise, before the early sun;
Each day, to see her daily duty done;
To cheer the partner of her household cares,
And mould her children, from their earliest years."

"Small is her house; but fill'd with stores of good;
Good, earn'd with toil, and with delight bestow'd.
In the clean cellar, rang'd in order neat,
Gay-smiling Plenty boasts her casks of meat,
Points, to small eyes, the bins where apples glow,
And marks her cyder-butts, in stately row.
Her granary, fill'd with harvest's various pride,
Still sees the poor man's bushel laid aside;
Here swells the flaxen, there the fleecy store,
And the long wood-pile mocks the winter's power:
White are the swine; the poultry plump and large;
For every creature thrives, beneath her charge."

"Plenteous, and plain, the furniture is seen;
All form'd for use, and all as silver clean.
On the clean dresser, pewter shines arow;
The clean-scower'd bowls are trimly set below;
While the wash'd coverlet, and linen white,
Assure the traveller a refreshing night."

"Oft have I seen, and oft still hope to see,
This friend, this parent to the poor and me,
Tho' bent with years, and toil, and care, and woe,
Age lightly silver'd on her furrow'd brow,
Her frame still useful, and her mind still young,
Her judgment vigorous, and her memory strong,
Serene her spirits, and her temper sweet,
And pleas'd the youthful circle still to meet,
Cheerful, the long-accustom'd talk pursue,
Prevent the rust of age, and life renew;
To church, still pleas'd, and able still, to come,
And shame the lounging youth, who sleep at home."

"Such as her toils, has been the bright reward;
For Heaven will always toils like these regard.
Safe, on her love, her truth and wisdom tried,
Her husband's heart, thro' lengthened life, relied;
From little, daily saw his wealth increase,
His neighbours love him, and his household bless;
In peace and plenty liv'd, and died resign'd,
And, dying, left six thousand pounds behind.
Her children, train'd to usefulness alone,
Still love the hand, which led them kindly on,
With pious duty, own her wise behest,
And, every day, rise up, and call her bless'd."

"More would ye know, of each poor hind enquire,
Who sees no sun go down upon his hire;
A cheerful witness, bid each neighbour come;
Ask each sad wanderer, where he finds a home;
His tribute even the vilest wretch will give,
And praise the useful life, he will not live."

"Oft have the prattlers, God to me has giv'n,
The flock, I hope, and strive, to train for Heaven,
With little footsteps, sought her mansion dear,
To meet the welcome, given with heart sincere;
And cheer'd with all, that early minds can move,

The smiles of gentleness, and acts of love,
At home, in lisping tales, her worth displayed,
And pour'd their infant blessings on her head."

"Ye kings, of pomp, ye nobles proud of blood,
Heroes of arms, of science sages proud!
Read, blush, and weep, to see, with all your store,
Fame, genius, knowledge, bravery, wealth, and power,
Crown'd, laurell'd, worshipp'd, gods beneath the sun,
Far less of real good enjoy'd, or done."

Such lessons, pleas'd he taught.   The precepts new
Oft the young train to early wisdom drew;
And, when his influence willing minds confess'd,
The children lov'd him, and the parents bless'd;
But, when by soft indulgence led astray,
His pupils' hearts had learn'd the idle way,
Tho' constant, kind, and hard, his toils had been,
For all those toils, small thanks had he, I ween.

Behold yon humbler mansion lift its head!
Where infant minds to science' door are led.
As now, by kind indulgence loos'd to play,
From place to place, from sport to sport, they stray,
How light their gambols frolic o'er the green!
How their shrill voices cheer the rural scene!
Sweet harmless elves! in Freedom's household born,
Enjoy the raptures of your transient morn;
And let no hour of anxious manhood see
Your minds less innocent, or bless'd, or free!

See too, in every hamlet, round me rise
A central school-house, dress'd in modest guise!
Where every child for useful life prepares,
To business moulded, ere he knows its cares;
In worth matures, to independence grows,
And twines the civic garland o'er his brows.

Mark, how invited by the vernal sky,
Yon cheerful group of females passes by!

Whose hearts, attun'd to social joy, prepare
A friendly visit to some neighbouring fair.
How neatness glistens from the lovely train!
Bright charm! which pomp to rival tries in vain.

Ye Muses! dames of dignified renown,
Rever'd alike in country, and in town,
Your bard the mysteries of a visit show;
For sure your Ladyships those mysteries know:
What is it then, obliging Sisters! say,
The debt of social visiting to pay?

'Tis not to toil before the idol pier;
To shine the first in fashion's lunar sphere;
By sad engagements forc'd, abroad to roam,
And dread to find the expecting fair, at home!
To stop at thirty doors, in half a day,
Drop the gilt card, and proudly roll away;
To alight, and yield the hand, with nice parade;
Up stairs to rustle in the stiff brocade;
Swim thro' the drawing room, with studied air;
Catch the pink'd beau, and shade the rival fair;
To sit, to curb, to toss, with bridled mien,
Mince the scant speech, and lose a glance between;
Unfurl the fan, display the snowy arm,
And ope, with each new motion, some new charm:
Or sit, in silent solitude, to spy
Each little failing, with malignant eye;
Or chatter, with incessancy of tongue,
Careless, if kind, or cruel, right, or wrong;
To trill of us, and ours, of mine, and me,
Our house, our coach, our friends, our family,
While all th' excluded circle sit in pain,
And glance their cool contempt, or keen disdain:
T' inhale, from proud Nanking, a sip of tea,
And wave a curtsey trim, and flirt away;
Or waste, at cards, peace, temper, health and life,
Begin with sullenness, and end in strife,

Lose the rich feast, by friendly converse given,
And backward turn from happiness, and heaven.

It is, in decent habit, plain and neat,
To spend a few choice hours, in converse sweet;
Careless of forms, to act th' unstudied part,
To mix in friendship, and to blend the heart;
To choose those happy themes, which all must feel,
The moral duties, and the household weal,
The tale of sympathy, the kind design,
Where rich affections soften, and refine;
T' amuse, to be amus'd, to bless, be bless'd,
And tune to harmony the common breast;
To cheer, with mild good-humour's sprightly ray,
And smooth life's passage, o'er its thorny way;
To circle round the hospitable board,
And taste each good, our generous climes afford;
To court a quick return, with accents kind,
And leave, at parting, some regret behind.

Such, here, the social intercourse is found;
So slides the year, in smooth enjoyment, round.

Thrice bless'd the life, in this glad region spent,
In peace, in competence, and still content;
Where bright, and brighter, all things daily smile,
And rare and scanty, flow the streams of ill;
Where undecaying youth sits blooming round,
And Spring looks lovely on the happy ground;
Improvement glows, along life's cheerful way,
And with soft lustre makes the passage gay.
Thus oft, on yonder Sound, when evening gales
Breath'd o'er th' expanse, and gently fill'd the sails,
The world was still, the heavens were dress'd in smiles,
And the clear moon-beam tipp'd the distant isles,
On the blue plain a lucid image gave,
And capp'd, with silver light, each little wave;
The silent splendour, floating at our side,

Mov'd as we mov'd, and wanton'd on the tide;
While shadowy points, and havens, met the eye,
And the faint-glimmering landmark told us home was nigh.

Ah, dire reverse! in yonder eastern clime,
Where heavy drags the sluggish car of time;
The world unalter'd by the change of years,
Age after age, the same dull aspect wears;
On the bold mind the weight of system spread,
Resistless lies, a cumbrous load of lead;
One beaten course, the wheels politic keep,
And slaves of custom, lose their woes in sleep;
Stagnant is social life; no bright design,
Quickens the sloth, or checks the sad decline.
The friend of man casts round a wishful eye,
And hopes, in vain, improving scenes to spy;
Slow o'er his head, the dragging moments roll,
And damp each cheerful purpose of the soul.

Thus the bewilder'd traveller, forc'd to roam
Through a lone forest, leaves his friends, and home;
Dun evening hangs the sky; the woods around
Join their sad umbrage o'er the russet ground;
At every step, new gloom inshrouds the skies;
His path grows doubtful, and his fears arise:
No woodland songstress soothes his mournful way;
No taper gilds the gloom with cheering ray;
On the cold earth he lays his head forlorn,
And watching, looks, and looks, to spy the lingering morn.

And when new regions prompt their feet to roam,
And fix, in untrod fields, another home,
No dreary realms our happy race explore,
Nor mourn their exile from their native shore.
For there no endless frosts the glebe deform,
Nor blows, with icy breath, perpetual storm:
No wrathful suns, with sickly splendour glare,
Nor moors, impoison'd, taint the balmy air,

But medial climates change the healthful year;
Pure streamlets wind, and gales of Eden cheer;
In misty pomp the sky-topp'd mountains stand,
And with green bosom humbler hills expand:
With flowery brilliance smiles the woodland glade;
Full teems the soil, and fragrant twines the shade.
There cheaper fields the numerous household charm,
And the glad sire gives every son a farm;
In falling forests, Labour's axe resounds;
Opes the new field; and winds the fence's bounds;
The green wheat sparkles; nods the towering corn;
And meads, and pastures, lessening wastes adorn.
Where howl'd the forest, herds unnumber'd low;
The fleecy wanderers fear no prowling foe;
The village springs; the humble school aspires;
And the church brightens in the morning fires!
Young Freedom wantons; Art exalts her head;
And infant Science prattles through the shade.
There changing neighbours learn their manners mild;
And toil and prudence dress th' improving wild:
The savage shrinks, nor dares the bliss annoy;
And the glad traveller wonders at the joy.

All hail, thou western world! by heaven design'd
Th' example bright, to renovate mankind.
Soon shall thy sons across the mainland roam;
And claim, on far Pacific shores, their home;
Their rule, religion, manners, arts, convey,
And spread their freedom to the Asian sea.
Where erst six thousand suns have roll'd the year
O'er plains of slaughter, and o'er wilds of fear,
Towns, cities, fanes, shall lift their towery pride;
The village bloom, on every streamlet's side;
Proud Commerce' mole the western surges lave;
The long, white spire lie imag'd on the wave;
O'er morn's pellucid main expand their sails,
And the starr'd ensign court Korean gales.
Then nobler thoughts shall savage trains inform;

Then barbarous passions cease the heart to storm;
No more the captive circling flames devour;
Through the war path the Indian creep no more;
No midnight scout the slumbering village fire;
Nor the scalp'd infant stain his gasping sire:
But peace, and truth, illume the twilight mind,
The gospel's sunshine, and the purpose kind.
Where marshes teem'd with death, shall meads unfold;
Untrodden cliffs resign their stores of gold;
The dance refin'd on Albion's margin move,
And her lone bowers rehearse the tale of love.
Where slept perennial night, shall science rise,
And new-born Oxfords cheer the evening skies;
Miltonic strains the Mexic hills prolong,
And Louis murmur to Sicilian song.

   Then to new climes the bliss shall trace its way,
And Tartar desarts hail the rising day;
From the long torpor startled China wake;
Her chains of misery rous'd Peruvia break;
Man link to man; with bosom bosom twine;
And one great bond the house of Adam join:
The sacred promise full completion know,
And peace, and piety, the world o'erflow.

END OF THE SECOND PART

PART III

THE BURNING OF FAIRFIELD

(lines 157–282)

MEANTIME, on yonder hills, forlorn,
The townsmen stood, with anguish torn,
Anguish for those, they left behind,
To fears, and ills, and foes, consign'd;

The husband, for his darling mate;
The father, for his children's fate;
While prescience wrung with keenest throe,
And fast enhanc'd suspended woe.
When lo! dark-rolling thro' the skies,
Unnumber'd smokes began to rise:
His mansion, long to each endear'd,
Where peace, and joy, alone appear'd,
Where all the charities of life,
Of parents, children, husband, wife,
With softest, tenderest bosoms strove,
For garlands, in the strife of love;
The morn with brighter beauty dress'd;
The evening gladden'd in the west;
Bade each gay sun more gaily roll,
And twin'd the sympathy of soul;
That mansion, malice' seven-fold ire
Now wrapp'd in swathes of circling fire,
Scatter'd his darling bliss in air,
And plung'd his heart in deep despair.
O vilest of the crimes of War,
Fell partner of his bloody car,
Dread ill, to guilty mortals given,
To mark the wrath of injur'd HEAVEN;
O Conflagration! curse intire;
The impoison'd sting of baffled ire;
Of kings, of chiefs, th' immortal shame;
The rasure of the reasoning name:
From thee, no aid the victor gains;
Nor wealth, nor strength, rewards his pains:
The fear, he fondly hopes impress'd,
Is chang'd to rage, in every breast:
The victim, maddening with his woe,
With vengence burns, a deadlier foe.
'Tis thine, to glean the wastes of war,
The landscape of HEAVEN's good to mar,
Life's latest refuge to consume,
And make the world a general tomb.

Say, Muse indignant! whose the hand
That hurl'd the conflagrative brand?
A foe to human feelings born,
And of each future age the scorn,
TRYON achiev'd the deed malign,
TRYON, the name of every sin.
Hell's basest fiends the flame survey'd,
And smil'd, to see destruction spread;
While Satan, blushing deep, look'd on,
And Infamy disown'd her son.

Now Night, of all her stars forlorn,
Majestic, up the sky was borne.
A cloud immense her misty car,
Slow-sliding thro' the burden'd air;
Her wreath of yew; a cypress wand
Uplifted by her magic hand;
Pale, shrouded fears her awful train,
And spectres gliding on the plain:
While Horror, o'er the sable world,
His ensigns, thro' the expanse, unfurl'd.
When lo! the southern skies around,
Expanded wide, with turrets crown'd,
With umber'd skirts, with wavy gleam,
Uprose, an awful ridge of flame,
Shed far its dreary lustre round,
And dimly streak'd the twilight ground.
Dark clouds, with many a dismal stain,
Hung hov'ring o'er the gleamy main;
While deep, the distant, hollow roar
Wav'd, echoing from the illumin'd shore;
And, from each heaven-directed spire,
Climb'd bending pyramids of fire.

Meantime, a storm, in western skies,
Thick, heavy, vast, began to rise,
Roll'd swift, on burden'd winds, along,
And brooded o'er the plundering throng,

In deeper night the heavens array'd
And stretch'd its pall of boundless shade.
Forth shot the fierce and lurid flame,
(The world dim-rising in the beam)
Lessen'd the conflagrative spires,
And blended, with their light, its fires.
Again new darkness spread the main,
The spelndors bright'ning rose again.
The thunder, with earth-rending sound,
Shook every vale, and hill around;
While, at each pause, with solemn voice,
The murmuring flames prolong'd the noise.
It seem'd, the final day was come,
The day of earth's protracted doom;
The Archangel's voice began to call
The nations of this guilty ball;
The hills to cleave; the skies to rend;
Tumultuous elements to blend;
And HEAVEN, in pomp tremendous, came
To light the last, funereal flame.

The tumult pass'd, the morn's meek eye
Look'd soft, and silent, from the sky.
Still on their hills the townsmen stood,
And mark'd the scene of strife, and blood,
Watching the progress of the day,
That bore their plundering foes away
Tumultuous, to the darkening strand
From vengeance shrunk the guilty band,
With loads of spoil, retir'd in haste,
The spoil of domes, and churches, ras'd;
Thence, to their ships, by boats convey'd,
Their sails unfurl'd, their anchors weigh'd,
Awak'd the Injurer's sullen ire,
And brooded o'er another fire.

Each to his home, the townsmen flew,
Where scenes of anguish met the view.

Here spread the sunk, still-blazing wall,
And there stood, nodding to its fall:
Here rose the slow-declining fire,
And smoke, reluctant to expire;
There sable brands lay scatter'd round,
And ashes vile defac'd the ground.
The sullen chimney frown'd alone;
The sad winds breath'd a hollow groan:
His joys were fled; his hopes were gone;
His household driven to haunts unknown:
There peaceful slumber'd Ruin wild,
And Horror rear'd his head, and smil'd . . .

PART VI

THE FARMER'S ADVICE TO THE VILLAGERS

THE ARGUMENT

Introduction. Farmer introduced. Villagers assembled. He recommends to them an industrious and economical life, the careful education and government of their children, and particularly the establishment of good habits in early life; enjoins upon them the offices of good neighbourhood, the avoidance of litigation, and the careful cultivation of parochial harmony. Conclusion.

Ye children of my fondest care,
With tenderest love, and frequent prayer,
This solemn charge, my voice has given,
To prompt, and guide, your steps to heaven.
Your present welfare now demands
A different tribute, from my hands.

Not long since liv'd a Farmer plain,
Intent to gather honest gain,
Laborious, prudent, thrifty, neat,

Of judgment strong, experience great,
In solid homespun clad, and tidy,
And with no coxcomb learning giddy.
Daily, to hear his maxims sound,
Th' approaching neighbours flock'd around;
Daily they saw his counsels prove
The source of union, peace, and love,
The means of prudence, and of wealth,
Of comfort, cheerfulness, and health:
And all, who follow'd his advice,
Appear'd more prosperous, as more wise.

Wearied, at length, with many a call,
The sage resolv'd to summon all:
And gathering, on a pleasant Monday,
A crowd not always seen on Sunday,
Curious to hear, while hard they press'd him,
In friendly terms, he thus address'd 'em.
"My friends, you have my kindest wishes:
Pray think a neighbour not officious,
While thus, to teach you how to live,
My very best advice I give."

"And first, *industrious* be your lives;
Alike employ'd yourselves, and wives:
Your children, join'd in labour gay,
With something useful fill each day.
Those little times of leisure save,
Which most men lose, and all men have;
The half days, when a job is done;
The whole days, when a storm is on.
Few know, without a strict account,
To what these little times amount:
If wasted, while the same your cost,
The sums, you might have earn'd, are lost."

"*Learn small things never to despise:*
You little think how fast they rise.

A rich reward the mill obtains,
'Tho' but two quarts a bushel gains:
Still rolling on its steady rounds,
The farthings soon are turn'd to pounds."

"*Nor think a life of toil severe:*
No life has blessings so sincere.
Its meals so luscious, sleep so sweet,
Such vigorous limbs, such health complete,
A mind so active, brisk, and gay,
As his, who toils the livelong day.
A life of sloth drags hardly on;
Suns set too late, and rise too soon;
Youth, manhood, age, all linger slow,
To him, who nothing has to do.
The drone, a nuisance to the hive,
Stays, but can scarce be said to live,
And well the bees, those judges wise,
Plague, chase, and sting him, 'till he dies.
Lawrence, like him, tho' sav'd from hanging,
Yet every day deserves a banging."

"Let *order* o'er your time preside,
And *method* all your business guide.
Early begin, and end, your toil;
Nor let great tasks your hands embroil.
One thing at once, be still begun,
Contriv'd, resolv'd, pursued, and done.
Hire not, for what yourselves can do;
And send not, when yourselves can go;
Nor, 'till to-morrow's light, delay,
What might as well be done to-day.
By steady efforts all men thrive,
And long by moderate labour live;
While eager toil, and anxious care,
Health, strength, and peace, and life, impair."

"What thus your hands with labour earn,
To save, be now your next concern.

What'er to health, or real use,
Or true enjoyment, will conduce,
Use freely, and *with pleasure* use;
But ne'er the gifts of HEAVEN abuse:
I joy to see your treasur'd stores,
Which smiling Plenty copious pours;
Your cattle sleek, your poultry fine,
Your cider in the tumbler shine,
Your tables, smoking from the hoard,
And children smiling round the board.
All rights to use in you conspire;
The labourer's worthy of his hire.
Ne'er may that hated day arrive,
When worse yourselves, or yours, shall live;
Your dress, your lodging, or your food,
Be less abundant, neat, or good;
Your dainties all to market go,
To feast the epicure, and beau;
But ever on your tables stand,
Proofs of a free and happy land."

"Yet still, with prudence, wear, and taste;
Use what you please, but nothing waste:
On little, better far to live,
Than, poor and pitied, much survive.
Like ants, lay something up in store,
Against the winter of threescore.
Disease may long your strength annoy;
Weakness and pain your limbs destroy;
On sorrow's bed your households lie;
Your debtors fail, your cattle die;
Your crops untimely seasons kill,
And life be worn with many an ill."

"Lo too, your little flocks demand
Much from the kind parental hand;
Your sons or learning, trades, or farms;
Your daughter's portions, with their charms:

From prudence, this provision flows,
And all, from little savings, grows."

"*And, O ye fair! this toil demands*
The efforts of your faithful hands.
If wealth, your husbands' hearts are wishing,
Of you, they first must ask permission.
By HEAVEN conjoin'd, to gain, and have,
'Tis theirs to earn; 'tis yours to save:
Whatever from their labour grows,
Careful, you keep, but, heedless, lose."

" 'Tis folly in th' extreme, *to till*
Extensive fields, and till them ill.
The farmer, pleas'd, may boast aloud
His bushels sown, his acres plough'd;
And, pleas'd, indulge the cheering hope,
That time will bring a plenteous crop.
Shrewd Common-sense sits laughing by,
And sees his hopes abortive die:
For, when maturing seasons smile,
Thin sheaves shall disappoint his toil.
Advis'd, this empty pride expel;
Till little, and that little well.
Of taxes, fencing, toil, no more,
Your ground requires, when rich, than poor;
And more one fertile acre yields,
Than the huge breadth of barren fields.
That mould, the leaves, for ages, spread,
Is, long since, with the forests, fled;
That slender ploughing, trifling care,
No longer will your fields prepare.
Some new manure must now be found;
Some better culture fit the ground.
Oft turn the soil to feel the weather;
Manure from every quarter gather,
Weeds, ashes, Paris-plaister, lime,
Marle, sea-weed, and the harbour slime.

Like Germans bid your acres thrive;
But not like stinting Germans live.

"Let *every grass of kindly seed*
Exterminate the noisome weed;
The clover round your pastures blow;
The rye-grass o'er your meadows bow:
Hence the rich mow your barns shall fill;
Hence with rich green your pastures smile;
The ox, untir'd, his toil sustain,
And fat steers frisk it, o'er the plain."

"*Your herds feed well, increase, amend,*
And from the wintry storm defend.
No source will surer profit give,
Or furnish easier means to live.
The grazier hugs his cool retreat,
And smiles, to see the farmer sweat;
To see much labour little yield,
The gleanings of a worn-out field;
While glistening beeves around him sport,
And drovers to his house resort;
Manur'd, huge swarths his meadows load,
And heavy harvests proudly nod."

"Let *useful flocks* your care demand,
Best riches of the happy land.
From them, shall swell the fleecy store,
And want, and rags, depart your door;
Your daughters find a sweet employ,
And, singing, turn the wheel with joy:
With homespun rich the loom be gay;
Your households clad in bright array;
And female toil more profit yield,
Than half the labours of the field."

"When first the market offers well,
At once your yearly produce sell.

A higher price you wait in vain,
And ten times lose, where once you gain.
The dog, that at the shadow caught,
Miss'd all he had, and all he sought.

Less, day by day, your store will grow,
Gone, you scarce know or when, or how;
Interest will eat, while you delay,
And vermin steal your hopes away.
In parcels sold, in ways unknown,
It melts, and, unobserv'd, is gone.
No solid purpose driblets aid,
Spent, and forgot, as soon as paid:
The sum, a year's whole earnings yield,
Will pay a debt, or buy a field."

"*In time*, whate'er your needs require,
Lay in, of clothing, food, or fire.
Your cellars, barns, and granaries fill;
Your wood, in winter, round you pile:
Let spring ne'er see th' exhausted mow,
Or oxen faint, before the plough;
Nor summer, when its hurries come,
Your wood, in harvest, carted home."

"Along the side of sloping hills,
Conduct your numerous living rills.
Thence bid them, sweetly-wandering, flow,
To wake the grass, in fields below.
Rich meadows in their course shall spring,
And mowers whet the scythe, and sing."

"Look round, and see *your wood's decay'd*,
Your fuel scarce, your timber fled.
What groves remain with care enclose,
Nor e'er to biting herds expose.
Your store with planted nuts renew,
And acorns o'er each barren strew.

Tho' spring now smiles, yet winter's blast
Will soon the frozen skies o'ercast;
And, pinch'd, your children crowding higher,
Hang shivering o'er the scanty fire:
Rouse! your reluctant sloth o'ercome,
And bid reviving forests bloom."

"Yearly the house, the barn, the fence,
Demand *much care*, and *some expense*.
Small sums, in time, with prudence paid,
Will profit more than great, delay'd;
Each year's decays in time repair,
Nor foolish waste, thro' want of care."

"*Neat be your farms:* 'tis long confess'd,
The neatest farmers are the best.
Each bog, and marsh, industrious drain,
Nor let vile balks deform the plain;
No bushes on your headlands grow,
Nor briars a sloven's culture show.
Neat be your barns; your houses neat;
Your doors be clean; your court-yards sweet;
No moss the sheltering roof inshroud;
No wooden panes the window cloud;
No filthy kennel foully flow;
Nor weeds with rankling poison grow:
But shades expand, and fruit-trees bloom,
And flowering shrubs exhale perfume.
With pales, your garden circle round;
Defend, enrich, and clean, the ground:
Prize high this pleasing, useful rood,
And fill with vegetable good."

"*With punctual hand your taxes pay,*
Nor put far off the evil day.
How soon to an enormous size,
Taxes, succeeding taxes, rise!
How easy, one by one, discharg'd!

How hardly, in the mass enlarg'd!
How humbling the intrusive dun!
How fast, how far, th' expenses run!
Fees, advertisements, travel, cost,
And that sad end of all the post!
This gulph of quick perdition flee,
And live, from duns and bailiffs free."

"In *merchants' books, from year to year,*
Be cautious how your names appear.
How fast their little items count!
How great, beyond your hopes, th' amount!
When shelves, o'er shelves, inviting stand,
And wares allure, on either hand;
While round, you turn enchanted eyes,
And feel a thousand wants arise,
(Ye young, ye fair, these counsels true
Are penn'd for all, but most for you),
Ere Fancy lead your hearts astray,
Think of the means you have, to pay;
What wants are nature's; fancy'd what;
What will yield real good, when bought;
What certain, future means you find,
To cancel contracts, left behind;
What means to make the first of May
To you, and yours, a welcome day."

"To you, let *each returning spring*
That day of certain reckoning bring;
All debts to cancel, books t' adjust,
And check the wild career of trust.
From frequent reckonings friendship grows,
And peace, and sweet communion, flows."

"Meanwhile, of all your toil, and care,
Your children claim the largest share.
In health, and sickness, much they need,
To nurse, to watch, to clothe, and feed;

Their education much demands
From faithful hearts, and active hands."

"First be *their health* your constant care;
Give them to breathe the freest air;
Their food be neither rich, nor dainty,
But plain, and clean, and good, and plenty;
Their clothes, let changing seasons rule,
In winter warm, in summer cool,
In your own houses spun, and dy'd,
For comfort made, and not for pride.
Hardy, not suffering, be their life,
With heat, and cold, and storm, at strife;
Accustom'd common ills to bear,
To smile at danger, laugh at fear,
Troubles to brave, with hardy breast,
And seek, thro' toilsome action, rest.
Teach them each *manly art to prize*,
And base effem'nacy despise,
Teach them to wrestle, leap, and run,
To win the palm, and prize it, won;
To seek, in acts like these, and find
A nervous frame, and vigorous mind."

"*My country's youth, I see with pain,*
The customs of their sires disdain,
Quit the bold pastimes of the green,
That strengthen striplings into men,
Grovel in inns, at cards, and dice,
The means of foul diseases, and vice,
And waste, in gaming, drink, and strife,
Health, honour, fame, and peace, and life."

"*With gentler hand, your daughters train,*
The housewife's various arts to gain;
O'er scenes domestic to preside;
The needle, wheel, and shuttle, guide;
The peacock's gaudry to despise,
And view vain sports with parents' eyes;

On things of use to fix the heart,
And gild, with every graceful art.
Teach them, with neatest, simplest dress,
A neat, and lovely mind t' express;
Th' alluring female mien to wear;
Gently to soothe corroding care;
Bid life with added pleasure glow,
And sweetly charm the bed of woe.
To show, the giddy fair-one train'd,
With every ugly spot is stain'd;
While she, who lives to worth, and duty,
Shines forth, in Wisdom's eye, a beauty."

"With steady hand your household sway,
And use them always to obey.
Always their worthy acts commend;
Always against their faults contend;
The mind inform; the conscience move;
And blame, with tenderness, and love.
When round they flock, and smile, and tell
Their lambkin sports, and infant weal,
Nor foolish laugh, nor fret, nor frown;
But all their little interests own;
Like them, those trifles serious deem,
And daily witness your esteem:
Yourselves their best friends always prove,
For filial duty springs from love.
Teach them, *with confidence t' impart,*
Each secret purpose of the heart:
Thrice happy parents, children bless'd,
Of mutual confidence possess'd!
Such parents shall their children see
From vice, and shame, and anguish, free."

"Correct not, 'til the coming day
Has fann'd resentment's heat away.
When passion rules, 'tis fear obeys;
But duty serves, when reason sways.

In earliest years, the rod will mend;
In later, fails to reach the end.
Still vary: let neglect, disgrace,
Confinement, censure, find their place.
Convince, ere you correct, and prove
You punish, not from rage, but love;
And teach them, with persuasion mild,
You hate the fault, but love the child."

"*All discipline*, as facts attest,
In private minister'd is best.
Vex'd to be seen disgrac'd, and sham'd,
His passion rous'd, his pride inflam'd,
Your child his guilt with care conceals,
And pertly talks, and stoutly feels;
From truth, with swift declension flies,
To arts, equivocations, lies;
And sullen broods, with sad design,
O'er sweet revenge of future sin.
Alone, before the parents bar,
His conscience with himself at war,
Of pride, and petulance, bereft,
Without a hope, or refuge, left,
He shrinks, beneath a father's eye,
And feels his firm perverseness die;
Reveres the love, his sighs implore,
And grateful turns, to sin no more."

"*On uniformity depends*
All government, that gains its ends.
The same things always praise, and blame,
Your laws, and conduct, be the same."

"Let no *discouragement* deter,
Nor *sloth* this daily task defer.
Sloth and discouragement destroy
The children's weal, the parents' joy.
For one, who labor lothes, we find

Ten thousand lothing toil of mind,
That close attention, careful tho't,
With every real blessing fraught.
Early the stubborn child trangresses;
Denies it; nor, 'till forc'd, confesses:
The fault, tho' punish'd, he renews;
His heart by nature prone to sin,
Agen he wounds you, and agen;
Amaz'd, dishearten'd, in despair,
To see so fruitless all your care,
And wearied, by such fix'd attention
To crimes, that suffer no prevention,
Reluctant, by degrees, you yield,
And leave him master of the field."

"Then with fond hope, that reason's sway
Will win him from his faults away,
For decent power, alone you strive,
Resign'd, if decently he'll live."

"Vain hope! by reason's power alone,
From guilt, no heart was ever won.
Decent, not good, may reason make him;
By reason, crimes will ne'er forsake him.
As weeds, self-sown, demand no toil,
But flourish in their native soil,
Root deep, grow high, with vigour bloom,
And send forth poison, for perfume;
So faults, inborn, spontaneous rise,
And daily wax in strength, and size,
Ripen, with neither toil, nor care,
And choke each germ of virtue there.
Virtues, like plants of nobler kind,
Transferred from regions more refin'd,
The gardener's careful hand must sow;
His culturing hand must bid them grow;
Rains gently shower; skies softly shine,
And blessings fall, from realms divine."

"Much time, and pain, and toil, and care,
Must virtue's habits plant, and rear:
Habits alone thro' life endure,
Habits alone your child secure:
To these be all your labours given;
To these, your fervent prayers to HEAVEN.
Nor faint, a thousand trials o'er,
To see your pains effect no more;
Love, duty, interest, bid you strive;
Contend, and yield not, while you live;
And know, for all your labours pass'd,
Your eyes shall see a crop, at last.
The smith beside his anvil stands,
The lump of silver in his hands,
A thousand strokes with patience gives,
And still unform'd the work perceives;
A thousand, and a thousand more,
Unfinish'd leaves it as before;
Yet, though, from each, no print is found,
Still toiling on his steady round,
He sees the ductile mass refine,
And in a beauteous vessel shine."

"*Taverns, and shops, and lounging places,*
Vile comrades, gaming tables, races,
Where youth to vice, and ruin, run,
Teach them, as pits of death, to shun.
At nine, when sounds the warning bell,
Use them to bid their sports farewell;
Health, order, temperance, every joy,
As blasts, untimely hours destroy;
At these dread hours, in places vile,
Where all things tempt, betray, defile,
Abroad, to every ill they roam,
But peace, and safety, find at home."

"*From licens'd talk their tongues restrain,*
And bridle, with discretion's rein;

Safety, and peace, reserve affords;
But evil hides in many words.
All wond'rous stories bid them shun,
And the *pernicious love of fun;*
In lies, great stories ever end,
And fun will every vice befriend.
What sports of real use you find,
To brace the form, or nerve the mind,
Freely indulge; such sports, as these,
Will profit youth, as well as please.
But from all arts and tricks dehort,
And check th' excessive love of sport.
All buzzing tales, of private life,
All scandals, form'd on household strife,
The idle chatterings of the street,
Early forbid them to repeat;
But teach them, kindness, praise, and truth,
Alone become the voice of youth."

"*Their hearts with soft affections warm;*
Their taste, to gentle manners form,
Let manly aims their bosoms fire,
And sweet civility inspire.
Bid them the stranger kindly greet,
The friend with faithful friendship meet,
And charm of life the little span,
By general courtesy to man."

"*Teach them to reverence righteous sway,*
With life defend, with love obey;
Nor join that wretched band of scoffers,
Who rail at every man in office.
With freedom's warmth their souls inspire,
And light their brave forefathers' fire.
Bid them their privileges know;
Bid them with love of country glow;
With skill, their arms defensive wield,
Nor shun the duties of the field."

"How bless'd this heaven-distinguish'd land!
Where schools in every hamlet stand;
Far spread the beams of learning bright,
And every child enjoys the light,
At school, beneath a faithful guide,
In teaching skill'd, of morals tried,
And pleas'd the early mind to charm
To every good, from every harm,
Learn they to read, to write, to spell,
And cast accompts, and learn them well:
For, on this microscopic plan,
Is form'd the wise, and useful man.
Let him a taste for books inspire;
While you, to nurse the young desire,
A social library procure,
And open knowledge to the poor.
This useful taste imbib'd, your eyes
Shall see a thousand blessings rise.
From haunts, and comrades vile secure,
Where gilden baits to vice allure,
No more your sons abroad shall roam,
But pleas'd, their evenings spend at home;
Allurements more engaging find,
And feast, with pure delight, the mind.
The realms of earth, their tho'ts shall scan,
And learn the works, and ways, of man;
See, from the savage, to the sage,
How nations ripen, age by age;
How states, and men, by virtue rise;
How both to ruin sink, by vice;
How thro' the world's great prison-bounds,
While one wide clank of chains resounds,
Men slaves, while Angels weep to see,
Some wise, and brave, and bless'd, are free.
Thro' moral scenes shall stretch their sight;
Discern the bounds of wrong, and right;
That lothe; this love; and, pleas'd, pursue
Whate'er from man to man is due;

And, from the page of HEAVEN derive
The motives, and the means, to live."

"Nor think the scope, or task, too great;
Coolly your leisure moments state;
These, nicely reckon'd, will appear
Enough for all, that's promis'd here.
Would you still higher proof behold?
Plain facts that higher proof unfold.
I know, and tell it with a smile,
No narrow list of men of toil,
Illum'd by no collegiate rays,
And forc'd to tread in busy ways,
Who yet, to read intensely loving,
And every leisure hour improving,
On wisdom's heights distinguish'd stand,
The boast, and blessing, of our land.
This mystery learn: in great, or small things,
'TIS APPLICATION MASTERS ALL THINGS."

"*Thus taught, in every state of life,*
Of child, of parent, husband, wife,
They'll wiser, better, happier, prove;
Their freedom better know, and love;
More pleasures gain, more hearts engage,
And feast their own dull hours, of age."

"*Use them, and early use, to have,*
To earn, and what they earn, to save.
From industry, and prudence, flow
Relief of want, and balm of woe,
Delightful sleep, enduring wealth,
The purest peace, the firmest health,
True independence of our peers,
Support for sickness, and for years,
Security from household strife,
The conscience sweet of useful life,
Esteem abroad, content at home,

At easy passage to the tomb,
With blessings numberless, that flow
To neighbour, stranger, friend, and foe,
That man to man resistless bind,
AnJ spread, and spread, to all mankind."

Would you for them this good acquire,
Prudence, and industry, inspire;
To habit bid the blessings grow;
Habits alone yield good below.
To these untrain'd, whate'er you give,
Whate'er inheritance you leave,
To every worthless passion given,
And scatter'd to the winds of heaven,
Will foes, and strangers, clothe, and feed;
While your own children pine with need,
Their friends, pain'd, pitied, slighted, fly,
Forgotten live, and wretched die.

"*In this New World, life's changing round,*
In three descents, is often found.
The *first*, firm, busy, plodding, poor,
Earns, saves, and daily swells, his store;
By farthings first, and pence, it grows;
In shillings next, and pounds, it flows;
Then spread his widening farms, abroad;
His forests wave; his harvests nod;
Fattening, his numerous cattle play,
And debtors dread his reckoning day.
Ambitious then t' adorn with knowledge
His son, he places him at college;
And sends, in smart attire, and neat,
To travel, thro' each neighbouring state;
Builds him a handsome house, or buys,
Sees him a gentleman, and dies."

"The *second*, born to wealth, and ease,
And taught to think, converse, and please,

Ambitious, with his lady-wife,
Aims at a higher walk of life.
Yet, in those wholesome habits train'd,
By which his wealth, and weight, were gain'd,
Bids care in hand with pleasure go,
And blends economy with show.
His houses, fences, garden, dress,
The neat and thrifty man confess.
Improv'd, but with improvement plain,
Intent on office, as on gain,
Exploring, useful sweets to spy,
To public life he turns his eye.
A townsman first, a justice soon;
A member of the house anon;
Perhaps to board, or bench, invited,
He sees the state, and subjects, righted;
And, raptur'd with politic life,
Consigns his children to his wife.
Of household cares amid the round,
For her, too hard the task is found.
At first she struggles, and contends;
Then doubts, desponds, laments, and bends;
Her sons pursue the sad defeat,
And shout their victory complete;
Rejoicing, see their father roam,
And riot, rake, and reign, at home.
Too late he sees, and sees to mourn,
His race of every hope forlorn,
Abroad, for comfort, turns his eyes,
Bewails his dire mistakes, and dies."

"His *heir, train'd only to enjoy,*
Untaught his mind, or hands, t' employ,
Conscious of wealth enough for life,
With business, care, and worth, at strife,
By prudence, conscience, unrestrain'd,
And none, but pleasure's habits, gain'd,
Whirls on the wild career of sense,

Nor danger marks, nor heeds expense.
Soon ended is the giddy round;
And soon the fatal goal is found.
His lands, secur'd for borrow'd gold,
His houses, horses, herds, are sold.
And now, no more for wealth respected,
He sinks, by all his friends neglected;
Friends, who, before, his vices flatter'd,
And liv'd upon the loaves he scatter'd.
Unacted every worthy part,
And pining with a broken heart,
To dirtiest company he flies,
Whores, gambles, turns a sot, and dies.
His children, born to fairer doom,
In rags, pursue him to the tomb."

   "Apprentic'd then to masters stern,
Some real good the orphans learn;
Are bred to toil, and hardy fare,
And grow to usefulness, and care;
And, following their great-grandsire's plan,
Each slow becomes a useful man."

   "Such here is life's swift-circling round;
So soon are all its changes found.
Would you prevent th' allotment hard,
And fortune's rapid whirl retard,
In all your race, industrious care
Attentive plant, and faithful rear;
With life, th' important task begin,
Nor but with life, the task resign;
To habit, bid the blessings grow,
Habits alone yield good below."

   "But, to complete the bless'd design,
Both parents must their efforts join;
With kind regard, each other treat:
In every plan, harmonious meet;
The conduct each of each approve;

Nor strive, but in the strife of love.
What one commands, let both require;
In counsels, smiles, and frowns, conspire;
Alike oppose; alike befriend;
And each the other's choice commend.
In sweetest union thus conjoin'd,
And one the life, as one the mind,
Your children cheerful will obey,
And reverence undivided pay;
The daily task be lightly done,
And half the household troubles gone:
While jars domestic weal destroy,
And wither every hope of joy."

"Meantime, let peace around you rest,
Nor feuds good neighbourhood molest.
Your neighbour's crops with justice eye,
Nor let his hopes by trespass die.
Your fence repair, your herds repel;
Much virtue's found in fencing well.
With care his reputation guard;
Sweet friendship will that care reward.
No idle tatler e'er receive;
No storied scandal e'er believe:
What's good, and kind, alone report;
Tell nothing, which can others hurt:
Oblige, lend, borrow—freely all—
Rejoice not in another's fall:
When others need, assistance lend:
Are others sick? their calls attend;
Their visits hospitably greet,
And pay, with cheerful kindness sweet.
These things, or I mistake, will form,
And keep the heart of friendship warm."

"But should contentions rise, and grudges,
Which call for arbitrating judges,
Still shun the law, that gulph of woe,

Whose waves without a bottom flow:
That gulph, by storms forever toss'd,
Where all, that's once afloat, is lost;
Where friends, embark'd, are friends no more,
And neither finds a peaceful shore:
While thousand wrecks, as warnings, lie,
The victims of an angry sky.

"*Each cause let mutual friends decide,*
With Common-sense alone to guide:
If right, in silent peace be glad;
If wrong, be neither sour, nor sad:
As oft you'll find full justice done,
As when thro' twenty terms you've run;
And when, in travel, fees, and cost,
Far more than can be won, is lost."

"Learn, this conclusion whence I draw.
Mark what estates are spent in law!
See men litigious business fly,
And loungers live, and beggars die!
What anger, hatred, malice fell,
And fierce revenge their bosoms swell!
What frauds, subornings, tamperings rife!
What slanders foul! what shameful lies!
What perjuries, blackening many a tongue!
And what immensity of wrong!
Where peace, and kindness, dwelt before,
See peace, and kindness, dwell no more!
Ills to good offices succeed,
And neighbours bid each other bleed!"

"Esop, the merry Phrygian sage,
Worth half the Wise-men of his age,
Has left to litigants a story,
Which, with your leave, I'll set before you."

" 'The bear, and lion, on the lawn,
Once found the carcase of a fawn.

Both claim'd the dainty; neither gave it;
But each swore roundly he would have it.
They growl'd; they fought; but fought in vain;
For neither could the prize obtain;
And, while, to breathe, they both retreated,
The lawyer fox. came in, and eat it.' "

"And would you useful live, and bless'd,
Parochial heats, and jars, detest.
Like you, their interests others feel;
Have price, and passions, warmth, and will.
Those interests clash; those wills contend;
And some, where all have votes, must bend.
A yielding spirit hence maintain;
Let all concede, that all may gain:
Hence, when fierce heat the mass inspires,
And Party blows her angry fires,
For weeks, or months, or years, postpone
What, prudence tells you, must be done:
Time will command the flames to cease,
And party soften into peace."

Thus spoke the sage. The crowd around,
Applauding, heard the grateful sound:
Each, deeply musing, homeward went,
T' amend his future life intent;
And, pondering past delays, with sorrow,
Resolv'd, he would begin, to-morrow.

END OF THE SIXTH PART

THE TRIUMPH OF INFIDELITY
A POEM

PRINTED IN *THE WORLD*

M,DCCLXXXVIII

To Mons. de Voltaire

Sir,

YOUR Creator endued you with shining talents, and cast your lot in a field of action, where they might be most happily employed: In the progress of a long and industrious life, you devoted them to a single purpose, the elevation of your character above his. For the accomplishment of this purpose, with a diligence and uniformity which would have adorned the most virtuous pursuits, you opposed truth, religion, and their authors, with sophistry, contempt, and obloquy; and taught, as far as your example or sentiments extended their influence, that the chief end of man was, to slander his God, and abuse him forever. To whom could such an effort as the following be dedicated, with more propriety, than to you. The subject it celebrates is the most pointed attack upon your old enemies; an attack more happily devised, at least, than any of yours; as yours were more advantageously concerted than the efforts of any of your predecessors. Reasoning is an unhappy engine to be employed against christianity; as, like elephants in ancient war, it usually, in this case, turns upon those who employ it. Ridicule is a more convenient weapon, as you have successfully evinced; but ingenious misinterpretation is a still more sure and effectual annoyance; for the sword and javelin, however keen, may be dreaded and shunned, while the secret and deadly dirk is plunged to the heart of unsuspecting friendship, unhappily trusting the smooth-faced assassin. Accept, then, as due, this tribute of acknowledgment from the

WRITER OF THIS POEM.

Audies, & veniet manes haec fama sub imos.

[The notes in this poem were written by the author.]

ERE yet the Briton left our happy shore,
Or war's alarming clarion ceas'd to roar,
What time the morn illum'd her purple flame,
Thro' air's dread wilds the prince of darkness came,
A cloud his gloomy car; his path around,
Attendant whirlwinds gave a fearful sound,
Before him dragons wound their bloody spires;
Far shot behind him death's Tartarean fires:
To image heaven's high state, he proudly rode,
Nor seem'd he less than hell's terrific God.
While, full before him, dress'd in beauteous day,
The realms of freedom, peace, and virtue lay;
The realms, where heav'n, ere Time's great empire fall,
Shall bid new Edens dress this dreary ball;
He frown'd; the world grew dark; the mountains shook,
And nature shudder'd as the spirit spoke.
What wasted years, with angry voice he cries,
I wage vain wars with yonder hated skies?
Still, as I walk th' unmeasur'd round of things,
From deepest ill what good perpetual springs;
What order shines, where blest confusion lay,
And from the night of death, what splendid day?
How* near me seem'd, ere Bethlehem's wonder rose,
The final victory o'er my struggling foes;
All nations won to ignorance, and sin,
Without the Gentile, and the Jew within?
How near, when cros'd, he met th' accursed doom,
Or lay, extinguish'd in the mortal tomb?
Yet then, even whilst I felt my pinions rise
Above the arches of a thousand skies,
Even then, deep plunged beneath the lowest hell,
As erst when hurl'd from heav'n, my kingdom fell.
And† oh, by what foul means! An angel I,
A god, the rival of yon haughty sky!

 * State of infidelity at the birth of ——
 † Injuries done to infidelity, by Peter, Paul, and others.

They the last sweepings of the clay-born kind,
The dunghill's offspring, and the reptile's mind.
Yet their creating voice, with startling sound,
From death and darkness wak'd the world's wide round;
Before it crumbled, mid my groans and tears,
The Pagan fabric of a thousand years;
The spells, the rites, the pomp, the victims fled,
The fanes all desert, and the lares dead.
In vain fierce persecution hedg'd their way;
In vain dread power's huge weight incumbent lay;
As sand-built domes dissolve before the stream,
As visions fleet upon th' awakening beam,
The structure fled; while hell was rack'd to save,
And all my heaven-bright glories sought the grave.
Amaz'd,* awhile, I saw the ruin spread,
My hopes, my efforts, with my kingdom, dead.
But soon I bade the floods of vengeance roll,
Soon rous'd anew my mightiness of soul,
With arts my own, th' opposer's power withstood,
And reign'd once more the universal God;
Mine, by all poisoning wealth, his sons I made,
And Satan preached, while proud Messiah fled.
Surpriz'd,† enrag'd, to see his wiles outdone,
His power all vanquish'd, and his kingdom gone,
From the stern North, he hail'd my darling host,
A whelming ocean, spread to every coast;
My Goths, my Huns, the cultur'd world o'er-ran,
And darkness buried all the pride of man.
On dozing realms he pour'd his vengeance dread,
On putrid bishops, and on priests half dead;
Blotted, at one great stroke, the work he drew,
And saw his gospel bid mankind adieu.
The‡ happy hour I seiz'd; the world my own:
Full in his church I fix'd my glorious throne;

* Progress of infidelity after the death of Constantine the Great.
† Infidels injured unwittingly by their friends, the northern bar-
barians.
‡ New progress of infidelity, under the papal hierarchy.

Thrice crown'd, I sate a God, and more than God;
Bade all earth's nations shiver at my nod;
Dispens'd to men the code of Satan's laws,
And made my priests the columns of my cause.
In their bless'd hands the gospel I conceal'd,
And new-found doctrines, in its stead, reveal'd;
Of gloomy visions drew a fearful round,
Names of dire look, and words of killing sound,
Where, meaning lost, terrific doctrines lay,
Maz'd the dim soul, and frighten'd truth away;
Where noise for truth, for virtue pomp was given,
Myself the God promulg'd, and hell the heaven.
To this bless'd scheme I forc'd the struggling mind;
Faith sunk beneath me; sense her light resign'd;
Before rebellious conscience clank'd the chain;
The rack, the wheel, unbosomed all their pain;
The dungeon yawn'd; uprose the faggot pyre,
And, fierce with vengeance, twin'd the livid fire.
These woes I form'd on earth; beyond the tomb,
Of dreams, I built the purgatorial doom;
Hurl'd round all realms the interdictive peal;
Shut kings from heaven, and nations scourg'd to hell;
All crimes forgave; those crimes indulg'd again;
Disclos'd the right divine to every sin;
To certain ecstasies the faithful led;
Damn'd Doubt, when living; double damn'd, when dead;
O'er bold Inquiry bade all horrors roll,
And to its native nothing shrunk the soul.
Thus, round the Gothic wild, my kingdom lay,
A night, soon clouded o'er a winter's day.
But* oh, by what fell fate, to be entomb'd
Are bright ambition's brightest glories doom'd?
While now my rival every hope foresook,
His arts, his counsels, and his sceptre broke,
This vast machine, so wondrous, so refin'd,
First, fairest offspring even of Satan's mind,

* Injuries done to infidelity by Luther, Calvin, and others.

This building, o'er all buildings proudly great,
Than Heaven more noble, and more fix'd than fate,
This glorious empire fell; the world grew pale,
And the skies trembled, at the dreadful tale.
In vain my arm, in vain my sword, I bar'd;
In vain my angels o'er example dar'd,
My priests, high-fed on all the spoils of man,
Outran belief and even my hopes outran;
Hell hop'd, and toil'd in vain: Thro' all her coast,
A general sigh declar'd her kingdom lost.
  Blush, Satan, blush, thou sovereign of mankind,
When, what thy reptile foes, thou call'st to mind.
New fishermen, mechanic worms, anew
The unfolded gospel from my kingdom drew.
From earth's wide realms, beneath the deluge bare,
As suns reviving bade the spring appear,
So, at their startling voice, from shore to shore,
A moral spring my winter cover'd o'er,.
The mind new sprang; rebudding virtue grew,
And trembling nations rose from death anew.
From them roll'd on, to bless this earth's cold clime,
A brighter season, and more vernal prime,
Where, long by wintry suns denied to rise,
Fair Right and Freedom open'd on the skies,
Virtue, and Truth, and joy, in nobler bloom,
Call'd earth and heaven to taste the sweet perfume,
Pleas'd, to the scene increasing millions ran,
And threaten'd Satan with the loss of man.
These* ills to ward I train'd my arts anew;
O'er truth's fair form the webs of sophism drew;
Virtue new chill'd, in growing beauties gay,
Wither'd her bloom, and puff'd her sweets away.
Against her friends I arm'd new bands of foes;
First, highest, all-subduing Fashion rose.
From courts to cottages, her sovereign sway,

* Progress of infidelity, under the auspicious influence of Charles II. and his cotemporaries.

With force resistless, bade the world obey.
She moulded faith, and science, with a nod;
Now there was not, and now there was, a God.
"Let black be white," she said, and white it seem'd,
"Hume a philosopher;" and straight he dream'd
Most philosophically. At her call,
Opinions, doctrines, learn'd to rise, and fall;
Before* her, bent the universal knee,
And own'd her sovereign, to the praise of me.
With† her, brave Ridicule, 'twixt ill and good,
Falshood and truth, satanic umpire stood.
He, Hogarth like, with hues and features new,
The form of providence, persuasive drew:
Round its fair face bade hells black colours rise.
Its limbs distorted, blear'd its heaven-bright eyes.
At the maim'd image gaz'd, and grinn'd aloud—
"Yon frightful hag's no semblance of a god."
　Mean‡time my friends, the veterans of my cause,

* Phil. ii, 10, 11.
† The doctrine that ridicule is a test of truth cannot, even on the scheme of infidels justify their application of it. Wherever any object, or if you please, proposition, when seen clearly and certainly in all its nature, parts, and relations, is evidently absurd, and ridiculous, it may be an objection against its reality, or truth. But a man, in his natural and proper appearance, may be a beautiful object; and a proposition, in its real nature, and necessary consequences, may contain a truth important and noble, altho' when a sign-post painter shall have drawn one with a pair of horns and a tail, and an infidel annexed his own dreams as appendages to the other, all the fraternity of blockheads will laugh at both.
‡ See the host of infidel writers, during the last age.
Such advantages does Infidelity enjoy over Revelation, that both sides of moral questions will equally support that, and weaken this. Thus one Infidel will overthrow Revelation by proving that there is not one honest man living; another will as successfully attack it by asserting, and the assertions of Infidels are always to be taken for proofs, that there are honest men of all religions and opinions. One sees intuitively that God never did, nor can, reveal his pleasure to mankind. Another finds the Koran and Shahstan in the list of

Rack'd every nerve, and gain'd all hell's applause,
To deist clubs familiar dar'd retire,
Or howl'd, and powaw'd, round the Indian fire,
Such feats my sons achiev'd, such honors won;
The shores, the blocking, of th' infernal throne!
And tho' yon haughty world their worth deny,
Their names shall glitter in the nether sky.
    But ah their wisdom, wit, and toils were vain,
A balm first soothing, then increasing pain.
Thro'† nature's fields while cloud-borne Bacon ran,
Doubtful his mind, an angel, or a man;
While high-soul'd Newton, wing'd by Heaven abroad,
Explain'd alike the works, and word, of God;
While patient Locke illum'd with newborn ray,

Revelations. Plato's devotion of himself to a courtizan, and Socrates' to Alcibiades were the effusions of honest, virtuous hearts; but Paul's dedication of his life to the Redeemer was a reverie of enthusiasm. God also, tho' dishonoured by adoration, presented to him in the character of a holy sin-hating God, and incapable of being pleased, when invoked in the name of Jesus Christ, is yet glorified, when honest votaries address him, in the elevated character of an ox, an onion, or a snake, and is highly delighted with invocations, when offered in the pleasing and prevailing name of the devil.

> Happy, happy, happy cause!
> None but the wise,
> None but the wise,
> Have such sharp eyes,
> Or tell such lies.   MORGAN*

The Devil's Feast, or the power of falsehood. An ode, by the very same Laureat, who wrote another, on the death of David Hume, Esq., in which, out of compassion to the Lord Jesus Christ, he forbears to tell how effectually said Hume has overthrown him.

* (Morgan) An unhappy man, who went to bed one night, and dreamed he was a great man, and a moral philosopher, which so turned his brain with surprise, that he never knew himself in the glass afterwards; but thought he was a moral philosopher, to the day of his death.   SCRIBLERUS.

† Names of a few silly men, whose minds were too small to comprehend the nature and evidences of Infidelity.   COLLINS.

The path of reason, and the laws of sway;
While Berkeley, bursting like the morning sun,
Look'd round all parching from his lofty throne,
In all events, and in all beings shew'd
The present, living, acting, speaking God,
Or cast resistless beams, the gospel o'er,
Union supreme of wisdom, love, and power!
Pain'd, shrivell'd, gasping, from the forceful ray
How crept my mite Philosophers away?
In vain my Methodist, brave Herbert, cried,
And whin'd, and wrote, pretended, pray'd, and lied,*
In vain my Shaftsbury, to his master true,
Dread† Humble bee! o'er burrs and thistles flew;
Incupped, and ravished with the fussful noise,
To praise the wondrous flowers, he rais'd his voice,
Of nature, beauty, dream'd and humm'd amain,
And sung himself, and buzz'd at truth, in vain.
Ah Bolingbroke, how well thy tatter'd robe,
Poor, Bedlam king of learning's little globe!
Amus'd thy fancy? He, with glory fir'd,
Myself in miniature! to heaven aspir'd
For fame, his heaven, thro' falshood's realms he ran,
And wish'd, and watch'd, and toil'd, and hop'd, in vain,
Misread, miswrote, misquoted, misapplied,
Yet fail'd of fame, and miss'd the skies, beside.
In views, in pride, in fate, conjoin'd with me,
Even Satan's self shall drop a tear for thee.
  My leaders these; yet Satan boasts his subs,
His Tolands, Tindals, Collinses, and Chubbs,
Morgans and Woolstons, names of lighter worth,
That stand, on falshood's list, for etc. [and so forth.]

  * See Lord Cherbury's Cock-Lane-Ghost Tale of Thunder's answer
to Prayer. SCRIBLERUS.
  † The characteristics of which insect are, busily to bustle about
with a great show of stateliness and mock majesty, with a noisy,
solemn hum, that sounds much, and means nothing, to be forever
poring over flowers, but never to gather, or yield, any honey.
                    LINNAEUS—properties of humble bees.

That sworn to me, to vice and folly given,
At truth and virtue growl'd, and bark'd at heaven.
Not men, 'tis true, yet manlings oft they won,
Against their God help'd blockheads oft to fun,
Help'd fops to folly, and help'd rakes to sin,
And* marr'd all sway, by mocking sway divine.
My list of authors too they help'd to count,
As cyphers eke the decimal amount.
As writers too they proffer'd useful aid
Believ'd unseen, and reverenc'd though unread.
Against their foe no proof my sons desire,
No reasoning canvass and no sense require.
Enough, the Bible is by wits arraign'd,
Genteel men doubt it, smart men say it's feign'd,
Onward my powder'd beaux and boobies throng,
As puppies float the kennel's stream along.
But their defects to varnish, and, in spite
Of pride and dignity, resolv'd to write,
I seiz'd the work myself. Straight, in a cloud
Of night involv'd, to Scotia's realms I rode.
There, in the cobwebs of a college room,
I found my best Amanuensis, Hume,
And bosom'd in his breast. On dreams afloat,
The youth soar'd high, and, as I prompted, wrote.
Sublimest nonsense there I taught mankind,
Pure, genuine dross, from gold seven times refin'd.
From realm to realm the strains exalted rung,
And thus the sage, and thus his teacher, sung.
All things roll on, by fix'd eternal laws;
Yet no effect depends upon a cause:
Hence every law was made by Chance divine,

* The same principles, which support or destroy christianity, alike
support or destroy political order and government. So manifest
is this, that Lord Bolingbroke, when contending against those whom he
esteems enemies of the British government, treats them unwittingly,
I presume, as enemies also to christianity, and loads them, for their
combined folly and perverseness, with many epithets of supreme
contempt.

Parent most fit of order, and design!
Earth was not made, but happen'd: Yet, on earth,
All beings happen, by most stated birth;
Each thing miraculous; yet strange to tell,
Not God himself can shew a miracle.

Meantime, lest these great things, the vulgar mind,
With learning vast, and deep research, should blind,
Lest dull to read, and duller still when known,
My favorite scheme should mould, and sleep, alone;
To* France I posted, on the wings of air,
And fir'd the labors of the gay Voltaire.
He, light and gay, o'er learning's surface flew,
And prov'd all things at option, false or true.
The gospel'd truths he saw were airy dreams,
The shades of nonsense, and the whims of whims.
Before his face no Jew could tell what past;
Or know the right from left, the first from last;
Conjecture where his native Salem stood,
Or find, if Jordan had a bank, or flood.
The Greeks, and Romans, never truth described;
But always (when they proved the gospel) lied.
He, he alone, the blest retreat had smelt,
The† Well, where long with frogs, the goddess dwelt;
In China dug, at Chihohamti's‡ call,
And curb'd with bricks, the refuse of his wall.
There, mid a realm of cheat, a world of lies,
Where alter'd nature wears one great disguise,
Where shrunk, misshapen bodies mock the eye,

* Satan seems guilty of an anachronism here, Voltaire being the eldest writer of the two. SCRIBLERUS.

† It appears by the testimony of all the ancient historians, that truth originally lived in a well; but Voltaire was the first geographer, who discovered where it was dug. LORD KAIMS's sketches of the weakness of man; article Voltaire.

‡ The Emperor, who burnt all the ancient records of his country, and built the great wall to defend it from the Tartars. Quere—In which instance did he do his countrymen the most good; if the books, he burnt, were like those written by them afterwards?

And shrivell'd souls the power of thought deny,
Mid idiot Mandarins, and baby Kings,
And dwarf Philosophers, in leading-strings,
Mid senseless votaries of less senseless Fo,*
Wretches who nothing even seem'd to know,
Bonzes, with souls more naked than their skin,
All brute without, and more than brute within,
From Europe's rougher sons the goddess shrunk,
Tripp'd in her iron shoes, and sail'd her junk.
Nice, pretty, wondrous stories there she told,
Of empires, forty thousand ages old,
Of Tohi, born with rainbows round his nose,—
Lao's long day—Ginseng† alchymic dose—
Stories, at which all Behmen's dreams awake,
Start into truth, and sense and virtue speak;
To which, all, lisping children e'er began
With, "At a time," or "Once there was a man,"
Is reason, truth, and fact; and sanctioned clear
With heaven's own voice, or proof of eye and ear.
He ‡ too reveal'd, that candour bade mankind
Believe my haughty rival weak, and blind;
That all things wrong a ruling God denied;
Or a satanic imp that God implied,
An imp, perchance of power and skill possest,
But not with justice, truth, or goodness blest.
Doctrines divine! would men their force receive,
And live to Satan's glory, as believe.

* Fo, the principal Idol of the Chinese.

† A plant, to which the Chinese ascribe all virtues of food and medicine, and proved by European scrutiny to be just as remote from them, as the date of the Chinese empire from 40,000 years. In the same manner, all Chinese extraordinaries, except a few mechanical ones, when examined, descend to plain dock and plantain. Yet, when swallowed by Voltaire, they will help to expel gripes of conscience, as a decoction of Ginseng will those of the flatulent cholic, full as well as warm water.

GARTH's alphabetical prophecies, article Ginseng.

‡ See Voltaire's Candide, the great purpose of which is to prove, that whatever is, is *not* right.

Nor these alone: from every class of man,
I gain'd new aids to build the darling plan.
But chief his favorite class, his priests, I won,
To undermine his course, and prop my own.
Here Jesuitic art its frauds combin'd
To draw ten thousand cobwebs o'er the mind.
In poisoned toils the flutterer to inclose,
And fix, with venom'd fangs, eternal woes.
On sceptic dross they stamp'd heavens image bright,
And nam'd their will a wisp, immortal light,
Thro' moors, and fens, the sightless wanderer led,
'Til down he plung'd, ingulph'd among the dead.
To life, * Socinus here his millions drew,
In ways, the art of Heaven conceal'd from view,
Undeified the world's almighty trust,
And lower'd eternity's great† fire to dust.
He taught, O first of men! the Son of God,
Who hung the globe, and stretch'd the heavens abroad,
Spoke into life the sun's supernal fire,
And mov'd to harmony the flaming choir,
Who in his hand immensity infolds,
And angels, worlds, and suns, and heavens, upholds,
Is—what? a worm, on far creation's limb,
A minim, in intelligence extreme.
O wondrous gospel, where such doctrines rise!
Discoveries wondrous of most wondrous eyes!
From him, a darling race descended fair,
Even to this day my first and chiefest care,

*Great men, if closely examined, will generally be found strongly
to resemble each other. Thus Milton, Homer and Ossian were blind.
Thus this great man exceedingly resembled Milton. There was however one or two trifling circumstances of difference. Milton, for
instance, was stone-blind in his bodily eyes, but had clear and intui-
tive moral optics. In Socinus the case was exactly reversed. Milton
also rose in his moral conceptions, with no unhappy imitation of the
scriptural sublimity: Socinus, on the contrary, anticlimaxed the
scriptural system down to nothing.   SCRIBLERUS.
  † Isai. ix. 6.

Where pertest Priestly* calls mankind, to see
His own corruptions of christianity.
   Mean time, less open friends my cause sustain'd,
More smoothly tempted and more slily gain'd;
Taught easier ways to climb the bright abode;
Less pure made virtue, and less perfect God;
Less guilty vice, the atonement less divine,
And pav'd, with peace and joy, the way to sin.
While† thus by art and perseverance won,
Again the old world seem'd almost my own.
   In this wild waste, where Albion's lights revive,
New dangers threaten and new evils live.
Here a dread race, my sturdiest foes design'd,
Patient of toil, of firm and vigorous mind,
Pinion'd with bold research to truth's far coast,
By storms undaunted, nor in oceans lost,
With dire invasion, error's realm assail,
And all my hardy friends before them fail.
   But my chief bane, my apostolic foe,
In life, in labours, source of every woe,
From scenes obscure, did heaven his * * * call,
That moral Newton, and that second Paul.
He, in clear view saw sacred systems roll,
Of reasoning worlds, around their central soul;
Saw love attractive every system bind,
The parent linking to each filial mind;
The end of heaven's high works resistless shew'd;
Creating glory, and created good;
And, in one little life, the gospel more
Disclos'd, than all earth's myriads kenn'd before.
Beneath his standard; lo what number rise,
To dare for truth, and combat for the skies!

   * A celebrated philosopher of the present day, who has carried chemical composition to a higher perfection than any other man living; for he has advanced so far, as to form a whole system of divinity out of fixed air.   Scriblerus.
   † Opposition to infidelity by disciples of Peter, Paul, etc., in this country.

Arm'd at all points, they try the battling field,
With reason's sword and faith's etherial shield.
To ward this fate all irreligion can,
Whate'er sustains, or flatters sinning man;
Whate'er can conscience of her thorns disarm,
Or calm, at death's approach, the dread alarm;
Whate'er like truth, with error cheats mankind;
Whate'er, like virtue, taints with vice the mind;
I preach'd, I wrote, I argued, pray'd, and lied,
What could my friends, or even myself, beside?
But, tho' with glad successes often crown'd,
Unceasing fears my troubled path surround.
While with each toil my friends the cause sustain,
Their toils, their efforts, and their arts are vain,
   Even plodding * * * did but little good,
Who* taught, the soul of man was made of mud:
Cold mud was virtue; warmer mud was sin;
And thoughts the angle-worms, that crawl'd within:
Nor taught alone; but wise, to precept join'd
A fair example, in his creeping mind.
In vain thro' † realms of nonsense * * * ran
The great Clodhopping‡ oracle of man.
Yet faithful were his toils: What could he more?
In Satan's cause he bustled, bruised, and swore;
And§ what the due reward, from me shall know,
For gentlemen of equal worth below.

  * See a late American treatise entitled a Philosophical Essay on
Matter, in which this great doctrine is fully proved.
  † Otherwise called Oracles of Reason.
  ‡ New name elegantly given to man, in Oracles of Reason.   Anon.
The annotator above mistakes, in calling this epithet a new name.
I could easily shew, by a series of learned deductions, that Clod-
hopper was the very original name of mankind, when they wore
tails, as Lord Monboddo has most ingeniously proved they did, at
their first creation.   SCRIBLERUS.
  § In A——n's Journal the writer observes, he presumes he shall
be treated, in the future world as well as other gentlemen of equal
merit are treated: A sentiment, in which all his countrymen will join
him.   SCRIBLERUS.

To vengeance then, my soul, to vengeance rise,
Assert thy glory and assault the skies.
What tho' dull seers have sung, in dreams sublime,
Thy ruin floats along the verge of time,
Tho' * without hands the stone from mountains riven,
Alarms my throne, and hastes the ire of heaven;
Tho' † bliss' dread heralds earth's far limits round,
Pardon, and peace, and joy, ere long shall sound;
How beautious are their feet! all regions cry,
And one great, natal song salutes the sky:
Still, should I sink, a glorious fate I'll find,
And sink amid the ruins of mankind.

But what blest onset shall I now begin,
To plunge the New World in the gulph of sin?
With sweet declension, down perdition's steep,
How, in one host, her cheated millions sweep?
I hail the glorious project, first, and best,
That ever Satan's bright invention blest;
That ‡ on this world my kingdom first began,
And lost my rival paradise, and man.
Twice fifteen suns are past, since C——'s mind,
Thro' doctrines deep, from common sense refin'd,
I led, a nice, mysterious work to frame,
With love of system, and with lust of fame.
Fair in his hand the pleasing wonder grew,
Wrought with deep art, and stor'd with treasures new:
There the sweet sophism led the soul astray;
There round to heaven soft bent the crooked way:
Saints, he confess'd, the shortest route pursue;
But, scarce behind, my children follow too.
Even Satan's self ere long shall thither hie;
On§ cap, huzza! and thro' the door go I!
Now palsied age has dimm'd his mental sight,

---

* Dan. ii. 44–45.   † Isai. lii. 7.
‡ Genesis iii. 4. *And the serpent said unto the woman. . . . Ye shall not surely die*, etc.

§ Magical incantation used formerly by the witches at Salem, when they went thro' key holes.   SCRIBLERUS.

I'll rouse the sage his master's laws to fight,
The injuries, long he render'd, to repair
And wipe from heaven's fair book his faith and prayer.
To wound the eternal cause with deepest harms,
A cheated gospel proves the surest arms:
Those arms, no hand can, like a preacher's wield;
False friends may stab, when foes must fly the field.
   This M——proves, in whom my utmost skill
Peer'd out no means of mischief, but the will.
He, in hard days, when ribbons gave no bread,
And Spitalfield's brave sons from Tyburn fled,
Scampering from bailiffs, wisely dropp'd the shuttle,
To preach down truth, and common sense to throttle.
With cunning, oft in scrapes and bustles tried,
Tongue at-your-service, in all stories plied,
The dirtiest ridicule of things most holy,
And dirtier flattery of sin and folly,
A mimickry, at which buffoons would blush,
Religion cent-per-cented, at a rush,
Boldness, that dares to make the Bible lie,
And brass, that would a foundery supply,
Mid gather'd rogues, and blockheads, oft he stood,
And rous'd to fun the genuine brotherhood;
Scripture, and argument, oblig'd to yield,
Made learning, sense, and virtue, quit the field,
While fainting decency sunk down to see
The desk of God a puppet-show for me.
   This said, invested with the robes of day,
To C——'s dome he wing'd his gladsome way,
And spread delightful to his wilder'd sense,
The pride of system, and the increase of pence.
Forth from its cobwebs straight the work he drew,
In mould still precious, and in dust still new.
This darling pet to usher to mankind,
High blown to ecstasy, the sage design'd;
And conn'd, with grand-parental love, the day,
When thro' the world the heir should make its way.
   The laughing spirit seized the lucky hour,

And round Columbia bade the* trumpet roar,
And thus thro' all her regions rang the song—
To† Pandemonia's plains, ye mortals, throng!
Here shall you, raptur'd, find there is no hell;
A priest shall teach it, and the gospel tell;
The pleasing truth, so long from earth conceal'd,
To bless desponding guilt, is now reveal'd.
Thus rang the thrilling voice the new world round;
Each villain started at the pleasing sound,
Hugg'd his old crimes, new mischiefs 'gan devise,
And turn'd his nose up to the threat'ning skies.

The perjur'd wretch, who met no honest eye,
But felt his own retreat, his spirit die,
Clear'd up his wither'd front, and true he cried
I've sometimes been forsworne, and often lied;
But all's a farce; as proves this doctrine new,
For God must help the perjur'd, as the true.

Up Florio sprang; and with indignant woes,
As thus he cried, his startled bosom rose—
I am the first of men in ways of evil,
The truest, thriftiest servant of the devil,
Born, educated, glory to engross,
And thine confess'd, the Devil's Man of Ross.
Here's three to one, I beat even him in pride;
Two whores already in my chariot ride:
Shall then this wretch?—forbid it Florio, heaven?
Shall sin's bright laurels to this priest be given?
No, still on Satan's roll shall shine my praise,
As erst on C——'s lists of yeas and nays.

Half pleas'd, the honest tar out bolted— "whew"!
"Good doctrine, Jack" "Aye, too good to be true."

* Otherwise called Salvation to all men. A treatise, published as a
harbinger to the great one having this motto on the title page,—
                    I leave you here a little book,
                    For you to look upon,
                    That you may learn to lie and swear,
                    When I am dead and gone.   SCRIBLERUS.
  † Otherwise called the field of mischief.   SCRIBLERUS.

P —— scowling heard, and growl'd—The day's our own!
I'll now tell two lies, where I told but one.
W —— more hard than flint, in sin grown old,
Clinch'd close his claws, and grip'd his bags of gold.
In vain, he cried, their woes let orphans tell;
In vain let widows weep; there is no hell.
Six, six per cent, each month, must now be given,
For pious usury now's the road to heaven.
All who, tho' fair without, yet black within,
Glued to their lips the choice liqueur of sin,
Whose conscience, oft rebuff'd, with snaky power,
Impoison'd still the gay and gleeful hour,
Check'd the loose wish, the past enjoyment stung,
And oft the alarm of retribution rung,
Thrill'd at each nerve, to find their fears were vain,
And swung triumphant caps at future pain.
  And now the morn arose; when o'er the plain
Gather'd, from every side, a numerous train;
To quell those fears, that rankled still within,
And gain new strength, and confidence, to sin.
There the half putrid Epicure was seen,
His cheeks of port, and lips with turtle green,
Who hop'd a long eternity was given,
To spread good tables, in some eating heaven.
The leacher there his lurid visage shew'd,
The imp of darkness, and the foe of good;
Who fled his lovely wife's most pure embrace,
To sate on hags, and breed a mongrel race;
A high-fed horse, for others wives who neigh'd;
A cur, who prowl'd around each quiet bed;
A snake, far spreading his impoison'd breath,
And charming innocence to guilt, and death.
Here stood Hypocrisy, in sober brown,
His sabbath face all sorrow'd with a frown.
A dismal tale he told of dismal times,
And this sad world brimful of saddest crimes,
Furrow'd his cheeks with tears for other's sin,
But clos'd his eyelids on the hell within.

There smil'd the smooth Divine, unus'd to wound
The sinners heart, with hell's alarming sound.
No terrors on his gentle tongue attend:
No grating truths the nicest ear offend.
That strange new-birth, that methodistic grace,
Nor in his heart, nor sermons, found a place.
Plato's fine tales he clumsily retold,
Trite, fireside, moral seesaws, dull as old;
His Christ, and bible, plac'd at good remove,
Guilt hell-deserving, and forgiving love.
'Twas best, he said, mankind should cease to sin;
Good fame requir'd it; so did peace within:
Their honours, well he knew, would ne'er be driven;
But hop'd they still would please to go to heaven.
Each week, he paid his visitation dues;
Coax'd, jested, laugh'd; rehears'd the private news;
Smok'd with each goody, thought her cheese excell'd;
Her pipe he lighted, and her baby held.
Or plac'd in some great town, with lacquer'd shoes,
Trim wig, and trimmer gown, and glistening hose,
He bow'd, talk'd politics, learn'd manners mild;
Most meekly questioned, and most smoothly smil'd;
At rich men's jests laugh'd loud, their stories prais'd;
Their wives new patterns gaz'd, and gaz'd, and gaz'd;
Most daintily on pamper'd turkies din'd;
Nor shrunk with fasting, nor with study pin'd:
Yet from their churches saw his brethren driven,
Who thunder'd truth, and spoke the voice of heaven,
Chill'd trembling guilt, in Satan's headlong path,
Charm'd the feet back, and rous'd the ear of death.
"Let fools," he cried, "starve on, while prudent I
Snug in my nest shall live, and snug shall die."
　　There stood the infidel of modern breed,
Blest vegetation of infernal seed,
Alike no Deist, and no Christian, he;
But from all principle, all virtue, free.
To him all things the same, as good or evil;
Jehovah, Jove, the Lama, or the Devil

Mohammed's braying, or Isaiah's lays;
The Indian's powaws, or the Christian's praise.
With him all *natural* desires are good;
His* thirst for stews; the Mohawk's thirst for blood:
Made, not to know, or love, the all beauteous mind;
Or wing thro' heaven his path to bliss refin'd:
But his dear self, choice Dagon! to adore;
To dress, to game, to swear, to drink, to whore;
To race his steeds; or cheat, when others run;
Pit tortur'd cocks, and swear 'tis glorious fun:
His soul not cloath'd with attributes divine;
But a nice watch-spring to that grand machine,
That work more nice than Rittenhouse can plan,
The body; man's chief part; himself, the man;
Man, that illustrious brute of noblest shape,
A swine unbristled, and an untail'd ape:
To couple, eat, and die—his glorious doom—
The oyster's church-yard, and the capon's tomb.

There —— grinn'd, his conscience fear'd anew,
And scarcely wish'd the doctrine false or true;
Scarce smil'd, himself secure from God to know,
So poor the triumph o'er so weak a foe.
In the deep midnight of his guilty mind,
Where not one solitary virtue shin'd,
Hardly, at times, his struggling conscience wrought
A few, strange intervals of lucid thought,
Holding her clear and dreadful mirrour nigher,
Where villain glow'd, in characters of fire.
Those few the tale dispers'd: His soul no more
Shall, once a year, the Beelzebub run o'er;
Nor more shall J——n's ghost her infant show,
Saw his hard nerves, and point the hell below;
Fixed in cold death, no more his eyeballs stare,
Nor change to upright thorns his bristly hair.

There Demas smil'd, who once the Christian name

* Both justified, as all other crimes are, on the great principle that
they are natural.   SCRIBLERUS.

Gravely assum'd, and wore with sober fame.
Meek, modest, decent, in life's lowly vale,
Pleas'd he walk'd on; nor now had grac'd this tale;
But, borne beyond the Atlantic ferry, he
Saw wondrous things, his schoolmates did not see.
Great houses, and great men, in coaches carried;
Great Ladies, great Lords' wives, tho' never married;
Fine horses, and fine pictures, and fine plays,
And all the finest things of modern days.
Camelion like, he lost his former hue,
And, mid such great men, grew a great man too;
Enter'd the round of silly, vain parade;
His hair he powder'd, and his bow he made.
Shall powder'd heads, he cried, be sent to hell?
Shall men in vain in such fine houses dwell?

    There Euclio—Ah my Muse, let deepest shame
Blush on thy cheek, at that unhappy name!
Oh write it not, my hand! the name appears
Already written: Wash it out, my tears!
Still, Oh all pitying Saviour! let thy love,
Stronger than death, all heights, and heaven above,
That on the accursed tree, in woes severe,
The thief's dire guilt extinguish'd with a tear,
Yearn o'er that mind, that, with temptations dire,
Rank appetites, and passions fraught with fire,
By each new call without, each thought within,
Is forc'd to folly, and is whirl'd to sin;
In conscience' spite, tho' arm'd with hissing fears,
Strong pangs of soul, and all his country's tears,
Is charm'd to madness by the old serpent's breath,
And hurried swiftly down the steep of death.
Burst, burst, thou charm! wake, trembler wake again,
Nor let thy parent's dying prayers be vain!

    The hour arriv'd, th' infernal trumpet blew;
Black from its mouth a cloud sulphureous flew;
The caverns groan'd; the startled throng gave way,
And forth the chariot rush'd to gloomy day.
On every side, expressive emblems rose,

The man, the scene, the purpose to disclose.
Here wrinkled dotage, like a fondled boy,
Titter'd, and smirk'd its momentary joy:
His crumbs there avarice grip'd, with lengthen'd nails,
And weigh'd clipp'd half pence in unequal scales.
Trim vanity her praises laugh'd aloud,
And snuff'd for incense from the gaping crowd.
While Age an eye of anguish cast around,
His crown of glory prostrate on the ground.
There C—— sate; aloud his voice declar'd,
Hell is no more, or no more to be fear'd.
What tho' the Heavens, in words of flaming fire,
Disclose the vengeance of eternal ire,
Bid anguish o'er the unrepenting soul,
In waves succeeding waves, forever roll;
The strongest terms, each language knows, employ
To teach us endless woe, and endless joy:
'Tis all a specious irony, design'd,
A harmless trifling with the human kind;
Or, not to charge the sacred books with lies,
A wile most needful of the ingenious skies,
On this bad earth their kingdom to maintain,
And curb the rebel, man; but all in vain.
First Origen, then Tillotson, then I
Learned their profoundest cunning to descry,
And shew'd this truth, tho' nicely cover'd o'er,
That hell's broad path leads round to heaven's door.
See* *kai's* and *epi's* build the glorious scheme!
And *gar's* and *pro's* unfold their proof supreme!
But such nice proof, as none but those can know,
Who oft have read the sacred volume thro',
And read in Greek: but chiefly those, who all
The epistles oft have search'd of cunning Paul.

* How much alike are great men, still say I? The Doctor has
found a whole system of divinity, in three or four Greek adverbs,
and prepositions; as Lord Coke had before discovered, that there
is much curious and cunning kind of learning, in an etc. . . .

SCRIBLERUS.

He, he alone, the mystery seem'd to know,
And none but wizard eyes can peep him thro'.
Then here, at second hand, receive from me
What in the sacred books you'll never see.
For* tho' the page reveal'd our cause sustains,
When search'd with cunning, and when gloss'd with pains,
Yet our first aids from human passions rise,
Blest friends to error, and blest props to lies!
And chief, that ruling principle within,
The love of sweet security in sin:
Beneath whose power all pleasing falsehoods blind,
And steal, with soft conviction, on the mind.
No good more luscious than their truth she knows.
And hence their evidence will ne'er oppose.
Aided by this, she mounts the Eternal Throne,
And makes the universe around her own.
Decides the rights of Godhead with her nod,
And wields for him dominion's mighty rod.
Whate'er he ought, or ought not, she descries,
Beholds all infinite relations rise,
Th' immense of time and space surveys serene,
And tells whate'er the bible ought to mean;
Whate'er she wishes, sees him bound to do,
Else is his hand unjust, his word untrue.
    Then would you lay your own, or others fears,
Search your own bosoms, or appeal to theirs.
Know, what those bosoms wish Heaven must reveal;
And sure no bosom ever wish'd a hell.
But, lest sustain'd by underpinning frail,
Our hopes and wits, our proofs and doctrines fail,
Admit a hell; but from its terrors take
Whate'er commands the guilty heart to quake.

    * Witness Matthew vii. 13–14—*Strait is the gate, and narrow the
way, that leadeth to destruction, and no body there is, who goes in thereat:
    Because wide is the gate, and broad is the way, that leadeth unto life,
and all they be, who find it.* Murray's new version of the Bible, very
proper to be kept by thieves, whoremongers, idolaters, and all liars;
with others, who mean to go to heaven, via hell.

Again the purgatorial whim revive,
And bid the soul by stripes and penance live.
And now, with search most deep, and wits most keen,
I've learn'd, that hell is but a school for sin;
Which yields, to heaven, the soul from guile refin'd,
And, tho' it mars the devil's, mends mankind.
And thus the matter stands. When God makes man,
He makes him *here* religious, if he can;
If he cannot, he bids him farther go,
And try to be religious, down below;
But as his failure is his fault, ordains
His soul to suffer dire repentance' pains,
Repentance, fearful doom of sinners vile!
The law's whole curse, and nature's highest ill!
If there the wretch repent, the work is done;
If not, he plunges to a lower zone,
A lower still, and still a lower, tries,
'Til with such sinking tir'd, he longs to rise;
And finding there the fashion to repent,
He joins the throng, and strait to heaven is sent.
Heaven now his own he claims; nor can the sky
Preserve its honour, and its claim deny.
Thus stands the fact; and if the proof should fail,
Let Heaven, next time, some better proof reveal.
I've done my part; I've given you here the pith;
The rest, the bark and sap, I leave to ——
    Thus spoke the sage; a shout, from all the throng,
Roll'd up to heaven, and roar'd the plains along;
Conscience, a moment, ceas'd her stings to rear,
And joy excessive whelm'd each rising fear.
But soon reflection's glass again she rear'd,
Spread out fell sin; and all her horrors bar'd;
There anguish, guilt, remorse, her dreadful train,
Tremendous harbingers of endless pain,
Froze the sad breast, amaz'd the withering eye,
And forc'd the soul to doubt the luscious lie.
    Yet soon sophistic wishes, fond and vain,
The scheme review'd, and lov'd, and hop'd again;

Soon, one by one, the flames of hell withdrew;
Less painful conscience, sin less dangerous grew;
Less priz'd the day, to man for trial given,
Less fear'd Jehovah, and less valued heaven.
　　No longer now by conscience' calls unmann'd,
To sin, the wretch put forth a bolder hand;
More freely cheated, lied, defam'd, and swore;
Nor wish'd the night to riot, drink, or whore;
Look'd up, and hiss'd his God; his parent stung,
And sold his friend, and country, for a song.
The new-fledg'd infidel of modern brood
Climb'd the next fence, clapp'd both his wings, and crow'd;
Confess'd the doctrines were as just, as new,
And doubted if the bible were not true.
The decent christian threw his mask aside,
And smil'd, to see the path of heaven so wide,
To church, the half of each fair sunday, went,
The rest, in visits, sleep, or dining, spent;
To vice and error nobly liberal grew;
Spoke kindly of all doctrines, but the true;
All men, but saints, he hop'd to heaven might rise,
And thought all roads, but virtue, reach'd the skies,
　　There truth and virtue stood, and sigh'd to find
New gates of falshood open'd on mankind;
New paths to ruin strew'd with flowers divine,
And other aids, and motives, gain'd to sin.
　　From a dim cloud, the spirit eyed the scene,
Now proud with triumph, and now vex'd with spleen,
Mark'd all the throng, beheld them all his own,
And to his cause no friend of virtue won:
Surpriz'd, enrag'd, he wing'd his sooty flight,
And hid beneath the pall of endless night.

COLUMBIA

COLUMBIA, Columbia, to glory arise,
The queen of the world, and child of the skies!
Thy genius commands thee; with rapture behold,
While ages on ages thy splendors unfold.
Thy reign is the last, and the noblest of time,
Most fruitful thy soil, most inviting thy clime;
Let the crimes of the east ne'er encrimson thy name.
Be freedom, and science, and virtue, thy fame.

To conquest, and slaughter, let Europe aspire;
Whelm nations in blood, and wrap cities in fire;
Thy heroes the rights of mankind shall defend,
And triumph pursue them, and glory attend.
A world is thy realm: for a world be thy laws,
Enlarg'd as thine empire, and just as thy cause;
On Freedom's broad basis, that empire shall rise,
Extend with the main, and dissolve with the skies.

Fair Science her gates to thy sons shall unbar,
And the east see thy morn hide the beams of her star.
New bards and new sages, unrival'd shall soar
To fame, unextinguish'd, when time is no more;
To fame, the last refuge of virtue design'd,
Shall fly from all nations the best of mankind;
Here, grateful to heaven, with transport shall bring
Their incense, more fragrant than odours of spring.

Nor less shall thy fair ones to glory ascend,
And Genius and Beauty in harmony blend;
The graces of form shall awake pure desire,
And the charms of the soul ever cherish the fire;
Their sweetness unmingled, their manners refin'd
And virtue's bright image, instamp'd on the mind,
With peace, and soft rapture, shall teach life to glow,
And light up a smile in the aspect of woe.

Thy fleets to all regions thy pow'r shall display,
The nations admire, and the ocean obey;
Each shore to thy glory its tribute unfold,
And the east and the south yield their spices and gold
As the day-spring unbounded, thy splendor shall flow,
And earth's little kingdoms before thee shall bow,
While the ensigns of union, in triumph unfurl'd,
Hush the tumult of war, and give peace to the world.

Thus, as down a lone valley, with cedars o'erspread,
From war's dread confusion I pensively stray'd—
The gloom from the face of fair heav'n retir'd;
The winds ceas'd to murmur; the thunders expir'd;
Perfumes, as of Eden, flow'd sweetly along,
And a voice, as of angels, enchantingly sung;
"Columbia, Columbia, to glory arise,
The queen of the world, and the child of the skies."

A SONG

Look, lovely maid, on yonder flow'r,
　And see that busy fly,
Made for the enjoyment of an hour
　And only born to die.

See, round the rose he lightly moves,
　And wantons in the sun,
His little life in joy improves,
　And lives, before 'tis gone.

From this instinctive wisdom, learn,
　The present hour to prize;
Nor leave to-day's supreme concern,
　'Till morrow's morn arise.

Say, lovliest fair, canst thou divine
　That morrow's hidden doom?
Know'st thou, if cloudless skies will shine,
　Or heaven be wrapt in gloom?

Fond man, the trifle of a day,
　Enjoys the morning light,
Nor knows, his momentary play
　Must end, before 'tis night.

The present joys are all we claim;
　The past are in the tomb;
And, like the poet's dream of fame
　The future never come.

No longer then, fair maid, delay
　The promis'd scenes of bliss;
Nor idly give another day,
　The joys assign'd to this.

If *then* my breast can soothe thy care,
  'Twill *now* that care allay;
If joy this hand can yield, my fair
  'Twill yield that joy to-day.

Quit then, oh quit! thou lovely maid,
  Thy bashful, virgin pride;
To-day the happy plot be laid,
  The bands, to-morrow, tied!

The purest joys shall be our own,
  That e'er to man were giv'n;
And those bright scenes, on earth begun,
  Shall brighter shine in heaven.

A HYMN

Sung at the PUBLIC EXHIBITION of the SCHOLARS belonging
to the Academy in Greenfield, May 2d, 1788.

HAIL child of light, returning Spring,
    Fair image, foretaste sweet, of heaven!
In thee our hearts thy Maker sing,
    By whose blest bounty thou wast given.

From thee the wintry glooms retire,
    The skies their purest beams display,
And winds, and showers, and suns conspire,
    To clothe the world with life and May.

Hail knowledge, hail, the moral spring
    That wakes the verdure of the mind!
To man, thy rays indulgent bring
    All fragrant flowers, and fruits refin'd.

Thy progress with the morn began,
    Before thee every region smil'd;
The savage brighten'd into man,
    And gardens blossom'd in the wild.

All hail fair Virtue, noblest good,
    The bliss and beauty of the skies!
By whom, to yonder blest abode,
    The humble, and the faithful rise.

While here fair Learning smiles benign,
    And Spring leads on the genial year,
From realms of life and peace divine,
    Descend, and bloom, and flourish here.

And O thou fount of good supreme,
    The sun that lights eternal spring,

At once of knowledge source and theme,
  Thee first, and last, our voices sing!

Virtue, in every charm array'd,
  For this dark world, thy sufferings won;
Those charms thy matchless life display'd,
  When here the incarnate splendor shone.

As dews refresh, as suns revive,
  When clear and cloudless shines the day,
Command our rising race to live,
  And win them from the world away.

With thee, the source of every grace,
  Our song shall end, as it began;
Our hope, our trust, our joy, and praise,
  The Saviour, and the Friend of Man.

THE CRITICS[1]

A FABLE

Written September 1785.

'To every general rule there are exceptions'—Common Sense.

'Tis said of every dog that's found,
Of mongrel, spaniel, cur, and hound;
That each sustains a doggish mind,
And hates the new, sublime, refin'd.
'Tis hence the wretches bay the moon,
In beauty throned at highest noon;
Hence every nobler brute they bite,
And hunt the stranger-dog with spite;
And hence, the nose's dictates parrying,
They fly from meat to feed on carrion.
'Tis also said, the currish soul
The critic race possesses whole;
As near they come, in tho'ts and natures,
As two legg'd can, to four legg'd creatures;
Alike the things they love and blame,
Their voice, and language, much the same.

The Muse this subject made her theme,
And told me in a morning dream.
Such dreams you sages may decry;
But Muses know they never lie.
Then hear, from me, in grave narration,
Of these strange facts, the strange occasion.

In Greece Cynethe's village lay,
Well known to all, who went that way,

[1] This Poem is reprinted from *The Gazette of the United States*, of July 13, 1791; where it was first published.

279

For dogs of every kindred famed,
And from true doggish manners named.
One morn, a greyhound pass'd the street;
At once the foul-mouth'd conclave met,
Huddling around the stranger ran,
And thus their smart *review* began.
"What tramper" with a grinner sneer,
Bark'd out the clumsy cur, "is here?
No native of the town, I see;
Some foreign whelp of base degree.
I'd shew, but that the record's torn,
We true Welsh curs are better born.
His coat is smooth; but longer hair
Would more become a dog by far.
His slender ear, how strait and flopping!
While ours is much improved by *cropping*."

"Right," cried the blood-hound, "that strait ear
Seems made for nothing, but to hear;
'Tis long agreed, thro' all the town,
That handsome ears, like mine, hang down;
And tho' his body's gaunt, and round,
'Tis no true rawboned gaunt of hound.
How high his nose the creature carries!
As if on bugs, and flies, his fare is;
I'll teach this strutting stupid dog,
To smell's the business of a dog."

"Baugh-waugh!" the shaggy spaniel cried,
"What wretched covering on his hide!
I wonder where he lives in winter;
His strait, sleek legs too, out of joint are;
I hope the vagrant will not dare
His fledging with my fleece compare.
He never plung'd in pond or river,
To search for wounded duck and diver;
By kicks would soon be set a skipping
Nor take, one half so well a whipping."

"Rat me," the lap-dog yelp'd, "thro' nature
Was ever seen so coarse a creature?
I hope no lady's sad mishap
E'er led the booby to her lap;
He'd fright PRIMRILLA into fits,
And rob FOOLERIA of her wits;
A mere barbarian, Indian whelp!
How clownish, countryish, sounds his yelp!
He never tasted bread and butter,
Nor play'd the petty squirm and flutter;
Nor e'er, like me, has learn'd to fatten,
On kisses sweet, and softest patting."

"Some parson's dog, I vow," whined puppy;
"His rusty coat how sun-burnt! stop ye!"
The beagle call'd him to the wood.
The bull-dog bellowed, "Zounds! and blood!"
The wolf-dog and the mastiff were,
The Muse says, an exception here;
Superior both to such foul play,
They wish'd the stranger well away.

From *spleen* the *strictures* rose to *fury*,
"Villain," growl'd one, "I can't endure you."
"Let's seize the truant," snarl'd another,
Encored by every foul-mouth'd brother.
" 'Tis done," bark'd all, we'll mob the creature,
And sacrifice him to ill-nature."

The greyhound, who despised their breath,
Still tho't it best to shun their teeth.
Easy he wing'd his rapid flight,
And left the scoundrels out of sight.

GOOD JUNO, by the ancients holden,
The genuine *notre-dame* of scolding,
Sate pleased, because there'd such a fuss been,
And in the hound's place wish'd her husband;

For her, even pleasure bade her own,
Her ladyship was once out-done.
"Hail dogs," she cried, "of every kind!
Retain ye still this snarling mind,
Hate all that's good, and fair, and new,
And I'll a goddess be to you.

Nor this the only good you prove;
Learn what the fruits of JUNO's love.
Your souls, from forms, that creep all four on,
I'll raise, by system Pythagorean,
To animate the human frame,
And gain my favorite tribe a name.
Be ye henceforth (so I ordain)
Critics, the genuine curs of men.
To snarl be still your highest bliss,
And all your criticism like this.
Whate'er is great, or just, in nature,
Of graceful form, or lovely feature;
Whate'er adorns the ennobled mind,
Sublime, inventive, and refin'd;
With spleen, and spite, forever blame,
And load with every dirty name.
All things of noblest kind and use,
To your own standard vile reduce,
And all in wild confusion blend,
Nor heed the *subject, scope,* or *end.*
But chief, when *modest young beginners,*
'Gainst *critic laws,* by *nature* sinners,
Peep out in verse, and dare to run,
Thro' towns and villages your own,
Hunt them, as when yon stranger dog
Set all your growling crew agog;
Till stunn'd, and scared, they hide from view,
And leave the country clear for you."

This said, the goddess kind caressing,
Gave every cur a double blessing.

Each doggish mind, tho' grown no bigger,
Hence forth assumed the human figure,
The body walk'd on two; the mind
To four, still chose to be confin'd;
Still creeps on earth, still scents out foes,
Is still led onward by the nose;
Hates all the good it used to hate,
The lofty, beauteous, new, and great;
The stranger hunts with spite quintessent,
And snarls, from that day to the present.

PSALM CXXXVII

I love thy kingdom, Lord,
The house of thine abode,
The church our blest Redeemer sav'd
With his own precious blood.

I love thy Church, O God!
Her walls before thee stand,
Dear as the apple of thine eye,
And graven on thy hand.

If e'er to bless thy sons
My voice, or hands, deny,
These hands let useful skill forsake,
This voice in silence die.

If e'er my heart forget
Her welfare, or her woe,
Let every joy this heart forsake,
And every grief o'erflow.

For her my tears shall fall;
For her my prayers ascend;
To her my care and toils be given,
'Till toils and cares shall end.

Beyond my highest joy
I prize her heavenly ways,
Her sweet communion, solemn vows,
Her hymns of love and praise.

Jesus, thou Friend divine,
Our Saviour and our King.
Thy hand from every snare and foe
Shall great deliverance bring.

Sure as thy truth shall last,
To Zion shall be given
The brightest glories, earth can yield,
And brighter bliss of heaven.

1800

JOEL BARLOW
(1754–1812)

The Columbiad is a revision and enlargement of the *Vision of Columbus*, published in 1782. In the opening lines Columbus is discovered sick, ruined, discouraged, an old man in chains in a dungeon in Valladolid. In his despair an angel of light appears to him, removes his chains and conducts him to the Mount of Vision, from whence he overlooks the earth and foresees the future. In Books I to IV he surveys the western hemisphere, its tribes and their social and political status; its discovery by Europeans and the founding of the English colonies; the European struggles for colonial possessions ending in the peace of 1763. In Books V to VII a dismal eclipse of the "march of troublous years" passes, opening to view the Continental Congress in session, "the Demon Form . . . War . . . swift hovering for the coast," the investiture of Yorktown, and the surrender of Cornwallis. In Book VIII the poet addresses his fellow countrymen as they emerge from the struggles of war:

> "Think not my friends, the patriot's task is done,
> Or Freedom safe, because the battle's won."

The poem rises in the end to prophecy and gives a vision of international peace and good will— "a general congress of all nations assembled to establish a political harmony of mankind." The great object which Barlow held in view in writing the work is set forth in the passage quoted in the Introduction.

THE COLUMBIAD

BOOK VII

ARGUMENT

Coast of France rises in vision. Louis, to humble the British
power, forms an alliance with the American states. This
brings France, Spain and Holland into the war, and rouses
Hyder Ally to attack the English in India. The vision
returns to America, where the military operations continue
with various success. Battle of Monmouth. Storming of
Stonypoint by Wayne. Actions of Lincoln, and surrender
of Charleston. Movements of Cornwallis. Actions of
Greene, and battle of Eutaw. French army arrives, and
joins the American. They march to besiege the English
army of Cornwallis in York and Gloster. Naval battle
of Degrasse and Graves. Two of their ships grappled and
blown up. Progress of the siege. A citadel Mined and
blown up. Capture of Cornwallis and his army. Their
banners furled and muskets piled on the field of battle.

THUS view'd the Pair; when lo, in eastern skies,
From glooms unfolding, Gallia's coasts arise.
Bright o'er the scenes of state a golden throne,
Instarr'd with gems and hung with purple, shone;
Young Bourbon there in royal splendor sat,
And fleets and moving armies round him wait.
For now the contest, with increased alarms,
Fill'd every court and roused the world to arms;
As Hesper's hand, that light from darkness brings,
And good to nations from the scourge of kings,
In this dread hour bade broader beams unfold,
And the new world illuminate the old.
  In Europe's realms a school of sages trace
The expanding dawn that waits the Reasoning Race;

On the bright Occident they fix their eyes,
Thro glorious toils where struggling nations rise;
Where each firm deed, each new illustrious name
Calls into light a field of nobler fame:
A field that feeds their hope, confirms the plan
Of well poized freedom and the weal of man.
They scheme, they theorise, expand their scope,
Glance o'er Hesperia to her utmost cope;
Where streams unknown for other oceans stray,
Where suns unseen their waste of beams display,
Where sires of unborn nations claim their birth,
And ask their empires in those wilds of earth.
While round all eastern climes, with painful eye,
In slavery sunk they see the kingdoms lie,
Whole states exhausted to enrich a throne,
Their fruits untasted and their rights unknown;
Thro tears of grief that speak the well taught mind,
They hail the era that relieves mankind.
Of these the first, the Gallic sages stand,
And urge their king to lift an aiding hand.
The cause of humankind their souls inspired,
Columbia's wrongs their indignation fired;
To share her fateful deeds their counsel moved,
To base in practice what in theme they proved:
That no proud privilege from birth can spring,
No right divine, nor compact form a king;
That in the people dwells the sovereign sway,
Who rule by proxy, by themselves obey;
That virtues, talents are the test of awe,
And Equal Rights the only source of law.
Surrounding heroes wait the monarch's word,
In foreign fields to draw the patriot sword,
Prepared with joy to join those infant powers,
Who build republics on the western shores.
    By honest guile the royal ear they bend,
And lure him on, blest Freedom to defend;
That, once recognised, once establisht there,
The world might learn her profer'd boon to share.

But artful arguments their plan disguise,
Garb'd in the gloss that suits a monarch's eyes.
By arms to humble Britain's haughty power,
From her to sever that extended shore,
Contents his utmost wish. For this he lends
His powerful aid, and calls the opprest his friends.
The league proposed, he lifts his arm to save,
And speaks the borrow'd language of the brave:
    Ye states of France, and ye of rising name
Who work those distant miracles of fame,
Hear and attend; let heaven the witness bear,
We wed the cause, we join the righteous war.
Let leagues eternal bind each friendly land,
Given by our voice, and 'stablisht by our hand;
Let that brave people fix their infant sway,
And spread their blessings with the bounds of day.
Yet know, ye nations; hear, ye Powers above,
Our purposed aid no views of conquest move;
In that young world revives no ancient claim
Of regions peopled by the Gallic name;
Our envied bounds, already stretch'd afar,
Nor ask the sword, nor fear encroaching war;
But virtue, coping with the tyrant power
That drenches earth in her best children's gore,
With nature's foes bids former compact cease;
We war reluctant, and our wish is peace;
For man's whole race the sword of France we draw;
Such is our will, and let our will be law.
    He spoke; his moving armies veil'd the plain,
His fleets rode bounding on the western main;
O'er lands and seas the loud applauses rung,
And war and union dwelt on every tongue.
    The other Bourbon caught the splendid strain,
To Gallia's arms he joins the powers of Spain;
Their sails assemble; Crillon lifts the sword,
Minorca bows and owns her ancient lord.
But while dread Elliott shakes the Midland wave,
They strive in vain the Calpian rock to brave.

Batavia's states with equal speed prepare
Thro western isles to meet the naval war;
For Albion there rakes rude the tortured main,
And foils the force of Holland, France and Spain.
　　Where old Indostan still perfumes the skies,
To furious strife his ardent myriads rise;
Fierce Hyder there, unconquerably bold,
Bids a new flag its horned moons unfold,
Spreads o'er Carnatic kings his splendid force,
And checks the Britons in their wasting course.
　　Europe's pacific powers their counsels join,
The laws of trade to settle and define.
The imperial Moscovite around him draws
Each Baltic state to join the righteous cause;
Whose arm'd Neutrality the way prepares
To check the ravages of future wars;
Till by degrees the wasting sword shall cease,
And commerce lead to universal peace.
　　Thus all the ancient world with anxious eyes
Enjoy the lights that gild Atlantic skies,
Wake to new life, assume a borrow'd flame,
Enlarge the lustre and partake the fame.
So mounts of ice, that polar heavens invade,
Tho piled unseen thro night's long wintry shade,
When morn at last illumes their glaring throne,
Give back the day and imitate the sun.
　　But still Columbus, on his war-beat shore,
Sees Albin's fleets her new battalions pour;
The states unconquer'd still their terrors wield,
And stain with mingled gore the embattled field.
On Pennsylvania's various plains they move,
And adverse armies equal slaughter prove;
Columbia mourns her Nash in combat slain,
Britons around him press the gory plain;
Skirmish and cannonade and distant fire
Each power diminish and each nation tire.
Till Howe from fruitless toil demands repose,
And leaves despairing in a land of foes

His wearied host; who now, to reach their fleet,
O'er Jersey hills commence their long retreat,
Tread back the steps their chief had led before,
And ask in vain the late abandon'd shore,
Where Hudson meets the main; for on their rear
Columbia moves, and checks their swift career.
　But where green Monmouth lifts his grassy height,
They halt, they face, they dare the coming fight.
Howe's proud successor, Clinton, hosting there,
To tempt once more the desperate chance of war,
Towers at their head, in hopes to work relief,
And mend the errors of his former chief.
Here shines his day; and here with loud acclaim
Begins and ends his little task of fame.
He vaults before them with his balanced blade,
Wheels the bright van, and forms the long parade;
Where Britons, Hessians crowd the glittering field,
And all their powers for ready combat wield.
As the dim sun, beneath the skirts of even,
Crimsons the clouds that sail the western heaven;
So, in red wavy rows, where spread the train
Of men and standards, shone the fateful plain.
　They shone, till Washington obscured their light,
And his long ranks roll'd forward to the fight.
He points the charge; the mounted thunders roar,
And rake the champaign to the distant shore.
Above the folds of smoke that veil the war,
His guiding sword illumes the fields of air;
And vollied flames, bright bursting o'er the plain,
Break the brown clouds, discovering far the slain:
Till flight begins; the smoke is roll'd away,
And the red standards open into day.
Britons and Germans hurry from the field,
Now wrapt in dust, and now to sight reveal'd;
Behind, swift Washington his falchion drives,
Thins the pale ranks, but saves submissive lives.
Hosts captive bow and move behind his arm,
And hosts before him wing the sounding storm;

When the glad sea salutes their fainting sight,
And Albion's fleet wide thundering aids their flight;
They steer to sad Newyork their hasty way,
And rue the toils of Monmouth's mournful day.
   But Hudson still, with his interior tide,
Laves a rude rock that bears Britannia's pride,
Swells round the headland with indignant roar,
And mocks her thunders from his murmuring shore;
When a firm cohort starts from Peekskill plain,
To crush the invaders and the post regain.
Here, gallant Hull, again thy sword is tried,
Meigs, Fleury, Butler, laboring side by side,
Wayne takes the guidance, culls the vigorous band,
Strikes out the flint, and bids the nervous hand
Trust the mute bayonet and midnight skies,
To stretch o'er craggy walls the dark surprise.
With axes, handspikes on the shoulder hung,
And the sly watchword whisper'd from the tongue,
Thro different paths the silent march they take,
Plunge, climb the ditch, the palisado break,
Secure each sentinel, each picket shun,
Grope the dim postern where the byways run.
Soon the roused garrison perceives its plight;
Small time to rally and no means of flight,
They spring confused to every post they know,
Point their poized cannon where they hear the foe,
Streak the dark welkin with the flames they pour,
And rock the mountain with convulsive roar.
   The swift assailants still no fire return,
But, tow'rd the batteries that above them burn,
Climb hard from crag to crag; and scaling higher
They pierce the long dense canopy of fire
That sheeted all the sky; then rush amain,
Storm every outwork, each dread summit gain,
Hew timber'd gates, the sullen drawbridge fall,
File thro and form within the sounding wall.
The Britons strike their flag, the fort forego,
Descend sad prisoners to the plain below.

A thousand veterans, ere the morning rose,
Received their handcuffs from five hundred foes;
And Stonypoint beheld, with dawning day,
His own starr'd standard on his rampart play.

　From sack'd Savanna, whelm'd in hostile fires,
A few raw troops brave Lincoln now retires;
With rapid march to suffering Charleston goes,
To meet the myriads of concentring foes,
Who shade the pointed strand. Each fluvial flood
Their gathering fleets and floating batteries load,
Close their black sails, debark the amphibious host,
And with their moony anchors fang the coast.

　The bold beleaguer'd post the hero gains,
And the hard siege with various fate sustains.
Cornwallis, towering at the British van,
In these fierce toils his wild career began;
He mounts the forky streams, and soon bestrides
The narrow neck that parts converging tides,
Sinks the deep trench, erects the mantling tower,
Lines with strong forts the desolated shore,
Hems on all sides the long unsuccour'd place,
With mines and parallels contracts the space;
Then bids the battering floats his labors crown,
And pour their bombard on the shuddering town.

　High from the decks the mortar's bursting fires
Sweep the full streets, and splinter down the spires.
Blaze-trailing fuses vault the night's dim round,
And shells and langrage lacerate the ground;
Till all the tented plain, where heroes tread,
Is torn with crags and cover'd with the dead.
Each shower of flames renews the townsmen's woe,
They wail the fight, they dread the cruel foe.
Matrons in crowds, while tears bedew their charms,
Babes at their sides and infants in their arms,
Press round their Lincoln and his hand implore,
To save them trembling from the tyrant's power.
He shares their anguish with a moistening eye,
And bids the balls rain thicker thro the sky;

Tries every aid that art and valor yield,
The sap, the countermine, the battling field,
The bold sortie, by famine urged afar,
That dreadful daughter of earth-wasting War.
But vain the conflict now; on all the shore,
The foes in fresh brigades around him pour;
He yields at last the well contested prize,
And freedom's banners quit the southern skies.

The victor Britons soon the champaign tread,
And far anorth their fire and slaughter spread;
Thro fortless realms, where unarm'd peasants fly;
Cornwallis bears his bloody standard high;
O'er Carolina rolls his growing force,
And thousands fall and thousands aid his course;
While in his march athwart the wide domain,
Colonial dastards join his splendid train.
So mountain streams thro slopes of melting snow,
Swell their foul waves and flood the world below.

Awhile the Patriarch saw, with heaving sighs,
These crimson flags insult the saddening skies,
Saw desolation whelm his favorite coast,
His children scatter'd and their vigor lost,
Dekalb in furious combat press the plain,
Morgan and Smallwood every shock sustain,
Gates, now no more triumphant, quit the field,
Indignant Davidson his lifeblood yield,
Blount, Gregory, Williamson, with souls of fire
But slender force, from hill to hill retire;
When Greene in lonely greatness takes the ground,
And bids at last the trump of vengeance sound.

A few firm patriots to the chief repair,
Raise the star standard and demand the war.
But o'er the regions as he turns his eyes,
What foes develop! and what forts arise!
Rawdon with rapid marches leads their course,
From state to state Cornwallis whirls their force,
Impetuous Tarleton like a torrent pours,
And fresh battalions land along the shores;

Where, now resurgent from his captive chain,
Phillips wide storming shakes the field again;
And traitor Arnold, lured by plunder o'er,
Joins the proud powers his valor foil'd before.
 Greene views the tempest with collected soul,
And fates of empires in his bosom roll;
So small his force, where shall he lift the steel?
(Superior hosts o'er every canton wheel)
Or how behold their wanton carnage spread,
Himself stand idle and his country bleed?
Fixt in a moment's pause the general stood,
And held his warriors from the field of blood;
Then points the British legions where to steer,
Marks to their chief a rapid wild career,
Wide o'er Virginia lets him foeless roam,
To search for pillage and to find his doom,
With short-lived glory feeds his sateless flame,
But leaves the victory to a nobler name,
Gives to great Washington to meet his way,
Nor claims the honors of so bright a day.
 Now to the conquer'd south he turns his force,
Renerves the nation by his rapid course;
Forts fall around him, hosts before him fly,
And captive bands his growing train supply;
A hundred leagues of coast, in one campaign,
Return reconquer'd to their lords again.
At last Britannia's vanguard, near the strand,
Veers on her foe to make one vigorous stand.
Her gallant Stuart here amass'd from far
The veteran legions of the Georgian war,
To aid her hard-pusht powers, and quick restore
The British name to that extended shore.
He checks their flight, and chooses well their field,
Flank'd with a marsh, by lofty woods conceal'd;
Where Eutaw's fountains, tinged of old with gore,
Still murmuring swell'd amid the bones they bore,
Destined again to foul their pebbly stream,
The mournful monuments of human fame;

There Albion's columns, ranged in order bright,
Stand like a fiery wall and wait the shock of fight.
  Swift on the neighboring hill as Greene arose,
He view'd, with rapid glance, the glittering foes,
Disposed for combat all his ardent train,
To charge, change front, each echellon sustain;
Roused well their rage, superior force to prove,
Waved his bright blade and bade the onset move.
As hovering clouds, when morning beams arise,
Hang their red curtains round our eastern skies,
Unfold a space to hail the promised sun,
And catch their splendors from his rising throne;
Thus glow'd the opposing fronts, whose steely glare
Glanced o'er the shuddering interval of war.
  From Albion's left the cannonade began,
And pour'd thick thunders on Hesperia's van,
Forced in her dexter guards, that skirmisht wide
To prove what powers the forest hills might hide;
They break, fall back, with measured quickstep tread,
Form close, and flank the solid squares they led.
Now roll, with kindling haste, the long stark lines,
From wing to wing the sounding battle joins;
Batteries and field-parks and platoons of fire,
In mingled shocks their roaring blasts expire.
Each front approaching fast, with equal pace,
Devours undaunted their dividing space;
Till, dark beneath the smoke, the meeting ranks
Slope their strong bayonets, with short firm shanks
Protruded from their tubes; each bristling van,
Steel fronting steel, and man encountering man,
In dreadful silence tread. As, wrapt from sight,
The nightly ambush moves to secret fight;
So rush the raging files, and sightless close
In plunging thrust with fierce conflicting foes.
They reach, they strike, they stagger o'er the slain,
Deal doubtful blows, or closing clench their man,
Intwine their twisting limbs, the gun forego,
Wrench off the bayonet and dirk the foe;

Then struggling back, reseize the musket bare,
Club the broad breech, and headlong whirl to war.
Ranks crush on ranks with equal slaughter gored;
Warm dripping streams from every lifted sword
Stain the thin carnaged crops, who still maintain,
With mutual shocks, the vengeance of the plain.
At last where Williams fought and Campbell fell,
Unwonted strokes the British line repel.
The rout begins; the shatter'd wings afar
Roll back in haste and scatter from the war;
They drop their arms, they scour the marshy field,
Whole squadrons fall and faint battalions yield.

The great Observer, fixt in his midsky,
View'd the whole combat, saw them fall and fly:
He mark'd where Greene with every onset drove,
Saw death and victory with his presence move,
Beneath his arm saw Marion, Sumter, Gaine,
Pickens and Sumner shake the astonish'd plain;
He saw young Washington, the child of fame,
Preserve in fight the honors of his name.
Lee, Jackson, Hampton, Pinckney, matcht in might,
Roll'd on the storm and hurried fast the flight:
While numerous chiefs, that equal trophies raise,
Wrought, not unseen, the deeds of deathless praise.

As Europe now the newborn states beheld
The shock sustain of many a hard fought field;
Swift o'er the main, with high spread sails advance
Our brave auxiliars from the coast of France.
On the tall decks their curious chiefs explore,
With optic tube, our camp-encumber'd shore;
And, as the lessening wave behind them flies
Wide scenes of conflict open on their eyes.
Rochambeau foremost with his gleamy brand
Points to each field and singles every band,
Sees Washington the power of nations guide,
And longs to toil and conquer by his side.
Two brother chiefs, Viominil the name,
Brothers in birth but twins in generous fame,

Behold with stedfast eye the plains disclose,
Uncase their arms and claim the promised foes.
Biron, beneath his sail, in armor bright,
Frown'd o'er the wave impatient for the fight;
A fiery steed beside the hero stood,
And his blue blade waved forward o'er the crowd.

   With eager haste descending on the coast,
Thro the glad states they march their veteran host,
From sea-nursed Newport file o'er western roads,
Pitch many a camp, and bridge a hundred floods,
Pass the full towns, where joyful crowds admire
Their foreign speech, gay mien and gilt attire,
Applaud their generous deeds, the zeal that draws
Their swords untried in freedom's doubtful cause.
Thro Hartford plains, on Litchfield hills they gleam,
Wave their white flags o'er Hudson's loaded stream,
Band after band with Delaware's current pour,
Shade Schuylkill's wave and Elk's indented shore,
Join their new friends, where allied banners lead,
Demand the foe and bid the war proceed.

   Again Columbus turned his anxious eye
Where Britain's banner waved along the sky;
And, graced with spoils of many fields of blood,
Cornwallis boastful on a bulwark stood.
Where York and Gloster's rocky towers bestride
Their parent stream, Virginia's midmost tide,
He camp'd his hundred nations, to regain
Their force, exhausted in the long campaign;
Paused for a moment on a scene so vast,
To plan the future and review the past.
Thro vanquisht provinces and towns in flame
He mark'd his recent monuments of fame,
His checker'd marches, long and various toils,
And camp well stored with wide collected spoils.

   High glittering to the sun his hands unfold
A map new drafted on a sheet of gold;
There in delusive haste his burin graved
A country conquer'd and a race enslaved.

Its middle realm, by fairer figures known
And rich with fruits, lay bounded for his own;
Deep thro the centre spreads a branching bay,
Full sails ascend and golden rivers stray;
Bright palaces arise relieved in gold,
And gates and streets the crossing lines unfold.
James furrows o'er the plate with turgid tide,
Young Richmond roughens on his masted side;
Reviving Norfolk from her ashes springs,
A golden phenix on refulgent wings;
Potowmak's yellow waves reluctant spread,
And Vernon rears his rich and radiant head.
Tis here the chief his pointed graver stays,
The bank to burnish with a purer blaze,
Gives all his art, on this bright hill to trace
His future seat and glory of his race;
Deems his long line of lords the realm shall own,
The kings predestined to Columbia's throne.

But while his mind thus quafft its airy food,
And gazing thousands round the rampart stood,
Whom future ease and golden dreams employ,
The songs of triumph and the feast of joy;
Sudden great Washington arose in view,
And allied flags his stately steps pursue;
Gaul's veteran host and young Hesperia's pride
Bend the long march concentring at his side,
Stream over Chesapeak, like sheets of flame,
And drive tempestuous to the field of fame.

Far on the wild expanse, where ocean lies,
And scorns all confines but incumbent skies,
Scorns to retain the imprinted paths of men
To guide their wanderings or direct their ken;
Where warring vagrants, raging as they go,
Ask of the stars their way to find the foe,
Columbus saw two hovering fleets advance,
And rival ensigns o'er their pinions dance.
Graves, on the north, with Albion's flag unfurl'd,
Waves proud defiance to the watery world;

Degrasse, from southern isles, conducts his train,
And shades with Gallic sheets the moving main.
   Now Morn, unconscious of the coming fray
That soon shall storm the crystal cope of day,
Glows o'er the heavens, and with her orient breeze
Fans her fair face and curls the summer seas.
The swelling sails, as far as eye can sweep,
Look thro the skies and awe the shadowy deep,
Lead their long bending lines; and, ere they close,
To count, recognise, circumvent their foes,
Each hauls his wind, the weathergage to gain
And master all the movements of the plain;
Or bears before the breeze with loftier gait,
And, beam to beam, begins the work of fate.
   As when the warring winds, from each far pole,
Their adverse storms across the concave roll,
Thin fleecy vapors thro the expansion run,
Veil the blue vault and tremble o'er the sun,
Till the dark folding wings together drive,
And, ridged with fire and rock'd with thunder, strive:
So, hazing thro the void, at first appear
White clouds of canvass floating on the air,
Then frown the broad black decks, the sails are stay'd,
The gaping portholes cast a frightful shade,
Flames, triple tier'd, and tides of smoke, arise,
And fulminations rock the seas and skies.
   From van to rear the roaring deluge runs,
The storm disgorging from a thousand guns,
Each like a vast volcano, spouting wide
His hissing hell-dogs o'er the shuddering tide,
Whirls high his chainshot, cleaves the mast and strows
The shiver'd fragments on the staggering foes;
Whose gunwale sides with iron globes are gored,
And a wild storm of splinters sweeps the board.
Husht are the winds of heaven; no more the gale
Breaks the red rolls of smoke nor flaps the sail;
A dark dead calm continuous cloaks the glare,
And holds the clouds of sulphur on the war,

Convolving o'er the space that yawns and shines,
With frequent flash, between the laboring lines.
Nor sun nor sea nor skyborn lightning gleams,
But flaming Phlegethon's asphaltic steams
Streak the long gaping gulph; where varying glow
Carbonic curls above, blue flakes of fire below.
  Hither two hostile ships to contact run,
Both grappling, board to board and gun to gun;
Each thro the adverse ports their contents pour,
Rake the lower decks, the interior timbers bore,
Drive into chinks the illumined wads unseen,
Whose flames approach the unguarded magazine.
Above, with shrouds afoul and gunwales mann'd.
Thick halberds clash; and, closing hand to hand,
The huddling troops, infuriate from despair,
Tug at the toils of death, and perish there;
Grenados, carcasses their fragments spread,
And pikes and pistols strow the decks with dead.
Now on the Gallic board the Britons rush,
The intrepid Gauls the rash adventurers crush;
And now, to vengeance stung, with frantic air,
Back on the British maindeck roll the war.
There swells the carnage; all the tar-beat floor
Is clogg'd with spatter'd brains and glued with gore;
And down the ship's black waist, fresh brooks of blood
Course o'er their clots and tinge the sable flood.
Till War, impatient of the lingering strife
That tires and slackens with the waste of life,
Opes with engulphing gape the astonish'd wave,
And whelms the combat whole, in one vast grave.
For now the imprison'd powder caught the flames,
And into atoms whirl'd the monstrous frames
Of both the entangled ships; the vortex wide
Roars like an Etna thro the belching tide,
And blazing into heaven, and bursting high,
Shells, carriages and guns obstruct the sky;
Cords, timbers, trunks of men the welkin sweep,
And fall on distant ships, or shower along the deep.

The matcht armadas still the fight maintain,
But cautious, distant; lest the staggering main
Drive their whole lines afoul, and one dark day
Glut the proud ocean with too rich a prey.
At last, where scattering fires the cloud disclose,
Hulls heave in sight and blood the decks o'er flows;
Here from the field tost navies rise to view,
Drive back to vengeance and the roar renew,
There shatter'd ships commence their flight afar,
Tow'd thro the smoke, hard struggling from the war;
And some, half seen amid the gaping wave,
Plunge in the whirl they make, and gorge their grave.
   Soon the dark smoky volumes roll'd away,
And a long line ascended into day;
The pinions swell'd, Britannia's cross arose
And flew the terrors of triumphing foes;
When to Virginia's bay, new shocks to brave,
The Gallic powers their conquering banners wave.
Glad Chesapeak unfolds his bosom wide,
And leads their prows to York's contracting tide;
Where still dread Washington directs his way,
And seas and continents his voice obey;
While brave Cornwallis, mid the gathering host,
Perceives his glories gone, his promised empire lost.
   Columbus here with silent joy beheld
His favorite sons the fates of nations wield.
Here joyous Lincoln rose in arms again,
Nelson and Knox moved ardent o'er the plain;
Scammel alert with force unusual trod,
Prepared to seal their victory with his blood;
Cobb, Dearborn, Laurens, Tilghman, green in years
But ripe in glory, tower'd amid their peers;
Death daring Hamilton with splendor shone,
And claim'd each post of danger for his own,
Skill'd every arm in war's whole hell to wield,
An Ithacus in camp, an Ajax in the field.
   Their Gallic friends an equal ardor fires;
Brisk emulation every troop inspires;

Where Tarleton turns, with hopes of flight elate,
Brave Biron moves and drives him back to fate,
Hems in his host, to wait, on Gloster plains,
Their finish'd labors and their destined chains.

Two British forts the growing siege outflank,
Rake its wide works and awe the tide-beat bank;
Swift from the lines two chosen bands advance,
Our light arm'd scouts, the grenadiers of France;
These young Viominil conducts to fame,
And those Fayette's unerring guidance claim.
No cramm'd cartouch their belted back attires,
No grains of sleeping thunder wait their fires;
The flint, the ramrod spurn'd, away they cast;
The strong bright bayonet, imbeaded fast,
Stands beaming from the bore; with this they tread,
Nor heed from high-wall'd foes their showers of lead.
Each rival band, tho wide and distant far,
Springs simultaneous to this task of war;
For here a twofold force each hero draws,
His own proud country and the general cause;
And each with twofold energy contends,
His foes to vanquish and outstrip his friends.
They summon all their zeal, and wild and warm
O'er flaming ramparts pour the maddening storm,
The mounted cannons crush, and lead the foe
Two trains of captives to the plain below;
An equal prize each gallant troop ameeds,
Alike their numbers and alike their deeds.

A strong high citadel still thundering stood,
And stream'd her standard o'er the field of blood,
Check'd long the siege with fulminating blare,
Scorn'd all the steel and every globe of war,
Defied fell famine, heapt her growing store,
And housed in bombproof all the host she bore.
No rude assault can stretch the scale so high,
In vain the battering siege-guns round her ply;
Mortars well poized their deafening deluge rain,
Load the red skies and shake the shores in vain;

Her huge rock battlements rebound the blow,
And roll their loose crags on the men below.
 But while the fusing fireballs scorch the sky,
Their mining arts the staunch besiegers ply,
Delve from the bank of York, and gallery far,
Deep subterranean, to the mount of war;
Beneath the ditch, thro rocks and fens they go,
Scoop the dark chamber plumb beneath the foe;
There lodge their tons of powder and retire,
Mure the dread passage, wave the fatal fire,
Send a swift messenger to warn the foe
To seek his safety and the post forego.
A taunting answer comes; he dares defy
To spring the mine and all its Etnas try;
When a black miner seized the sulphur'd brand,
Shriek'd high for joy, and with untrembling hand
Touch'd quick the insidious train; lest here the chief
Should change his counsel and afford relief:
For hard the general's task, to speak the doom
That sends a thousand heroes to the tomb;
Heroes who know no wrong; who thoughtless speed
Where kings command or where their captains lead.
—Burst with the blast, the reeling mountain roars,
Heaves, labors, boils, and thro the concave pours
His flaming contents high; he chokes the air
With all his warriors and their works of war;
Guns, bastions, magazines confounded fly,
Vault wide their fresh explosions o'er the sky,
Encumber each far camp, and plough profound
With their rude fragments every neighboring ground.
 Britain's brave leader, where he sought repose,
And deem'd his hill-fort still repulsed the foes,
Starts at the astounding earthquake, and descries
His chosen veterans whirling down the skies.
Their mangled members round his balcon fall,
Scorch'd in the flames, and dash't on every wall:
Sad field of contemplation! here, ye great,
Kings, priests of God, and ministers of state,

Review your system here! behold and scan
Your own fair deeds, your benefits to man!
You will not leave him to his natural toil,
To tame these elements and till the soil,
To reap, share, tithe you what his hand has sown,
Enjoy his treasures and increase your own,
Build up his virtues on the base design'd,
The well toned harmonies of humankind.
You choose to check his toil, and band his eyes
To all that's honest and to all that's wise;
Lure with false fame, false morals and false lore,
To barter fields of corn for fields of gore,
To take by bands what single thieves would spare,
And methodise his murders into war.
 Now the prest garrison fresh danger warms;
They rush impetuous to each post of arms,
Man the long trench, each embrasure sustain,
And pour their langrage on the allied train;
Whose swift approaches, crowing on the line,
Each wing envelop and each front confine.
O'er all sage Washington his arm extends,
Points every movement, every work defends,
Bids closer quarters, bloodier strokes proceed,
New batteries blaze and heavier squadrons bleed.
Line within line fresh parallels enclose;
Here runs a zigzag, there a mantlet grows,
Round the pent foe approaching breastworks rise,
And bombs, like meteors, vault the flaming skies.
Night, with her hovering wings, asserts in vain
The shades, the silence of her rightful reign;
High roars her canopy with fiery flakes,
And War stalks wilder thro the glare he makes.
 With dire dismay the British chief beheld
The foe advance, his veterans shun the field,
Despair and slaughter where he turns his eye,
No hope in combat and no power to fly;
Degrasse victorious shakes the shadowy tide,
Imbodied nations all the champaign hide,

Fosses and batteries, growing on the sight,
Still pour new thunders and increase the fight;
Shells rain before him, rending every mound,
Crags, gunstones, balls o'er turn the tented ground,
From post to post his driven ranks retire,
The earth in crimson and the skies on fire.

Death wantons proud in this decisive round,
For here his hand its favorite victim found;
Brave Scammel perisht here. Ah! short, my friend,
Thy bright career, but glorious to its end.
Go join thy Warren's ghost, your fates compare,
His that commenced, with thine that closed the war;
Freedom, with laurel'd brow but tearful eyes,
Bewails her first and last, her twinlike sacrifice.

Now grateful truce suspends the burning war,
And groans and shouts promiscuous load the air;
When the tired Britons, where the smokes decay,
Quit their strong station and resign the day.
Slow files along the immeasurable train,
Thousands on thousands redden all the plain,
Furl their torn bandrols, all their plunder yield,
And pile their muskets on the battle field.
Their wide auxiliar nations swell the crowd,
And the coop'd navies, from the neighboring flood,
Repeat surrendering signals, and obey
The landmen's fate on this concluding day.

Cornwallis first, their late all conquering lord,
Bears to the victor chief his conquer'd sword,
Presents the burnisht hilt, and yields with pain
The gift of kings, here brandisht long in vain.
Then bow their hundred banners, trailing far
Their wearied wings from all the skirts of war.
Battalion'd infantry and squadron'd horse
Dash the silk tassel and the golden torse;
Flags from the forts and ensigns from the fleet
Roll in the dust, and at Columbia's feet
Prostrate the pride of thrones; they firm the base
Of freedom's temple, while her arms they grace.

Here Albion's crimson Cross the soil o'er spreads,
Her Lion crouches and her Thistle fades;
Indignant Erin rues her trampled Lyre,
Brunswick's pale Steed forgets his foamy fire,
Proud Hessia's Castle lies in dust o'erthrown,
And venal Anspach quits her broken Crown.

   Long trains of wheel'd arttilery shade the shore,
Quench their blue matches and forget to roar;
Along the encumber'd plain, thick planted rise
High stacks of muskets glittering to the skies,
Numerous and vast. As when the toiling swains
Heap their whole harvest on the stubbly plains,
Gerb after gerb the bearded shock expands,
Shocks, ranged in rows, hill high the burden'd lands;
The joyous master numbers all the piles,
And o'er his well earn'd crop complacent smiles:
Such growing heaps this iron harvest yield,
So tread the victors this their final field.

   Triumphant Washington, with brow serene,
Regards unmoved the exhilarating scene,
Weighs in his balanced thought the silent grief
That sinks the bosom of the fallen chief,
With all the joy that laurel crowns bestow,
A world reconquer'd and a vanquish'd foe.
Thus thro extremes of life, in every state,
Shines the clear soul, beyond all fortune great,
While smaller minds, the dupes of fickle chance,
Slight woes o'erwhelm and sudden joys entrance.
So the full sun, thro all the changing sky,
Nor blasts nor overpowers the naked eye;
Tho transient splendors, borrow'd from his light,
Glance on the mirror and destroy the sight.

   He bids brave Lincoln guide with modest air
The last glad triumph of the finish'd war;
Who sees, once more, two armies shade one plain,
The mighty victors and the captive train.

BOOK VIII

Hail, holy Peace, from thy sublime abode
Mid circling saints that grace the throne of God.
Before his arm, around our embryon earth,
Stretch'd the dim void, and gave to nature birth,
Ere morning stars his glowing chambers hung,
Or songs of gladness woke an angel's tongue,
Veil'd in the splendors of his beamful mind,
In blest repose thy placid form reclined,
Lived in his life, his inward sapience caught,
And traced and toned his universe of thought.
Borne thro the expanse with his creating voice
Thy presence bade the unfolding worlds rejoice,
Led forth the systems on their bright career,
Shaped all their curves and fashion'd every sphere,

Spaced out their suns, and round each radiant goal,
Orb over orb, compell'd their train to roll,
Bade heaven's own harmony their force combine,
Taught all their host symphonious strains to join,
Gave to seraphic harps their sounding lays,
Their joys to angels, and to men their praise.

    From scenes of blood, these verdant shores that stain,
From numerous friends in recent battle slain,
From blazing towns that scorch the purple sky,
From houseless hordes, their smoking walls that fly,
From the black prison ships, those groaning graves,
From warring fleets that vex the gory waves,
From a storm'd world, long taught thy flight to mourn,
I rise, delightful Peace, and greet thy glad return.

    For now the untuneful trump shall grate no more;
Ye silver streams, no longer swell with gore,
Bear from your war-beat banks the guilty stain
With yon retiring navies to the main.
While other views, unfolding on my eyes,
And happier themes bid bolder numbers rise;
Bring, bounteous Peace, in thy celestial throng,
Life to my soul, and rapture to my song;
Give me to trace, with pure unclouded ray,
The arts and virtues that attend thy sway,
'To see thy blissful charms, that here descend,
Thro distant realms and endless years extend.

    Too long the groans of death and battle's bray
Have rung discordant thro my turgid lay:
The drum's rude clang, the war wolf's hideous howl
Convulsed my nerves and agonised my soul,
Untuned the harp for all but misery's pains,
And chased the Muse from corse-encumber'd plains.
Let memory's balm its pious fragrance shed
On heroes' wounds and patriot warriors dead;
Accept, departed Shades, these grateful sighs,
Your fond attendants thro your homeward skies.

    And thou, my earliest friend, my Brother dear,
Thy fall untimely still renews my tear.

In youthful sports, in toils, in taste allied,
My kind companion and my faithful guide,
When death's dread summons, from our infant eyes,
Had call'd our last loved parent to the skies.
Tho young in arms, and still obscure thy name,
Thy bosom panted for the deeds of fame;
Beneath Montgomery's eye, when by thy steel
In northern wilds the frequent savage fell.
Fired by his voice, and foremost at his call,
To mount the breach or scale the flamy wall,
Thy daring hand had many a laurel gain'd,
If years had ripen'd what thy fancy feign'd.
Lamented Youth! when thy great leader bled,
Thro the same wound thy parting spirit fled,
Join'd the long train, the self-devoted band,
The gods, the saviors of their native land.

On fame's high pinnacle their names shall shine,
Unending ages greet the group divine,
Whose holy hands our banners first unfurl'd,
And conquer'd freedom for the grateful world.

And you, their peers, whose steel avenged their blood,
Whose breasts with theirs our sacred rampart stood,
Illustrious relics of a thousand fields!
To you at last the foe reluctant yields.
But tho the Muse, too prodigal of praise,
Dares with the dead your living worth to raise,
Think not, my friends, the patriot's task is done,
Or Freedom safe, because the battle's won.
Unnumber'd foes, far different arms that wield,
Wait the weak moment when she quits her shield,
To plunge in her bold breast the insidious dart,
Or pour keen poison round her thoughtless heart.
Perhaps they'll strive her votaries to divide,
From their own veins to draw the vital tide;
Perhaps, by cooler calculation shown,
Create materials to construct a throne,
Dazzle her guardians with the glare of state,
Corrupt with power, with borrow'd pomp inflate,

Bid thro the land the soft infection creep,
Whelm all her sons in one lethargic sleep,
Crush her vast empire in its brilliant birth,
And chase the goddess from the ravaged earth.
  The Dragon thus, that watch'd the Colchian fleece,
Foil'd the fierce warriors of wide-plundering Greece;
Warriors of matchless might and wondrous birth,
Jove's sceptred sons and demigods of earth.
High on the sacred tree, the glittering prize
Hangs o'er its guard, and fires the warriors' eyes;
First their hurl'd spears his spiral folds assail,
Their spears fall pointless from his flaky mail;
Onward with dauntless swords they plunge amain;
He shuns their blows, recoils his twisting train,
Darts forth his forky tongue, heaves high in air
His fiery crest, and sheds a hideous glare,
Champs, churns his poisonous juice, and hissing loud
Spouts thick the stifling tempest o'er the crowd;
Then, with one sweep of convoluted train,
Rolls back all Greece, and besoms wide the plain,
O'erturns the sons of gods, dispersing far
The pirate horde, and closes quick the war.
From his red jaws tremendous triumph roars,
Dark Euxine trembles to its distant shores,
Proud Jason starts, confounded in his might,
Leads back his peers, and dares no more the fight.
But the sly Priestess brings her opiate spell,
Soft charms that hush the triple hound of hell,
Bids Orpheus tune his all enchanting lyre,
And join to calm the guardian's sleepless ire.
Soon from the tepid ground blue vapors rise,
And sounds melodious move along the skies;
A settling tremor thro his folds extends,
His crest contracts, his rainbow neck unbends,
O'er all his hundred hoops the languor crawls,
Each curve develops, every volute falls,
His broad back flattens as he spreads the plain,
And sleep consigns him to his lifeless reign.

Flusht at the sight the pirates seize the spoil,
And ravaged Colchis rues the insidious toil.

   Yes! fellow freemen, sons of high renown,
Chant your loud peans, weave your civic crown;
But know, the goddess you've so long adored,
Tho now she scabbards your avenging sword,
Calls you to vigilance, to manlier cares,
To prove in peace the men she proved in wars:
Superior task! severer test of soul!
Tis here bold virtue plays her noblest role
And merits most of praise. The warrior's name,
Tho peal'd and chimed on all the tongues of fame,
Sounds less harmonious to the grateful mind
Than his who fashions and improves mankind.

   And what high meed your new vocation waits!
Freedom, parturient with a hundred states,
Confides them to your hand; the nascent prize
Claims all your care, your soundest wisdom tries.
Ah nurture, temper, train your infant charge,
Its force develop and its life enlarge,
Unfold each day some adolescent grace,
Some right recognise or some duty trace;
Mould a fair model for the realms of earth,
Call moral nature to a second birth,
Reach, renovate the world's great social plan,
And here commence the sober sense of man.

   For lo, in other climes and elder states,
What strange inversion all his works awaits!
From age to age, on every peopled shore,
Stalks the fell Demon of despotic power,
Sweeps in his march the mounds of art away,
Blots with his breath the trembling disk of day,
Treads down whole nations every stride he takes,
And wraps their labors in his fiery flakes.

   As Anarch erst around his regions hurl'd
The wrecks, long crush'd, of time's anterior world;
While nature mourn'd, in wild confusion tost,
Her suns extinguisht and her systems lost;

Light, life and instinct shared the dreary trance,
And gravitation fled the field of chance;
No laws remain'd of matter, motion, space;
Time lost his count, the universe his place;
Till Order came, in her cerulean robes,
And launch'd and rein'd the renovated globes,
Stock'd with harmonious worlds the vast Inane,
Archt her new heaven and fixt her boundless reign:
So kings convulse the moral frame, the base
Of all the codes that can accord the race;
And so from their broad grasp, their deadly ban,
Tis yours to snatch this earth, to raise regenerate man.
   My friends, I love your fame, I joy to raise
The high toned anthem of my country's praise;
To sing her victories, virtues, wisdom, weal,
Boast with loud voice the patriot pride I feel;
Warm, wild I sing; and, to her failing blind,
Mislead myself, perhaps mislead mankind.
Land that I love! is this the whole we owe?
Thy pride to pamper, thy fair face to show;
Dwells there no blemish where such glories shine?
And lurks no spot in that bright sun of thine?
Hark! a dread voice, with heaven-astounding strain,
Swells like a thousand thunders o'er the main,
Rolls and reverberates around thy hills,
And Hesper's heart with pangs paternal fills.
Thou hearst him not; 'tis Atlas, throned sublime,
Great brother guardian of old Afric's clime;
High o'er his coast he rears his frowning form,
O'erlooks and calms his sky-borne fields of storm,
Flings off the clouds that round his shoulders hung,
And breaks from clogs of ice his trembling tongue;
While far thro space with rage and grief he glares,
Heaves his hoar head and shakes the heaven he bears:
—Son of my sire! Oh latest brightest birth
That sprang from his fair spouse, prolific earth!
Great Hesper, say what sordid ceaseless hate
Impels thee thus to mar my elder state.

Our sire assign'd thee thy more glorious reign,
Secured and bounded by our laboring main;
That main (tho still my birthright name it bear)
Thy sails o'ershadow, thy brave children share;
I grant it thus; while air surrounds the ball,
Let breezes blow, let oceans roll for all.
But thy proud sons, a strange ungenerous race,
Enslave my tribes, and each fair world disgrace,
Provoke wide vengeance on their lawless land,
The bolt ill placed in thy forbearing hand.—
Enslave my tribes! then boast their cantons free,
Preach faith and justice, bend the sainted knee,
Invite all men their liberty to share,
Seek public peace, defy the assaults of war,
Plant, reap, consume, enjoy their fearless toil,
Tame their wild floods, to fatten still their soil,
Enrich all nations with their nurturing store,
And rake with venturous fluke each wondering shore.—
Enslave my tribes! what, half mankind imban,
Then read, expound, enforce the rights of man!
Prove plain and clear how nature's hand of old
Cast all men equal in her human mould!
Their fibres, feelings, reasoning powers the same,
Like wants await them, like desires inflame.
Thro former times with learned book they tread,
Revise past ages and rejudge the dead,
Write, speak, avenge, for ancient sufferings feel,
Impale each tyrant on their pens of steel,
Declare how freemen can a world create,
And slaves and masters ruin every state.—
Enslave my tribes! and think, with dumb disdain,
To scape this arm and prove my vengeance vain!
But look! methinks beneath my foot I ken
A few chain'd things that seem no longer men;
Thy sons perchance! whom Barbary's coast can tell
The sweets of that loved scourge they wield so well.
Link'd in a line, beneath the driver's goad,
See how they stagger with their lifted load;

The shoulder'd rock, just wrencht from off my hill
And wet with drops their straining orbs distil,
Galls, grinds them sore, along the rampart led,
And the chain clanking counts the steps they tread.
  By night close bolted in the bagnio's gloom,
Think how they ponder on their dreadful doom,
Recal the tender sire, the weeping bride,
The home, far sunder'd by a waste of tide,
Brood all the ties that once endear'd them there,
But now, strung stronger, edge their keen despair.
Till here a fouler fiend arrests their pace:
Plague, with his burning breath and bloated face,
With saffron eyes that thro' the dungeon shine,
And the black tumors bursting from the groin,
Stalks o'er the slave; who, cowering on the sod,
Shrinks from the Demon and invokes his God,
Sucks hot contagion with his quivering breath,
And, rack'd with rending torture, sinks in death.
  Nor shall these pangs atone the nation's crime;
Far heavier vengeance, in the march of time,
Attends them still; if still they dare debase
And hold inthrall'd the millions of my race;
A vengeance that shall shake the world's deep frame,
That heaven abhors, and hell might shrink to name.
Nature, long outraged, delves the crusted sphere,
And moulds the mining mischief dark and drear;
Europa too the penal shock shall find,
The rude soul-selling monsters of mankind:
  Where Alps and Andes at their bases meet,
In earth's mid caves to lock their granite feet,
Heave their broad spines, expand each breathing lobe,
And with their massy members rib the globe,
Her cauldron'd floods of fire their blast prepare;
Her wallowing womb of subterranean war
Waits but the fissure that my wave shall find,
To force the foldings of the rocky rind,
Crash your curst continent, and whirl on high
The vast avulsion vaulting thro the sky,

Fling far the bursting fragments, scattering wide
Rocks, mountains, nations o'er the swallowing tide.
Plunging and surging with alternate sweep,
They storm the day-vault and lay bare the deep,
Toss, tumble, plough their place, then slow subside,
And swell each ocean as their bulk they hide;
Two oceans dasht in one! that climbs and roars,
And seeks in vain the exterminated shores,
The deep drencht hemisphere. Far sunk from day,
It crumbles, rolls, it churns the settling sea,
Turns up each prominence, heaves every side,
To pierce once more the landless length of tide:
Till some poized Pambamarca looms at last
A dim lone island in the watery waste,
Mourns all his minor mountains wreck'd and hurl'd,
Stands the sad relic of a ruin'd world,
Attests the wrath our mother kept in store,
And rues her judgments on the race she bore.
No saving Ark around him rides the main,
Nor Dove weak-wing'd her footing finds again;
His own bald Eagle skims alone the sky,
Darts from all points of heaven her searching eye,
Kens, thro the gloom, her ancient rock of rest,
And finds her cavern'd crag, her solitary nest.
    Thus toned the Titan his tremendous knell,
And lash'd his ocean to a loftier swell;
Earth groans responsive, and with laboring woes
Leans o'er the surge and stills the storm he throws.
    Fathers and friends, I know the boding fears
Of angry genii and of rending spheres
Assail not souls like yours; whom Science bright
Thro shadowy nature leads with surer light;
For whom she strips the heavens of love and hate,
Strikes from Jove's hand the brandisht bolt of fate,
Gives each effect its own indubious cause,
Divides her moral from her physic laws,
Shows where the virtues find their nurturing food,
And men their motives to be just and good.

You scorn the Titan's threat; nor shall I strain
The powers of pathos in a task so vain
As Afric's wrongs to sing; for what avails
To harp for you these known familiar tales?
To tongue mute misery, and re-rack the soul
With crimes oft copied from that bloody scroll
Where Slavery pens her woes; tho 'tis but there
We learn the weight that mortal life can bear.
The tale might startle still the accustom'd ear,
Still shake the nerve that pumps the pearly tear,
Melt every heart, and thro the nation gain
Full many a voice to break the barbarous chain.
But why to sympathy for guidance fly,
(Her aids uncertain and of scant supply)
When your own self-excited sense affords
A guide more sure, and every sense accords?
Where strong self-interest, join'd with duty, lies,
Where doing right demands no sacrifice,
Where profit, pleasure, life-expanding fame
League their allurements to support the claim,
Tis safest there the impleaded cause to trust;
Men well instructed will be always just.

From slavery then your rising realms to save,
Regard the master, notice not the slave;
Consult alone for freemen, and bestow
Your best, your only cares, to keep them so.
Tyrants are never free; and, small and great,
All masters must be tyrants soon or late;
So nature works; and oft the lordling knave
Turns out at once a tyrant and a slave,
Struts, cringes, bullies, begs, as courtiers must,
Makes one a god, another treads in dust,
Fears all alike, and filches whom he can,
But knows no equal, finds no friend in man.

Ah! would you not be slaves, with lords and kings,
Then be not masters; there the danger springs.
The whole crude system that torments this earth,
Of rank, privation, privilege of birth,

False honor, fraud, corruption, civil jars,
The rage of conquest and the curse of wars,
Pandora's total shower, all ills combined
That erst o'erwhelm'd and still distress mankind,
Box'd up secure in your deliberate hand,
Wait your behest, to fix or fly this land.
    Equality of Right is nature's plan;
And following nature is the march of man.
Whene'er he deviates in the least degree,
When, free himself, he would be more than free,
The baseless column, rear'd to bear his bust,
Falls as he mounts, and whelms him in the dust.
    See Rome's rude sires, with autocratic gait,
Tread down their tyrant and erect their state;
Their state secured, they deem it wise and brave
That every freeman should command a slave,
And, flusht with franchise of his camp and town,
Rove thro the world and hunt the nations down;
Master and man the same vile spirit gains,
Rome chains the world, and wears herself the chains.
    Mark modern Europe with her feudal codes,
Serfs, villains, vassals, nobles, kings and gods,
All slaves of different grades, corrupt and curst
With high and low, for senseless rank athirst,
Wage endless wars; not fighting to be free,
But *cujum pecus*, whose base herd they'll be.
    Too much of Europe, here transplanted o'er,
Nursed feudal feelings on your tented shore,
Brought sable serfs from Afric, call'd it gain,
And urged your sires to forge the fatal chain.
But now, the tents o'erturn'd, the war dogs fled,
Now fearless Freedom rears at last her head
Matcht with celestial Peace,—my friends, beware
To shade the splendors of so bright a pair;
Complete their triumph, fix their firm abode,
Purge all privations from your liberal code,
Restore their souls to men, give earth repose,
And save your sons from slavery, wars and woes.

Based on its rock of Right your empire lies,
On walls of wisdom let the fabric rise;
Preserve your principles, their force unfold,
Let nations prove them and let kings behold.
EQUALITY, your first firm-grounded stand;
Then FREE ELECTION; then your FEDERAL BAND;
This holy Triad should forever shine
The great compendium of all rights divine,
Creed of all schools, whence youths by millions draw
Their themes of right, their decalogues of law;
Till men shall wonder (in these codes inured)
How wars were made, how tyrants were endured.

Then shall your works of art superior rise,
Your fruits perfume a larger length of skies,
Canals careering climb your sunbright hills,
Vein the green slopes and strow their nurturing rills,
Thro tunnel'd heights and sundering ridges glide,
Rob the rich west of half Kenhawa's tide,
Mix your wide climates, all their stores confound,
And plant new ports in every midland mound.
Your lawless Mississippi, now who slimes
And drowns and desolates his waste of climes,
Ribb'd with your dikes, his torrent shall restrain,
And ask your leave to travel to the main;
Won from his wave while rising cantons smile,
Rear their glad nations and reward their toil.

Thus Nile's proud flood to human hands of yore
Raised and resign'd his tide-created shore,
Call'd from his Ethiop hills their hardy swains,
And waved their harvests o'er his newborn plains;
Earth's richest realm from his tamed current sprung;
There nascent science toned her infant tongue,
Taught the young arts their tender force to try,
To state the seasons and unfold the sky;
Till o'er the world extended and refined,
They rule the destinies of humankind.

Now had Columbus well enjoy'd the sight
Of armies vanquisht and of fleets in flight,

From all Hesperia's heaven the darkness flown,
And colon crowds to sovereign sages grown.
To cast new glories o'er the changing clime,
The guardian Power reversed the flight of time,
Roll'd back the years that led their course before,
Stretch'd out immense the wild uncultured shore;
Then shifts the total scene, and rears to view
Arts and the men that useful arts pursue.
As o'er the canvass when the painter's mind
Glows with a future landscape well design'd,
While Panorama's wondrous aid he calls,
To crowd whole realms within his circling walls,
Lakes, fields and forests, ports and navies rise,
A new creation to his kindling eyes;
He smiles o'er all; and in delightful strife
The pencil moves and calls the whole to life.
So while Columbia's patriarch stood sublime,
And saw rude nature clothe the trackless clime;
The green banks heave, the winding currents pour,
The bays and harbors cleave the yielding shore,
The champaigns spread, the solemn groves arise,
And the rough mountains lengthen round the skies;
Thro' all their bounds he traced, with skilful ken,
The unform'd seats and future walks of men;
Mark'd where the field should bloom, the pennon play,
Great cities grow and empires claim their sway;
When, sudden waked by Hesper's waving hand,
They rose obedient round the cultured land.

    In western tracts, where still the wildmen tread,
From sea to sea an inland commerce spread;
On the dim streams and thro the gloomy grove
The trading bands their cumbrous burdens move;
Furs, peltry, drugs, and all the native store
Of midland realms descended to the shore.

    Where summer suns, along the northern coast,
With feeble force dissolve the chains of frost,
Prolific waves the scaly nations trace,
And tempt the toils of man's laborious race.

Tho rich Brazilian strands, beneath the tide,
Their shells of pearl and sparkling pebbles hide,
While for the gaudy prize, a venturous train
Plunge the dark deep and brave the surging main,
Drag forth the shining gewgaws into air,
To stud a sceptre or emblaze a star;
Far wealthier stores these genial tides display,
And works less dangerous with their spoils repay.
The Hero saw the hardy crews advance,
Cast the long line and aim the barbed lance;
Load the deep floating barks, and bear abroad
To every land the life-sustaining food;
Renascent swarms by nature's care supplied,
Repeople still the shoals and fin the fruitful tide.
    Where southern streams thro broad savannas bend,
The rice-clad vales their verdant rounds extend;
Tobago's plant its leaf expanding yields,
The maize luxuriant clothes a thousand fields;
Steeds, herds and flocks o'er northern regions rove,
Embrown the hill and wanton thro the grove.
The woodlands wide their sturdy honors bend,
The pines, the liveoaks to the shores descend,
There couch the keels, the crooked ribs arise,
Hulls heave aloft and mastheads mount the skies;
Launcht on the deep o'er every wave they fly,
Feed tropic isles and Europe's looms supply.
    To nurse the arts and fashion freedom's lore
Young schools of science rise along the shore;
Great without pomp their modest walls expand,
Harvard and Yale and Princeton grace the land,
Penn's student halls his youths with gladness greet,
On James's bank Virginian Muses meet,
Manhattan's mart collegiate domes command,
Bosom'd in groves, see growing Dartmouth stand;
Bright o'er its realm reflecting solar fires,
On yon tall hill Rhode Island's seat aspires.
    Thousands of humbler name around them rise,
Where homebred freedmen seize the solid prize;

Fixt in small spheres, with safer beams to shine,
They reach the useful and refuse the fine,
Found, on its proper base, the social plan,
The broad plain truths, the common sense of man,
His obvious wants, his mutual aids discern,
His rights familiarize, his duties learn,
Feel moral fitness all its force dilate,
Embrace the village and comprise the state.
Each rustic here who turns the furrow'd soil,
The maid, the youth that ply mechanic toil,
In equal rights, in useful arts inured,
Know their just claims, and see their claims secured;
They watch their delegates, each law revise,
Its faults designate and its merits prize,
Obey, but scrutinize; and let the test
Of sage experience prove and fix the best.
  Here, fired by virtue's animating flame,
The preacher's task persuasive sages claim,
To mould religion to the moral mind,
In bands of peace to harmonize mankind,
To life, to light, to promised joys above
The soften'd soul with ardent hope to move.
No dark intolerance blinds the zealous throng,
No arm of power attendant on their tongue;
Vext Inquisition, with her flaming brand,
Shuns their mild march, nor dares approach the land.
Tho different creeds their priestly robes denote,
Their orders various and their rites remote,
Yet one their voice, their labors all combined,
Lights of the world and friends of humankind.
So the bright galaxy o'er heaven displays
Of various stars the same unbounded blaze;
Where great and small their mingling rays unite,
And earth and skies exchange the friendly light.
  And lo, my son, that other sapient band,
The torch of science flaming in their hand!
Thro nature's range their searching souls aspire,
Or wake to life the canvass and the lye.

Fixt in sublimest thought, behold them rise
World after world unfolding to their eyes,
Lead, light, allure them thro the total plan,
And give new guidance to the paths of man.

   Yon meteor-mantled hill see Franklin tread,
Heaven's awful thunders rolling o'er his head;
Convolving clouds the billowy skies deform,
And forky flames emblaze the blackening storm.
See the descending streams around him burn,
Glance on his rod and with his finger turn;
He bids conflicting fulminants expire
The guided blast, and holds the imprison'd fire.
No more, when doubling storms the vault o'erspread,
The livid glare shall strike thy race with dread,
Nor towers nor temples, shuddering with the sound,
Sink in the flames and shake the sheeted ground.
His well tried wires, that every tempest wait,
Shall teach mankind to ward the bolts of fate,
With pointed steel o'ertop the trembling spire,
And lead from untouch'd walls the harmless fire;
Fill'd with his fame while distant climes rejoice,
Wherever lightning shines or thunder rears its voice.

   And see sage Rittenhouse, with ardent eye,
Lift the long tube and pierce the starry sky;
Clear in his view the circling planets roll,
And suns and satellites their course control.
He marks what laws the widest wanderers bind,
Copies creation in his forming mind,
Sees in his hall the total semblance rise,
And mimics there the labors of the skies.
There student youths without their tubes behold
The spangled heavens their mystic maze unfold,
And crowded schools their cheerful chambers grace
With all the spheres that cleave the vast of space.

   To guide the sailor in his wandering way,
See Godfrey's glass reverse the beams of day.
His lifted quadrant to the eye displays
From adverse skies the counteracting rays;

And marks, as devious sails bewilder'd roll,
Each nice gradation from the stedfast pole.
   West with his own great soul the canvass warms,
Creates, inspires, impassions human forms,
Spurns critic rules, and seizing safe the heart,
Breaks down the former frightful bounds of Art;
Where ancient manners, with exclusive reign,
From half mankind withheld her fair domain.
He calls to life each patriot, chief or sage,
Garb'd in the dress and drapery of his age.
Again bold Regulus to death returns,
Again her falling Wolfe Britannia mourns;
Lahogue, Boyne, Cressy, Nevilcross demand
And gain fresh lustre from his copious hand;
His Lear stalks wild with woes, the gods defies,
Insults the tempest and outstorms the skies;
Edward in arms to frowning combat moves,
Or, won to pity by the queen he loves,
Spares the devoted *Six*, whose deathless deed
Preserves the town his vengeance doom'd to bleed.
   With rival force, see Copley's pencil trace
The air of action and the charms of face.
Fair in his tints unfold the scenes of state,
The senate listens and the peers debate;
Pale consternation every heart appals,
In act to speak, when death-struck Chatham falls.
He bids dread Calpe cease to shake the waves,
While Elliott's arm the host of Bourbon saves;
O'er sail-wing'd batteries sinking in the flood,
Mid flames and darkness, drench'd in hostile blood,
Britannia's sons extend their generous hand
To rescue foes from death, and bear them to the land.
   Fired with the martial deeds that bathed in gore
His brave companions on his native shore,
Trumbull with daring hand their fame recalls;
He shades with night Quebec's beleagured walls,
Thro flashing flames, that midnight war supplies,
The assailants yield, their great Montgomery dies.

On Bunker height, thro floods of hostile fire,
His Putnam toils till all the troops retire,
His Warren, pierced with balls, at last lies low,
And leaves a victory to the wasted foe.
Britannia too his glowing tint shall claim,
To pour new splendor on her Calpean fame;
He leads her bold sortie, and from their towers
O'erturns the Gallic and Iberian powers.
　　See rural seats of innocence and ease,
High tufted towers and walks of waving trees,
The white waves dashing on the craggy shores,
Meandring streams and meads of mingled flowers,
Where nature's sons their wild excursions tread,
In just design from Taylor's pencil spread.
　　Stuart and Brown the moving portrait raise,
Each rival stroke the force of life conveys;
Heroes and beauties round their tablets stand,
And rise unfading from their plastic hand;
Each breathing form preserves its wonted grace,
And all the soul stands speaking in the face.
　　Two kindred arts the swelling statue heave,
Wake the dead wax, and teach the stone to live.
While the bold chisel claims the rugged strife,
To rouse the sceptred marble into life,
Wee Wright's fair hands the livelier fire control,
In waxen forms she breathes impassion'd soul;
The pencil'd tint o'er moulded substance glows,
And different powers the peerless art compose.
Grief, rage and fear beneath her fingers start,
Roll the wild eye and pour the bursting heart;
The world's dead fathers wait her wakening call,
And distant ages fill the storied hall.
　　To equal fame ascends thy tuneful throng,
The boast of genius and the pride of song;
Caught from the cast of every age and clime,
Their lays shall triumph o'er the lapse of time.
　　With lynx-eyed glance thro nature far to pierce,
With all the powers and every charm of verse,

Each science opening in his ample mind,
His fancy glowing and his taste refined,
See Trumbull lead the train. His skilful hand
Hurls the keen darts of satire round the land.
Pride, knavery, dullness feel his mortal stings,
And listening virtue triumphs while he sings;
Britain's foil'd sons, victorious now no more,
In guilt retiring from the wasted shore,
Strive their curst cruelties to hide in vain;
The world resounds them in his deathless strain.
    On wings of faith to elevate the soul
Beyond the bourn of earth's benighted pole,
For Dwight's high harp the epic Muse sublime
Hails her new empire in the western clime.
Tuned from the tones by seers seraphic sung,
Heaven in his eye and rapture on his tongue,
His voice revives old Canaan's promised land,
The long-fought fields of Jacob's chosen band.
In Hanniel's fate, proud faction finds its doom,
Ai's midnight flames light nations to their tomb,
In visions bright supernal joys are given,
And all the dark futurities of heaven.
    While freedom's cause his patriot bosom warms,
In counsel sage, nor inexpert in arms,
See Humphreys glorious from the field retire,
Sheathe the glad sword and string the soothing lyre;
That lyre which erst, in hours of dark despair,
Roused the sad realms to finish well the war.
O'er fallen friends, with all the strength of woe,
Fraternal sighs in his strong numbers flow;
His country's wrongs, her duties, dangers, praise,
Fire his full soul and animate his lays:
Wisdom and War with equal joy shall own
So fond a votary and so brave a son.

THE HASTY PUDDING

A Poem in Three Cantos.

Written at Chambery in Savoy, January, 1793,

Omne tulit punctum qui miscuit utile dulci,
He makes a good breakfast who mixes pudding with molasses

To Mrs. Washington.

MADAM:—A simplicity in diet, whether it be considered with reference to the happiness of individuals or the prosperity of a nation, is of more consequence than we are apt to imagine. In recommending so great and necessary a virtue to the rational part of mankind, I wish it were in my power to do it in such a manner as would be likely to gain their attention. I am sensible that it is one of those subjects in which example has infinitely more power than the most convincing arguments, or the highest charms of poetry. Goldsmith's *Deserted Village*, though possessing these two advantages in a greater degree than any other work of the kind, has not prevented villages in England from being deserted. The apparent interest of the rich individuals, who form the taste as well as the laws in that country, has been against him; and with that interest it has been vain to contend.

The vicious habits which in this little piece I endeavor to combat, seem to me not so difficult to cure. No class of people has any interest in supporting them, unless it be the interest which certain families may feel in vieing with each other in sumptuous entertainments. There may indeed be some instances of depraved appetites which no arguments will conquer; but these must be rare. There are very few persons but would always prefer a plain dish for themselves, and would prefer it likewise for their guests, if there were no risk of reputation in the case. This difficulty can only be removed by example; and the example should proceed from those whose situation enables them to take the lead in forming the manners of a nation. Persons of this description in America,

I should hope, are neither above nor below the influence of truth and reason when conveyed in language suited to the subject.

Whether the manner I have chosen to address my arguments to them be such as to promise any success, is what I cannot decide. But I certainly had hopes of doing some good, or I should not have taken the pains of putting so many rhymes together; and much less should I have ventured to place your name at the head of these observations.

Your situation commands the respect and your character the affections of a numerous people. These circumstances impose a duty upon you, which I believe you discharge to your own satisfaction and that of others. The example of your domestic virtues has doubtless a great effect among your countrywomen. I only wish to rank *simplicity of diet* among the virtues. In that case it will certainly be cherished by you, and I should hope more esteemed by others than it is at present.

THE AUTHOR.

THE HASTY PUDDING [1]

CANTO I

Ye Alps audacious, through the heavens that rise,
To cramp the day and hide me from the skies;
Ye Gallic flags, that o'er their heights unfurled,
Bear death to kings, and freedom to the world,
I sing not you. A softer theme I choose,
A virgin theme, unconscious of the Muse,
But fruitful, rich, well suited to inspire
The purest frenzy of poetic fire.

Despise it not, ye bards to terror steel'd,
Who hurl your thunders round the epic field;
Nor ye who strain your midnight throats to sing
Joys that the vineyard and the still-house bring;
Or on some distant fair your notes employ,

[1] The notes in this poem were written by the author.

And speak of raptures that you ne'er enjoy.
I sing the sweets I know, the charms I feel,
My morning incense, and my evening meal,
The sweets of Hasty-Pudding. Come, dear bowl,
Glide o'er my palate, and inspire my soul.
The milk beside thee, smoking from the kine,
Its substance mingled, married in with thine,
Shall cool and temper thy superior heat,
And save the pains of blowing while I eat.

   Oh! could the smooth, the emblematic song
Flow like thy genial juices o'er my tongue,
Could those mild morsels in my numbers chime,
And as they roll in substance, roll in rhyme,
No more thy awkward, unpoetic name
Should shun the muse, or prejudice thy fame;
But rising grateful to the accustom'd ear,
All bards should catch it, and all realms revere!

   Assist me first with pious toil to trace
Through wrecks of time, thy lineage and thy race;
Declare what lovely squaw, in days of yore,
Ere great Columbus sought thy native shore
First gave thee to the world; her works of fame
Have lived indeed, but lived without a name.
Some tawny Ceres, goddess of her days,
First learn'd with stones to crack the well dried maize,
Through the rough sieve to shake the golden shower,
In boiling water stir the yellow flour:
The yellow flour, bestrew'd and stirr'd with haste,
Swells in the flood and thickens to a paste,
Then puffs and wallops, rises to the brim,
Drinks the dry knobs that on the surface swim;
The knobs at last the busy ladle breaks,
And the whole mass its true consistence takes.

   Could but her sacred name, unknown so long,
Rise, like her labors, to the son of song,
To her, to them, I'd consecrate my lays,
And blow her pudding with the breath of praise.
If 'twas Oella whom I sang before,

I'd here ascribe her one great virtue more.
Nor through the rich Peruvian realms alone
The fame of Sol's sweet daughter should be known,
But o'er the world's wide clime should live secure,
Far as his rays extend, as long as they endure.

Dear Hasty-Pudding, what unpromised joy
Expands my heart, to meet thee in Savoy!
Doom'd o'er the world through devious paths to roam,
Each clime my country, and each house my home,
My soul is soothed, my cares have found an end,
I greet my long lost, unforgotten friend.

For thee through Paris, that corrupted town,
How long in vain I wandered up and down,
Where shameless Bacchus, with his drenching hoard,
Cold from his cave usurps the morning board.
London is lost in smoke and steep'd in tea;
No Yankee there can lisp the name of thee;
The uncouth word, a libel on the town,
Would call a proclamation from the crown.*
From climes oblique, that fear the sun's full rays,
Chilled in their fogs, exclude the generous maize:
A grain whose rich, luxuriant growth requires
Short, gentle showers and bright, ethereal fires.

But here, though distant from our native shore,
With mutual glee we meet and laugh once more,
The same! I know thee by that yellow face,
That strong complexion of true Indian race,
Which time can never change, nor soil impair,
Nor Alpine snows, nor Turkey's morbid air;
For endless years, through every mild domain,
Where grows the maize, there thou art sure to reign.

But man, more fickle, the bold license claims,
In different realms to give thee different names.
Thee, the soft nations round the warm Levant
Polenta call, the French, of course, *Polente*.

* A certain king, at the time when this was written, was publishing
proclamations to prevent American principles from being propagated
in his country

E'en in thy native regions, how I blush
To hear the Pennsylvanians call thee *Mush!*
On Hudson's banks, while men of Belgic spawn
Insult and eat thee by the name Suppawn,
All spurious appellations, void of truth;
I've better known thee from my earliest youth:
Thy name is *Hasty-Pudding!* thus my sire
Was wont to greet thee fuming from the fire;
And while he argued in thy just defence
With logic clear, he thus explained the sense:—
"In *haste* the boiling cauldron, o'er the blaze,
Receives and cooks the ready powdered maize;
In *haste* 'tis served, and then in equal *haste*,
With cooling milk, we make the sweet repast.
No carving to be done, no knife to grate
The tender ear, and wound the stony plate;
But the smooth spoon, just fitted to the lip,
And taught with art the yielding mass to dip,
By frequent journeys to the bowl well stored,
Performs the hasty honors of the board."
Such is thy name, significant and clear,
A name, a sound to every Yankee dear,
But most to me, whose heart and palate chaste
Preserve my pure hereditary taste.

There are who strive to stamp with disrepute
The luscious food, because it feeds the brute;
In tropes of high-strain'd wit, while gaudy prigs
Compare thy nursling man, to pamper'd pigs;
With sovereign scorn I treat the vulgar jest,
Nor fear to share thy bounties with the beast.
What though the generous cow gives me to quaff
The milk nutritious; am I then a calf?
Or can the genius of the noisy swine,
Though nursed on pudding, claim a kin to mine?
Sure the sweet song, I fashion to thy praise,
Runs more melodious than the notes they raise.

My song resounding in its grateful glee,
No merit claims: I praise myself in thee.

My father loved thee through his length of days!
For thee his fields were shaded o'er with maize;
From thee what health, what vigor he possess'd,
Ten sturdy freemen from his loins attest;
Thy constellation ruled my natal morn,
And all my bones were made of Indian corn.
Delicious grain! whatever form it take,
To roast or boil, to smother or to bake,
In every dish 'tis welcome still to me,
But most, my *Hasty-Pudding*, most in thee.

　　Let the green succotash with thee contend,
Let beans and corn their sweetest juices blend,
Let butter drench them in its yellow tide,
And a long slice of bacon grace their side;
Not all the plate, how famed soe'er it be,
Can please my palate like a bowl of thee.

　　Some talk of Hoe-Cake, fair Virginia's pride,
Rich Johnny-Cake, this mouth has often tried;
Both please me well, their virtues much the same,
Alike their fabric, as allied their fame,
Except in dear New England, where the last
Receives a dash of pumpkin in the paste,
To give it sweetness and improve the taste.
But place them all before me, smoking hot,
The big, round dumpling, rolling from the pot,
The pudding of the bag, whose quivering breast,
With suet lined, leads on the Yankee feast,
The Charlotte brown, within whose crusty sides
A belly soft the pulpy apple hides;
The yellow bread whose face like amber glows,
And all the Indian that the bake-pan knows,—
Ye tempt me not, my fav'rite greets my eyes,
To that loved bowl my spoon by instinct flies.

CANTO II

　　To mix the food by vicious rules of art,
To kill the stomach and to sink the heart,

To make mankind to social virtue sour,
Cram o'er each dish and be what they devour;
For this the Kitchen Muse first framed her book,
Commanding sweets to stream from every cook;
Children no more their antic gambols tried,
And friends to physic wondered why they died.

Not so the Yankee—his abundant feast,
With simples furnished and with plainness drest,
A numerous offspring gathers round the board,
And cheers alike the servant and the lord;
Whose well-bought hunger prompts the joyous taste
And health attends them from the short repast.

While the full pail rewards the milk-maid's toil,
The mother sees the morning cauldron boil;
To stir the pudding next demands their care;
To spread the table and the bowls prepare;
To feed the children as their portions cool,
And comb their heads and send them off to school.

Yet may the simplest dish some rules impart,
For nature scorns not all the aids of art.
E'en *Hasty-Pudding*, purest of all food,
May still be bad, indifferent, or good,
As sage experience the short process guides,
Or want of skill, or want of care presides.
Whoe'er would form it on the surest plan,
To rear the child and long sustain the man;
To shield the morals while it mends the size,
And all the powers of every food supplies,
Attend the lessons that the Muse shall bring,
Suspend your spoons, and listen while I sing.

But since, O man! thy life and health demand
Not food alone but labor from thy hand,
First in the field, beneath the sun's strong rays,
Ask of thy Mother Earth the needful maize;
She loves the race that courts her yielding soil,
And gives her bounties to the sons of toil.

When now the ox, obedient to thy call,
Repays the loan that filled the winter stall,

Pursue his traces o'er the furrow'd plain,
And plant in measur'd hills the golden grain.
But when the tender germ begins to shoot,
And the green spire declares the sprouting root,
Then guard your nursling from each greedy foe,
The insidious worm, the all-devouring crow.
A little ashes, sprinkled round the spire,
Soon steep'd in rain, will bid the worm retire;
The feather'd robber with his hungry maw
Swift flies the field before your man of straw,
A frightful image, such as schoolboys bring,
When met to burn the pope, or hang the king.

    Thrice in the season, through each verdant row
Wield the strong ploughshare and the faithful hoe:
The faithful hoe; a double task that takes,
To till the summer corn and roast the winter cakes.

    Slow springs the blade while check'd by chilling rains,
E'er yet the sun the seat of Cancer gains;
But when his fiercest fires emblaze the land,
Then start the juices, then the roots expand;
Then, like a column of Corinthian mould,
The stalk struts upward and the leaves unfold;
The busy branches all the ridges fill,
Entwine their arms, and kiss from hill to hill.
Here cease to vex them, all your cares are done:
Leave the last labors to the parent sun;
Beneath his genial smiles, the well-drest field,
When autumn calls, a plenteous crop shall yield.

    Now the strong foliage bears the standards high,
And shoots the tall top-gallants to the sky;
The suckling ears their silky fringes bend,
And pregnant grown, their swelling coats distend;
The loaded stalk, while still the burthen grows,
O'erhangs the space that runs between the rows.
High as a hop-field waves the silent grove,
A safe retreat for little thefts of love,
When the fledged roasting-ears invite the maid,
To meet her swain beneath the new-formed shade;

His generous hand unloads the cumbrous hill,
And the green spoils her ready basket fill;
Small compensation for the two-fold bliss,
The promised wedding and the present kiss.
　Slight depredations these: but now the moon
Calls from his hollow tree the sly raccoon;
And while by night he bears his prize away,
The bolder squirrel labors through the day.
Both thieves alike, but provident of time—
A virtue rare that almost hides their crime.
Then let them steal the little stores they can,
And fill their granaries from the toils of man;
We've one advantage where they take no part:
With all their wiles they ne'er have found the art
To boil the *Hasty-Pudding;* here we shine
Superior far to tenants of the pine;
This envied boon to man shall still belong,
Unshared by them in substance or in song.
　At last the closing season browns the plain,
And ripe October gathers in the grain;
Deep loaded carts the spacious corn-house fill,
The sack distended marches to the mill;
The lab'ring mill beneath the burthen groans,
And showers the future pudding from the stones;
Till the glad housewife greets the powder'd gold,
And the new crop exterminates the old.
Ah! who can sing what every wight must feel,
The joy that enters with the bag of meal.
A general jubilee pervades the house,
Wakes every child and gladdens every mouse.

CANTO III

　The days grow short; but though the falling sun
To the glad swain proclaims his day's work done,
Night's pleasing shades his various tasks prolong,
And yield new subjects to my various song.
For now, the corn-house filled, the harvest home,

The invited neighbors to the *Husking* come;
A frolic scene, where work, and mirth, and play,
Unite their charms to chase the hours away.

Where the huge heap lies centred in the hall,
The lamp suspended from the cheerful wall,
Brown corn-fed nymphs, and strong hard-handed **beaus,**
Alternate ranged, extend in circling rows,
Assume their seats, the solid mass attack;
The dry husks rustle, and the corn-cobs crack;
The song, the laugh, alternate notes resound,
And the sweet cider trips in silence round.

The laws of husking every wight can tell—
And sure no laws he ever keeps so well:
For each red ear a general kiss he gains,
With each smut ear he smuts the luckless swains;
But when to some sweet maid a prize is cast,
Red as her lips and taper as her waist,
She walks the round, and culls one favored beau,
Who leaps, the luscious tribute to bestow.
Various the sport as are the wits and brains
Of well pleased lasses and contending swains;
Till the vast mound of corn is swept away,
And he that gets the last ear wins the day.

Meanwhile the housewife urges all her care,
The well-earned feast to hasten and prepare.
The sifted meal already waits her hand,
The milk is strained, the bowls in order stand,
The fire flames high; and, as a pool (that takes
The headlong stream that o'er the mill-dam breaks)
Foams, roars, and rages, with incessant toils,
So the vexed cauldron rages, roars and boils.

First with clean salt she seasons well the food,
Then strews the flour and thickens all the flood.
Long o'er the simmering fire she lets it stand—
To stir it well demands a stronger hand:
The husband takes his turn, and round and round
The adlle flies; at last the toil is crown'd;

When to the board the thronging huskers pour,
And take their seats as at the corn before.
  I leave them to their feast.   There still belong
More useful matters to my faithful song;
For rules there are, though ne'er unfolded yet,
Nice rules and wise, how pudding should be eat.
  Some with molasses grace the luscious treat,
And mix, like bards, the useful and the sweet.
A wholesome dish, and well deserving praise,
A great resource in those bleak wintry days,
When the chilled earth lies buried deep in snow,
And raging Boreas dries the shivering cow.
  Blest cow! thy praise shall still my notes employ,
Great source of health, the only source of joy,
Mother of Egypt's god;—but sure, for me,
Were I to leave my God, I'd worship thee.
How oft thy teats these pious hands have pressed!
How oft thy bounties proved my only feast!
How oft I've fed thee with my favorite grain!
And roared, like thee, to see thy children slain!
  Ye swains who know her various worth to prize,
Ah! house her well from Winter's angry skies.
Potatoes, pumpkins, should her sadness cheer,
Corn from your crib, and mashes from your beer;
When spring returns, she'll well acquit the loan,
And nurse at once your infants and her own.
  Milk then with pudding, I should always choose;
To this in future I confine my Muse,
Till she, in haste, some further hints unfold,
Good for the young, nor useless to the old.
First in your bowl the milk abundant take,
Then drop with care along the silver lake
Your flakes of pudding; these, at first, will hide
Their little bulk beneath the swelling tide;
But when their growing mass no more can sink,
When the soft island looms above the brink,
Then check your hand; you've got the portion due,
So taught my Sire, and what he taught is true.

There is a choice in spoons. Though small appear
The nice distinction, yet to me 'tis clear.
The deep-bowled Gallic spoon, contrived to scoop
In ample draughts the thin diluted soup,
Performs not well in those substantial things,
Whose mass adhesive to the metal clings;
Where the strong labial muscles must embrace,
The gentle curve, and sweep the hollow space.
With ease to enter and discharge the freight,
A bowl less concave, but still more dilate,
Becomes the pudding best. The shape, the size,
A secret rests, unknown to vulgar eyes;
Experienced feeders can alone impart
A rule so much above the lore of art.
These tuneful lips, that thousand spoons have tried,
With just precision could the point decide.
Though not in song; the Muse but poorly shines
In cones and cubes, and geometric lines,
Yet the true form, as near as she can tell,
Is that small section of a goose-egg shell
Which in two equal portions shall divide
The distance from the centre to the side.

Fear not to slaver; 'tis no deadly sin:—
Like the free Frenchman, from your joyous chin
Suspend the ready napkin; or, like me,
Poise with one hand your bowl upon your knee;
Just in the zenith your wise head project,
Your full spoon, rising in a line direct,
Bold as a bucket, heed no drops that fall,
The wide-mouthed bowl will surely catch them all! *

* There are various ways of preparing and eating it; with molasses, butter, sugar, cream, and fried. Why so excellent a thing cannot be eaten alone? Nothing is perfect alone, even man who boasts of so much perfection is nothing without his fellow substance. In eating, beware of the lurking heat that lies deep in the mass; dip your spoon gently, take shallow dips and cool it by degrees. It is sometimes necessary to blow. This is indicated by certain signs which every experienced feeder knows. They should be taught to young begin-

THE CONSPIRACY OF KINGS [1]

SUPPOSED TO HAVE BEEN WRITTEN IN THE YEAR 1792

ETERNAL TRUTH, thy trump undaunted lend,
People and priests and courts and kings, attend:
While, borne on western gales (from that far shore
Where justice reigns, and tyrants tread no more)
Th' unwonted voice, that no dissuasion awes,
That fears no frown, and seeks no blind applause,
Shall tell the bliss that Freedom sheds abroad,
The rights of nature and the gift of God.
Think not, ye knaves, whom meanness stiles the Great,
Drones of the Church, and harpies of the State,—
Ye, whose curst fires, for blood and plunder fam'd,
Sultans or kings or czars or emp'rors nam'd,
Taught the deluded world their claims to own,
And raise the crested reptiles to a throne,—
Ye who pretend to your dark host was given
The lamp of life, the mystic keys of heaven;
Whose impious arts, with magic spells, began
When shades of ign'rance veil'd the race of man;
Who change, from age to age, the sly deceit,
As Science beams, and Virtue learns the cheat;
Tyrants of double powers, the soul that blind,
To rob, to scourge, and brutalize mankind,—

ners. I have known a child's tongue blistered for want of this attention, and the schooldame would insist that the poor thing had told
a lie. A mistake: the falsehood was in the faithless pudding. A
prudent mother will cool it for her child with her own sweet breath.
The husband, seeing this, pretends his own wants blowing too from
the same lips. A sly deceit of love. She knows the cheat, but feign-
ing ignorance, lends her pouting lips and gives a gentle blast, which
warms the husband's heart more than it cools his pudding."

[1] The notes in this poem were written by the author.

Think not I come to croak, with omen'd yell,
The dire damnations of your future hell;
To bend a bigot or reform a knave,
By op'ning all the scenes beyond the grave.
I know your crested souls: while one defies,
In sceptic scorn, the vengeance of the skies,
The other boasts,—"I ken thee, Power divine,
"But fear thee not; th' avenging bolt is mine."
   No! 'tis the present world that prompts the song;
The world we see; the world that feels the wrong,
The world of men, whose arguments ye know,
Of men, long curb'd to servitude and woe;
Men, rous'd from sloth, by indignation stung,
Their strong hands loos'd, and found their fearless tongue;
Whose voice of fire, whose deep-descending steel,
Shall speak to souls, and teach dull nerves to feel.
   Think not—(ah no! the weak delusion shun;
Burke leads you wrong, the world is not his own)
Indulge not once the thought, the vapory dream,
The fool's repast, the madman's thread-bare theme,
That nations, rising in the light of truth,
Strong with new life and pure regen'rate youth,
Will shrink from toils so splendidly begun,
Their bliss abandon and their glory shun;
Betray the trust by Heaven's own hand consign'd,
The great concentred stake, the interest of man-kind.
   Ye speak of kings combin'd, some league that draws
Europe's whole force, to save your sinking cause;
Of fancy'd hosts by myriads that advance,
To crush the untry'd pow'r of new-born France.
Misguided men! these idle tales despise;
Let one bright ray of reason strike your eyes;
Show me your kings, the sceptred horde parade,—
See their pomp vanish! see your visions fade!
Indignant man resumes the shaft he gave,
Disarms the tyrant, and unbinds the slave,
Displays the unclad skeletons of kings,*

   * Offa vides regum vacuis exhausta medullis. Juv. Sat. 8.

Spectres of power, and serpents without stings.
And shall mankind, shall France, whose giant might
Rent the dark veil, and dragg'd them forth to light;
Heed now their threats in dying anguish tost?
And She who fell'd the monster, fear the ghost?
Bid young Alcides, in his grasp who takes,
And gripes with naked hand the twisting snakes,
Their force exhausted, bid him prostrate fall,
And dread their shadows trembling on the wall.
But grant to kings and courts their ancient play,
Recall their splendour and revive their sway;
Can all your cant and all your cries persuade
One power to join you, in your wild crusade?
In vain ye search to earth's remotest end;
No court can aid you, and no king defend.

Not the mad knave that S—— sceptre stole,
Nor she, whose thunder shakes the northern pole;
For Frederick's widow'd sword, that scorns to tell
On whose weak brow his crown reluctant fell;
Not the tri-sceptred Prince, of Austrian mould,
The ape of wisdom and the slave of gold,
Theresa's son, who, with a feeble grace,
Just mimics all the vices of his race;
For him no charm can foreign strife afford,
Too mean to spend his wealth, too wise to trust his sword.

Peep o'er the Pyrenees,—but you'll disdain
To break the dream that sooths the monk of Spain.
He counts his beads, and spends his holy zeal
To raise once more th' inquisitorial wheel,
Prepares the faggot and the flame renews,
To roast the French, as once the Moors and Jews;
While able hands the busy task divide,
His Queen to dandle, and his State to guide.

Ye ask great Pitt to join your desp'rate work,—
See how his annual aid confounds the Turk!
Like a war-elephant his bulk he shows,
And treads down friends, when frighten'd by his foes.
Where then, forsaken villains, will ye turn?

Of France the outcast and of earth the scorn;
What new-made charm can dissipate your fears?
Can Burke's mad foam, or Calonne's house of Peers? *
Can Artois' sword, that erst near Calpe's wall,
Where Crillion fought and Elliot was to fall,
Burn'd with the fire of fame, but harmless burn'd,
For sheath'd the sword remain'd, and in its sheath return'd? †
Oh Burke, degen'rate slave! with grief and shame,
The muse indignant must repeat thy name.
Strange man, declare,—since, at creation's birth,
From crumbling chaos sprang this heav'n and earth,
Since wrecks and outcast relics still remain,
Whirl'd ceaseless round confusion's dreary reign,
Declare, from all these fragments, whence you stole
That genius wild, that monstrous mass of soul;
Where spreads the widest waste of all extremes,
Fell darkness frowns, and heav'n's own splendour beams;
Truth, Error, Falsehood, Rhetoric's raging tide,
And Pomp and Meanness, Prejudice and Pride,
Strain to an endless clang thy voice of fire,
Thy thoughts bewilder and thy audience tire.

* M. de Calonne, at an immense labour, and by the aid of his friends
in England, has framed a constitution for France, after the English
model; the chief ornament of which is that "CORINTHIAN CAPI-
TAL OF POLISHED SOCIETY," A House of Peers. . . .

† Among the disadvantages attending the lives of Princes, must be
reckoned the singular difficulties with which they have to struggle
in acquiring a military reputation. A Duke of Cumberland, in order
to become an Alexander, had to ride all the way to Culloden, and
back again to London. Louis the fourteenth was obliged to submit
to the fatigue of being carried on board of a splendid barge, and
rowed across the Rhine, about the same time that the French army
crossed it. . . .

The Count d'Artois. . . . stiled "*le digne rejeton du grand Henri*,"
. . . and champion of Christendom, set out, at the age of twenty-
five, and travelled by land with a princely equipage, from Paris to
Gibraltar; where he arrived just in time to see, at a convenient distance, Elliot's famous bonfire of the floating batteries. He then returned, covered with glory. . . .

Like Phoebus' son, we see thee wing thy way,
Snatch the loose reins and mount the car of day;
To earth now plunging plough thy wasting course,
The great sublime of weakness and of force.
But while the world's keen eye, with gen'rous glance,
Thy faults could pardon and thy worth enhance,
When foes were hush'd, when justice dar'd commend,
And e'en fond Freedom claim'd thee as a friend,
Why in a gulph of baseness sink forlorn,
And change pure praise for infamy and scorn?

   And didst thou hope, by thy infuriate quill,
To rouse mankind the blood of realms to spill?
Then to restore, on death-devoted plains,
Their scourge to tyrants, and to man his chains
To swell their souls with thy own bigot rage,
And blot the glories of so bright an age?
First stretch thy arm, and, with less impious might,
Wipe out the stars, and quench the solar light:
"*For heav'n and earth,*" the voice of God ordains,
"*Shall pass and perish, but my word remains.*"
The eternal Word, which gave, in spite of thee,
Reason to man, that bids the man be free.

   Thou could'st not hope: 'twas Heav'n's returning grace,
In kind compassion to our injur'd race,
Which stript that soul, ere it should flee from hence,
Of the last garb of decency or sense.
Left thee its own soul horrors to display,
In all the blackness of its native day,
To sink at last, from earth's glad surface hurl'd,
The sordid sov'reign of the letter'd world.

   In some sad hour, ere death's dim terrors spread,
Ere seas of dark oblivion whelm thy head,
Reflect, lost man—If those, thy kindred knaves,
O'er the broad Rhine, whose flag rebellious waves,
Once draw the sword; its burning point shall bring
To thy quick nerves a never-ending sting;
The blood they shed thy weight of woe shall swell,
And their grim ghosts for ever with thee dwell.

Learn hence, ye tyrants, ere ye learn too late,
Of all your craft th' inevitable fate.
The hour is come, the world's unclosing eyes
Discern with rapture where its wisdom lies;
From western heav'ns th' inverted Orient springs,
The morn of man, the dreadful night of kings.
Dim, like the day-struck owl, ye grope in light,
No arm for combat, no resource in flight;
If on your guards your lingering hopes repose,
Your guards are men, and men you've made your foes;
If to your rocky ramparts ye repair,
De Launay's* fate can tell your fortune there.
No turn, no shift, no courtly arts avail,
Each mask is broken, all illusions fail;
Driv'n to your last retreat of shame and fear,
One counsel waits you, one relief is near:
By worth internal, rise to self-wrought fame,
Your equal rank, your human kindred claim;
'Tis Reason's choice, 'tis Wisdom's final plan,
To drop the monarch and assume the man.
Hail man, exalted title! first and best,
On God's own image by his hand imprest;
To which at last the reas'ning race is driv'n
And seeks anew what first it gain'd from Heav'n.
O Man, my brother, how the cordian flame
Of all endearments kindles at the name!
In every clime, thy visage greets my eyes,
In every tongue, thy kindred accents rise;
The thought expanding swells my heart with glee,
It finds a friend, and loves itself in thee.
Say then, fraternal family divine,
Whom mutual wants and mutual aids combine,

---

* De Launay was the last governor of the Bastile. His well-known
exit, serving as a warning to others, saved the lives of many commanders of fortresses in different parts of France during the Revolution. It may probably have the same salutary effect in other
countries.

Say from what source the dire delusion rose,
That souls like ours were ever made for foes;
Why earth's maternal bosom, where we tread,
To rear our mansions and receive our bread,
Should blush so often for the race she bore,
So long be-drench'd with floods of filial gore;
Why to small realms for ever rest confin'd
Our great affections, meant for all mankind?
Though climes divide us, shall the stream or sea
That forms a barrier 'twixt my friend and me,
Inspire the wish his peaceful state to mar,
And meet his falchion in the ranks of war?

    Not seas, nor climes, nor wild ambition's fire,
In nations minds, could e'er the wish inspire;
Where equal rights each sober voice should guide,
No Blood would stain them, and no war divide.
'Tis dark deception, 'tis the glare of state,
Man sunk in titles, lost in Small and Great;
'Tis Rank, Distinction, all the hell that springs,
From those prolific monsters, Courts and kings.
These are the vampires nurs'd on nature's spoils;
For these with pangs the starving peasant toils;
For these the earth's broad surface teems with grain;
Theirs the dread labours of the devious main:
And when the wasted world but dares refuse
The gifts oppressive and extorted dues,
They bid wild slaughter spread the gory plains,
The life blood gushing from a thousand veins;
Erect their thrones amid the sanguine flood,
And dip their purple in the nation's blood.

    The gazing croud, of glitt'ring State afraid,
Adore the pow'r their coward meanness made;
In war's short intervals, while regal shows
Still blind their reason and insult their woes,
What strange events for proud processions call!
See kingdoms crowding to a birth-night ball!
See the long pomp in gorgeous glare display'd,
The tinsel'd guards, the squadron'd horse parade;

See heralds gay, with emblems on their vest;
In tissu'd robes, tall, beauteous pages drest;
Amid superior ranks of splendid slaves,
Lords, Dukes and Princes, titulary knaves;
Confusedly shine their crosses, gems and stars,
Sceptres and globes and crowns and spoils of wars.
On gilded orbs see thund'ring chariots roll'd,
Steeds, snorting fire, and champing bits of gold,
Prance to the trumpet's voice, while each assumes
A loftier gait, and lifts his neck of plumes.
High on a moving throne, and near the van,
The tyrant rides, the chosen scourge of man;
Clarions and flutes and drums his way prepare,
And shouting millions rend the troubled air;
Millions, whose ceaseless toils the pomp sustain,
Whose hour of stupid joy repays an age of pain.

    Of these no more. From orders, slaves and kings,
To thee, O Man! my heart rebounding springs;
Behold th' ascending bliss that waits your call,
Heav'n's own bequest, the heritage of all:
Awake to wisdom, seize the proffer'd prize;
From shade to light, from grief to glory rise.
Freedom at last, with Reason in her train,
Extends o'er earth her everlasting reign;
See Gallia's sons, so late the tyrant's sport,
Machines in war and sycophants at court,
Start into men, expand their well-taught mind,
Lords of themselves and leaders of mankind;
On equal rights their base of empire lies,
On walls of wisdom see the structure rise;
Wide o'er the gazing world it tow'rs sublime,
A modell'd form for each surrounding clime.
To useful toils they bend their noblest aim,
Make patriot views and moral views the same;
Renounce the wish of war, bid conquest cease,
Invite all men to happiness and peace;
To faith and justice rear the youthful race,
With strength exalt them and with science grace;

Till truth's blest banners, o'er the regions hurl'd,
Shake tyrants from their thrones, and cheer the waking world.
   In northern climes, where feudal shades of late
Chilled every heart and palsied every State,
Behold, illumin'd by th' instructive age,
That great phenomenon, a sceptred sage:
There Stanislaus unfolds his prudent plan,
Tears the strong bandage from the eyes of man,
Points the progressive march, and shapes the way
That leads a realm from darkness into day.
   And deign, for once, to turn a transient eye
To that wide world that skirts the western sky;
Hail the mild morning, where the dawn began,
The full fruition of the hopes of man;
Where sage experience seals the sacred cause,
And that rare union, Liberty and Laws,
Speaks to the reas'ning race, "To freedom rise,
Like them be equal, and like them be wise."

ADVICE TO THE PRIVILEGED ORDERS IN THE SEVERAL STATES OF EUROPE, RESULTING FROM THE NECESSITY AND PROPRIETY OF A GENERAL REVOLUTION IN THE PRINCIPLES OF GOVERNMENT

INTRODUCTION

THE French Revolution is at last not only accomplished, but its accomplishment universally acknowledged, beyond contradiction abroad, or the power of retraction at home.*

It has finished its work, by organizing a government, on principles approved by reason; an object long contemplated by different writers, but never before exhibited, in this quarter of the globe. The experiment now in operation will solve a question of the first magnitude in human affairs: Whether *Theory* and *Practice*, which always agree together in things of slighter moment, are really to remain eternal enemies in the highest concerns of men?

The change of government in France is, properly speaking, a renovation of society; an object peculiarly fitted to hurry the mind into a field of thought, which can scarcely be limited by the concerns of a nation, or the improvements of an age. As there is a tendency in human nature to imitation; and as all the apparent causes exist in most of the governments of the world, to induce the people to wish for a similar change; it becomes interesting to the cause of humanity, to take a

* The reader will bear in mind that this was written in the latter end of the year 1791, just as the French had established their first constitution, and were determined to try the experiment of a limited monarchy. It is in this sense that the author considered the revolution as finished; though he did not believe, as will appear in this introduction, that a government so constructed; and so little congenial to the spirit of the times, would be of long duration.

He did not believe in the necessity of a war to introduce and establish the republic. . . .

deliberate view of the real nature and extent of this change, and find what are the advantages and disadvantages to be expected from it.

There is not that necromancy in politics, which prevents our foreseeing, with tolerable certainty, what is to be the result of operations so universal, in which all the people concur. Many truths are as perceptible when first presented to the mind, as an age or a world of experience could make them; others require only an indirect and collateral experience; some demand an experience direct and positive.

It is happy for human nature, that in morals we have much to do with this first class of truths, less with the second, and very little with the third; while in physics we are perpetually driven to the slow process of patient and positive experience.

The Revolution in France certainly comes recommended to us under one aspect which renders it at first view extremely inviting: it is the work of argument and rational conviction, not of the sword. The *ultima ratio regum* had nothing to do with it. It was an operation designed for the benefit of the people; it originated in the people, and was conducted by the people. It had therefore a legitimate origin; and this circumstance entitles it to our serious contemplation, on two accounts: because there is something venerable in the idea, and because other nations, in similar circumstances, will certainly be disposed to imitate it.

I shall therefore examine the nature and consequences of a similar revolution in government, as it will affect the following principal objects, which make up the affairs of nations in the present state of Europe:

    I.   The Feudal System,
    II.   The Church,
    III. The Military,
    IV. The Administration of Justice,
    V.   Revenue and Public Expenditure.

It must be of vast importance to all the classes of society, as it now stands classed in Europe, to calculate before-hand what they are to gain or to lose by the approaching change;

that, like prudent stock-jobbers, they may buy in or sell out, according as this great event shall affect them.

Philosophers and contemplative men, who may think themselves disinterested spectators of so great a political drama, will do well to consider how far the catastrophe is to be beneficial or detrimental to the human race; in order to determine whether in conscience they ought to promote or discourage, accelerate or retard it, by the publication of their opinions. It is true, the work was set on foot by this sort of men; but they have not all been of the same opinion relative to the best organization of the governing power, or how far the reform of abuses ought to extend. Montesquieu, Voltaire, and many other respectable authorities, have accredited the principle, that republicanism is not convenient for a great state. Others take no notice of the distinction, between great and small states, in deciding, that this is the only government proper to ensure the happiness, and support the dignity of man. Of the former opinion was a great majority of the constituent national assembly of France. Probably not many years will pass, before a third opinion will be universally adopted, never to be laid aside: That the republican principle is not only proper and safe for the government of any people; but that its propriety and safety are in proportion to the magnitude of the society and extent of the territory.

Among sincere enquirers after truth, all general questions on this subject reduce themselves to this: Whether men are to perform their duties by an easy choice or an expensive cheat; or, whether our reason be given us to be improved or stifled, to render us greater or less than brutes, to increase our happiness or aggravate our misery.

Among those whose anxieties arise only from interest, the inquiry is, how their privileges or their professions are to be affected by the new order of things. These form a class of men respectable both for their numbers and sensibility; it is our duty to attend to their case. I sincerely hope to administer some consolation to them in the course of this essay. And though I have a better opinion of their philanthropy, than political opponents generally entertain of each other, yet I do not altogether rely upon their presumed sympathy with their fellow-citizens, and their supposed willingness to sacrifice to the public good; but I hope to convince them, that the establishment of general liberty will be less injurious to those who now live by abuses, than is commonly imagined; that protected industry will produce effects far more astonishing than have ever been calculated; that the increase of enjoyments will be such, as to ameliorate the condition of every human creature.

To persuade this class of mankind, that it is neither their duty nor their interest to endeavour to perpetuate the ancient forms of government, would be an high and holy office; it would be the greatest act of charity to them, as it might teach them to avoid a danger that is otherwise unavoidable; it would preclude the occasion of the people's indulging what is sometimes called a ferocious disposition, which is apt to grow upon the revenge of injuries, and render them less harmonious in their new station of citizens; it would prevent the civil wars, which might attend the insurrections of the people, where there should be a great want of unanimity,—for we are not to expect in every country that mildness and dignity which have uniformly characterized the French, even in their most tumultuous movements;* it would remove every obsta-

* Whatever reason may be given for the fact, I believe all those who have been witnesses of what are called *mobs* in France (during the revolution) will join with me in opinion, that they are by no means to be compared with English mobs, in point of indiscriminate ferocity and private plunder. A popular commotion in Paris was uniformly directed to a certain well-explained object; from which it never was known to deviate. Whether this object were to hang a man, to arrest the king, to intimidate the court, or to break the furniture of a hotel, all other persons and all other property, that fell in the way of the mob, were perfectly safe.

The truth is, those collections were composed of honest and industrious people, who had nothing in view but the public good. They believed that the cause of their country required an execution of justice more prompt than could be expected from any established tribunal. Besides, they were in the crisis of a revolution, when they

cle and every danger that may seem to attend that rational
system of public felicity to which the nations of Europe are
moving with rapid strides, and which in prospect is so consoling to the enlightened friends of humanity.

To induce the men who now govern the world to adopt
these ideas, is the duty of those who now possess them. I
confess the task, at first view, appears more than Herculean;
it will be thought an object from which the eloquence of the
closet must shrink in despair, and which prudence would
leave to the more powerful arguments of events. But I believe at the same time that some success may be expected;
that though the harvest be great, the labourers may not be
few; that prejudice and interest cannot always be relied on to
garrison the mind against the assaults of truth. This belief,
ill-grounded as it may appear, is sufficient to animate me in
the cause; and to the venerable host of republican writers,
who have preceded me in the discussions occasioned by the
French revolution, this belief is my only apology for offering
to join the fraternity, and for thus practically declaring my
opinion, that they have not exhausted the subject.

Two very powerful weapons, the force of reason and the
force of numbers, are in the hands of the political reformers.
While the use of the first brings into action the second, and
ensures its coöperation, it remains a sacred duty, imposed on
them by the God of reason to wield with dexterity this mild
and beneficent weapon, before recurring to the use of the other;
which, though legitimate, may be less harmless; though infallible in operation, may be less glorious in victory.

The tyrannies of the world, whatever be the appellation
of the government under which they are exercised, are all
aristocratical tyrannies. An ordinance to plunder and murder,
whether it fulminate from the Vatican, or steal silently forth
from the Harem; whether it come clothed in the *certain*

were sensible, that the crimes of their enemies would remain unpun-
ished, for want of a known rule by which they could be judged.
Though a violation of *right*, is not always a violation of *law;* yet, in
their opinion, occasions might exist, when it would be dangerous to
let it pass with impunity. . . .

science of a Bed of Justice, or in the legal solemnities of a
bench of lawyers; whether it be purchased by the caresses of
a woman, or the treasures of a nation;—never confines its
effects to the benefit of a single individual; it goes to enrich
the whole combination of conspirators, whose business it is
to dupe and to govern the nation. It carries its own bribery
with itself through all its progress and connexions,—in its
origination, in its enaction, in its vindication, in its execution;
it is a fertilizing stream, that waters and vivifies its happy
plants in the numerous channels of its communication. Ministers and secretaries, commanders of armies, contractors, col-
lectors and tide-waiters, intendants, judges and lawyers,—
whoever is permitted to drink of the salutary stream,—are
all interested in removing the obstructions and in praising
the fountain from which it flows.

The state of human nature requires that this should be the
case. Among beings so nearly equal in power and capacity
as men of the same community are, it is impossible that a
solitary tyrant should exist. Laws that are designed to operate unequally on society, must offer an exclusive interest to
a considerable portion of its members, to ensure their execution upon the rest. Hence has arisen the necessity of that
strange complication in the governing power, which has made
of politics an inexplicable science; hence the reason for arm-
ing one class of our fellow creatures with the weapons of bodily
destruction, and another with the mysterious artillery of the
vengeance of heaven; hence the cause of what in England is
called the independence of the judges, and what on the continent has created a judiciary nobility, a set of men who purchase the privilege of being the professional enemies of the
people, of selling their decisions to the rich, and of distribut-
ing individual oppression; hence the source of those Draconian
codes of criminal jurisprudence which enshrine the idol property in a bloody sanctuary, and teach the modern European,
that his life is of less value than the shoes on his feet; hence
the positive discouragements laid upon agriculture, manufacture, commerce, and every method of improving the condition of men; for it is to be observed, that in every country

the shackles imposed upon industry are in proportion to the degree of general despotism that reigns in the government. This arises not only from the greater debility and want of enterprise in the people, but from the superior necessity that such governments are under, to prevent their subjects from acquiring that ease and information, by which they could discern the evil and apply the remedy.

To the same fruitful source of calamities we are to trace that perversity of reason, which, in governments where men are permitted to discuss political subjects, has given rise to those perpetual shifts of sophistry, by which they vindicate the prerogative of kings. In one age it is the *right of conquest*, in another the *divine right*, then it comes to be a *compact between king and people*, and last of all, it is said to be founded on general convenience, *the good of the whole community*. In England these several arguments have all had their day; though it is astonishing that the two former could ever have been the subjects of rational debate: the first is the logic of the musquet, and the second of the chalice; the one was buried at Runnimede on the signature of Magna Charta, the other took its flight to the continent with James the Second. The compact of king and people has lain dormant the greater part of the present century; till it was roused from slumber by the French revolution, and came into the service of Mr. Burke.

Hasty men discover their errors when it is too late. It had certainly been much more consistent with the temperament of that writer's mind, and quite as servicable to his cause, to have recalled the fugitive claim of the divine right of kings. It would have given a mystic force to his declamation, afforded him many new epithets, and furnished subjects perfectly accordant with the copious charges of *sacrilege*, *atheism*, *murders*, *assassinations*, *rapes*, and *plunders* with which his three volumes abound.* He then could not have disappointed his friends by his total want of argument, as he now does in his

---

* These three works are, his *Reflections on the Revolution in France*, his *Letter to a Member of the National Assembly*, and his *Appeal from the New to the Old Whigs*.

two first essays; for on such a subject no argument could be expected; and in his third, where it is patiently attempted, he would have avoided the necessity of showing that he has none, by giving a different title to his book; for the "Appeal," instead of being "from the New to the Old Whigs," would have been *from the new whigs to the old tories;* and he might also well have appealed to Caesar; he could have found at this day no court to take cognizance of his cause.

But the great advantage of this mode of handling the subject would have been, that it could have provoked no answers; the gauntlet might have been thrown, without a champion to have taken it up; and the last solitary admirer of chivalry have retired in negative triumph from the field.

Mr. Burke, however, in his defence of royalty, does not rely on this argument of the compact. Whether it be, that he is conscious of its futility, or that in his rage he forgets that he has used it, he is perpetually recurring to the last ground that has yet been heard of, on which we are called upon to consider kings even as a tolerable nuisance, and to support the existing forms of government: this ground is *the general good of the community.* It is said to be dangerous to pull down systems that are already formed, or even to attempt to improve them; and it is likewise said, that, were they peaceably destroyed, and we had society to build up anew, it would be best to create hereditary Kings, hereditary orders, and exclusive privileges.

These are sober opinions, uniting a class of reasoners too numerous and too respectable to be treated with contempt. I believe, however, that their number is every day diminishing, and I believe the example which France will soon be obliged to exhibit to the world on this subject, will induce every man to reject them, who is not personally and exclusively interested in their support.

The inconsistency of the constituent assembly, in retaining an hereditary king, armed with an enormous civil list, to wage war with a popular government, has induced some persons to predict the downfall of their constitution. But this measure had a different origin from what is commonly assigned to it, and will probably have a different issue. It was the result rather of local and temporary circumstances, than of any general belief in the utility of kings, under any modifications or limitations that could be attached to the office.

It is to be observed, *first*, that the French had a king upon their hands. This king had always been considered as a well-disposed man; so that, by a fatality somewhat singular, though not unexampled in *regal history*, he gained the love of the people, almost in proportion to the mischief which he did them. *Secondly*, their king had very powerful family con-nexions, in the sovereigns of Spain, Austria, Naples and Sardinia; besides his relations within the kingdom, whom it was necessary to attach, if possible, to the interests of the com-munity. *Thirdly*, the revolution was considered by all Europe as a high and dangerous experiment. It was necessary to hide as much as possible the appearance of its magnitude from the eye of the distant observer. The reformers consid-ered it as their duty to produce an internal regeneration of society rather than an external change in the appearance of the court; to set in order the counting-house and the kitchen, before arranging the drawing room. This would leave the sovereigns of Europe totally without a pretext for interfering; while it would be consoling to that class of philosophers, who still believed in the compatibility of royalty and liberty. *Fourthly*, this decree, *That France should have a king*, and that he *could do no wrong*, was passed at an early period of their operations; when the above reasons were apparently more urgent than they were afterwards, or probably will ever be again.

From these considerations we may conclude that royalty is preserved in France for reasons which are fugitive; that a majority of the constituent assembly did not believe in it, as an abstract principle; that a majority of the people will learn to be disgusted with so unnatural and ponderous a deformity in their new edifice, and will soon hew it off.

After this improvement shall have been made, a few years' experience in the face of Europe, and on so great a theatre as that of France, will probably leave but one opinion in the minds of honest men, relative to the republican principle, or the great simplicity of nature applied to the organization of society.

The example of America would have had great weight in producing this conviction; but it is too little known to the European reasoner, to be a subject of accurate investigation. Besides, the difference of circumstances between that country and the states of Europe has given occasion for imagining many distinctions which exist not in fact, and has prevented the application of principles which are permanently founded in nature, and follow not the trifling variations of the state of society.

But I have not prescribed to myself the task of entering into arguments on the utility of kings, or of investigating the meaning of Mr. Burke, in order to compliment him with an additional refutation. My subject furnishes a more extensive scope. It depends not on me, or Mr. Burke, or any other writer, or description of writers, to determine the question, whether a change of government shall take place, and extend through Europe. It depends on a much more important class of men, the class that cannot write; and in a great measure, on those who cannot read. It is to be decided by men who reason better without books, than we do with all the books in the world. Taking it for granted, therefore, that a general revolution is at hand, whose progress is irresistible, my object is to contemplate its probable effects, and to comfort those who are afflicted at the prospect.

CHAPTER IV [1]

THE ADMINISTRATION OF JUSTICE

It would be a curious speculation, and perhaps as useful as curious, to consider how far the moral nature of man is affected by the organization of society; and to what degree his

[1] Chapters I, II, III have been omitted, and of Chapters IV and V only those portions which reveal Barlow's social theory, have been included.—EDITOR.

predominant qualities depend on the nature of the government under which he lives. The adage, *That men are everywhere the same*, though not wholly false, would doubtless be
found to be true only in a limited sense. I love to indulge the
belief, that it is true so far as to ensure permanency to institutions that are good; but not so far as to discourage us
from attempting to reform those that are bad. To consider
it is true in an unlimited sense, would be to serve the purposes
of despotism; for which this, like a thousand other maxims,
has been invented and employed. It would teach us to sit
down with a gloomy satisfaction on the state of human affairs, to pronounce the race of man emphatically "fated to be
curst," a community of self-tormentors and mutual assassins,
bound down by the irresistible destiny of their nature to be
robbed of their reason by priests, and plundered of their
property by Kings. It would teach us to join with Soame
Jenyns, and furnish new weapons to the oppressors, by our
manner of pitying the misfortunes of the oppressed.

In confirmation of this adage, and as an apology for the
existing despotisms, it is said, That all men are by nature
tyrants, and will exercise their tyrannies whenever they find
opportunity. Allowing this assertion to be true, it is surely
cited by the wrong party. It is an apology for equal, not for
unequal governments; and the weapon belongs to those who
contend for the republican principle. If government be
founded on the vices of mankind, its business is to restrain
those vices in all, rather than to foster them in a few. The
disposition to tyrannize is effectually restrained under the
exercise of the equality of rights; while it is not only rewarded
in the few, but invigorated in the many, under all other forms
of the social connexion. But it is almost impossible to decide,
among moral propensities, which of them belong to nature,
and which are the offspring of habit; how many of our vices
are chargeable on the permanent qualities of man, and how
many result from the mutable energies of state.

If it be in the power of a bad government to render men
worse than nature has made them, why should we say it is
not in the power of a good one to render them better? and if

the latter be capable of producing this effect in any perceivable degree, where shall we limit the progress of human wisdom, and the force of its institutions, in ameliorating, not only the social condition, but the controlling principles of man?

Among the component parts of government, that, whose operation is the most direct on the moral habit of life, is the Administration of Justice. In this every person has a peculiar isolated interest, which is almost detached from the common sympathies of society. It is this which operates with a singular concentrated energy, collecting the whole force of the state from the community at large, and bringing it to act upon a single individual, affecting his life, reputation, or property; so that the governing power may say with peculiar propriety to the minister of justice, *divide et impera;* for, in case of oppression, the victim's cries will be too feeble to excite opposition; his cause having nothing in common with that of the citizens at large. If, therefore, we would obtain an idea of the condition of men on any given portion of the earth, we must pay a particular attention to their judiciary system, not in its form and theory, but in its spirit and practice. It may be said in general of this part of the civil polity of a nation, that, as it is a stream flowing from the common fountain of the government, and must be tinged with whatever impurities are found in the source from whence it descends, the only hope of cleaning the stream is by purifying the fountain.

If I were able to give an energetic sketch of the office and dignity of a rational system of jurisprudence, describe the full extent of its effects on the happiness of men, and then exhibit the perversions and corruptions attendant on this business in most of the governments of Europe, it would furnish one of the most powerful arguments in favour of a general revolution, and afford no small consolation to those persons who look forward with certainty to such an event. But my plan embraces too many subjects, to be particular on any; all that I can promise myself is to seize the rough features of systems, and mark the moral attitudes of man as placed in the necessary posture to support them.

It is generally understood, that the object of government, in this part of its administration, is merely to *restrain* the vices of men. But there is another object prior to this: an office more sacred, and equally indispensible, is to *prevent* their vices,—to correct them in their origin, or eradicate them totally from the adolescent mind. The latter is performed by instruction, the former by coercion; the one is the tender duty of a father, the other, the unrelenting drudgery of a master; but both are the business of government, and ought to be made concurrent branches of the system of jurisprudence.

The absurd and abominable doctrine, *that private vices are public benefits*, it is hoped will be blotted from the memory of man, expunged from the catalogue of human follies, with the systems of government which gave it birth. The ground of this insulting doctrine is, that advantage may be taken of the extravagant foibles of individuals to increase the revenues of the State; as if the chief end of society were, to steal money for the government's purse! to be squandered by the govern-ors, to render them more insolent in their oppressions! it is humiliating, to answer such arguments as these; where we must lay open the most degrading retreats of prostituted logic, to discover the positions on which they are founded. But *Orders* and *Privileges* will lead to any thing: once teach a man, that *some are born to command and others to be commanded;* and after that, there is no camel too big for him to swallow.

This idea of the objects to be kept in view by the system of Justice, involving in it the business of prevention as well as of restriction, leads us to some observations on the particular subject of criminal jurisprudence. Every society, considered in itself as a moral and physical entity, has the undoubted faculty of self-preservation. It is an independent being; and, towards other beings in like circumstances of independence, it has a right to use this faculty of defending itself, without previous notice to the party; or without the observance of any duty, but that of abstaining from offensive operations. But when it acts towards the members of its own family, towards those dependent and defenceless beings that make part of itself, the *right* of coercion is preceded by the *duty* of instruction. It may be safely pronounced, *that a State has no right to punish a man, to whom it has given no previous instruction;* and consequently, any person has a right to do any action, unless he has been informed that it has an evil tendency. It is true, that, as relative to particular cases, the having given this information is a thing that the society must sometimes *presume*, and is not always obliged to *prove*. But these cases are rare, and ought never to form a general rule. This presumption has, however, passed into a general rule, and is adopted as universal practice. With what justice or propriety it is so adopted, a very little reflection will enable us to decide.

The great outlines of morality are extremely simple and easy to be understood; they may be said to be written on the heart of a man antecedent to his associating with his fellow-creatures. As a self-dependent being he is self-instructed; and as long as he should remain a simple child of *nature*, he would receive from nature all the lessons necessary to his condition. He would be a complete moral agent; and should he violate the rights of another independent man like himself, he would sin against sufficient light, to merit any punishment that the offended party might inflict upon him. But society opens upon us a new field of contemplation; it furnishes man with another class of rights, and imposes upon him an additional system of duties; it enlarges the sphere of his moral agency, and makes him a kind of artificial being, propelling and propelled by new dependencies, in which nature can no longer serve him as a guide. Being removed from her rudimental school, and entered in the college of society, he is called to encounter problems which the elementary tables of his heart will not always enable him to solve. Society then ought to be consistent with herself in her own institutions; if she sketches the lines of his duty with a variable pencil, too slight for his natural perception, she should lend him her optical glasses to discern them; if she takes the ferule in one hand, she is bound to use the fescue with the other.

We must observe farther,—that though society itself be a state of nature, as relative to the nation at large,—though it

be a state to which mankind naturally recur to satisfy their
wants and increase the sum of their happiness,—though all
its laws and regulations may be perfectly reasonable, and
calculated to promote the good of the whole,—yet, with regard to an individual member, his having *consented* to these
laws, or even chosen to live in the society, is but a *fiction;* and
a rigid discipline, founded on a fiction, is surely hard upon its
object.　In general it may be said, that a man comes into
society by birth; he neither consents nor dissents respecting
his relative condition; he first opens his eyes on that state of
human affairs in which the interests of his moral associates are
infinitely complicated; with these his duties are so blended
and intermingled, that nature can give him but little assistance in finding them out.　His morality itself must be
arbitrary; it must be varied at every moment, to comprehend
some local and positive regulation; his science is to begin
where that of preceding ages has ended; his alpha is their
omega; and he is called upon to act by instinct what they have
but learnt to do from the experience of all mankind.　Natural
reason may teach me not to strike my neighbour without a
cause; but it will never forbid my sending a sack of wool from
England, or printing the French constitution in Spain.　These
are positive prohibitions, which nature has not written in her
book; she has therefore never taught them to her children.
The same may be said of all regulations that arise from the
social compact.

It is a truth, I believe, not to be called in question, that
every man is born with an imprescriptible claim to a portion
of the elements; which portion is termed his *birth-right.*　Society may vary this right, as to its form, but never can destroy it in substance.　She has no control over the man, till
he is born; and the right being born with him, and being
necessary to his existence, she can no more annihilate the one
than the other, though she has the power of new-modelling
both.　But on coming into the world, he finds that the ground
which nature has promised him is taken up, and in the oc-
cupancy of others; society has changed the form of his birth-
right; the general stock of elements, from which the lives of

men are to be supported, has undergone a new modification; and his portion among the rest. He is told that he cannot claim it in its present form, as an independent inheritance; that he must draw on the stock of society, instead of the stock of nature; that he is banished from the mother and must cleave to the nurse. In this unexpected occurrence he is unprepared to act; but *knowledge* is a part of the stock of society; and an indispensable part to be allotted in the portion of the claimant is *instruction* relative to the new arrangement of natural right. To withhold this instruction therefore would be, not merely the ommission of a duty, but the commission of a crime; and society in this case would sin against the man, before the man could sin against society.

I should hope to meet the assent of all unprejudiced readers, in carrying this idea still farther. In cases where a person is born of poor parents, or finds himself brought into the community of men without the means of subsistence, society is bound in duty to furnish him the means. She ought not only to instruct him in the artificial laws by which property is secured, but in the artificial industry by which it is obtained. She is bound, in *justice* as well as policy, to give him some art or trade. For the reason of his incapacity is, that *she* has usurped his birth-right; and this is restoring it to him in another form, more convenient for both parties. The failure of society in this branch of her duty is the occasion of much the greater part of the evils that call for criminal jurisprudence. The individual feels that he is robbed of his natural right; he cannot bring his process to reclaim it from the great community, by which he is overpowered; he therefore feels authorized in reprisal; in taking another's goods to replace his own. And it must be confessed, that in numberless instances the conduct of society justifies him in this proceeding; she has seized upon his property, and commenced the war against him.

Some, who perceive these truths, say that it is unsafe for society to publish them; but I say it is unsafe not to publish them. For the party from which the mischief is expected to arise has the knowledge of them already, and has acted upon them in all ages. It is the wise who are ignorant of these things, and not the foolish. They are truths of nature; and in them the teachers of mankind are the only party that remains to be taught. It is a subject on which the logic of indigence is much clearer than that of opulence. The latter reasons from contrivance, the former from feeling; and God has not endowed us with false feelings, in things that so weightily concern our happiness.

None can deny that the obligation is much stronger on me, to support my life, than to support the claim that my neighbour has to his property. Nature commands the first, society the second:—in one I obey the laws of God, which are universal and eternal; in the other, the laws of man, which are local and temporary.

It has been the folly of all old governments, to begin every thing at the wrong end, and to erect their institutions on an inversion of principle. This is more sadly the case in their systems of jurisprudence, than is commonly imagined. *Compelling* justice is always mistaken for *rendering* justice. But this important branch of administration consists not merely in compelling men to be just to each other, and individuals to society,—this is not the whole, nor is it the principal part, nor even the beginning, of the operation. The source of power is said to be the source of justice; but it does not answer this description, as long as it contents itself with *compulsion*. Justice must begin by flowing from its source; and the first as well as the most important object is, to open its channels from society to all the individual members. This part of the administration being well devised and diligently executed, the other parts would lessen away by degrees to matters of inferior consideration.

It is an undoubted truth, that our duty is inseparably connected with our happiness. And why should we despair of convincing every member of society of a truth so important for him to know? Should any person object, by saying, that nothing like this has ever yet been done; I answer, that nothing like this has ever yet been tried. Society has hitherto been curst with governments, whose existence depended on the extinction of truth. Every moral light has been smothered under the bushel of perpetual imposition; from whence it emits but faint and glimmering rays, always insufficient to form any luminous system on any of the civil concerns of men. But these covers are crumbling to the dust, with the governments which they support; and the probability becomes more apparent, the more it is considered, that society is capable of curing all the evils to which it has given birth.

It seems that men, to diminish the physical evils that surround them, connect themselves in society; and from this connection their moral evils arise. But the *immediate* occasion of the moral evils is nothing more than the *remainder* of the physical, that still exist even under the regulations that society makes to banish them. The direct object therefore of the government ought to be, to destroy as far as possible the remaining quantity of physical evils: and the moral would so far follow their destruction. But the mistake that is always made on this subject is, that governments, instead of laying the axe at the root of the tree, aim their strokes at the branches; they attack the moral evils *directly* by vindictive justice, instead of removing the physical by distributive justice.

There are two distinct kinds of physical evils; one arises from want, or the apprehension of want; the other from bodily disease. The former seems capable of being removed by society; the latter is inevitable. But the latter gives no occasion to moral disorders; it being the common lot of all, we all bear our part in silence, without complaining of each other, or revenging ourselves on the community. As it is out of the power of our neighbour's goods to relieve us, we do not covet them for this purpose. The former is the only kind from which moral evils arise; and to this the energies of government ought to be chiefly directed; especially that part which is called the administration of justice.

No nation is yet so numerous, nor any country so populous, as it is capable of becoming. Europe, taken together, would support at least five times its present number, even on its present system of cultivation; and how many times this increased population may be multiplied by new discoveries in the infinite science of subsistence, no man will pretend to calculate. This of itself is sufficient to prove, that society at present has the means of rendering all its members happy in every respect, except the removal of bodily disease. The common stock of the community appears abundantly sufficient for this purpose. By common stock, I would not be understood to mean the goods exclusively appropriated to individuals. Exclusive property is not only consistent with good order among men, but it is conceived by some to be necessary to the existence of society. But the common stock of which I speak consists, first, in *knowledge*, or the improvement which men have made in the means of acquiring a support; and secondly, in the *contributions* which it is necessary should be collected from individuals, and applied to the maintenance of tranquillity in the State. The property exclusively belonging to individuals can only be the surplusage remaining in their hands, after deducting what is necessary to the real wants of society. Society is the first proprietor; as she is the original cause of the appropriation of wealth, and its indispensable guardian in the hands of the individual.

Society then is bound, in the first place, to distribute knowledge to every person according to his wants, to enable him to be useful and happy; so far as to dispose him to take an active interest in the welfare of the State. *Secondly*, where the faculties of the individual are naturally defective, so that he remains unable to provide for himself, she is bound still to support and render him happy. It is her duty in all cases to induce every human creature, by rational motives, to place his happiness in the tranquillity of the public, and in the security of individual peace and property. But *thirdly*, in cases where these precautions shall fail of their effect, she is driven indeed to the last extremity,—she is to use the rod of correction. These instances would doubtless be rare; and if we could suppose a long continuance of wise administration, such as a well-organized government would ensure to every nation in the world, we may almost persuade ourselves to believe that the necessity for punishment would be reduced to nothing.

Proceeding however on the supposition of the existence of crimes, it must still remain an object of legislative wisdom, to discriminate between their different classes, and apply to each its proper remedy, in the quantity and mode of punishment. It is no part of my subject to enter into this inquiry, any farther than simply to observe, that it is the characteristic of arbitrary governments, to be jealous of their power. And, as jealousy is, of all human passions, the most vindictive and the least rational, these governments seek the revenge of injuries in the most absurd and tremendous punishments that their fury can invent. As far as any rule can be discovered in their gradation of punishments, it appears to be this, That the severity of the penalty is in proportion to the injustice of the law. The reason of this is simple,—the laws which counteract nature the most, are the most likely to be violated.

*   *   *   *   *   *

After considering what is the duty of society, and what *would be* the practice of a well organized government, relative to the subject of this chapter, it is almost useless to inquire what *is* the practice of all the old governments of Europe. We may be sure beforehand, that it is directly the contrary,—that, like all other parts of the system, it is the inversion of every thing that is right and reasonable. The pyramid is every where placed on the little end, and all sorts of extraneous rubbish are constantly brought to prop it up.

Unequal governments are necessarily founded in ignorance, and they must be supported by ignorance; to deviate from their principle would be voluntary suicide. The first great object of their policy is to perpetuate that undisturbed ignorance of the people, which is the companion of poverty, the parent of crimes, and the pillar of the State.

In England, the people at large are as perfectly ignorant of the acts of parliament after they are made, as they possibly can be before. They are printed by one man only, who is called the King's printer,—in the old German character, which few men can read,—and sold at a price that few can afford to pay. But lest some scraps or comments upon them should come to the people through the medium of public newspapers, every such paper is stamped with a heavy duty; and an act of parliament is made to prevent men from letting their papers to read; * so that not one person in a hundred sees a newspaper once in a year. If a man at the bottom of Yorkshire discovers by instinct that a law is made, which is interesting for him to know, he has only to make a journey to London, find out the King's printer, pay a half-penny a page for the law, and learn the German alphabet. He is then prepared to spell out his duty.

As to the general system of the laws of the land, on which all property depends, no man in the kingdom knows them, and no man pretends to know them. They are a fathomless abyss, that exceeds all human faculties to sound. They are studied, not to be understood, but to be disputed; not to give information, but to breed confusion. The man, whose property is depending on a suit at law, dares not look into the gulph that separates him from the wished-for decision; he has no confidence in himself, nor in reason, nor in justice; he mounts on the back of a lawyer, like one of Mr. Burke's heroes of chivalry between the wings of a griffin, and trusts the pilotage of a man, who is superior to himself only in the confidence which results from having nothing at stake.

To penetrate into what are called the courts of justice on the continent, and expose the general system of their administration in those points which are common to most countries in Europe, would be to lay open an inconceivable scene of iniquity; it would be,

" *To pour in light on Pluto's drear abodes,*
" *Abhorr'd by men, and dreadful e'en to gods.*"

 *   *   *   *   *   *

* As this work may chance to fall into the hands of some people who never see the acts of parliament (the same precautions not being taken to prevent its circulation), it is out of compassion to that class of readers, that I give this information. It is a duty of humanity to save our fellow-creatures from falling into snares, even those that are spread for them by the government. Therefore: Notice is hereby given to all persons, to whom these presents shall come, that the penalty for letting a newspaper, within the Kingdom of Great-Britain, is fifty pounds.

All governments that lay any claim to respectability or justice, have proscribed the idea of *ex-post-facto laws*, or laws made after the performance of an action, constituting that action a crime, and punishing a party for a thing that was innocent at the time of its being done. Such laws would be so flagrant a violation of natural right, that in the French and several of the American State Constitutions they are solemnly interdicted in their Declarations of Rights. This proscription is likewise considered as a fundamental article of English liberty, and almost the only one that has not been habitually violated, within the present century. But let us resort to reason and justice, and ask what is the difference between a violation of this article and the observance of that tremendous maxim of jurisprudence, common to all the nations above mentioned,* *ignorantia legis neminem excusat?*

Most of the laws of society are positive regulations, not taught by nature. Indeed, such only are applicable to the subject now in question. For *ignorantia legis* can have reference only to laws arising out of society, in which our natural feelings have no concern; and where a man is ignorant of such a law, he is in the same situation as if the law did not exist. To read it to him from the tribunal, where he stands arraigned for the breach of it, is to him precisely the same thing as it would be to originate it at the time by the same tribunal, for the express purpose of his condemnation. The law till then, as relative to him, is not in being. He is therefore in the same predicament that the society in general would be, under the operation of an *ex-post-facto* law.† Hence

---

* *Ignorance of the law is no excuse for the breach of it.*

† *What shocking ideas of morals those governments must have inculated, which first invented that exemption in penal statutes, called the benefit of clergy! To be able to write and read, was at that time an evidence of an uncommon degree of knowledge. Out of respect to learning (as it is presumed) it was therefore enacted, that any person convicted of a felony should be pardoned, on showing that he could write his name. As this talent was then chiefly confined to the clerks, or clergy, this circumstance gave name to the law. The language of the exemption is simply this, that those persons only who know the law are at liberty*

we ought to conclude that, as it seems difficult for a government to dispense with the maxim above-mentioned, a free
people ought, in their declaration of rights, to provide for
universal public instruction. If they neglect to do this, and
mean to avoid the absurdity of a self-destroying policy, by
adhering to a system of justice which would preserve a dignity
and inspire a confidence worthy the name of liberty, they
ought to reject the maxim altogether; and insert in their
declaration of rights, that instruction alone can constitute a
duty; and that laws can enforce no obedience, but where they
are explained.

It is truly hard and sufficiently to be regretted that any
part of society should be obliged to yield obedience to laws,
to which they have not literally and personally consented.
Such, however, is the state of things; it is necessary that a
majority should govern. If it be an evil to obey a law to
which we have not consented, it is at least a necessary evil;
but to compel a compliance with orders which are unknown, is
carrying injustice beyond the bounds of necessity; it is absurd,
and even impossible. Laws in this case may be avenged, but
cannot be obeyed; they may inspire terror, but can never command respect.

CHAPTER V

REVENUE AND EXPENDITURE

A Nation is surely in a wretched condition, when the
principal object of its government is the increase of its public
revenue. Such a state of things is in reality a perpetual warfare between the few individuals who govern, and the great
body of the people who labour. Or, to call things by their
proper names, and use the only language that the nature of
the case will justify, the real occupation of the governors is
either to plunder or to steal, as will best answer their purpose; while the business of the people is to secrete their property by fraud, or to give it peaceably up, in proportion as the

*to violate it. There is indeed much reason for a distinction; but it should
have been the other way.*

other party demands it; and then, as a consequence of being driven to this necessity, they slacken their industry, and become miserable through idleness; in order to avoid the mortification of labouring for those they hate.

The art of constructing governments has usually been to organize the State in such a manner, as that this operation could be carried on to the best advantage for the administrators; and the art of administering those governments has been, so to vary the means of seizing upon private property, as to bring the greatest possible quantity into the public coffers, without exciting insurrections. Those governments which are called despotic, deal more in open plunder; those that call themselves free, and act under the cloak of what they teach the people to reverence as a constitution, are driven to the arts of stealing. These have succeeded better by theft than the others have by plunder; and this is the principal difference by which they can be distinguished. Under these *constitutional* governments the people are more industrious, and create property faster; because they are not sensible in what manner and in what quantities it is taken from them. The administration, in this case, operates by a compound movement; one is to induce the people to work, and the other to take from them their earnings.

In this view of government, it is no wonder that it should be considered as a curious and complicated machine, too mysterious for vulgar contemplation, capable of being moved by none but experienced hands, and subject to fall in pieces by the slightest attempt at innovation or improvement. It is no wonder that a church and an army should be deemed necessary for its support; and that the double guilt of impiety and rebellion should follow the man who offers to enter its dark sanctuary with the profane light of reason. It is not surprising that kings and priests should be supposed to have derived their authority from God, since it is evidently not given them by men; that they should trace to a supernatural source claims which are at war with every principle of society.

I constantly bear in mind, that there is a respectable class of men in every country in Europe, who, whether immediately interested in the administration of the governments or not, are conscientiously attached to the old established forms. I know not how much pain it may give them to see exposed to public view the various combinations of iniquity which appear to me to compose the system. But I should pay a real compliment to their sensibility, in supposing that their anguish can be as great on viewing the picture, as mine has been in attempting to draw it; or, that they can shudder as much at the prospect of a change, as I have done in contemplating society under the distortions of its present organization. I see the noble nature of man so cruelly debased,—I see the horse and the dog in so many instances raised to a rank far superior to beings whom I must acknowledge as my fellow-creatures, and whom my heart cannot but embrace with a fraternal affection which must increase with the insults I see them suffer,—I see the pride of power and of rank mounted to so ungovernable a height in those whom accident has called to direct the affairs of nations,—I see the faculty of reason so completely dormant in both these classes, and morality, the indispensible bond of union among men, so effectually banished by the unnatural combinations, which in Europe are called Society,—that I have been almost determined to relinquish the disagreeable task which I had prescribed to myself in the first part of this work, and, returning to my country, endeavour in the new world to forget the miseries of the old.

But I reflect that the contemplation of these miseries has already left an impression on my mind too deep to be easily effaced.—I am likewise convinced that all the moral evils under which we labour, may be traced without difficulty, to their proper source,—that the spirit of investigation, which the French revolution has awakened in many parts of Europe, is stimulating the people to pursue the enquiry, and will consequently lead them to apply the remedy. Under this prospect, every person who but thinks he can throw the least light upon the subject, is called upon for his assistance; and this duty to his fellow-creatures becomes more imperious, as it is increased by the probability of success.

In considering the subject of *Revenue and Expenditure*, as in other articles that I have treated, I shall confine myself chiefly to the great outlines of the system; only noticing its effect on the moral habits which must be considered as the vital principles of society, and which ought always to be kept in view as the first object of government, both in its original constitution and in every part of its administration. I was indeed sensible that this subject would require more details; and that it might be useful to form an estimate of the quantity of contributions necessary for any given portion of mankind united in a national interest; as we might thus be convinced how small a revenue would be sufficient for all the purposes of a rational government. But I find myself happily relieved from this part of my task, by the appearance of the second part of the *Rights of Man*, in which this branch of the subject is treated in that perspicuous manner which might be expected from its author; a man whom I consider as a luminary of the age, and one of the greatest benefactors of mankind. Neither my work, nor any other that shall be written for ages to come, will surely find a reader, who will not have read the *Rights of Man*.

Men are gregarious in their nature; they form together in society, not merely from necessity, to avoid the evils of solitude, but from inclination and mutual attachment. They find a positive pleasure in yielding assistance to each other, in communicating their thoughts and improving their faculties. This disposition in man is the source of morals; they have their foundation in nature, and receive their nourishment from society. The different portions of this society, that call themselves nations, have generally established the principle of securing to the individuals who compose a nation, the exclusive enjoyment of the fruits of their own labour; reserving however to the governing power the right to reclaim from time to time so much of the property and labour of individuals as shall be deemed necessary for the public service. This is the general basis on which *property*, public and private, has hitherto been founded. Nations have proceeded no farther. Perhaps in a more improved state of

society, the time will come when a different system may be
introduced; when it shall be found more congenial to the
social nature of man to exclude the idea of separate property,
and with that the numerous evils which seem to be entailed
upon it. But it is not my intention in this work to enter upon
that inquiry.

When the feudal system, with all its ferocities, was in full
operation, the superior lord, who represented the power of the
state, granted the lands to his immediate vassals, on condition
of military service. They engaged to serve in the wars of
the lord paramount a certain number of days in the year, at
their own expense. Thus they stipulated as to the quantity
of service; but gave up the right of private judgment, as to
the *object of the war*. This is the origin of the revenue of
modern Europe; and it began by debasing the minds of the
whole community; as it hurried them into actions, of which
they were not to enquire into the justice or propriety. Then
came the *socage-tenures;* which were lands granted to another
class of vassals, on condition of ploughing the lord's fields
and performing his husbandry. This was a more rational
kind of service; though, by a shocking perversion of terms,
it was called less honorable.

In proportion as war became less productive, and its profits more precarious, than those of husbandry, the tenures
upon knight-service were converted into socage-tenures; and
finally it was found convenient in most cases, especially in
England, to make a commutation of the whole money, in
certain fixed sums; and this, by its subsequent modifications
and extensions, has obtained the name of a land-tax. The
feudal revenues of the crown, though they were supposed to
be sufficient for the ordinary purposes of government, were
capable of being increased on any extraordinary occasion;
and such extraordinary occasions were sure to happen, as
often as the government chose to draw more money from the
people. It began this operation under the name of aids to
the king, *subsidia regis;* and, in England (before it was found
necessary to work the engine by regular parliaments) various
expedients were used to raise from different classes of the com-

munity these extraordinary aids. In many cases the authority of the pope was brought in to the assistance of the
king, to enable him to levy money for the court. The pope,
as head of the church, received a revenue from the people of
England through the English clergy; and the king, on certain
occasions, agreed with him that he should double his demand;
on condition that the additional sum to be raised, should be
divided between themselves.*

A perpetual pretext for these additional impositions was
always to be found in foreign wars.—Edward the first must
subdue the Welsh; a long succession of kings made the glory
of the British nation to consist in the reduction of Ireland;
others, in conquering the tomb of Christ; and others, the
crown of France. But in common occurrences, where the
call for money could not be predicated on any national object
sufficiently glaring to excite the enthusiasm or rouse the fears
of the people, it was the policy of the king to detach some
particular classes of the community from the common interest, and to extort money from them, as from a common
enemy. Thus all strangers were heavily taxed on coming
into the realm; thus Jews, with all the wealth they possessed,
were declared to be the absolute property of the king; † thus
after the religion of the government was changed, the papists
and non-jurors were taxed double to the professors of the
national religion; and thus the king could take a savage advantage of the misfortunes of individuals, and seize their
property, under the title of *wrecks, waifs, treasure-trove,
strays, amercements,* and *forfeitures.*

These, and a vast variety of other inventions, have been
practised by the English government, to legalize partial robberies, and take possession of the people's money, without
the trouble of asking for it. But all these means were insuf-

* *Cunningham's History of Taxes, page 6.*

† *In one of the laws of Edward the Confessor (which was repeatedly
enforced long after the conquest, and perhaps it is not repealed to this
day) the clause respecting the Jews is in these words: Judaei et omnia sua
sunt regis; quod in quispiam detinuerit eos, vel pecuniam corum, per-
quirat rex, si vult, tanquam suum proprium.*

ficient to supply the unlimited expenses of a government founded on orders, privileges, rank, and ignorance. The most effectual way to carry on the great business of revenue was found to be through the intervention of a parliament; and for this purpose the farce of representation has been acted over in this country, to much better effect than any species of fraud or violence has been in any other.

It would be an insult to the understanding of any reader at this day, to describe to him a thing so well known, as the manner in which this game is played between the different branches of the government. The secret is out; and the friends of the system, who used to be occupied in concealing its operation, are now engaged in defending it. The drift of their defence is to change the mode of the deception; and persuade the people by *argument*, to suffer to pass before their eyes in open day-light, scenes which have hitherto been acted only in the dark. The curtain has fallen from their hands; and they now declare that the play can go on without it. This for England, forms a new æra in cabinet politics. While the system remains the same, the scheme for carrying it on is totally new-modelled; and, like other novelties in the course of human improvement, it becomes a proper subject of our investigation.

I have known a juggler, who, after having for a long time excited wonder and drawn money from the multitude, by tricks which were supposed to be the effect of magic, would come forward with an engaging frankness, and declare that there was really nothing supernatural in the art; that it was only the effect of a little experience and attention to physical causes, not beyond the capacity of any one in the company; that, though he had deceived them thus far, he was now ready to undeceive them; and, for another fee, he would go through the same course again, with the explanations. This ingenious confession redoubled their curiosity; the spectators continued their attention, and renewed their contributions.

The government of Great Britain, under king, lords and boroughs, is now defended both in and out of parliament, by arguments unknown to former politicians. As nearly as any

words, except the right ones, can express the full force of these
arguments, they are stated by their authors in the following
language: "No people ever has been or ever can be capable
of knowing what is for their own good, of making their own
laws, or of understanding them after they are made: as the
people of England, during the time of the commonwealth,
imbibed a different opinion, it has been thought best, especially
since the last revolution, to cherish them in their error, in
order to come more easily at their money. We therefore told
them that they were free; that they, as Englishmen, ought
to be free, because their ancestors were so; that English
liberty was the envy and admiration of the world; that the
French were their natural enemies, because they were slaves;
and it was necessary to make a war once in seven years, to
keep up this idea; that we were sorry for the increasing burthen of their taxes; but that was a circumstance not to be
regarded by a free people, as they had the privilege of taxing
themselves, and their taxes were the price of their freedom in
church and state; that, we intended to lessen their burthens
as soon as the enemies to our religion and to our happy constitution were destroyed. But now, gentlemen, we see you have
discovered, and we are willing to acknowledge, that this was
all a deception: as to liberty, it is but a name; man gives it up
on entering into society, in order to enjoy the benefits of being
governed; it never was nor ever will be, realized by any nation
under heaven; witness the horrors of pretended liberty in
France, the daily assassinations and perpetual robberies
which you see in Mr. Burke's book from beginning to end;
witness the late infatuation of the Americas; who, already
recovering their senses, and sick of their boasted independence,* are now wishing to return to the protection of their
mother-country, where they could purchase their laws ready
made by us, who understand the business; as to the church,
we are convinced it is no matter on what sort of religion it is

* *This is a serious argument, used by several writers as well as parlia-
mentary and coffee-house orators, to prove that liberty cannot exist in any
country. See Dr.* Tatham *and others.*

founded, provided it be well connected with the state. We shall say nothing in future of the *burthen of taxes*, as it has been falsely called, the phrase itself has no longer any meaning; it is now clearly known that public taxes are, in themselves, a public benefit; every well-wisher to this country must wish them to increase; and for that purpose he will do all in his power to multiply the occasions for creating them; for it is acknowledged by all good subjects, that a national debt is national prosperity, and that we grow rich in proportion to the money we pay out. We are as frank to confess, as any caviller is to assert, that the House of Commons is not a representation of the people; it has no connection with them, and it is no longer to our purpose to suppose that it has; for the people have nothing to do with the government, except to be governed; but the House of Commons is retained in the State for the same reason that the other branches of the legislature, and that courts and armies are retained, for the sake of increasing the wealth and happiness of the people in the augmentation of the revenue."

* * * * * *

The true object of the social compact is to improve our moral faculties, as well as to supply our physical wants; and where it fails in the first of these, it certainly will fail in the last. But where the moral purpose is attained, there can be no fear but that the physical one will be the inseparable consequence; place society on this footing, and there will be no aid or duty that the general interest can require from individuals, but what every individual will understand. His duties, when first proposed, will all be voluntary, and being clearly understood to be founded on the good of the whole community, he will find a greater personal interest in the performance than he would in the violation. There is no position more undeniable in my apprehension, than that this would always be the case with a great majority of any people; and if we suppose a small portion of refractory persons, who, from want of original consent, or from a subsequent change of opinion, should refuse to perform their duties; in this case, the opinions of the great majority assume the shape of government, and procure a compliance by compulsion and restraint. This is the only sure foundation on which we can ever build the real dignity of society, or the corresponding energy of government. It is establishing the moral relations of men on the moral sense of men; and it is this union alone that can cherish our esteem or command our respect.

On this plan, it is of the utmost importance that the wants of the state should never be disguised, and that the duty of the individual, in supplying those wants, should never be performed by deception. If the state be properly organized, such disguise and deception will be unnecessary; and if we wish to preserve it from degeneration, they will be extremely dangerous; as, by attacking the moral sense of the people, they sap the foundation of the state.

When a company of merchants, or other private men, engage in an enterprise that requires contributions in money, we hear of no difficulties in raising the stipulated sums among the different partners in the company. Every partner makes it his business to understand the nature of the concern; he expects an advantage from the enterprise, and pays his money with the same willingness, as he would pay it in his private business. He would feel himself insulted, if any disguise were thrown upon the subject, to cheat him into his duty. Indeed, when the enterprise has come to an end, or when there is an apprehension of loss, or a suspicion of mismanagement in the agents, it is natural to expect a reluctance in payment, which is only to be overcome by the arts of deception or the compulsion of law. But this is not the case while the company is in a prosperous condition, and while its members are united by mutual confidence in pursuit of a common interest. A nation, whose government should be habitually in the hands of the whole community, would always be a company in this prosperous condition; its concerns would be a perpetual and promising enterprise, in which every individual would find his interest and repose his confidence. Personal protection and public happiness would be the objects aimed at in the administration; and these would be infallibly attained, because no human accidents could prevent it. There could be no suspicion of mismanagement in the agents, they being perpetually under the control of the whole people. Every reason, therefore, which could induce individuals to withhold their pecuniary contributions, would be entirely removed; and the same motives which influence a man to give his attention and pay his money in his own personal concerns, would engage him to do the same things in the concerns of the public.

DAVID HUMPHREYS
(1753–1818)

A POEM ON THE INDUSTRY OF THE UNITED STATES OF AMERICA *

[Reprinted from the 1804 edition, with the author's notes.]

ARGUMENT

The Genius of Culture invoked—prodigious effect of toil in changing the face of nature—state of our country when it was first settled by our ancestors—their manly efforts crowned with success—contrast between North and South-America—the latter remarkable for mines, as the former is for agriculture—in what manner labour embellishes the land—different branches of cultivation recommended—the fabrication of maple sugar dwelt upon, as having a gradual tendency to the abolition of slavery—commerce to succeed—strong propensities of the people of the United States for extensive navigation—effeminate nations are always in danger of losing their independence—several specified which have experienced the debilitating consequences of sloth—its destructive influence on states—Congress called upon to encourage industry in the United States; and Washington, as President, to protect manufactures—machinery for diminishing the operations of manual labour—the loom—wool—sheep—flax and hemp—remonstrance against suffering our manufacturing establishments to be frustrated by an unreasonable predilection for foreign fabrics—the fair sex invited to give the example of encouraging home manufactures—their province in the United States—their influence on civilized society—deplorable condition of savage life—moral effect of industry on constitution and character—bold and adventurous spirit of our citizens—prepared by hardiness to distinguish themselves on the ocean and in war

* Written in Lisbon when the Author was Minister at the Court—To His Royal Highness the Prince Regent of Portugal.

—allusion to our contest with Britain—happiness of our present peaceful situation—the Poem is concluded with the praises of Connecticut as an agricultural State.

GENIUS of Culture! thou, whose chaster taste
Can clothe with beauty ev'n the dreary waste;
Teach me to sing, what bright'ning charms unfold,
The bearded ears, that bend with more than gold;
How empire rises, and how morals spring,
From lowly labour, teach my lips to sing;
Exalt the numbers with thy gifts supreme,
Ennobler of the song, my guide and theme!

Thou, toil! that mak'st, where our young empire grows,
The wilderness bloom beauteous as the rose,
Parent of wealth and joy! my nation's friend!
Be present, nature's rudest works to mend;
With all the arts of polish'd life to bless,
And half thy ills, Humanity! redress.
On this revolving day, that saw the birth
Of a whole nation glad th' astonished earth;
Thee I invoke to bless the recent reign
Of independence—but for thee how vain
Each fair advantage liberty has giv'n,
And all the copious bounties show'r'd by heav'n?
Hail, mighty pow'r! whose vivifying breath
Wakes vegetation on the barren heath;
Thou changest nature's face; thy influence such
Dark deserts brighten at thy glowing touch;
Creation springs where'er thy plough-share drives,
And the dead grain, an hundred fold, revives.
Thy voice, that dissipates the savage gloom,
Bade in the wild unwonted beauty bloom;
By thee and freedom guided, not in vain,
Our great fore-fathers dar'd the desert main;
O'er waves no keel had cut they found the shore,

Where desolation stain'd his steps with gore,
Th' immense of forest! where no tree was fell'd,
Where savage-men at midnight orgies yell'd;
Where howl'd round burning pyres each ravening **beast,**
As fiend-like forms devour'd their bloody feast,
And hoarse resounded o'er the horrid heath,
The doleful war-whoop, or the song of death.
Soon our progenitors subdu'd the wild,
And virgin nature, rob'd in verdure, smil'd.
They bade her fruits, through rifted rocks, from **hills**
Descend, misnam'd innavigable rills:
Bade houses, hamlets, towns, and cities rise,
And tow'rs and temples gild Columbian skies.
Success thence crown'd that bold, but patient **band,**
Whose undegen'rate sons possess the land;
Their great fore-fathers' principles avow,
And proudly dare to venerate the plough.

Where slaughter's war-dogs many a tribe **destroy'd,**
Not such the race who fill'd the southern void:
For them unbidden harvests deck the soil,
For them in mines unhappy thousands toil,
Where Plata's waves o'er silvery sands are roll'd,
Or Amazonia's path is pav'd in gold.
There suns too fiercely o'er the surface glow,
And embryon metals form and feed below;
Where, shut from day, in central caverns deep,
Hopeless of freedom, wretches watch and weep;
Compell'd for gold to rip the womb of earth,
And drag the precious mischief into birth.

Yet where those vertic suns intensely shine,
Whose fires the metals more than men refine,
To drain their limbs of strength the climate serves,
And not our vigour strings their slacken'd nerves.

While all your gains the social pact secures,
Columbians! say, what happiness is yours?

Say, ye who, not as tenants, till the soil,
The joys that freedmen find in rural toil?
In what blest spot, through all terraqueous space,
Exists a hardier or a happier race?
Ye bid your glebes with future germs rejoice,
And seeds that sleep inhum'd strait hear your voice.
How change the prospects at your blithe command!
Where weeds and brambles stood now flowrets stand.
How blooms the dell, as spreads the rippling rill,
While mottled cattle top the moving hill!
Bid marshall'd maize the tassell'd flag unfold,
And wheat-ears barb their glistening spears with gold:
In northern plains the orchard's produce glow,
Or with its beverage pure the press o'erflow:
In southern climes, beneath a fervid sky,
Savannas, green with rice, refresh the eye;
There, from th' adopted stranger-tree, despoil
The branch that cheers for peace, the fruit with oil.
O'er fens, reform'd, let verdant grass succeed
The blue-ting'd indigo—pestiferous weed!
Where dun, hoed fields, afford subsistence scant
For those who tend Tobago's luxury plant,
Bid other crops with brighter hues be crown'd,
And herb for beast, and bread for man abound.
With little fingers let the children cull,
Like flakes of snow, the vegetable wool;
Or nurse the *chrysalis* with mulberry leaves,
The *worm* whose silk the curious artist weaves:
Let buzzing bees display the winnowing wing,
Seek freshest flowers, and rifle all the spring:
Let brimming pails beside the heifers stand,
With milk and honey flow the happy land;
And turn the wildest growth to human use,
Ambrosial sugar find from maple-juice!

Thou, dulcet tree, imbue the flowing song
With thy distilling drops, untried too long!
Thee, dancing round in many a mazy ring,

The rustic youths and sylvan maids shall sing.
In sacch'rine streams thou pour'st the tide of life,
Yet grow'st still stronger from th' innocuous knife;
Thy sap, more sweet than Hybla's honey, flows,
Health for the heart-sick—cure of slavery's woes—
Then, as th' unfailing source, balsamic, runs,
Dispense that cordial, hope, for Afric's sons!

Oh, could my song impressive horror bring,
Of conscious guilt th' insufferable sting;
From eyes untaught to weep the tear should start,
And mercy melt the long obdur'd of heart.
See naked negroes rear the sugar'd reeds!
Behold! their flesh beneath their driver bleeds!
And hear their heart-heav'd groans! then say, how good,
How sweet, the dainties drugg'd with human blood!

Though night's dark shades o'ercast th' ill-favour'd race,
Nor transient flushes change the vacant face;
Though nature ne'er transforms their woolly hair
To golden ringlets, elegantly fair!
Yet has not God infus'd immortal powers,
The same their organs and their souls as ours?
Are they not made to ruminate the sky?
Or must they perish like the beasts that die?
Perish the thought that men's high worth impairs,
Sons of Omnipotence, and Glory's Heirs!

Come, ye who love the human race divine,
Their bleeding bosoms bathe with oil and wine,
Bind up their wounds—then bless the dulcet tree,
Whose substituted sweets one slave may free;
Till new* discoveries more man's wrath assuage,
And heav'n restrain the remnant of his rage.

* The recent invention in Prussia of extracting sugar from the
Beterave, or *Beet*, it is to be hoped will be followed by useful results.
. . . It is a well known fact that many families in the new settle-
ments of the United States are entirely supplied with sugar manufac-
tured from maple-sap.

Thou, slavery, (maledictions blast thy name!)
Fell scourge of mortals, reason's foulest shame!
Fly, fiend infernal! to thy Stygean shore,
And let thy deeds defile my song no more.

Heav'ns! still must men, like beasts, be bought and sold,
The charities of life exchang'd for gold!
Husbands from wives, from parents children torn,
In quivering fear, with grief exquisite, mourn!
No, soon shall commerce, better understood,
With happier freight promote the mutual good.
As fed by snows of winter, show'rs of spring,
Whate'er the seasons in succession bring;
What summer ripens and *what* autumn yields,
Th' *immeasurable growth* of fertile fields!
Our rapid fleets to realms that want convey,
And new-born stars in wond'ring skies display.
Ev'n now innumerous ships, their flags unfurl'd,
With flying convass cloud the wat'ry world;
Commercing, steer beneath the burning line,
Near icy mountains, on the polar brine;
From cheerless cliffs, where not a blossom blows,
Whose wild craggs whiten in eternal snows,
To where the smooth Pacific Ocean smiles,
Cheer'd by the fragrance of the spicy isles.

Not thus enervate nations tempt the seas,
By luxury lull'd in soft voluptuous ease;
Thence sloth begets servility of soul,
Degrades each part, contaminates the whole;
And taints in torpid veins the thickening blood,
Like the green mantle on a mire of mud.
Where convents deal the poor their daily broth,
See charity herself encourage sloth!
Though helpless some, more lazy join the troop,
And healthful beggars swell the shameless groupe.
Will heav'n benignant on those nations smile,
Where sloth and vice are less disgrace than toil?

With opiates drunk, in indolence reclin'd,
Unbrac'd their sinews, and debauch'd their mind,
Can crowds, turn'd cowards, self-esteem retain,
Or long unspoil'd of freedom's gifts remain?
'Tis by the lofty purpose, desperate deed,
Of men who dare for liberty to bleed,
By long endurance, fields with crimson stain'd,
That independence won, must be maintain'd.

   Where art thou, Athens! thy high spirit lost!
Where, Sparta! that defied all Asia's host!
And where (in dust her mould'ring trophies hurl'd)
Imperial Rome, the mistress of the world!
How Lusitania, queen of diamond mines,
(Her glorious Gamas dead) a widow pines!
And will not grave Iberia learn, at length,
In toil, not gold, consists a nation's strength?
How long shall empires feel, destructive sloth!
Thy cank'ring breath, that checks and kills their growth?
If sloth to dissolution yields the prey,
Take but the cause, we take th' effect away.

   Sages, conven'd from delegating states,
Who bear the charge of unborn millions' fates;
From early systems states their habits take,
And morals more than climes a difference make:
Then give to toil a bias, aid his cause
With all the force and majesty of laws;
So shall for you long generations raise,
The sweetest incense of unpurchas'd praise!

   Thou, Washington, by heav'n for triumphs nurs'd,
In war, in peace, of much lov'd mortals first!
In public as in private life benign,
Still be the people heav'n's own care and thine!
While thou presid'st, in useful arts direct,
Create new fabrics and the old protect.
Lo! at thy word, subdued for wond'ring man,

What mighty elements advance the plan;
While fire and wind obey the Master's call,
And water labours in his forceful fall!
Teach tiny hands with engin'ry to toil,
Cause failing age o'er easy tasks to smile;
Thyself that best of offices perform,
The hungry nourish and the naked warm;
With gladness picture rescued beauty's eye,
And cheek with health's inimitable dye;
So shall the young, the feeble find employ,
And hearts with grief o'erwhelm'd emerge to joy.

    First let the loom each lib'ral thought engage,
Its labours growing with the growing age;
Then true utility with taste allied,
Shall make our homespun garbs our nation's pride.
See *wool*, the boast of Britain's proudest hour,
Is still the basis of her wealth and pow'r!
From her the nations wait their wintry robe,
Round half this idle, poor, dependant globe.
Shall we, who foil'd her sons in fields of fame,
In peace add noblest triumphs to her name?
Shall we, who dar'd assert the rights of man,
Become the vassals of her wiser plan?
Then, rous'd from lethargies—up! men! increase,
In every vale, on every hill, the fleece!
And see the fold, with thousands teeming, fills
With flocks the bleating vales and echoing hills.
Ye harmless people! man your young will tend,
While ye for him your coats superfluous lend.
Him nature form'd with curious pride, while bare,
To fence with finery from the piercing air:
This fleece shall draw its azure from the sky,
This drink the purple, that the scarlet dye;
Another, where immingling hues are giv'n,
Shall mock the bow with colours dipt in heav'n:
Not guarded Colchis gave admiring Greece
So rich a treasure in its golden fleece.

Oh, might my* guidance from the downs of Spain,
Lead a white flock across the western main;
Fam'd like the bark that bore the Argonaut,
Should be the vessel with the burden fraught!
Clad in the raiment my Merinos yield,
Like Cincinnatus fed from my own field;
Far from ambition, grandeur, care and strife,
In sweet fruition of domestic life;
There would I pass with friends, beneath my trees,
What rests from public life, in letter'd ease.

To toil encourag'd, free from tythe and tax,
Ye farmers sow your fields with hemp and flax:
Let these the distaff for the web supply,
Spin on the spool, or with the shuttle fly.
But what vile cause retards the public plan?
Why fail the fabrics patriot zeal began?
Must nought but tombs of industry be found,
Prostrated arts expiring on the ground?
Shall we, of gewgaws gleaning half the globe,
Disgrace our country with a foreign robe?
Forbid it int'rest, independence, shame,
And blush that kindles bright at honour's flame!

Should peace, like sorcery, with her spells controul
Our innate springs and energies of soul;
To you, Columbian dames! my accents call,
Oh, save your country from the threaten'd fall!
Will ye, blest fair! adopt from every zone
Fantastic fashions, noxious in your own?
At wintry balls in gauzy garments drest,
Admit the dire destroyer in your breast?
Oft when nocturnal sports your visage flush,
As gay and heedless to the halls ye rush,
Then death your doom prepares: cough, fever, rheum,
And pale consumption nip your rosy bloom.

* . . . The Merino breed of Sheep.

Hence many a flow'r in beauty's damask pride,
Wither'd, at morn, has droop'd its head and died.*
While youthful crimson hurries though your veins,
No cynic bard from licit joys restrains;
Or bids with nature hold unequal strife,
And still go sorrowing through the road of life.
Nor deem him hostile who of danger warns,
Who leaves the rose, but plucks away its thorns.

    In our new world not birth and proud pretence,
Your sex from skill in household cares dispense.
Yet those where fortune smiles, whom fancy warms,
May paint historic or ideal forms;
Teach the fair flow'r on lucid lawn to spring,
The lute to languish or the tongue to sing.
With letters, arts, botanic, chemic skill,
Some shall their leisure hours delighted fill;
While some, for studies more sublime design'd,
Expatiate freely o'er the world of mind:
Another class on boldest wing shall soar,
The wand'ring stars and ways of heav'n explore;
Still skill'd not less in captivating arts,
To move our passions and to mend our hearts.
While tiptoe spirits buoy each graceful limb,
See down the dance the lovely fair-one swim;
Her own neat needle-work improves her bloom,
Cloth'd in the labours of Columbia's loom:
Her lover sees express'd upon her face,
Angelic goodness, loveliness and grace;
And hopes, in bridal bow'rs, to meet those charms,
Bliss to his soul and rapture in her arms!
Then, oh, ye fair! refin'd each grosser sense,
'Gainst delicacy shun the least offence.

    * This, it is wished, may be received as a useful warning by young
persons against exposing themselves, when too thinly clad, to the
winter air. Many deaths have been occasioned by imprudencies of
this nature.

What though not call'd to mix in cares of state,
To brave the storm of battle or debate;
Yet in our revolution greatly brave,
What high examples to our sex ye gave?
And still 'tis yours with secret, soft controul,
To hold a gentler empire o'er the soul;
In polish'd states to make, with sweet behest,
The hero happy and the patriot blest;
To charm their anxious hours with cheering smiles,
Relieve their suff'rings and reward their toils.

And are there men, with civil bliss at strife,
Who lavish wanton praise on savage life?
Is licence freedom? Can the general good
Bid each barbarian quench revenge in blood?
While wrongs, ev'n fancied, set his soul on fire,
Can judgment cool unite with burning ire?
Or numb'd in apathy, can that alone
Afford the fond endearments I have known?
See the rude Indian, reason's dictates braves,
And treats the females as his abject slaves:
He, round his hearth, no circle calls, at ev'n,
To share the sweetest pleasures under heav'n.
Regard yon desert, dark and drear, where roam
Hordes who ne'er knew a comfortable home:
On them no peaceful arts their influence shed,
But fierce as panthers on the mountains bred,
They prowl for prey. For them the hunted wood
Now yields redundant, now penurious food—
Regorg'd or famish'd oft—a miscreant crew—
If few their wants, their comforts still more few!
Ah! when will virtue's evangelic flame
The frigid wildness of their tempers tame?
Till that bright hour, no hope beyond the sky—
Forlorn they live, and like the brute they die!

Of savage life so spring the bitter fruits,
For savage indolence the man imbrutes.

From industry the sinews strength acquire,
The limbs expand, the bosom feels new fire.
Unwearied industry pervades the whole,
Nor lends more force to body than to soul.
Hence character is form'd, and hence proceeds
Th' enlivening heat that fires to daring deeds:
Then animation bids the spirit warm,
Soar in the whirlwind and enjoy the storm.
For our brave tars what clime too warm, too cold,
What toil too hardy, or what task too bold?
O'er storm-vex'd waves our vent'rous vessels roll,
Round artic isles or near th' antartic pole;
Nor fear their crews the fell tornado's ire,
Wrapp'd in a deluge of Caribbean fire.
The wonders of the deep they see, while tost
From earth's warm girdle to the climes of frost:
Full soon to bid the battle's thunder roar,
And guard with wooden walls their native shore.

What like rough effort fortifies each part,
With steel the limbs and adamant the heart!
What gives our seamen steadiness of soul,
When bursting thunders rend the redd'ning pole,
When down the black'ning clouds, in streams that bend
Athwart the tall shrouds, livid fires descend,
When howling winds in wild gyrations fly,
And night sits frantic on the scowling sky?

What makes the patriot scorn the menac'd blow,
His courage rising as the dangers grow!
What bade our bands—to shield the commonweal—
Bare their bold bosoms to the lifted steel;
What time Virginia's light, with steady ray,
Led through the darksome gloom our desp'rate way;
When Britain, like a night-storm, hovering, hurl'd
The red-wing'd vengeance on the western world!

Lo! in that western world how chang'd the scene!
There peace now shines uncloudedly serene;

While, red with gore, through Europe's realms afar,
Sails the dread storm of desolating war.
In Lusitania's clime, while we behold
The orange gleam with vegetating gold;
Where buds and fruits in gay confusion join,
And the glad vintage purples on the vine;
Where sleeps on beds of rose the moon-light calm,
Honey'd the dew and steep'd the air in balm!
Where wild-heath blooms perfume the passing gales,
And Tagus whitens with unnumber'd sails;
Say, shares my friend,* my fond desires that rise
For distant scenes beneath the western skies?
Say, canst thou love those scenes in lonely pride,
The beauteous shores that bound th' Atlantic tide;
Where hills and vales, and villages and farms,
In lovely landscapes blend their mingled charms?

Me, languid long, new ardour fires at length,
(With thee my soul collecting all her strength)
New raptures seize, with patriot pride elate,
To sing the charms that grace my native state.

Hail favour'd state! CONNECTICUT! thy name
Uncouth in song, too long conceal'd from fame;
If yet thy filial bards the gloom can pierce,
Shall rise and flourish in immortal verse.
Inventive genius, imitative pow'rs,
And, still more precious, common-sense, is ours;
While knowledge useful, more than science grand,
In rivulets still o'erspreads the smiling land.

Hail, model of free states! too little known,
Too lightly priz'd for *rural arts* alone:
Yet hence from savage, social life began,
Compacts were fram'd and man grew mild to man.
Thee, Agriculture! source of every joy.

* Addressed to a lady in Lisbon.

Domestic sweets and bliss without alloy;
Thee, friend of freedom, independence, worth,
What raptur'd song can set conspicuous forth?
Thine every grateful gift, my native soil!
That ceaseless comes from *agricultural toil;*
This bids thee, dress'd, with added charms appear,
And crowns with glories, not its own, the year.
Though, capp'd with cliffs of flint, thy surface rude,
And stubborn glebe the slothful race exclude;
Though sultry summer parch thy gaping plains,
Or chilling winter bind in icy chains;
Thy patient sons, prepar'd for tasks sublime,
Redress the rigours of th' inclement clime,
Clothe arid earth in green, for glooms supply
The brightest beauties to th' astonish'd eye.

What though for us no fields Arcadian bloom,
Nor tropic shrubs diffuse a glad perfume;
No fairy regions picturesque with flow'rs,
Elysian groves, or amaranthine bow'rs,
Breathe sweet enchantment—but still fairer smile,
Once savage wilds now tam'd by tut'ring toil.
The rolling seasons saw with rapture strange,
The desert blossom and the climate change.
Roll on, thou sun! and bring the prospect bright,
Before our ravish'd view in liveliest light.
Arise in vernal pride, ye virgin plains!
With winning features which no fiction feigns.
Arise, ye laughing lawns! ye gladd'ning glades!
Poetic banks! and philosophic shades!
Awake, ye meads! your bosoms ope, ye flow'rs!
Exult, oh earth! and heav'n descend in show'rs!

Where the dun forest's thickest foliage frown'd,
And night and horror brooded o'er the ground;
While matted boughs impenetrably wove
The sable curtains of th' impervious grove;
Where the swart savage fix'd his short abode,

Or wound through tangled wilds his thorny road;
Where the gaunt wolves from crag-roof'd caverns prowl'd,
And mountains echoed as the monsters howl'd;
Where putrid marshes felt no solar beams,
And mantling mire exhal'd mephitic steams;
See, mid the rocks, a Paradise arise,
That feels the fostering warmth of genial skies!
While gurgling currents lull th' enchanted soil,
The hill-tops brighten and the dingles smile.

    Then hail for us, ye transatlantic scenes,
Soul-soothing dwellings! sight-refreshing greens!
And chiefly hail, thou state! where virtue reigns,
And peace and plenty crown the cultur'd plains.

    Nor lacks there aught to soothe the pensive mind,
Its taste on nature form'd, by truth refin'd;
For pure simplicity can touch the heart,
Beyond the glitter and the gloss of art.
Not wanting there the fountain's bubbling tide,
Whence flows the narrow stream and river wide,
With gladsome wave to drench the thirsty dale,
Or waft through wond'ring woods the flitting sail.
Not wanting there the cottage white-wash'd clean,
Nor town with spires that glimmmer o'er the green:
Nor rich variety's uncloying charm,
The steeds that prance, the herds that graze the farm;
The flocks that gambol o'er the dark-green hills,
The tumbling brooks that turn the busy mills;
The clover pastures deck'd with dappled flow'rs,
Spontaneous; gardens gay with roseate bow'rs;
The tedded grass in meadows newly shorn,
The pensile wheat-heads and stiff Indian corn;
The grafts with tempting fruit, and thick-leav'd groves,
Where timid birds conceal their airy loves:
Along th' umbrageous walk, enamour'd meet
The artless pairs, in courtship chaste as sweet,
In wedlock soon to join—hail, sacred rite!

Delicious spring! exhaustless of delight!
No poor, for wealth withheld, accuses heav'n,
Nor rich, insulting, spurns the bounties giv'n.
No wretched outcast—happy, till beguil'd—
Pollution's sister, and affliction's child!
Shivering and darkling strays through wintry streets,
And lures (for bread) to brothels all she meets;
Or tir'd and sick, with fain and fearful cry,
At her betrayer's door lies down to die.
No scenes of woe the pleasing prospect blight,
And no disgusting object pains the sight;
For calm *content*, the sunshine of the soul,
With bright'ning *ease*, embellishes the whole.

   'Tis rural innocence, with rural toil,
Can change the frown of fortune to a smile.
Ah, let the sons of insolence deride
The simple joys by humble toil supplied:
Not him whose breast with false refinement pants,
Factitious pleasures, artificial wants,
Such scenes delight—nor boasts that state a claim,
For man's or nature's grandest works, to fame.

   Of life sequester'd, fond and frequent theme!
Th' instructed few with higher reverence deem:
For o'er its moral part a lustre shines,
That all around enlivens and refines.
'Twas there the joys of wedded love began,
And health and happiness there dwelt with man:
The city's palaces though man has made,
The country's charming views a God display'd—
Still the best site from art derives new charms,
In villas fair and ornamented farms.

   There, while our freemen share thy blessings, health!
In that blest mean dividing want from wealth;
How sweet their food appears! how lightsome seems
Their daily labour! and how bright their dreams!

Not inexpert to till or guard their farms,
Patient in toil, but terrible in arms,
When stung by wrong, and fir'd with patriot rage,
They in the battle's brunt with hosts engage!
What Rome, once virtuous, saw, this gives us now—
Heroes and statesmen, awful from the plough.

   And ye, compatriots! who for freedom fought,
Preserve that prize your toil and blood have bought.
(Fraternal troop long tried by storms of fate,
Surviving soldiers of my native state,
From me your cherish'd image ne'er shall part,
'Till death's cold hand shall wring it from my heart!)
Heav'ns! how your fields were heap'd with kindred slain,
While many a stream ran crimson to the main!
Where a new* Thames distain'd with carnage flow'd,
How the sea redden'd to receive the load?
How Danb'ry's burning turrets dimm'd the day,
How Fairfield, Norwalk, dark in ashes lay?
Ye tearless saw your coasts to deserts turn'd,
Your substance pillag'd, and your buildings burn'd;
Your flocks and herds become th' invaders' spoil,
And the fair harvest ravish'd from the soil.
Ye saw th' infuriate foe, with impious ire,
Consume Jehovah's hallow'd fanes in fire.
What Gothic rage assail'd the muses' seat,†
And hunted science in her lov'd retreat?
Her very porch‡ with vital purple stain'd,
Her courts polluted and her shrine prophan'd!
'Twas then th' obstrep'rous drum, th' ear-tinkling fife,
Pierc'd the still shades of academic life;
There Tryon left on ruins, mark'd with flame,
A dread memorial of his hated name.

   * New London in Connecticut.
   † Princeton and New Haven Colleges.
   ‡ Mr. Beers, a respectable inhabitant of New Haven, was killed
when standing peaceably at his own door, contiguous to Yale
College.

But, lo! what present growth exceeds the past,
While population adds improvements vast;
For population doubles still our force,
Ere thrice eight annual suns complete their course.
How teems the fresh mould with luxuriant green!
There, not a vestige of the war is seen;
And ev'n late blazing towns that blush'd with gore,
Smile brighter far and lovelier than before.
Not so for man will life's once faded spring,
Return more sweet and fairer blossoms bring.
No more will friendship's buried hopes return!
Say, mem'ry! mourning o'er each hero's urn,
Where now the dreams that cheer'd my youth in vain,
And where my youthful friends in battle slain?
See, vernal blooms, as soon as born, decay,
And each wing'd moment bear some flow'r away!
So fly the years that charm'd in early life,
So fade the laurels won in martial strife.
Ye vanish'd scenes! ye visionary toys!
Delusive hopes! and transitory joys!
Adieu!—but, virtue! cheer our little lives,—
For, from the wreck, religion still survives.
Religious zeal our ancestors that warm'd,
With passions cool'd, their temp'rate habits form'd:
Hence in that state is seen (sight passing strange!)
Choice free and frequent, yet no lust of change.
The foreigner admires of bliss the cause,
In fair elections and the reign of laws;
And joys to find on shores long waste and wild,
A race in manners undebauch'd, yet mild;
Between too rude and polish'd life, a stage
That claims new actors for a golden age.

Such sober habits industry prepares,
And order guarantees for freedom's heirs.
Say, in what state, so soon imbib'd the youth
Th' eternal principles of right and truth?
Where education such instruction spread?

Where on the mind such influence morals shed?
Where modesty with charms so fair appear'd?
So honour'd age, and virtue so rever'd?

   Thou fount of learning where I drank, thou Yale!
Fount of religion and of knowledge, hail!
There, happy parents! bid our thirsting youth
Quaff copious immortality and truth;
While Dwight, with soaring soul, directs their way
To the full well of life, in climes of endless day.

   Rejoice in strength of youth! rejoice, sweet band!
To rise the hope and glory of our land.
First shall the legates in th' Almighty's name,
Like seers whose lips were touch'd with living flame,
Announce the WORD *from* HEAV'N sublime, refin'd,
And bring mild consolations to the mind;
Of future being the glad tidings bear,
And God's high will with holy zeal declare!

   Ye champions, prompt to check the course of fate,
And give man's days their longest, healthiest date;
Go forth, the sick-man's sleepy couch to smooth,
With potent drugs the pang of anguish soothe;
The dart of death avert—his victim save—
And rescue thousands from th' untimely grave!
For this, from nature's mixture, chemic art
Extracts the healing from the pois'nous part.
And where our woods contain salubrious pow'rs,
In life-prolonging roots, and barks, and flow'rs;
Ye botanists! with sapient toil explore
Our continent's interminable store,—
A boundless field! ne'er view'd by human eye,
Where vegetation lives alone to die.
There search the sylvan world with eager view,
And call by name each plant that sips the dew;
From the proud pine, his lofty head who shrouds
In misty regions mid condensing clouds,

To tufted shrubs and gadding vines that crawl,
Or humble hyssop springing by the wall.

Ye advocates for justice thence proceed,
With pow'rful voice for innocence to plead;
Not warp'd by favour, flatt'ry, gold or awe,
The firm support and ornament of law!
Hence oft elect from your enlighten'd band,
Judges and senators shall rule the land.

With fancy vivid as with judgment strong,
Our pride in genius, as our first in song,
Thy intellectual stores, blest Dwight! impart,
And taste correct for every finer art:
Bid wisdom's higher lore with ethics giv'n,
For greatness form the race, belov'd of heav'n:
Bring to their breasts her energies divine,
The grovelling thought to raise, the gross refine!
Bid bards melodious charm the listening throng,
Thrill'd with the raptures of ecstatic song;
Bid, while the spark of animation warms,
Imagination body finest forms;
Creative artists paint our martial strife,
And wake the slumb'ring marble into life!

Or should the hollow brass be heard to roar,
And hostile navies hover round our shore,
Then bid our youth along th' extended coast,
Their country's bulwark, and their country's boast,
Horrent in arms, an iron rampart stand,
To shield from foes th' inviolable land!

Ere ye begin to tread life's wider stage,
In manhood's prime, dear, interesting age!
Attend a time-taught bard, to toils inur'd,
With those bold chiefs whose blood your rights secur'd:
Ye junior patriots, listen! learn, my friends!
How much your lot on industry depends:

For God, a God of order, ne'er design'd,
Equal conditions for the human kind.
Equality of rights your bliss maintains,
While law protects what honest labour gains.,
Your great exertions by restraint uncheck'd,
Your gen'rous heat undamp'd by cold neglect;
The wide career for freemen open lies,
Where wealth, and pow'r, and honour yield the prize.
Yet should dark discord's clouds your land o'ercast,
Lost is your freedom and your empire past.
Be union yours! To guard your union, heav'n
The general government, in *trust*, has giv'n:
Then, when ere long your fathers sleep in dust,
Preserve, like vestal fire, that *sacred* TRUST!

THE MONKEY,
Who shaved himself and his Friends

A FABLE

Addressed to the Hon. —— ——.

A MAN who own'd a barber's shop
At York, and shav'd full many a fop,
A monkey kept for their amusement;
He made no other kind of use on't—
This monkey took great observation,
Was wonderful at imitation,
And all he saw the barber do,
He mimic'd straight, and did it too.

It chanc'd in shop, the dog and cat,
While friseur din'd, demurely sat,
Jacko found nought to play the knave in,
So thought he'd try his hand at shaving.
Around the shop in haste he rushes,
And gets the razors, soap, and brushes;
Now puss he fix'd (no muscle miss stirs)
And lather'd well her beard and whiskers,)
Then gave a gash, as he began—
The cat cry'd "waugh!" and off she ran.

Next Towser's beard he try'd his skill in,
Though Towser seem'd somewhat unwilling:
As badly here again succeeding,
The dog runs howling round, and bleeding.

Nor yet was tir'd our roguish elf;
He'd seen the barber shave himself;
So by the glass, upon the table,
He rubs with soap his visage sable,

Then with left hand holds smooth his jaw,—
The razor in his dexter paw;
Around he flourishes and slashes,
Till all his face is seam'd with gashes.
His cheeks dispatch'd—his visage thin
He cock'd, to shave beneath his chin;
Drew razor swift as he could pull it,
And cut, from ear to ear, his gullet.

MORAL

Who cannot write, yet handle pens,
Are apt to hurt themselves and friends.
Though others use them well, yet fools
Should never meddle with edge tools.

AN ODE

OH, lovely Laura! may a youth,
Inspir'd by beauty, urg'd by truth,
    Disclose the heart's alarms,
The fire in youthful blood that glows,
Th' impassion'd pang on love that grows,
    And dare to sing thy charms!

Enough with war my lay has rung;
A softer theme awakes my tongue;
    'Tis beauty's force divine;
Can I resist that air, that grace,
The charms of motion, figure, face?
    For ev'ry charm is thine.

Of health, of youth, th' expanding flush,
Of virgin fear the flying blush,
    Distain thy lily cheek:
The bee such nectar never sips,
As yields the rose-bud of thy lips,
    Thy lips that sweetly speak.

'Tis thine the heaviest heart to cheer,
Those accents caught with eager ear,
    So musically roll:
While swells the breast, the snow-white skin
Scarce hides the secret thoughts within,
    Nor needs disguise that soul.

Where down thy waist, and o'er thy breast,
In light brown ringlets neatly drest,
    Devolves thy beauteous hair:
Eager I gaze—and, gazing, dream

Of halcyon days; while on me beam
   Those blue-eyes, mild and fair.

Unblam'd, oh let me gaze and gaze,
While love-sick fancy fondly strays
   And feasts on many a kiss;—
For us let tides of rapture roll,
Thus intermingling soul with soul,
   In ecstacies of bliss!

SONNET I

ADIEU, thou Yale! where youthful poets dwell,
No more I linger by thy classic stream.
Inglorious ease and sportive songs farewell!
Thou startling clarion! break the sleeper's dream!

And sing, ye bards! the war-inspiring theme.
Heard ye the din of battle? clang of arms?
Saw ye the steel 'mid starry banners beam?
Quick throbs my breast at war's untried alarms,
Unknown pulsations stirr'd by glory's charms.

While dear Columbia calls, no danger awes,
Though certain death to threaten'd chains be join'd.
Though fails this flesh devote to freedom's cause,
Can death subdue th' unconquerable mind?
Or adamantine chains ethereal substance bind?

SONNET IV

ON DISBANDING THE ARMY*

YE brave Columbian bands! a long farewell!
Well have ye fought for freedom—nobly done
Your martial task—the meed immortal won—
And time's last records shall your triumphs tell.

Once friendship made their cup of suff'rings sweet—
The dregs how bitter now those bands must part!
Ah! never, never more on earth to meet:

* It will be difficult for any person who was not present with the
troops at the conclusion of the war, to form an adequate idea of the
affecting circumstances which attended the disbanding of the army.

Distill'd from gall that inundates the heart,
What tears from heroes' eyes are seen to start!

   Ye, too, farewell, who fell in fields of gore,
And chang'd tempestuous toil for rest serene;
Soon shall we join you on the peaceful shore,
(Though gulfs irremeable roll between)
Thither by death-tides borne, as ye full soon have been.

SONNET V

ON LIFE

ERE we can think of time—the moment's past—
And straight another since that thought began:
So swift each instant mingles with the last,
The flying *now* exists—no more* for man.

   With consciousness suspended ev'n by sleep,
To what this phantom, life, then likest seems?
Say, thou! whose doubtful being (lost in dreams)
Allows the wilder'd but to wake and weep,
So thoughtless hurried to th' eternal deep!

   'Tis like a moon-light vision's airy shade,
A bubble driving down the deep beneath—
Then, ere the bubble burst, the vision fade,
Dissolv'd in air this evanescent breath!
Let man, not mortal, learn true life begins at death.

SONNET XII

ON RECEIVING THE NEWS OF THE DEATH OF GENERAL WASHINGTON

   HARK! friends! what sobs of sorrow, moans of grief,
On every gale, through every region spread!

* With the Deity, past, present, and future (as they respect man,
who recognizes the parts of duration by succession), are the same.

Hark! how the western world bewails our chief,
Great Washington, his country's father dead!

Our living light expiring with his breath,
His bright example still illumes our way
Through the dark valley of thy shadow, death!
To realms on high of life without decay,

Faint, he relied on heav'nly help alone,
While conscience cheer'd th' inevitable hour;
When fades the glare of grandeur, pomp of pow'r,
And all the pageantry that gems a throne:
Then from his hallow'd track, who shall entice
Columbia's sons to tread the paths of vice?

LEMUEL HOPKINS
(1750–1808)

EPITAPH

HERE lies a fool flat on his back,
The victim of a Cancer Quack;
Who lost his money and his life,
By plaister, caustic, and by knife.
The case was this—a pimple rose,
South-east a little of his nose;
Which daily redden'd and grew bigger,
As too much drinking gave it vigour:
A score of gossips soon ensure
Full three score diff'rent modes of cure;
But yet the full-fed pimple still
Defied all petticoated skill;
When fortune led him to peruse
A hand-bill in the weekly news;
Sign'd by six fools of diff'rent sorts,
All cur'd of cancers made of warts;
Who recommend, with due submission,
This cancer-monger as magician;
Fear wing'd his flight to find the quack,
And prove his cancer-curing knack;
But on his way he found another,—
A second advertising brother:
But as much like him as an owl
Is unlike every handsome fowl;
Whose fame had rais'd as broad a fog,
And of the two the greater hog:
Who us'd a still more magic plaister,
That sweat forsooth, and cur'd the faster.
This doctor view'd, with moony eyes
And scowl'd up face, the pimple's size;
Then christen'd it in solemn answer,

415

And cried, "This pimple's name is CANCER."
"But courage, friend, I see you're pale,
"My sweating plaisters never fail;
"I've sweated hundreds out with ease,
"With roots as long as maple trees;
"And never fail'd in all my trials—
"Behold these samples here in vials!
"Preserv'd to shew my wond'rous merits,
"Just as my liver is—in spirits.
"For twenty joes the cure is done—"
The bargain struck, the plaister on,
Which gnaw'd the cancer at its leisure,
And pained his face above all measure.
But still the pimple spread the faster,
And swell'd, like toad that meets disaster.
Thus foil'd, the doctor gravely swore,
It was a right rose-cancer sore;
Then stuck his probe beneath the beard,
And shew'd them where the leaves appear'd;
And rais'd the patient's drooping spirits,
By praising up the plaister's merits.—
Quoth he, "The roots now scarcely stick—
"I'll fetch her out like crab or tick;
"And make it rendezvous, next trial,
"With six more plagues, in my old vial."
Then purg'd him pale with jalap drastic,
And next applies th' infernal caustic.
But yet, this semblance bright of hell
Serv'd but to make the patient yell;
And, gnawing on with fiery pace,
Devour'd one broadside of his face—
"Courage, 'tis done," the doctor cried,
And quick th' incision knife applied:
That with three cuts made such a hole,
Out flew the patient's tortur'd soul!

Go, readers, gentle, eke and simple,
If you have wart, or corn, or pimple;

To quack infallible apply;
Here's room enough for you to lie.
His skill triumphant still prevails,
For DEATH's a cure that never fails.

THE HYPOCRITE'S HOPE

Blest is the man, who from the womb,
    To saintship him betakes,
And when too soon his child shall come,
    A long confession makes.

When next in Broad Church-alley, he
    Shall take his former place,
Relates his past iniquity,
    And consequential grace.

Declares how long by Satan vex'd,
    From truth he did depart,
And tells the time, and tells the text,
    That smote his flinty heart.

He stands in half-way-cov'nant sure;
    Full five long years or more,
One foot in church's pale secure,
    The other out of door.

Then riper grown in gifts and grace,
    With ev'ry rite complies,
And deeper lengthens down his face,
    And higher rolls his eyes.

He tones like Pharisee sublime,
    Two lengthy prayers a day,
The same that he from early prime,
    Had heard his father say.

Each Sunday perch'd on bench of pew,
    To passing priest he bows,
Then loudly 'mid the quav'ring crew,
    Attunes his vocal nose.

With awful look then rises slow,
  And pray'rful visage sour,
More fit to fright the apostate foe,
  Than seek a pard'ning power.

Then nodding hears the sermon next,
  From priest haranguing loud;
And doubles down each quoted text,
  From Genesis to Jude.

And when the priest holds forth address,
  To old ones born anew,
With holy pride and wrinkled face,
  He rises in his pew.

Good works he careth nought about,
  But *faith* alone will seek,
While Sunday's pieties blot out
  The knaveries of the week.

He makes the poor his daily pray'r,
  Yet drives them from his board:
And though to his own good he swear,
  Thro' habit breaks his word.

This man advancing fresh and fair,
  Shall all his race complete;
And wave at last his hoary hair,
  Arrived in Deacon's seat.

There shall he all church honours have,
  By joyous brethren given—
Till priest in fun'ral sermon grave,
  Shall send him straight to heaven.

PSALM CXXXVII PARAPHRASED *

Along the banks where Babel's current flows
   Our captive bands in deep despondence strayed,
While Zion's fall in sad remembrance rose,
   Her friends, her children, mingled with the dead.

The tuneless harp that once with joy we strung,
   When praise employed, and mirth inspired the lay,
In mournful silence on the willows hung,
   And growing grief prolonged the tedious day.

The barbarous tyrants, to increase our woe,
   With taunting smiles a song of Zion claim,
Bid sacred praise in strains melodious flow
   While they blaspheme the great Jehovah's name.

But how, in heathen climes and lands unknown,
   Shall Israel's sons a song of Zion raise?
O hapless Salem, God's terrestial throne,
   Thou land of glory, sacred mount of praise.

If e'er my memory lose thy lovely name,
   If my cold heart neglect my kindred race,
Let dire destruction seize this guilty frame—
   My hand shall perish, and my voice shall cease.

Yet, shall the Lord, who hears when Zion calls,
   O'ertake her foes with terror and dismay;
His arm avenge her desolated walls,
   And raise her children to eternal day.

* By Dr. Lemuel Hopkins for Joel Barlow in 1785—usually accredited to Barlow.—EDITOR.

RICHARD ALSOP
(1751–1816)

AN ELEGY

WRITTEN IN FEBRUARY, 1791

Dark is the hour and lone, o'er icy plains
  The wandering meteors gleam a deadly light;
Wild howls the blast, and descending rains,
  And forms funereal flit along the night.

Retir'd from scenes where Pleasure's airy wand
  Fills the light moments with delusive joy,
Where Mirth exulting leads her festive band,
  Far other scenes my pensive soul employ.

The clouds of death that gloom the baleful year,
  The days of joy, alas, so lately fled!
While Friendship bids its sympathetic tear
  Stream in remembrance of the much-lov'd dead.

My friend, but now, of every bliss possest
  That love connubial can on man bestow,
When mutual wishes warm the mutual breast;
  Behold the prey of life-consuming woe.

Of late, how fair the beauteous prospect show'd,
  How lovely glittering in the morning's eye;
But long ere noon, like April's painted cloud,
  Or hues that tinge the summer's evening sky,

The fairy hopes that raptur'd Fancy drew,
  The dream of future bliss that shone so bright,
On Fate's swift pinions vanish'd from the view,
  And sunk in shadows of eternal night.—

What notes of woe in mournful cadence swell
  Along the Western breeze from climes afar,

Mix'd with the dying groan, the savage yell,
  And all the horrid dissonance of war!

And lo! mid gliding spectres dimly seen,
  Pale as the mists that Autumn's car surround,
A form superior lifts his pensive mien,
  While on his bosom glares the shadowy wound.

"Behold," he cries, "the band who lately bled,
  "Mid western wilds in glorious conflict slain;
"While recreant troops in pale confusion fled,
  "Ignobly left unburied on the plain."—

Far opes the view, sublime in savage pride
  A wild unbounded frowns on Fancy's eye;
Tall rise the trees, and o'er savannahs wide
  The rank grass trembles to the breeze on high.

With torrent sweep, amid a night of woods
  Where scarce the sun a livid glimmering lends,
A blood-stain'd river rolls his foaming floods,
  And o'er the plains in wild meanders bends.

Lo! this the scene where War, with bloody hand,
  Wav'd his red standard o'er the carnag'd ground;
Where wild-eyed Horror led the tawny band,
  And fell the brave with dear-bought laurels crown'd.

Here, grim with gore, beneath the inclement sky,
  Smote by the parching ray and driving rain,
The mangled forms of breathless warriors lie,
  All pale extended on the lonely plain.

In slaughter'd heaps, around promiscuous cast,
  Mid savage chiefs Columbia's sons are spread,
While, breath'd from polar snows, the northern blast
  Shakes ice cold pinions o'er the unburied dead.

For them no more shall morning gild the sky,
  No more shall May unveil her radiant charms,

No more shall Joy illume the sparkling eye,
  Or Glory's voice excite the soul to arms.

Near yon grey rock by withering leaves conceal'd,
  Amyntor lies, benevolent and brave;
Whose duteous hand a father's age upheld,
  And smooth'd his dreary passage to the grave.

Not far, a corse distinguish'd o'er the rest,
  Of noble stature and heroic mien;
Deep opes the wound that gor'd his manly breast,
  And his pale features wear a smile serene.

Too well alas! that much-lov'd form I know,
  Those features pale with gory dust o'erspread,
O'er whom has Friendship mourn'd in bitterest woe,
  For whom Affection's tenderest tears are shed.

Still, still in Fancy's view recurs the day
  When war's black demons pour'd their hideous yell,
When left expos'd to savage rage a prey,
  Thy gallant band beside their leader fell.

Opprest with toil, while countless foes surround,
  Thy arm, thy voice, the fainting troop inspir'd;
And e'en when sinking with the deadly wound,
  Thy latest breath their martial ardor fir'd.

Lamented Hero, far from weeping friends!
  No funeral honours to thy corse were paid,
And no memorial o'er thy grave extends
  To mark the lonely spot where low thou'rt laid.

Yet what avails to please the senseless clay,
  "The trophied tomb," the monumental bust,
Or recks the spirit and the realms of day,
  The empty rites attendant on its dust.

A fairer wreath shall friendship's hand bestow,
  A fairer tribute shall thy shade receive,

Than all the idle pageantry of woe,
  Than all its pompous monuments can give.

Long, long shall Memory's ardent eye recall
  Thy worth, thy milder virtues to her view;
Thy Country long lament her hero's fall,
  And o'er thee Fame her brightest laurels strew.

O'er the lone spot where rests thy mouldering form,
  Shall opening spring her mildest breezes wave;
And Flora's hand with every fragrant charm
  Deck the soft turf that forms thy verdant grave.

There the Wild-Rose in earliest pride shall bloom,
  There the Magnolia's gorgeous flowers unfold,
The purple Violet shed its sweet perfume,
  And beauteous Meadia wave her plumes of gold.

Rest much-lov'd Chief with thy Jer****a blest,
  Amid yon realms of light, yon seats of joy,
Where hush'd is sorrow in perpetual rest,
  And pleasure smiles unconscious of alloy.

From that calm shore with pitying eye survey
The varying schemes of man, the busy strife,
The vain pursuits that fill his "little day,"
  And toss with ceaseless storms the sea of life.

While seraphs, bending from their thrones of gold,
  With songs of triumph hymn thy soul to peace;
And to thy raptur'd eye, with smiles, unfold
  The happy mansions of eternal bliss.

WORKS DONE IN COLLABORATION

The Anarchiad appeared in *The New Haven Gazette* and *The Connecticut Magazine* in a series of twelve papers, the first in the issue of October 26, 1786, and the concluding number in the issue of September 13, 1787. In 1861 it was reprinted with notes and appendices by Luther G. Riggs, under the title, *The Anarchiad: A New England Poem.* In the introduction Mr. Riggs states: "While *The Anarchiad* was published originally and complete in the *Gazette*, still many numbers of it were reprinted in the Hartford, and indeed, in most of the Massachusetts, New Hampshire, and Rhode Island papers. Four of the Hartford group took part in the production of this mock-heroic poem: David Humphreys, Joel Barlow, John Trumbull, and Dr. Lemuel Hopkins; but, because the papers were anonymously sent to the publishers at New Haven, the authorship of any particular paper has never been definitely ascertained. The plan of *The Anarchiad* was suggested by the *Rolliad*, a satire of English Tory politics . . . By cleverly adopting the English original to the social and political unrest in New England, the Hartford group were able to level relentless satire against the men and conditions that gave rise to demagogy, Paper Money, Shays' Rebellion, and other evils." Mr. Riggs then gives a critical estimate of the poem in these words: "*The Anarchiad* is pre-eminently a NEW ENGLAND POEM. Its publication, at a time when New England was convulsed by the evils growing out of the war of our Revolution, and when insurrectionary mobs had arisen in various parts of the land, and fears were entertained in others—at such a time, this fearless satire, being scattered broadcast into the homes of the people, through the columns of the weekly press, is supposed to have exerted great and beneficial influence upon the public mind, and to have tended in no small degree to check the leaders of insubordination and infidel philosophy. . . . we say, also, that it is no less a NATIONAL POEM, battling nobly for the right universal, for the majesty of law, and for the federal government . . . these soul-inspiring sentiments are too numerous for us to particularize. The reader will find them in plenteous profusion as he reviews its pages."

The conclusion reached by the present editor is that the plan of the work was originally conceived by Humphreys. While in England he seems to have read *The Rolliad* and been greatly impressed by it. On his return in 1786 he probably communicated his design to some of his old associates who were evidently concerned at the menace of

Populism. Barlow had lost money through the functioning of the Rhode Island currency law, Humphreys himself buckled on his sword to take the field against the mob movement, and Hopkins was a hater of whatever he conceived to be quackery. The resulting satire would seem to have been largely the work of Hopkins, supplemented by contributions from Humphreys, Barlow, and Trumbull.

The text, as here reprinted, is from the edition of 1861, with the notes omitted, the introductory and explanatory remarks much deleted, and with one or two deletions in the text.

THE ANARCHIAD

AMERICAN ANTIQUITIES. No I

[By David Humphreys and Lemuel Hopkins]

Messrs Meigs and Dana:—I have the felicity to belong to a society of critics and antiquarians, who have made it their business and delight for some years past to investigate the ancient as well as natural history of America . . . It has fallen to my lot to communicate, . . . a recent discovery . . . to the republic of letters. . . . The ruins of fortifications yet visible, and other vestiges of art, in the Western country, had sufficiently demonstrated that this delightful region had once been occupied by a civilized people. For upon digging into the ruins . . . the laborers were surprised to find a casement, a magazine, and a cistern, almost entire. . . . Near the northeast corner of the bastion, . . . they found a great number of utensils, more curious and elegant than those of Palmyra or Herculaneum. But what rendered their good fortune complete, was the discovery of a great number of papers, manuscripts, etc., whose preservation through such a long lapse of years, . . . must be deemed marvellous indeed, perhaps little short of miraculous.

. . . Among the relics of antiquity I was overjoyed to find a folio manuscript which appeared to contain an epic poem, complete; . . . the extraneous concretions with which it was in some parts enveloped, defaced and rendered (*it*) illegible.

430   WORKS DONE IN COLLABORATION

By means of a chemic preparation . . . I found it was called
THE ANARCHIAD, a Poem on the restoration of Chaos and substantial Night, in twenty-four books.

. . . I might also add, . . . that this work was well known
to the ancients. . . . Perhaps, in a future essay, I shall attempt to prove that Homer, Virgil, and Milton, have borrowed many of their capital beauties from it.   At present, to
show that the matter is not fabulous, . . . I shall cite a few
lines from the eighth book, which is denominated the Book
of Vision. . . . The prophetic bard seems to have taken for the
point of vision one of the lofty mountains of America. . . .

> In visions fair the scenes of fate unroll,
> And Massachusetts opens on my soul;
> There Chaos, Anarch old, asserts his sway,
> And mobs in myriads blacken all the way:
> See Day's stern port—behold the martial frame
> Of Shays' and Shattuck's mob-compelling name:
> See the bold Hampshirites on Springfield pour,
> The fierce Tauntonians crowd the alewife shore.
> O'er *Concord* fields the bands of *discord* spread,
> And Wor'ster trembles at their thundering tread:
> See from proud Egremont the woodchuck train,
> Sweep their dark files, and shade with rags the plain.
> Lo, THE COURT FALLS; th' affrighted judges run,
> Clerks, Lawyers, Sheriffs, every mother's son.
> The stocks, the gallows lose th' expected prize,
> See the jails open, and the thieves arise.
> Thy constitution, Chaos, is restor'd;
> Law sinks before thy uncreating word;
> Thy hand unbars th' unfathom'd gulf of fate,
> And deep in darkness 'whelms the new-born state.

I know not whether it is necessary to remark, in this place
. . . that the celebrated English poet, Mr. Pope, has proven
himself a noted plagiarist, by copying the preceding ideas, and
even the couplets almost entire, into his famous poem called
"The Dunciad."

. . . Other extracts . . . will be published, should the preceding specimen meet with the applause . . . it merits. The blessings of paper money and confusion, as now experienced in Rhode Island, are predicted in the most awful and beautiful manner. . . .

I am &c.,

AMERICAN ANTIQUITIES. No. II

Messrs Meigs and Dana:— . . . I thought I ought not to delay to gratify the Connecticut readers with a fragment of the speech which the old Anarch makes to Beelzebub, for the purpose of persuading him to come over and help his faithful friends in our Macedonia, since his affairs were in so thriving a posture in Massachusetts and Rhode Island. . . .

After describing in a very pathetic manner, the necessity of his presence and personal influence, he encourages him to hope for every reasonable countenance from his faithful adherents and allies in this state. He gives as long and significant a list of their names and characters as Homer does . . . I can only have room to select a few of the most remarkable. . . .

SURVEY the State, behold the flame that draws
Chiefs, mobs, conventions, to support thy cause.
See where the frogs' loquacious realms extend,
Instructions on their *deputies* attend,
O'er all the east new fangled magi rise,
Join croaking choirs and boast the name of wise.

The north by myriads pours her mighty sons,
Great nurse of mobs, of bankrupts, and of duns:
There Froth, the sep'rate, glows with pop'lar rage,
And G——n, type of dotards in old age.

Where lard and brimstone gild the itch-vat shore,
The soil that trays and wooden dishes bore,
His full-globed paunch the brainless *Bubo* draws,
And solid ignorance threats the feeble laws.

Near Hartford stream, where groves perpetual bloom,
And onion gardens breathe a glad perfume,
Though sunk in dust, to his own stench a prey,
Again our *Laz'rus* shall ascend *to day;*
Thy potent voice shall burst the deathful chain,
And raise him active in thy toils again.
Where *purslain harvests* charm th' extended sight,
Clothe the fair fields and feed thy sons for fight;
In act to speak, his eyes a smoky fire,
His face of shadow, and his shins of wire,
See *Copper* graceful ride, and, o'er his cane,
Look like a pale moon sick'ning in its wane.

Why sleep'st thou, *Blacklegs*, child of knavery, why?
Seest thou, blest Wronghead, helpless how we lie?
And where is Wimble, earliest squib of fame!
Your tongues and pens must wake the factious flame!
And thou, poor Quack, behold thy efforts fail;
Could one address thy o'erstrain'd wits exhale?
Wake, scribble, print; arouse thee from thy den,
And raise conventions with thy blust'ring pen!

No more the Boatman's call alarms the shore,
Old *Ben*, exhausted, wields the quill no more;
The *Chairman's* snuff expir'd as erst was sung,
And gouts have quelled the *Irish Blunderer's* tongue.
Yet, can a faction cease in craft to thrive,
Where such high talents, such strong brains, survive?
These, and a thousand yet unnam'd we find—
Fame waits the thousand yet unnam'd behind.

The poetic seer has then the address, by a happy transition,
to group his principal characters in *solemn conclave*, and to
display their abilities in high debate. . . . I have not been
able to cleanse that part of the manuscript which contains
their speeches, . . . That part of the manuscript which is
still legible. . . progresses . . . in unfolding the catastrophe
by predicting that a majority should be persuaded, by the

power of intrigues and sophistry, to refuse a compliance with the *requisitions of Congress*—that a determination should be formed and announced to the world, that we will not pay the interest on our foreign or domestic debt—that we should furnish nothing for the support of the federal government—*that we should withdraw ourselves from the Union*—that all government should be prostrated in the dust—that *mobs, conventions,* and *anarchy,* should prevail for a limited time, and then—. . . But I draw the curtain; the picture is too melancholy to be viewed by a patriot eye. . . .

I am , &c.,

American Antiquities. No. III

Extracts from the Anarchiad, on Paper Money

Messrs Meigs and Dana:—The readers of . . . the two first numbers of American Antiquities . . . will doubtless remember that the subject of Paper Money was more than once mentioned. . . . For it will scarcely be denied, in any part of the United States, that paper money, in an unfunded and depreciating condition, is happily calculated to introduce the long expected scenes of misrule, dishonesty, and perdition. . . . The citizens of the Union . . . are inhabitants of the only country under heaven, where paper (of that predicament) is, by compulsory laws, made of equal value with gold and silver. . . .

It is to be remarked that the following speech is addressed, by the old Anarch, to a council of war, consisting of his compeers, his general officers, and counselors of state:

Hail! fav'rite State, whose nursing fathers prove
Their fairest claim to my paternal love!
Call'd from the deck with pop'lar votes elate,
The mighty *Jacktar* guides the helm of state;
Nurs'd on the waves, in blust'ring tempests bred,

His heart of marble, and his brain of lead,
My foes subdued while knavery wins the day,
He rules the senate with inglorious sway;
Proud, *for one year*, my orders to perform,
Sails in the whirlwind, and enjoys the storm.

Yet not alone the per'lous watch he keeps,
His mate, great O—n, bustles while he sleeps;
There G[oodwi]n stands, his head with quibbles fill'd;
His tongue in lies, his hand in forg'ry skill'd;
To him, my darling knave, my lore I teach,
While he to C[ollin]s lends in many a pompous speech.

Oh, roguery! their being's end and aim,
Fraud, tendry, paper bills, whate'er thy name;
That medium still, which prompts th' eternal sigh,
By which great villains flourish, small ones die.
Plant of infernal seed, without hell's heat,
Say in what mortal soil thou deign'st to cheat?
Fair from the Gen'ral Court's unpardon'd sin,
Ap'st thou the gold Peruvian mines within?
Wak'd to new life, by my creative power,
The press thy mint, and dunghill rags thy ore.
Where grow'st thou not? If vain the villain's toil,
We ought to blame the culture, not the soil;
Fix'd to that isle, it nowhere passes free,
But fled from Congress, C[ollin]s dwells with thee.

Hail! realm of rogues, renown'd for fraud and guile,
All hail! ye knav'ries of yon little isle.
There prowls the rascal, cloth'd with legal pow'r,
To snare the orphan, and the poor devour;
The crafty knave his creditor besets,
And advertising paper pays his debts;
Bankrupts their creditors with rage pursue,
No stop, no mercy from the debtor crew.
Arm'd with new tests, the licens'd villain bold,
Presents his bills, and robs them of their gold;

Their ears, though rogues and counterfeiters lose,
No legal robber fears the gallows noose.

Look through the State, the unhallow'd ground appears
A pen of dragons, and a cave for bears;
A nest of vipers, mix'd with adders foul;
The screeching night-bird, and the greater owl:
For now, unrighteousness, a deluge wide,
Pours round the land an overwhelming tide;
And dark injustice, wrapp'd in paper sheets,
Rolls a dread torrent through the wasted streets;
While net of law th' unwary fry draws in
To damning deeds, and scarce they know they sin.
New paper struck, new tests, new tenders made,
Insult mankind, and help the thriving trade.
Each weekly print new lists of cheats proclaims,
Proud to enroll their knav'ries and their names;
The wiser race, the snares of law to shun,
Like Lot from Sodom, from Rhode Island run.

. . . The society to avoid the imputation of impartiality,
. . . direct me, . . . to eternize those subaltern heroes
[worthies who were principal actors in the epic poem] . . . by
informing the public that honorable mention is made of Mr.
G— I——, as well as of most of the horse jockies and bankrupts in the state; and particularly, . . . those persons who
have given due notice in the public gazette, of their having
lodged, agreeably to law, with some justice of the peace, paper
bills, for the payment of certain honest debts. These good
people are specified individually, in proportion to the sums
deposited, as proper to be captains over tens, over fifties, . . .
[in] the army . . . of anarchy, or whenever that new state
(whereof the rumour runs so rife on earth) *the State of Confusion*, shall be properly organized and admitted into the
confederacy. The characters of the Judges of the Supreme
Court, of the Governors, . . . the officers of the late army,
with a long catalogue of names (comprising all the honest
men in the state), are represented as the antipodes of the

preceding. These are the thousands who have never bowed
the knee to Baal, and who have never sacrificed their honor
or their honesty at the shrine of Paper Money.

AMERICAN ANTIQUITIES. No. IV

Extract from the Anarchiad, Book XXIII

Bow low, ye heavens, and all ye lands, draw near,
The voice prophetic of great Anarch hear!
From Eastern climes, by light and order driven,
To me, by fate, this Western world was giv'n;
My standard rear'd, the realm imperial rules,
The last asylum for my knaves and fools.
Here shall my best and brightest empire rise,
Wild riot reign, and discord greet the skies.
Awake, my chosen sons, in folly brave,
Stab Independence! dance o'er Freedom's grave!
Sing choral songs, while conq'ring mobs advance,
And blot the debts to Holland, Spain, and France—
Till ruin come, with fire, and sword, and blood,
And men shall ask where your republic stood.

Thrice happy race! how blest are discord's heirs!
Blest while they know what anarchy is theirs;
Blest while they feel to them alone 'tis given
To know no sovereign, neither law nor Heaven.
From all mankind, by traits peculiar known,
By frauds and lies distinguish'd for mine own,
Wonder of worlds! like whom, to mortal eyes,
None e'er have risen, and none e'er shall rise!

Lo, the poor Briton, who, corrupted, sold,
Sees God in courts, or hears him chink in gold:
Whose soul, proud empire oft has taught to stray
Far as the Western world, and gates of day;
Though plagu'd with debts, with rage of conquest curst,

In rags and tender-acts he puts no trust;
But in the public weal his own forgets,
Finds heaven for him who pays the nation's debts;
A heaven like London, his fond fancy makes,
Of nectar'd porter and ambrosial steaks.

Not so, Columbia, shall thy sons be known
To prize the public weal above their own;
In faith and justice least, as last in birth,
Their race shall grow, a by-word through the earth.
Long skill'd to act the hypocritic part,
Grace on the brow, and knav'ry at the heart,
Perform their frauds with sanctimonious air,
Despise good works, and balance sins by pray'r—
Forswear the public debt, the public cause;
Cheat heaven with forms, and earth with tender-laws,
And leave the empire, at its latest groan,
To work salvation out by *faith alone*.

Behold the reign of anarchy, begun,
And half the business of confusion done.
From hell's dark caverns discord sounds alarms,
Blows her loud trump, and calls my *Shays* to arms,
O'er half the land the desperate riot runs,
And maddening mobs assume their rusty guns.
From councils feeble, bolder faction grows,
The daring corsairs, and the savage foes;
O'er Western wilds, the tawny bands allied,
Insult the States of weakness and of pride;
Once friendly realms, unpaid each generous loan,
Wait to divide and share them for their own.

Now sinks the public mind; a death-like sleep
O'er all the torpid limbs begins to creep;
By dull degrees decays the vital heat,
The blood forgets to flow, the pulse to beat;
The powers of life, in mimic death withdrawn,
Closed the fixed eyes with one expiring yawn;

Exposed in state, to wait the funeral hour,
Lie the pale relics of departed power;
While conscience, harrowing up their souls, with dread,
Their ghost of empire stalks without a head.

No more stands forth to check the rising feud,
Their great DEFENDER of the public good;
Retired, in vain his sighs their fate deplore,
He hears, unmoved, the distant tempest roar;
No more to save a realm, dread GREENE appears,
Their second hope, prime object of my fears;
Far in the south, from his pale body riven,
The deathful angel wings his soul to heaven.

Here shall I reign, unbounded and alone,
Nor men, nor demons, shake my baseless throne;
Till comes the day—but late, oh, may it spring—
When their tumultuous mobs shall ask a king;
A king, in wrath, shall heaven, vindictive send,
And my confusion and my empire end.

With arms, where bickering fires innumerous shine,
Like the torn surface of the midnight brine;
In sun-bright robes, that dazzled as he trod,
The stature, motion, armor of a god,
Great HESPER rose; the guardian of the clime—
O'er shadowy cliffs he stretch'd his arm sublime,
And check'd the Anarch old: "Malicious fiend,
Eternal curses on thy head descend!
Heaven's darling purpose can thy madness mar,
To glut thy eyes with ruin, death, and war!
I know thee, Anarch, in thy cheerless plight,
Thou eldest son of Erebus and Night!
Yes, bend on me thy brows of hideous scowl;
Roll thy wild eyeballs like the day-struck owl;
In Zion blow the trump, resound it far;
Fire the red beacons of intestine war;
The jealous breasts inflame; set hell at work,

And crown the labors of E—s B—e;
Yet, know for this, thyself to penance called,
Thy troops in terrors, their proud hearts appall'd,
E'en *Shays*, that moment when eternal night
Rolls dark'ning shadows o'er his closing sight,
Shall feel, 't were better on a plank to lie,
Where surging billows kiss the angry sky;
'T were better, through a furnace, fiery red,
With naked feet, on burning coals, to tread—
Than point his sword, with parricidious hand,
Against the bosom of his native land.

"Where is the spirit of bold freedom fled?
Dead are my warriors; all my sages dead?
Is there, Columbia, bending o'er her grave,
No eye to pity, and no arm to save?

"Sister of Freedom! heaven's imperial child!
Serenely stern, beneficently mild,
Blest Independence! rouse my sons to fame,
Inspire their bosoms with thy sacred flame!
Teach, ere too late, their blood-bought rights to prize,
Bid other GREENES and WASHINGTONS arise!
Teach those who suffer'd for their country's good,
Who strove for freedom, and who toil'd in blood,
Once more, in arms, to make a glorious stand,
And bravely die, or save their natal land.

"Yes, they shall rise, terrific in their rage,
And crush the factions of the faithless age;
Bid laws again exalt th' imperial scale,
And public justice o'er her foes prevail;
Restore the reign of order and of right,
And drive thee, howling, to the shades of night."

They ended parley, and both for fight address'd,
On Anarch's helm a comet blaz'd his crest;
Infernal arms the shadowy demon steel'd,

And half the Andes form'd his ample shield;
Through parting clouds, high gleam'd his dreadful spear,
And shuddering earth proclaim'd the onset near;
Unmov'd, great HESPER drew th' immortal sword,
And rush'd, in vengeance,——

. . . The fragments still legible are truly sublime. And we have reason to conjecture that the combat ended with some disadvantage to the old Anarch.

AMERICAN ANTIQUITIES. No. V

Extract from the Miscellaneous Papers found in the same fort with the Anarchiad

. . . If Americans could be taught to revere themselves; if they could be made to realize their consequence, . . . the inhabitants of such a country, . . . might be considered as the peculiar favorites of heaven, and actors on the most conspicuous theater that ever was allotted to mankind. Such is the fact. And so the GENIUS OF AMERICA is represented to have sung, in mystical numbers, at the moment when the New World was discovered. . . . This Ode is preserved, entire. They make no doubt that [the contents] . . . which give sufficient demonstration of its originality, will recommend it to the *amateurs* of poetry and music. Should the *taste* of their countrymen, in general, be uncorrupted, as they flatter themselves it is, they expect this song will be introduced into most of the polite circles of the United States. . . . Until the public mind shall be known, no further gratification of the same kind will be offered.

THE GENIUS OF AMERICA: A SONG

[By David Humphreys]

TO THE TUNE OF

"*The watery god, great Neptune, lay
In dalliance soft, and amorous play,
On Amphytrite's breast,*" etc.

I

WHERE spirits dwell, and shadowy forms,
On Andes' cliffs, 'mid black'ning storms,
    With livid lightnings curl'd;
The awful Genius of our clime,
In thunder rais'd his voice sublime,
    And hush'd the list'ning world.

II

In lonely waves, and wastes of earth,
A mighty empire claims its birth,
    And Heaven asserts the claim;
The sails that hang in yon dim sky,
Proclaim the promis'd era nigh,
    Which wakes a world to fame.

III

Hail! ye first bounding ships that roam
Blue tumbling billows topp'd with foam,
    That keel ne'er plowed before!
Here suns perform their useless round,
Here rove the naked tribes embrown'd,
    Who feed on living gore.

IV

To midnight orgies, off'rings dire,
The human sacrifice in fire,
    A heavenly light succeeds:
But, lo! what horrors intervene,
The toils severe, the carnage scene,
    And more than mortal deeds!

V

Ye FATHERS! spread your fame afar!
'Tis yours to still the sounds of war,
    And bid the slaughter cease;
The peopling hamlets wide extend,
The harvests spring, the spires ascend,
    'Mid grateful songs of peace!

VI

Shall steed to steed, and man to man,
With discord thundering in the van,
    Again destroy the bliss!
Enough my mystic words reveal;
The rest the shades of night conceal,
    In fate's profound abyss!

American Antiquities. No. VI

Extract from the Anarchiad, Book XX

The soliloquy and invocation of WRONGHEAD, with the appearance and consolatory speech of the ANARCH

Now marshal'd hosts assembling from afar,
Prelude the onset of approaching war
In Wronghead's jealous soul; while thus, in sighs,
He breathes hoarse accents to the mother skies:

"O thou dark world, where chance eternal reigns,
And wide misrule, the Anarch, old, maintains;
Orcus, and Hades! hear my fervent prayer,
And aid, if Wrongheads still deserve your care:
If you receiv'd me dark'ning from the womb,
And nurs'd the hope of mischiefs yet to come;
If busied, daily, planning pop'lar schemes,
And nightly rapt in democratic dreams,
Fair discord as a goddess I revere,
And in her vineyards toil from year to year;
Still active, as the princely power of air,
To sow each jealousy, and till with care;
If I each long-face in the land assail,
At Congress, Courts, and legal powers to rail;
If I at trade, great men and lawyers' fees,
Have so harangu'd as vulgar ears to please;
If *cant pretense* of *Liberty*, the while,
Has been the universal burden of my style;
If this has gain'd me all the posts I hold,

With numerous salaries heap'd my chest with gold,
And fed my hopes that fed'ral ties no more
Shall bind the nations of the western shore;
That local schemes shall lift their narrow scale,
And our own statesmen through the land prevail;
Then, hear again, ye powers that stretch the sway,
Through the wide vast, beneath the solar day,
Hear, and dispel my anxious doubts and fears,
To me more dread than certain loss of ears.

"Since the Convention fell, no more to rise,
And grey'd these locks, and dimm'd these tearful eyes,
This more minute, less blust'ring plan, I tried,
Till wish'd success began to feed my pride:
But now, alas! stern justice rears her head,
And crowds my days with fears, my nights with dread;
Those congregated sages, who, ere now,
Had I my wish, were doom'd to guide the plow,
Are planning, still, to build a fed'ral name,
And blast my laurels with eternal shame;
The pride of courts still brightens in their eyes,
And scorning still to pay our debts with lies,
Have raised these martial bands to aid their cause,
To awe each mob, and execute the laws.
Shall these succeed? and shall my labor'd schemes,
Ye sov'reign powers! disperse in empty dreams?"
He spoke, and breath'd a care-corroding sigh,
Then, through a dark, deep vale, bent down his eye;
When, lo! a lurid fog began to move,
And mount in solemn grandeur o'er the grove,
Convolving mists enroll'd a demon's form,
But headless, monstrous, shapeless as a storm;
While *Wronghead* gaz'd, the fiend sublimer grew,
Known for the Anarch, to his raptur'd view;
Sudden, as rumbling thunder heard remote,
These stunning sounds rose, grating, through his throat:

"Beloved sage, the powers of Chaos know
Your every fear, and number every woe;

Their ken sweeps broader than the bounds of day,
And thrice ten lengths of hell, their nether sway;
Where now your world has gain'd that little hight,
Just o'er the precincts of chaotic night,
We held, of old, the reign; nor yet despair
To hold a wilder mental chaos there.

"Those warlike bands, whose music grates thine ear,
Are ills, at best, but not the worst we hear;
(Though they our much-lov'd mobs may sorely awe,
Give Union aid, and tone to fed'ral law,)—
More dang'rous foes arise, in learning's dress,
Arm'd with the pen, and ambush'd in the press.
The laughing youth, as lessons, learn their page,
And age, approving smiles, while dullards rage;
Their shafts all poison'd in Pierian springs,
Seem now impatient, on the bending strings,
To pierce their foes;—their arrows drink the fame
Of each unfederal politician's name.
See our best heroes, stagg'ring from the plain,
With eyes aghast, in curses vent their pain.
But give your toils not o'er—the human soul
Sinks, by strong instinct, far beneath her goal;
Fierce, bickering tribes, acknowledg'd once my sway,
From rising morning to the setting day;
Low bow'd the north, and all the spacious south
Receiv'd the precepts warm from Anarch's mouth;
And when, o'er eastern climes, proud science shone,
And millions bow'd before her splendid throne,
My storm of Goths quench'd her meridian light,
And whelm'd her sons in anarchy and night:
There had she mourn'd her everlasting doom,
But the curs'd press dispell'd the midnight gloom.
Hence, learn, my seer, we shadowy powers who dwell
Far in the wilds of space, 'twixt this and hell,
Thron'd on unnumber'd whirlwinds, through the void,
Nor yet by distance, time, or place, annoy'd,
Save where our envious foe, with swift surprise,

Snatch'd that small spot where now creation lies:
Learn, though strict order guides His world on high,
Where suns emblaze, and systems vault the sky;
Yet there, we oft, in wayward whirls, control
The mystic, mad'ning mazes of the soul:
But chief, where science sheds her taintless beams,
And men are haunted worst with waking dreams;
Where prejudice is headstrong, reason blind,
The soul unpolish'd, all its views confin'd;
Where self is all-in-all; and stubborn will
Shuts out each good, through jealousy of ill.
Though in thy soul these choicest gifts preside,
With an unbounded share of *humble pride*;
Though all the lesser virtues we can give,
Instinctive, in thy mind, immortal live;
Each one his duty, task, and drudgery knows,
As plann'd by thee; yet know, my faithful seer,
These plans alone can scarce survive the year:
The lamp of science must be quench'd in night,
Till none, or next to none, can read or write;
The press, anon, in brazen chains must groan,
First watch'd and guarded by our saints alone;
The numerous schools that live along the shore,
Must fall, successive, and must rise no more;
The wits be hang'd; the Congress forc'd to flee
To western wilds, or headlong to the sea.

"Then shall ten thousand whirlwinds lead the way,
And he, true Anarch, here exalt his sway;
Before his face a flood of darkness roll,
Blot the dim day, and whelm the sinking pole;
Confusion, chaos, chance, his course attend,
Hoarse rumor rave, and hell's own mobs ascend;
His sons, on fierce tornadoes, hail from far
The black effulgence of his wasting car,
And throng his courts; old Night's dark eye shall glow,
Like seas of boiling tar, or hills of lampblack snow."

AMERICAN ANTIQUITIES. No. VII

Extracts from the Anarchiad, Book XII

In this Book the Anarch, on the first success of his mobs in demolishing the courts of justice,[1] institutes heroic games, after the ancient epic manner. Among other extraordinary contests, a prize is proposed to those of his heroes who would see the farthest into total darkness, and shut their eyes longest to the clear light of day. *Wronghead* is the sole conqueror in this game, and is, thereupon, rewarded by the Anarch with a pair of spectacles, which showed every object inverted, and wrapped in a mist of darkness. On this occasion, *Tweedle*, a poet, reared under the patronage of *Copper*, and now principal bard of his chaotic majesty, filled with the poetic flatus, bursts forth with an eulogium on the victor.[2]

Oh, thou! whatever title please thine ear,
Judge, General, Delegate, or Registrar,
Whether thou choose the high Comptroller's air,
Or frown more grimly in thy Council chair;
Catch some new salary from each opening job,
At Congress rail or vindicate the mob;
Thou *millpede of office*, hear my lays,
And aid the bard that sings thy welcome praise!

Oh for a muse of fire! sublime to draw
The judge unfetter'd by the rules of law;
The self-taught General, valiant to control
The dangerous passions of the daring soul;
In Compo's scene, whose Christian spirit shone,
Spar'd the foes' lives, and gladly screen'd his own,

[1] Refers to the popular uprising in Massachusetts which ended in the Shays' Rebellion.—EDITOR.

[2] Wronghead was General Erastus Wolcott, Judge of the Superior Court and Representative in the federal Congress; William Wimble was William Williams; Joe Copper was Joseph Hopkins, Esq., of Waterbury, so called because he took part in private coinage of "coppers."—EDITOR.

Or sing in strains unus'd to mortal ear,
Th' unletter'd Statesman and Anarchian seer.
Thine the dread task, on thy immortal plan,
From federal ties to guard the rights of man;
At power's deep root to lay the patriot ax,
Oppose the impost and prevent the tax;
Bid depreciation pay the public debt,
And teach the noblest art, the art to cheat;
Thro' all the States thy dark'ning mists to spread,
And shroud their scenes in [thy] chaotic shade;
O'er their true interest close the curtain draw,
Hide them from light and cover them from law;
With jealous arts misguide the wayward throng,
Supremely blind, and obstinately wrong!
With insect ken to local views confin'd,
Display thy pigmy penury of mind;
To other shores bid wealthy commerce pass,
"*The State* surrounding with thy wall of brass;"
Bid insurrection claim thy noblest praise,
O'er WASHINGTON exalt thy darling Shays;
With thy contagion, embryo mobs inspire,
And blow to tenfold rage the kindling fire;
Till the wide realm of *discord* bow the knee,
And hold true faith in *Anarch* and in thee.

Still may'st thou thus support th' unfederal cause,
The scourge of Congress, and the dread of laws;
May never age, pain, sickness, or despair
Attack thy life with unsuccessful war;
Or late, when all thy race of fame is run,
All parts accomplish'd, and all duties done—
Proud rulers crush'd by thy supreme decree—
Our Governor, Council, Judges, men like thee;
Our debts all cancel'd in one fav'ring hour,
And Congress bared of every plume of power;
Their *requisitions*, by thy bold attack,
Sunk in the whirlpool of the gen'ral wreck;
From dreadful arts of *Cincinnati* free,

Foiled by the breath of Wimble and of thee;
All souls reduc'd, that e'er presum'd to shine,
To one just level, and the rank of thine;
This world forsaking, fairly may'st thou *rise*
Above the earth, and *pointing* to the skies;
While the great *finisher of mortal strife*,
Shall close thy glories with the *line* of life;
Where *seraphs*, then, in *brighter* regions *burn*,
Go thou, a *glowing seraph*, in thy turn;
With souls congenial, in those realms that dwell,
Receive the meed you long deserv'd so well;
Then draw thy comrades, in the *closing string*,
And glad those regions with the sons you bring;
And in thy patriot bosom yield a room
For all the race of *Wrongheads* yet to come.

AMERICAN ANTIQUITIES. No. VIII

. . . On Friday last, agreeably to his sentence, William
Wimble was conveyed, by the Sheriff, to the place of execution . . .

At half past eleven o'clock, A. M., Wimble pulled the handkerchief over his eyes, and was launched from the tail of a
cart, on his voyage towards that country from whose bourne
no traveler returns. His friend, *Tweedle*, the poet laureate,
has composed an Elegy in his praise. A correspondent has
favored us with a genuine copy of it, which we offer, with
unfeigned pleasure, for the gratification of our kind readers:

AN ELEGY ON A PATRIOT

Occasioned by the awful and untimely Death of the Honorable
WILLIAM WIMBLE, who, by the coroner's inquest, was found to have
come to his end by suffocation.

"*Hic cinis, ubique fama.*"

I

IN yonder dark and narrow lodging,
There rests a patriot's body,

Which, after many a slip and dodging,
  Death took in safe custody.

II

What though to earth his corse consign'd
  Must moulder and be rotten;
His name, while it is kept in mind,
  Will never be forgotten.

III

O'er him the muse a tomb shall raise,
  (Or she's an idle strumpet,)
And fame (if she won't sound his praise)
  May throw away her trumpet.

IV

Mine be the task to celebrate
  This hero sly and nimble;
Whose praise shall last, in spite of fate—
  Who knows not WILLIAM WIMBLE?

V

To fellow creatures he was kind,
  To brethren, staunch and hearty;
He help'd the *weak*, and led the *blind*,
  Whene'er he led his party.

VI

Nor is it true, what some have said,
  His kindness did not stop here—
The mean in spirit, oft he fed,
  To wit, *himself* and *Copper*.

VII

Though he was lib'ral, wise, and gallant,
  As warmest friends could wish one;
'Twas own'd by all, his chiefest talent
  Lay most in composition.

VIII

No one could equal him for style,
  For art and elocution;

For dismal periods of a mile,
    The *genius of confusion*.

IX

His race of ancestors was long—
    Indeed, it was pretended
His race was young—but that was wrong;
    From *Gimblet* he descended.

X

The heralds prov'd his ancient blood,
    By race of sire and madam,
Had crept through scoundrels from the flood,
    And reach'd almost to Adam.

XI

Two pillars rampany were his *arms*—
    A beam, with slender cable,
(I think I've got the herald's terms,)
    A cart and coffin sable.

XII

Should man from ills be free, t'were strange,
    'Twould be on earth a rarity;
So our good hero had the *mange*,
    The *itch* of popularity.

XIII

He was so courteous and so bland,
    Throughout the whole dominion;
He shook each lubber by the hand,
    And stole his good opinion.

XIV

He shone in many an office fair,
    By honorable seeking;
The Army, Church, and State, his care,—
    A Delegate and Deacon.

XV

Adman, of Congress, asked, thus:
"How comes it, *Poet Timbrel!*

"Your State doth send a fool to us,
  "Whose name is WILLIAM WIMBLE?"

XVI

The poet did this speech relate—
  "From honest views, we sent him;
"The fools are many in our State—
  "He goes to represent 'em."

XVII

And yet, though wicked wits kept sneering,
  'Tis plain as nose in face is;
'Twas only by *electioneering*,
  He got and held his places.

XVIII

So once, upon the Ides of May,
  When great men quit their spouses,
To Hartford come, in best array,
  And sit in *both the Houses:*

XIX

To take a seat, then, WIMBLE came,
  As every man supposes;
But soon 't was found he'd lost the same,
  When they had counted noses.

XX

How strangely does dame fortune frown,
  How strangely do times alter!
What long ago would buy a crown,
  Will purchase now a halter.

XXI

Then straightway evils came apace:
  By sheriff being cited,
And judges taking each his place,
  He stood of crimes indicted:

XXII

Then he, among the goose-cap tribes,
  With one *Joe Copper*, leaguing,

Bought votes, and sold the geese for bribes,
  With other vile intriguing.

XXIII

Then, forc'd against his will, to stand
  Before twelve sturdy fellows;
And only holding up his hand,
  They all turn'd fortune tellers.

XXIV

Who said, (ah, wonderful to tell!)
  By what they could discover,
Though now the man was sound and well,
  His days would soon be over.

XXV

And so it did this wight betide,
  Just like to Tyburn's fashion,
Sublime, on two-wheel'd car, to ride,
  And make a fine oration.

XXVI

But sad and mournful was his part;
  He scarce had made an end on't,
When off they drove the two-wheel'd cart,
  And left the speaker pendent.

XXVII

Still, as great men to death draw nigher,
  They rise, and prove they're true wits;
So his last day he mounted higher,
  Like Haman, fifty cubits.

XXVIII

Ye statesmen all, so blithe and gay,
  In life's delusive morning,
Here learn each dog must have his day,
  And from this fate take warning:

XXIX

No further seek his faults to learn,
  No further search his glory—

Our fame, how short! and, mortal man,
   Good lack, how transitory!

XXX

Yet shall the foolish folks, *for aye,*
   Whose brains would fill a thimble,
Striking their pensive bosoms, say,
   "Here lies poor WILLIAM WIMBLE."

N.B.—A few copies of the last words of WILLIAM WIMBLE, accurately compiled, and now first printed in a handbill at large, may be had at the *Huron Printing Office.* Price, one *Copper.*

AMERICAN ANTIQUITIES. No. IX

Extract from the ANARCHIAD, Book XXIII

The situation and soliloquy of Anarch, after having been vanquished in single combat by Hesper. . . .

IN fight sore foil'd by Hesper's vengeful sword,
His shield to havoc hewn, his armor gor'd.
His bulk immense by wounds unseemly marr'd,
His helmless front by furrowing thunders scarr'd,
Clotted with dark red gore, his horrent hair,
Like meteors streaming on the troubled air,
As heaves to heaven the huge volcano's smoke,
From his long trance immortal Anarch broke;
Nor less appear'd, escap'd from deadly fight,
Than the dread son of Erebus and Night;
Around in wrath his baleful eyes he throws,
And vents loud curses o'er his hopeless woes.
Oh, rage! oh, torture! limbs and armor riven,
On earth an exile, and the scorn of heaven!
Robb'd of a world, by lying fates bestow'd,
Hesper victorious! I a vanquish'd god!
Gape wide, profoundest hell! in Stygian flame
Hide your lost Anarch from undying shame!

He spoke! Astonish'd from the central bound
Heav'd the dark gulf and ope'd the rocking ground;

From all the extremes of chaos, wild and waste,
With hollow murmur swell'd the roaring blast;
Ting'd with sulphureous flames, obscurely curl'd,
Black clouds, expanding, swept the nether world;
Thron'd on the ascending pyramid of storm,
Rose, wrapp'd in vapors, Night's majestic form;
O'er her lov'd son she hung with pitying air,
And sooth'd his sadness with maternal care.

Oh, blind to fate, to happier visions blind,
While past disasters rankle in thy mind!
While future woe thy boding bosom rends,
Lo, Orcus wakes a new-form'd host of friends;
To nobler champions change thy fiercest foes,
And splendid triumph on thy ruin grows.

Where yonder isle the meeting tides embrace,
And commerce smiles on Belgia's thrifty race—
Once bowry isle, whose woodless summits far
Now lift the relics of barbarian war;
Whose laurel vales with bleaching bones abound,
Where slaughter drench'd the saturated ground;
When a few heroes, wedg'd in firm array,
Held Hessian hosts and British bands at bay;
Till wider carnage round the empire spread,
For nine long years, while sad Columbia bled,
To save one central region, and restore
Each glorious exile to his natal shore.
But now, while victory greets their glad return,
The *Power* that sav'd, th' ungrateful miscreants spurn;
I see, through Hellgate, where the whirlpool pours,
How the day darkens, how confusion lowers;
Where Congress dwells, I see portentous signs—
Of total nature, there th' eclipse begins.
Hail! sacred spot, imperial city, hail!
Here shall our reign commence, our throne prevail;
Whence hate and discord, erst by * * * hurl'd,
Clung to the British prow, and fought the elder world.

Oh! lost to virtue's heaven-descended flame,
Lost to those realms that boast his early fame,
I see his friends, (but now his friends no more,)
And Vernon's sage his fated lapse deplore;
Columbia's self the tear of anguish shed,
And mourns the glories of her * * * fled!
'Tis he, my son, shall stretch thy dark domain,
By me inspir'd with dreams of boundless gain;
'Tis he, illustrious changeling, shall control
Each generous thought that swell'd his active soul;
Court the low crowd, his free-born spirit brav'd,
And blast the realms his former valor saved.

Lo! at his side, and guardian of his way,
Our fav'rite * * * directs his steps astray;
In that vile shape, predictive fate assign'd
A frame well suited to so base a mind;
To him no form, no grace, nor genius given,
But mark'd for mischief by the hand of heaven;
Him plodding patience taught to con the laws,
And knavery sold to serve the British cause,
To wealth and power in *courts marine* to rise,
And glut his avarice on each rebel prize;
Then foil'd, he chang'd, at our superior call,
To lure his cringing pupil to his fall;
With steady aim, his former toils to crown,
Subvert the Congress, and exalt the throne.

Fair to thine eyes, and number'd with thy friends,
The train of selfish jealousy ascends;
Blind Belisarius leads the mighty round,
And gropes in darkness o'er the mystic ground;
Rous'd at his call, advance an airy group,
Thin, shadowy shapes, and ghastly phantoms troop;
In fancy dress, the hands fantastic join'd,
Revel to madness on his moody mind;
He sees cadets in pigmy armies rise,
And Boston fifers swarm like Hessian flies,

Creative frenzy painting on his brain,
By Congress rais'd, and paid the innumerous train,
Himself neglected, needy, blind, and old,
The R—— B—— balanced by the ——
In wild profusion spent each liberal grant,
While war alone can rescue him from want.

The blunt *Rough-hewer*, from his savage den,
With learned dullness loads his lab'ring pen;
In muddy streams his rumbling wits combine
Big words convolving on the turbid line.
Yet spare thy scorn, for, lo! by friendly hands,
In Congress rear'd, the reptile *Scarecrow* stands;
Strange to himself, for now, no more the prig,
Swells in the powder'd majesty of wig,
But gay, like snake from wintry garb releas'd,
Shines the stiff coxcomb in his courtly vest;
From side to side there struts, and smiles, and prates,
And seems to wonder what's become of ——

To check their force, our desperate foes in vain
Attempt thy ruin and oppose thy reign;
Ardent and bold, the sinking land to save,
In council sapient as in action brave,
I fear'd young HAMILTON's unshaken soul,
And saw his arm our wayward host control;
Yet, while the Senate with his accents rung,
Fire in his eye, and thunder on his tongue,
My *band of mutes* in dumb confusion throng,
Convinc'd of right, yet obstinate in wrong,
With stupid reverence lift the guided hand,
And yield an empire to thy wild command.

Rise, then, my son! the frowns of fate to dare;
Blest with such aid, shall Anarch's soul despair?
Hark! how my heroes to the field invite,
Go, more victorious in thy mother's might;
Still one last conflict waits; one gleam of day

Shall pierce thine empire with expiring ray,
Ere light and order from their seats be hurl'd,
And shade and silence veil thy vanquish'd world.

AMERICAN ANTIQUITIES   No X

Extract from the Anarchiad, Book XXIV

THE SPEECH OF HESPER

. . . his last solemn address to his principal counselors and
sages, whom he had convened at Philadelphia.

Ye fires of nations, call'd in high debate
From kindred realms, to save the sinking State,
A boundless sway on one broad base to rear—
My voice paternal claims your listening ear;
O'er the wide clime my fostering cares extend,
Your guardian genius, and your deathless friend.

When splendid victory, on her trophy'd car
Swept from these shores the last remains of war—
Bade each glad State that boasts Columbia's name,
Exult in freedom and ascend to fame;
To bliss unbounded stretch their ardent eyes,
And wealth and empire from their labor rise—
My raptur'd sons beheld the discord cease,
And sooth'd their sorrows in the songs of peace.

Shall these bright scenes, with happiest omens born,
Fade like the fleeting visions of the morn?
Shall this fair fabric from its base be hurl'd,
And whelm in dust the glories of the world?
Will ye, who saw the heavens tempestuous lower—
Who felt the arm of irritated power—
Whose souls, descending with the wasting flood,
Prepar'd the firm foundations, built in blood;
By discord seiz'd, will ye desert the plan—
Th' unfinish'd Babel of the bliss of man?

Go search the field of death, where heroes lost,
In graves obscure, can tell what freedom cost,
Tho' conquest smil'd; there slain amid the crowd,
And plunged, promiscuous, with no winding shroud,
No friendly hand their gory wounds to lave,
The thousands moulder in a common grave.
Not so thy son, oh LAURENS! gasping lies,
Too daring youth, war's latest sacrifice;
His snow-white bosom heaves with writhing pain,
The purple drops his snow-white bosom stain;
His cheek of rose is wan; a deadly hue
Sits on his face, that chills with lucid dew.
There WARREN, glorious with expiring breath,
A comely corse, that smiles in ghastly death:
See MERCER bleed; and o'er yon wintry wall,
'Mid heaps of slain, see great MONTGOMERY fall!

Behold these veterans, worn with want and care,
Their sinews stiffen'd, silver'd o'er their hair;
Weak in their steps of age, they move forlorn,
Their toils forgotten by the sons of scorn;
This hateful truth still aggravates their pain,
In vain they conquer'd! and they bled in vain!
Go, then, ye remnants of inglorious wars,
Disown your marks of merit, hide your scars,
Of lust, of power, of titled pride accurs'd;
Steal to your graves, dishonored, and abus'd.

For, see! proud Faction waves her flaming brand,
And discord riots o'er the ungrateful land;
Lo! to the north, a wild, adventurous crew,
In desperate mobs, the savage state renew;
Each felon chief his maddening thousands draws,
And claims bold license from the bond of laws;
In other States the chosen fires of shame
Stamp their vile knaveries with a legal name;
In honor's seat, the sons of meanness swarm,
And Senates base the work which mobs perform;

To wealth, to power, the foes of union rise,
While foes deride you, and while friends despise.

Stand forth, ye traitors! at your country's bar,
Inglorious authors of intestine war;
What countless mischiefs from their labors rise!
Pens dipp'd in gall, and lips inspir'd with lies!
Ye fires of ruin, prime detested cause
Of bankrupt faith, annihilated laws—
Of selfish systems, jealous, local schemes,
And union'd empire lost in empty dreams;
Your names, expanding with your growing crime,
Shall float, disgustful, down the stream of time;
Each future age applaud th' avenging song,
And outraged nature vindicate the wrong.

Yes, there are men, who, touch'd with heavenly fire,
Beyond the confines of these climes aspire—
Beyond the praises of a transient age,
To live, immortal, in the patriot page;
Who greatly dare, though warring worlds oppose,
To pour just vengeance on their country's foes.

And lo! th' ethereal worlds assert your cause;
Celestial aid, the voice of virtue draws;
The curtains blue, of yon expansion, rend—
From opening skies heroic shades descend.
See, rob'd in light, the forms of heaven appear;
The warrior spirits of your friends are near—
Each on his steed of fire, (his quiver stor'd
With shafts of vengeance,) grasps his flaming sword:
The burning blade waves high, and, dipt in blood,
Hurls plagues and death on discord's faithless brood.

Yet, what the hope? The dreams of Congress fade,
The federal UNION sinks in endless shade;
Each feeble call, that warns the realms around,
Seems the faint echo of a dying sound;

Each requisition wastes in fleeting air,
And not one State regards the powerless prayer.

Ye wanton States, by heaven's best blessings curst,
Long on the lap of softening luxury nurst,
What fickle frenzy raves! what visions strange
Inspire your bosoms with the lust of change,
And frames the wish to fly from fancy's ill,
And yield your freedom to a monarch's will?

Go, view the lands to lawless power a prey,
Where tyrants govern with unbounded sway;
See the long pomp, in gorgeous state display'd—
The tinsel's pomp, the squadron's horse parade;
See heralds gay, with emblems on their vest—
In tissued robes, tall, beauteous pages, drest;
Where moves the pageant throng, unnumber'd slaves,
Lords, Dukes, and Princes, titulary knaves,
Confus'dly thine, the purple gemm'd with stars,
Sceptres, and globes, and crowns, and ruby'd cars,
On gilded orbs the thundering chariots roll'd,
Steeds snorting fire, and champing bits of gold,
Prance to the trumpet's voice—while each assumes
A loftier gait, and lifts his neck of plumes.
High on the moving throne, and near the van,
The tyrant rides, the chosen scourge of man:
Clarions, and flutes, and drums, his way prepare,
And shouting millions rend the conscious air—
Millions, whose ceaseless toils the pomp sustain,
Whose hour of stupid joy repays an age of pain.

From years of darkness springs the regal line—
Hereditary kings, by right divine;
'Tis theirs to riot on all nature's spoils—
For them, with pangs unblest, the peasant toils;
For them, the earth prolific teems with grain;
Their's the dread labors of the devious main;
Annual, for them, the wasted land renews
The gifts oppressive, and extorted dues;

For them, when slaughter spreads the gory plains,
The life-blood gushes from a thousand veins—
While the dull herd, of earth-born pomp afraid,
Adore the power that coward meanness made . . .

Nor less abhor'd, the certain woe that waits
The giddy rage of democratic States,
Whose pop'lar breath, high-blown in restless tide,
No laws can temper, and no reason guide:
An equal sway, their mind indignant spurns,
To wanton change, the bliss of freedom turns;
Led by wild demagogues, the factious crowd,
Mean, fierce, imperious, insolent and loud,
Nor fame, nor wealth, nor power, nor system draws—
They see no object, and perceive no cause;
But feel, by turns, in one disastrous hour,
Th' extremes of license, and th' extremes of power.

What madness prompts, or what ill-omen'd fears,
Your realm to parcel into petty States?
Shall lordly Hudson part contending powers,
And broad Potomac lave two hostile shores?
Must Alleghany's sacred summits bear
The impious bulwarks of perpetual war?—
His hundred streams receive your heroes slain,
And bear your sons inglorious to the main?
Will States cement, by feebler bonds allied,
Or join more closely, as they more divide?
Will this vain scheme bid restless factions cease,
Check foreign wars, or fix internal peace?—
Call public credit from her grave to rise,
Or gain in grandeur what they lose in size?
In this weak realm, can countless kingdoms start,
Strong with new force, in each divided part—
While empire's head, dissected into four,
Gains life by severance of diminish'd power?
So, when the philosophic hand divides
The full-grown polypus, in genial tides,

Each severed part, infused with latent life,
Acquires new vigor from the friendly knife;
O'er peopled sands the puny insects creep,
Till the next wave absorbs them in the deep.

What, then, remains? Must pilgrim FREEDOM fly
From these lov'd regions, to her native sky?
When the fair fugitive the orient chased,
She fixed her feet beyond the watery waste;
Her docile sons (enough of power resign'd,
And natural rights in social leagues combin'd)
In virtue firm, though jealous in her cause,
Gave Senates force, and energy to laws;
From ancient habit, local powers obey,
Yet feel no reverence for one general sway;
For breach of faith, no keen compulsion feel,
And find no interest in the federal weal.
But know, ye favor'd race, one potent head
Must rule your States, and strike your foes with dread,
The finance regulate, the trade control,
Live through the empire, and accord the whole.

Ere death invades, and night's deep curtain falls,
Through ruined realms the voice of UNION calls;
Loud as the trump of heaven through darkness roars,
When gyral gusts entomb Caribbean towers—
When nature trembles, through the deeps convuls'd,
And ocean foams, from craggy cliffs repuls'd;
On you she calls! attend the warning cry:
"YE LIVE UNITED, OR DIVIDED DIE!"

AMERICAN ANTIQUITIES. No. XI

Extract from the Anarchiad, Book XVII

THE LAND OF ANNIHILATION

. . . The society of critics and antiquarians have successfully deciphered the Seventeenth Book of The Anarchiad, in

which the poet makes a descent into the infernal regions.
It is curious to observe how closely he has been followed (as,
indeed, might naturally be expected) by Homer, Virgil, and
their successors in modern ages. . . . The Land of Annihilation, described in so picturesque a manner, is a valuable addition to the subterranean geography; but the theory of a
race of beings, properly the denizens of that country, who,
after having mixed, undistinguished, with mankind, and performed all human functions, then returned to their primitive
nihility, might pass for a burlesque, if it were not found in so
serious a performance.

Beyond the realms where stygian horrors dwell,
And floods sulphureous whelm the vales of hell;
Where Naiad furies, yelling as they lave,
In fiery eddies roll the turbid wave:
Beyond the verge of chaos' utmost clime,
The dubious bounds of nature, space, and time;
A realm extends its unessential gloom,
The vast creation's universal tomb!
There no fair suns emblaze the courts on high,
Nor moon, nor starry fires, the evening sky;
No matin clouds in ether hang their sails,
Nor moving spirit wakes the vernal gales;
But endless twilight, with a feeble ray,
Browns the dim horrors of the dusky day;
And silence, sameness, and eternal shade,
Th' unbounded wild inanity pervade.

In night, pavilion'd o'er the shadowy plains,
The peerless *power*, ANNIHILATION, reigns!
Eldest of fiends! whose uncreating breath,
Peoples the shores of darkness and of death;
Down the deep gulf's absorbing vortex whirl'd,
Sink the vain splendors of each upper world;
Ambition's toils, the statesman's gloried name,
The hero's triumph, and the poet's fame;
Insatiate throngs, who, fired with lust of gain,

Rive the firm earth, and force the faithless main;
Here, lulled to rest, eternal stillness keep,
And curtain'd close in dead oblivion, sleep.

Beneath his scepter, in imperial state,
His stern commands ten thousand demons wait;
Prompt, like their prince, in elemental wars
To tread out empires, and to quench the stars;
Extinguish'd worlds in delug'd fires to lave—
Sweep ruin'd systems to a common grave;
Exterminate existence, and restore
The vanquish'd vacuum to the tyrant's power.

These the great *hierarchs*, whose prowess leads
The vassal throng to desolating deeds;
But far beneath them spreads a junior fry—
The pigmy populace of the nether sky;
With feeble powers, for petty toils design'd,
Their humble province is to plague mankind,
Pervade the world, excite all mortal strife,
Inspire the wrongs, and blast the joys, of life.

Matured for birth, at times on earth they rise,
Incarnate *imps*, and veiled in human guise;
Like man appear in stature, shape, and face—
Mix, undistinguished, with the common race;
Fill every *rank*, in each *profession* blend,
Power all their aim, and ruin all their end.

Of these, the least, in medicine's garb arrayed,
With deadly art pursues the healing trade—
The lancet wield, prescribe the poisonous pill,
Invent the nostrum, and, unlicensed, kill;
O'erload the stygian bark with frequent freight,
And crowd with angry ghosts the realm of fate.
In sable robes, and stiff with reverend air,
Some vent their dogmas in the house of prayer;
With pious cant, or persecution's flame,

To vilest ends abuse each sacred name;
On rites and forms, with zeal eternal dwell,
Ope heaven for self, and doom the rest to hell:
To banish blest religion, all agree,
A work, *O, Murray!* fate reserves for thee!

Oft at the wrangling bar, in loud renown,
The demon lurks beneath the lawyer's gown;
Confounds all right, and, arrogant in lies,
Spreads a dark mist before the judge's eyes;
Less dangerous thief, who, limited by fate,
Leaves soul and body free, and ruin but th' estate.

But chief the race allured by fleeting fame,
Who seek on earth the politician's name;
Auspicious race! whom folly joys to bless,
And wealth and honor crown with glad success;
Formed, like ballons, by emptiness to rise
On pop'lar gales, to waft them through the skies,
In wond'ring air the fog-born meteors stand,
And shine the *Wimbles* of th' applauding land.
And, lo! th' expected scene advances near—
The promised age, the *fiends' millenial year!*
At that famed era, raised by angry fates,
What countless *imps* shall throng the new-born States!
See, from the shades, on tiny pinions swell
And rise, the young DEMOCRACY of *hell!*
Before their face the *powers of Congress* fade,
And *public credit* sinks, an empty shade;
Wild severance rages, wars intestine spread,
Their boasted UNION hides her dying head;
The forms of government in ruin hurled,
Reluctant empire quits the western world.

O, glorious throng! beyond all wisdom wise!
Expert to act, eccentric to devise!
In retrogressive march, what schemes advance!
What vast resources, and what strange finance!

Chimeras sage, with plans commercial fraught,
Sublime abortions of projecting thought!
To paper coin, how copper mints succeed—
How Indian wars in brains prolific breed!
What strength, what firmness, guide the public helm!
How troops disbanded guard the threaten'd realm!
How treaties thrive! and, 'mid the sons of Ham,
The LYBIAN LION shrinks before the LAMB!
New modes of taxing spring from *Woglog's* hands,
And peerless *Wimble* sells the western lands!
Their task performed; again, by sovereign doom,
The *fiend* compels them to their native home.
Where *Lethe's streams* through glooms tartarean roll,
And seek th' expansion of th' oblivious pool—
From all the clime th' innumerable crowd
Float, half-embosom'd in the genial flood;
Down the dark deep, in friendly union, flows
Tweedle's soft verse, and *Copper's* sounding prose;
Light *Commutation*, dancing on the wave
With federal *Impost*, finds the eternal grave;
Like bubble bright, the *nation's glory* rides,
And *Acts of Congress* load the downward tides;
By *Collins* steered, *Rhode Island* joins the train,
With all things else as transient, vile, and vain.

There mansions wait, prepared in pomp, to grace
The coming heroes of the illustrious race;
When *Wronghead's* steps shall seek their natal shore,
And Night her *Blacklegs* to his fire restore.
Thither, again, they tend; and there, at last,
Their projects, changes, and elections past,
Wimble shall turn to *froth*, to *Bubo Zack*;
Ben change to *Copper*; *Woglog* end in *Quack*:
From shade to shade, from nought to nought, decoyed,
All center whence they sprang—in one eternal void.

AMERICAN ANTIQUITIES. No. XII

Extracts from the Anarchiad, Book XVII

THE REGION OF PREËXISTENT SPIRITS

. . . Some further extracts from the . . . Book . . . "The Land of Annihilation." In his progress through the shades, the Bard is attended by an ancient seer, the Merlin of the West, who explains to him the nature of the country, and the character of its inhabitants. . . . The account of the various regions and circles into which the Subterranean World is divided, has in many parts been copied by the famous Italian poet, Dante, in his "Inferno." The American Bard seems to have been the first who entered the Region of the Preëxistent Spirits, which has since been explored by the celebrated voyager, Æneas, whose observations may be found in the Sixth Book of Virgil. . . . That part of the Book which we shall now transcribe, contains the description of many illustrious personages . . . both in Europe and America in the eighteenth century from the Christian era. . . . Those writers who were destined to spend their lives . . . both in philosophy and history, . . . demonstrating the debility and diminution of nature in the western hemisphere, . . . He beholds, with admiration, the souls of those learned sages [who discovered] . . . that in this part of the globe the animal and vegetable creation are far inferior . . . ; that man has wonderfully degenerated in courage, activity, and other marks of virility; and that "America has never produced one good Poet, one able Mathematician, or one man of genius in one single Art, or one single Science" as the sagacious Abbe Raynal has so wisely observed. These he finds grouped in [a] . . . circle . . . He describes his entrance into the circle, in the following sublime and awful manner:

Darkling they plied o'er many a burning heath,
Down the low shores of Erebus and Death—
When, through th' obscure they saw the glim'ring glades

'Twixt Orcus central, and th' Elysian shades:
As hov'ring dreams the slumb'ring eye assail,
Unnumber'd phantoms flit among the vale;
And sounds as vague and hollow meet the ear,
As startled fancy hears, or seems to hear,
What time the mourner, through the midnight gloom,
Sees shadowy spectres issuing from the tomb:
The unreal forms the bard, astonish'd, eyed,
And ask'd the wonder from the friendly guide.
Behold, the seer replies, on those dark coasts
The vagrant hordes of preëxistent ghosts—
Elect for earth, and destined to be born
When time's slow course shall wake the natal morn:
Approach and view, in this, their embryo home,
Wits, poets, chiefs, and sages yet to come.

See yonder group, that scorn the vulgar crowd,
Absorb'd in thought, of conscious learning proud,
Who, rapt with foretaste of their glorious day,
Now seiz'd the pen, impatient of delay:
These shades shall late in Europe's clime arise,
And scan new worlds with philosophic eyes:
Immured at home, in rambling fancy brave,
Explore all lands beyond th' Atlantic wave;
Of laws for unknown realms invent new codes,
Write natural histories for their antipodes;
Tell how th' enfeebled powers of life decay,
Where falling suns defraud the western day;
Paint the dank, steril globe, accurst by fate,
Created, lost, or stolen from ocean late;
See vegetation, man, and bird, and beast,
Just by the distance' squares in size decreased;
See mountain pines to dwarfish reeds descend,
Aspiring oaks in pigmy shrub oaks end;—
The heaven-topp'd Andes sink a humble hill,—
Sea-like Potomac run a tinkling rill;—
Huge mammoth dwindle to a mouse's size—
Columbian turkeys turn European flies;—

Exotic birds, and foreign beasts, grow small,
And man, the lordliest, shrink to least of all:
While each vain whim their loaded skulls conceive
Whole realms shall reverence, and all fools believe.

In passing farther, the seer points out the father of this
system, in the soul of the famous *Abbé de Pau*, who was then
busied in prying into futurity, by the aid of a philosophic
telescope, calculated to diminish all objects, according to the
squares of the distances, as has been hinted. And thus con-
tinues the prediction:

There, with sure ken, th' inverted optics show
All nature lessening to the sage *De Pau;*
E'en now his head the cleric tonsures grace,
And all the *abbé* blossoms in his face;
His peerless pen shall raise, with magic lore,
The long-lost pigmies on th' Atlantic shore;
Make niggard nature's noblest gifts decline
Th' indicial marks of bodies masculine;
Nor seek the proof of those who best can tell
The well-taught duchess, and Parisian belle.

He then points out the *Compte de Buffon*, the *Abbé Raynal*,
Dr. Robertson, and the whole train of imitators, . . . He
appears to have exactly forseen *Dr. Robertson's* "History of
America," and his observation that the soil of America is
prolific in nothing but reptiles and insects. The allusion to
Moses, . . . seems to confirm the opinion of some learned
writers, that the natives of this country were descended from
the Jews, or the Jews from them:

See Scotland's livy in historic pride,
Rush, with blind fury, o'er th' Atlantic tide;
He lifts, in wrath, his plague-compelling wand,
And deadly murrain blasts the fated land:
His parent call awakes the insect train—
Gnats cloud the skies, and ants devour the plain;

Thick swarming frogs attend his magic voice—
Rods change to serpents, and the dust to lice.

Here the seer took occasion to inform the bard how . . .
that a great [MORRIS] should arise . . . who, never having
enjoyed . . . THE ANARCHIAD, or any other American poem,
should dogmatically decide, in his capacity of Senator, that
America never had produced a good poet. . . .

That plodding shade, who, ere he starts from hence,
By mammon taught, in shillings, pounds, and pence,
In Philadelphia's happy soil, shall claim
Gold for his GOD, and [MORRIS] for his name;
With purse-proud wit, and Senatorial rank,
His critic talents glowing from the bank;
From famed *Raynal's* wise labors, shall declare,
That not one poet breathes Columbian air!

Yet not all wits who there to fame advance,
Shall take their cue from dictatorial France;
But, like sincere allies, each needy friend
Shall sometimes borrow lies, and sometimes lend.
Scared at the shape of CINCINNATUS' name,
The envious *Burke* denied that road to fame;
Stars, ribbands, mantles, crowding on his brain,
"*Blows the loud trump!*" and calls the jealous train;
Fills gaping herds with visionary fears
Of landless nobles, and of penceless peers;
From social rites, and charity, debars
The unpaid veterans of successful wars—
Proscribes all worth, by ostracising doom,
To death or exile, as in Greece or Rome;
While safe himself, he boasts a strong defense,
Clear from the crime of merit or of sense.

From him shall Gallic scribblers learn their lore,
And write, like him, as man ne'er wrote before;
Grave Demeunier, with borrowed tales, and weak,

Th' encyclopedias' endless tomes shall eke—
Assert with falsehood, and with froth disclaim,
Forebode the issues, and foresee the aim;
Through time's dark vale, the plans of fate explore,
By ign'rance aided in prophetic power;
As old Tiresias, favor'd of the skies,
Gain'd gifts oracular by the loss of eyes.

. . . He makes an easy transition to the shade of the redoubtable *Comte Mirabeau*, who, having lately emerged from the Bastile, has employed his tremendous pen on "the Cincinnati," "the Navigation of the Scheldt," . . . and innumerable other knotty points: . . . . seconded and opposed, by his brother in scribbling and the Bastile, the perjured *Linguet*. . . . The Mirabeaus were predestined to be infamous for unnatural vices. . . . The seer points out these characters: . . .

When souls select, near Jordan rose to dwell,
And people Sodom with the dregs of hell,
Great was the doubt, and great the learn'd debates,
Through the grand conclave of th' infernal States,
With that vile crew, if these should rise to earth,
Or future Europe better claim'd their birth;
The latter vote prevail'd; on this dark stage
Each incubus awaits the destined age;
Then shall their souls to human forms advance,
And spring to light the *Mirabeaus* of France.
Yet not alone to carnal views confined;
The younger shades, for mental toils designed,
Profuse of lies, and obstinate in ill,
On every theme shall try his gall-dipt quill:
In *Burke's* proud steps shall equal honors claim,
A learn'd associate of Demeunier's fame.

The next group of souls who pass in review, consists of those wise civilians who have generously wasted such fountains of ink in endeavoring to instruct poor America in her

own history and politics. The *Abbé Mably* is mentioned . . .
[also] the modest *Target*, who, supposing that no laws existed
in the United States, . . . humanely proposed to Congress
to . . . furnish a code for the use of the empire.   The seer
. . . thus apostrophizes:

Inflated pride! all-feeling ignorance!
Ye grand inspirers of the wits of France!
On blest *Target* exhaust your utmost power;
Shower all your gifts, and lavish all your store!
I see him, tow'ring 'mid th' applauding throng,
Pomp in his air, and bluster on his tongue;
Wave-dangling far, his wig-official curl'd—
A sign of sapience, to the western world.
Throned 'mid the forty wise, by partial fates,
A self-made Solon for the rising States.

Next . . . appear . . . those European historians and
biographers who have amused their readers with many fairy
tales, the scenes of which . . . lay in America . . . The
seer . . . even condescends to notice the *history of Connecticut*, invented by *Parson Peters, the fag-end man of M'Fingal*. But he pays particular attention to the great genius of
D'Auberteul, who has . . . described the manner of cutting
up the crown into thirteen pieces, and sending it to the several
States, and given the interesting novel of the amours of
General WASHINGTON . . . He concludes with the following sublime address to his shade, which has been closely
copied by Pope: . . .

Swift fly the years, and rise the expected morn!
Oh spring to light! auspicious sage, be born!
The new-found world shall all your cares engage;
The promised lyre of the future age.
No more shall glory gild the hero's name,
Nor envy sicken at the deeds of fame;
Virtue no more the generous breast shall fire,
Nor radiant truth the historic page inspire;

But lost, dissolved in thy superior shade,
One tide of falsehood o'er the world be spread;
In wit's light robe shall gaudy fiction shine,
And all be lies, as in a work of thine.

The Echo was published in a series of twenty numbers in *The American Mercury* from 1791 to 1805. It was reissued in an abridged form by the surviving members of the group, "with curious illustrations painted by Tisdale, engraved by Levey," from the Porcupine Press in 1807. Numbers II and III were reprinted as originally written, but portions were omitted from the other numbers, "without essentially injuring the constituent parts." The original intention was to ridicule the bad literary taste of the time, but after the first number the work became largely political, directing its attack upon Republican leaders and the "prevalent infidel ideas of the French Revolution." It followed the plan of reprinting some absurd passage from a political speech or a newspaper article, and echoing it in a burlesque poem. It is often clever and far better humored than *The Anarchiad*, although some of the democratic leaders come in for rather severe handling, in particular John Hancock, whose pompous ways were a fair target, Samuel Adams, and Judge Hugh Henry Brackenridge, author of *Modern Chivalry*, a racy satire of frontier politics. With the exception of a few lines by Cogswell and Smith, and a part of one or two numbers by Hopkins, the entire work was the production of Alsop and Theodore Dwight. Kettell attributes the conception and the greater part of the whole to the former.

The portions of *The Echo* here reprinted, with the original notes, are from the edition of 1807.

THE ECHO

NUMBER I

[By Richard Alsop and Theodore Dwight]

Boston, July 14th, 1791.

"On Tuesday last, about 4 o'clock, P. M. came on a smart shower of rain attended with lightning and thunder, no ways remarkable. The clouds soon dissipated, and the appearance of the azure vault, left trivial hopes of further needful supplies from the *uncorked bottles of heaven.* In a few moments the horizon was again overshadowed, and an almost impenetrable gloom mantled the face of the skies. The wind frequently shifting from one point to another, wafted the clouds in various directions, until at last they united in one common centre and shrouded the visible globe in thick darkness. The attendant lightning, with the accompanying thunder, brought forth from the treasures that embattled elements to awful conflict, were extremely vivid, and amazing loud. Those buildings that were defended by electric rods, appeared to be wrapped in sheets of livid flame, and a flood of the pure fire rolled its burning torrents down them with alarming violence. The majestic roar of disploding thunders, now bursting with a sudden crash, and now wasting the rumbling Echo of their sounds in other lands, added indescribable grandeur to the sublime scene. The windows of the upper regions appeared as thrown wide open, and the trembling cataract poured impetuous down. More salutary showers, and more needed, have not been experienced this summer. Several previous weeks had exhibited a melancholy sight: the verdure of fields was nearly destroyed; and the patient husbandman almost experienced despair. Two beautiful rainbows, the one existing in its native glories, and the other a splendid reflection of primitive colours, closed the magnificent picture, and presented to the contemplative mind, the angel of mercy, cloathed with the brilliance of this irradiated arch, and dispensing felicity to assembled worlds.

475

"It is not unnatural to expect that the thunder storm would be attended with some damage. We hear a barn belonging to Mr. Wythe of Cambridge caught fire from the lightning, which entirely consumed the same, together with several tons of hay, &c."

Hartford, August 8, 1791.

"Those mighty tales which great events rehearse,
"To fame we consecrate in deathless verse."

On Tuesday last great Sol, with piercing eye,
Pursued his journey thro' the vaulted sky,
And in his car effulgent roll'd his way
Four hours beyond the burning zone of day;
When lo! a cloud, o'ershadowing all the plain,
From countless pores perspir'd a *liquid* rain,
While from its cracks the lightnings made a peep,
And chit-chat thunders rock'd our fears asleep.
But soon the vapoury fog dispers'd in air,
And left the azure blue-eyed concave bare:
Even the last drop of hope, which dripping skies
Gave for a moment to our straining eyes,
Like *Boston Rum*, from heaven's *junk bottles* broke,
Lost all the corks, and vanish'd into smoke.
    But swift from worlds unknown, a fresh supply
Of vapour dimm'd the great horizon's eye;
The crazy clouds, by shifting zephyrs driven,
Wafted their courses through the high-arch'd heaven,
Till pil'd aloft in one stupendous heap,
The seen and unseen worlds grew dark, and nature 'gan to
        weep.
Attendant lightnings stream'd their tails afar,
And social thunders wak'd ethereal war,
From dark deep pockets brought their treasur'd store,
Embattled elements increas'd the roar—
Red crinkling fires expended all their force,
And tumbling rumblings steer'd their headlong course.

Those guarded frames by thunder poles* secur'd,
Tho' wrapp'd in sheets of flame, those sheets endur'd,
O'er their broad roofs the fiery torrents roll'd,
And every shingle seem'd of burning gold.
Majestic thunders, with disploding roar,
And sudden crashing, bounc'd along the shore,
Till, lost in other lands, the whispering sound
Fled from our ears and fainted on the ground.
Rain's house† on high its window sashes op'd,
And out the cataract impetuous hopp'd,
While the grand scene by far more grand appear'd
With lightnings never seen and thunders never heard.

More salutary showers have not been known,
To wash dame Nature's dirty homespun gown—
For several weeks the good old Joan's been seen,
With filth bespatter'd like a lazy quean.
The husbandman fast travelling to despair,
Laid down his hoe and took his rocking chair,
While his fat wife the well and cistern dried,
Her mop grown useless hung it up and cry'd.

Two rain-bows fair that Iris brought along,
Pick'd from the choicest of her colour'd throng;
The first-born deck'd in pristine hues of light,
In all its native glories glowing bright,
The next adorn'd with less refulgent rays,
But borrowing lustre from its brother's blaze;
Shone a bright reflex of those colours gay
That deck'd with light creation's primal day,
When infant Nature lisp'd her earliest notes,
And *younker Adam* crept in petticoats:
And to the people to reflection given,
"The sons of Boston, the elect of heaven."
Presented Mercy's Angel smiling fair,
Irradiate splendors frizzled in his hair,

* Vulgarly lightning rods.
† The old gentleman from whose cellar the junk bottles and demi-johns were taken.

Uncorking demijohns,* and pouring down
Heaven's liquid blessings on the gaping town.
    N.B. At Cambridge town, the self-same day,
A barn was burnt well-filled with hay.
Some say the light'ning turn'd it red,
Some say the thunder struck it dead,
Some say it made the cattle stare,
And some it kill'd an aged mare;
But we expect the truth to learn,
From Mr. Wythe, who own'd the barn.

ECHO. NO. IX

[The ECHO, unwilling that the sublime and cautionary
speeches of the Governor of the State of Massachusetts,
should be lost to posterity, has thought proper, as they possess such uncommon excellencies, to introduce them together,
to the notice of the public; and has only omitted such passages as did not seem so immediately to concern the two
grand objects of her laudable apprehensions.]

From the Columbian Centinel, of Nov. 10, 1792

Concord, November 8

"*Gentlemen of the Senate, and*
    "*Gentlemen of the House of Representatives,*

"I Should for my own, as well as for your convenience,
have been glad to have met you at the ancient seat of our
Government; but as it has pleased the Most High, to visit
that, as well as many other of our towns, with a troublesome
and contagious disease, I have, with the advice of the Council
thought it most for your safety and comfort to convene at
this place.

    * Otherwise called demi-jars; but the above is preferred as the
most elegant, being a species of the prosopopeia.

"Gentlemen,

"I am urged, by the sense of duty, to communicate with you my mind upon a transaction, which I cannot but consider as an open insult upon the Laws and Government of the commonwealth.

"In the year one thousand seven hundred and fifty, the legislature of this then province of Massachusetts-Bay, passed an act, entitled, "An Act to prevent Stage Plays, and other Theatrical Entertainments."

"The preamble of this Act is in these words, "For preventing and avoiding many great mischiefs, which arise from public Stage-Plays, Interludes, and other Theatrical Entertainments; which not only occasion great and unnecessary expenses, and discourage industry and frugality; but likewise tend generally to increase immorality, impiety, and a contempt of religion."

"The act is now a law of the commonwealth; the principles upon which it is predicated, have been recognized by, and derive support from the consideration of several legislatures; and surely it ought to claim the respect and obedience of all persons who live or happen to be within the Commonwealth. Yet a number of aliens and foreigners, have lately entered the State, and in the metropolis of the Government, under advertisements insulting to the habits and education of the citizens, have been pleased to invite them to, and to exhibit before such as attended, *Stage-Plays, Interludes, and Theatrical Entertainments*, under the stile and appellation of "Moral Lectures." This fact is so notorious, that it is in vain to attempt a concealment of its coming to our knowledge.

"Whether the Judicial Departments, whose business it is, have attended to this subject or not, I am unable to determine; but this I am convinced of, that no measures have been taken to punish a most open breech of the Laws, and a most contemptuous insult upon the powers of the Government.

"You, Gentlemen, are the guardians of the Commonwealth's dignity and honour; and our fellow-citizens rely upon your vigilance and wisdom, for the support of the sovereignty and importance of the Government. I therefore refer this matter to your determinations; and cannot but hope that your resolutions and measures will give efficacy to the laws, and be the means of bringing to condign punishment those who dare to treat them with contempt or open opposition.

"*Gentlemen of the Senate, and of the*
"*House of Representatives,*

"By the Constitution of the United States of America, each State is to appoint, in such manner as the legislature shall direct, Electors of President and Vice-President. By a late act of Congress, it is enacted, "That the Supreme "Executive of each State SHALL cause three lists of the names "of the Electors of such State to be made and certified, and "to be delivered to the Electors on or before the first Wednes-"day in December."

"I feel the importance of giving every constitutional sup- port to the General Government: and I also am convinced that the existence and well-being of that Government de- pends upon preventing a confusion of the authority of it with that of the States separately. But that Government applies itself to the People of the United States in their natural, individual capacity, and cannot exert any force upon, or by any means control the officers of the State Governments as such: Therefore, when an act of Congress uses compulsory words with regard to any Act to be done by the Supreme Executive of this Commonwealth, I shall not feel myself obliged to obey them, because I am not, in my official capac- ity, amenable to that Government.

"My duty as Governor, will most certainly oblige me to see that proper and efficient Certificates are made of the ap- pointment of Electors of President and Vice-President; and perhaps the mode suggested in the Act above-mentioned, may be found to be the most proper. If you, Gentlemen, have any mode to propose with respect to the conduct of this busi- ness, I shall pay every attention to it.

"*Gentlemen,*

"I do not address you at this time from a disposition to regard the proceedings of the general government with a jealous eye, nor do I suppose that Congress could intend that clause in their Act as a compulsory provision: but I wish to prevent any measure to proceed through inattention, which may be drawn into precedents hereafter, to the injury of the people, or to give a constructive power where the Federal Constitution has not expressly given it."

Hartford, January 14th, 1793

"*Again shall* ECHO *strike the lyre,*
"*While deeds sublime the song inspire:*
"*To* HANCOCK *pass from* JOHN MONIER,
"*And give the* ROYAL JOHN *a cheer.*"
Western Star.]

GENTLES, of either kind, both small and great,
Props of *our* laws, and pillars of *our* state;
Tho' words would fail, and language' self prove weak,
My joy, in seeing you once more, to speak;
While in this fleshly bottle closely pent,
So strong expression struggles for a vent,
Ere I can draw the cork, I fear, alas!
'Twill burst the frail contexture of my glass:
Yet, had this joy been even *more* complete
Could I have met you at our ancient Seat,
Near Faneuil Hall, to me forever dear,
Where first I enter'd on *my* great career;
Whose walls, so oft, *my* presence bade rejoice,
Which oft in transport echoed to *my* voice,
When rose, 'gainst Britain, its tremendous roar,
And shook her distant isle, from shore to shore;
So when stern Jove, to vengeful anger driven,
Rolls the black tempest o'er the expanse of heaven,
Loud peals of thunder on the storm arise,
And the red lightning quivers o'er the skies;
From central depths disturbed the ocean raves,
And high to heaven upheaves his briny waves;
From its deep base the cloud-veil'd mountain shakes;
The firm rock trembles, and the valley quakes;
All nature, shuddering, owns the dreadful nod,

And shrinks before the terrors of the God.
There FREEDOM, then a chick, unfledg'd and bare,
I kindly brooded with a mother's care;
Taught her to creep, to hop, to run, to fly,
And gave her wings to lift herself on high,
'Till perfect grown, she came at length, to soar
To heights unthought of, but by *me*, before.
In that loved spot, O could you but have met!
"But fate denies, and man must yield to fate;"
Since the SMALL-POX, *Death's* Vicar here on earth,
Who, stern, respects nor dignities, nor worth,
O'er that sad place, now sunk in dire dismay,
Waves his pale banners, and extends his sway,
Deforms the face, and shuts the eyes in death,
And still uncheck'd, his grisly triumph leads,
Nor votes regards, nor resolution heeds;
Those *votes*, by which, that man of patriot soul
Who o'er Town-Meetings held unmatch'd controul,
Far-fam'd SAM ADAMS thought to fright away
This curst disease, for ever, and for aye:
Therefore it is, by heaven's peculiar grace,
That I've thought fit to call you to this place.

But Gentlemen! a thing unmention'd yet,
Enough to throw you in a dog-day sweat;
A thing, perchance, which you, as well as *I*,
Have seen, some time, with many an aching eye;
Since, above measure bold, it scorns disguise;
And proudly stares us in the face and eyes;
A thing, most vile, most dreadful of its kind,
Hangs, like a mill-stone, heavy on my mind:
By conscience urged, in duty's cause made bold,
To you this wicked thing I shall unfold,
Since plain enough to *me* is its intent,
An open insult on *my* government.

Long since, while Britain, with maternal hand,
Cheer'd the lov'd offspring of Columbia's land;
Ere proud oppression bade that offspring brave
Assert their rights, and scorn the name of slave;

Ere o'er the world had flown my mob-rais'd fame,
And George and Britain trembled at *my* name;
This State, then Province, pass'd with wise intent,
An Act, *Stage-Plays*, and such things to prevent:
You'll find it Sirs, among the Laws sky blue,
Made near that time on brooms when Witches flew,
That blessed *time* when Law kept wide awake,
Proscribed the *faithless*, and made the *Quakers quake*;
And thus, in terms sublime *I* state the fact,
Runs the *Preamble* of this precious *Act*.
  Both for the preventing, and avoiding, all
Those various evils which would sure befall
Our sober people, and their sober ways,
From *Interludes*, and vile *Theatric Plays;*
To wit, all fiddling, fighting, gaming, raking,
Swearing profane, high broils, and sabbath breaking;
  This ACT, so full of wisdom and so good,
Has now become a Law well understood;
Since it has often been confirm'd, you see,
By many a Legislature great as we.
Yet, notwithstanding this, some chaps uncivil,
Grand Emissaries of our foe the Devil,
Aliens, and *Foreigners*, and *Actors* funny,
Who less esteem our morals than our money;
Even in *our* holy Capital, of late,
Have dared insult the majesty of state,
And to exhibit publicly, propose,
Stage-Plays, and *Interludes*, and *Heathen Shows;*
Which, in the garb of *Moral Lectures* drest,
Of our good sober manners make a jest.
Yet so obnoxious to the people's notions,
So strange, so foreign to their constitutions,
That well *I* am convinced they never go,
From motives of amusement, to the Show;
But, like good, honest folks, with mere intent,
To keep these Actors under some restraint.
Judge, Gentlemen! *my* feelings, when at first,
This information, on my ear-drum burst:

Not more was Israel's hapless King appall'd,
When Endor's Witch the Ghost of Samuel call'd,
And slowly rising from the shades of night,
The frowning spectre met his startled sight.
Not more *bold* ELDERKIN* with terror shook,
Not more dismay was pictured in his look,
When Windham's Sons, at midnight's awful hour,
Heard, from afar, the hoarse discordant roar
Of Bull-Frog sorrow groaning on the wind,
Denouncing death and ruin to mankind;
While one supposed the *tawny Myriads* near,
And heard their War-whoops thunder in his ear;
Another thought *Old Nick* was sure a coming,
Since none but Belial's bands could make such drumming;
Yet each, prepar'd his proper weapon took,
While one his bible hugg'd, and one his musket shook.
Wild consternation on my visage hung,
Congeal'd my blood, and every nerve unstrung;
O'er my whole frame a palsying horror flew,
And *sense*, retiring, bade a long adieu.
So CAIN, the fratricide, when deep disgrace
Fix'd its black brand upon his guilty face,
Fled from the crime of brother ABEL's blood,
And took lone lodgings in the *Land of Nod*.
    Whether the Magistrates all this have known
I do not know; but this I know, that none
Have taken care, whatever their intent,
These Fellows' *pranks* and *postures*, to prevent;
    Ne'er have laid hold of them with Law's strong hand,
And fairly brought the scoundrels to a stand,
Nor to the whipping-post the rogues have tied,
Where oft cash-pay is chang'd to pay in hide.
With joy extreme, O Gentlemen! in you
The firm upholders of the Law I view,

---

* For a particular account of this remarkable occurrence, extracted from Peters' History of Connecticut, see Supplementary
Notes.

On you devolves the *task* (I grant it great,)
To keep unstain'd the chasteness of our *State:*
Since that *good Lady* is beset so sore
By rakes and libertines full many a score,
That much I fear me, do whate'er you can,
She'll be debauch'd by that unrighteous clan.
But this at least I hope, that, if unable
To keep with all your might, her virtue stable,
You will not fail to show this wicked sect,
You know to punish, though you can't protect;
And whate'er punishment you shall devise,
As to your noble judgments seemeth wise;
Whether you burn, drown, knock them on the head,
Or hang them by the neck, 'till dead, dead, dead—
Or with a neighbor State, so very tender,
Loth to extend the neck of an offender,
Prefer the hanging business to commute
For *private prayers* and some *small goods** to boot—
I hope a great example it will stand,
And *in terrorem* guard *our* pious land.

Once more, ye Gentiles! to my voice give heed,
While things unthought of from my lips proceed,
Things of high import and of utmost weight,
Which much concern *our* Sovereignty of State.
The Constitution most expressly says:
  "Each several *State* shall, in such modes and ways,
  "As to adopt *its* Rulers are content,
  "Appoint ELECTORS for the PRESIDENT."
Yet in an act has Congress said of late,
That the Supreme Executive of State
SHALL—what a word to *Governors to use*,
By men unworthy to unloose their shoes!
SHALL—I repeat the *abusive term* once more,

---

* For an explanation of the above, vide the Archives of Connecticut, wherein it may be found that on a certain occasion of commutative justice, the sheriff was directed to furnish the criminal with the consolation of his prayers.

That dreadful offspring of usurping pow'r—
Cause with th' Electors names to be supply'd
Three proper lists all duly certified;
These to be given them *on* or *ere* that day
The Wednesday first that owns December's sway.
Though not unconscious of what mighty weight
Would prove my count'nance, and my aid how great,
Should I stretch forth my hand, with kind intent,
To prop the frame of General Government—
And eke am conscious that the public good
Would better be consulted if *I* should;
Yet when the Congress in compulsive phrase,
Pretend to teach *me* how to guide *my* ways,
SHALL I obey them, tremble at their nod,
And, school-boy like, most humbly kiss the rod?
I who first led the way to wond'rous things,
To humbling nobles and unkinging kings?
I who have done what man ne'er did before,
Quell'd the old British Lion's frightful roar?
I who first taught the Pole* t' ascend on high,
While flaming Tar-tubs kindled up the sky;
When, thick as feathery snows fast-flitting fall,
Or quails and manna at the Prophet's call,
The *Tar* and *Feathers* at my voice appear'd
And every Tory thought himself a bird?
 I who most nobly burst the *chests* of *tea*,
And with those wicked cargoes strew'd the sea,
Till Boston's dock might rival in its store
Kiangsi's plains, or Canton's busy shore—
That drink Circean, whose bewitching charm,
Had tied our tongue, unnerv'd our sinewy arm,
Chill'd the warm breast, transform'd the man to ape,
And given to Freedom Slavery's brutish shape?
No—I ne'er will— for *Governors* I'm sure
If any thing are from their power secure.
 As Presidents it seems must be elected,

* Liberty Pole.

Perhaps the mode which Congress has directed
Is full as good as any we can find:—
Yet Gentlemen! if any strikes your mind
Of different feature, mien, shape, air, or stature,
By which you would conduct this weighty matter,
Congress shall know it—and from *me* shall hear
That once they've caught the wrong pig by the ear.

    Pray, Gentlemen! do not suppose that *I*
Regard the Government with jealous eye;
Or have the smallest hope, or wish, that you
Should with a jealous eye regard it too.
I do not think that Congress ever meant
That *Clause* to construe to such base intent;
It must be a mistake, the careless work
Of careless Printers, or more careless Clerk.
I only meant a gentle hint, or so;
For, to the wise, a hint's enough you know;
I only wish'd such measures to prevent,
As might, in time, grow up to precedent,
To raise *constructive power*, as high as steeple,
On the tir'd shoulders of the grumbling people.

ECHO. No. X

[By Richard Alsop]

From the Virginia Gazette

Richmond, December 6, 1792

"Mr. Carey,
"The following impromptu was written on the report that the Electors of this State in consequence of their having unanimously voted for Governor Clinton as Vice-President, were contumeliously called Jacobins.

"Having remarked and admired the freedom of your press, I have submitted it through your medium to the public.

"If any one shall suppose it personal as to himself, with him you are at liberty to effect an interview with the author.

"REJOICE! Republicans rejoice! your inestimable privileges are secure. The genius of America is awake. The tutelary saint of Virginia is roused. The electors of this state have unanimously given their suffrages to Governor Clinton, as Vice-President. Governor Clinton is a republican both in principle and practice. The principles of Mr. Adams, the late Vice-President, are reprobated—his book—his writings—his sentiments—his late conduct—his love of, and his having recommended hereditary monarchy, and hereditary aristocracy, are all, all reprobated. The monocrats, aristocrats, highflyers, mushrooms, all hang their heads; and while the friends of men sing psalms, hallelujahs, and anthems, to the tune of regenerating freedom, they who were conspiring to dethrone the sacred majesty of the people may perform the last funeral obsequy and sing the last melancholy dirge to Adamitical principles.

"Yes! ye men of Belial, regeneration is at your heels, and ere long she will hold you up hated and avoided, as you are now suspected and despised. Your chariots, your pomp, your galadays, your court etiquette, your cries of sedition, and your reproaches against tried republican characters, will not avail. All eyes will be opened; the fatal issue of your abominable schemes will be developed; then you will hate and execrate each other, yourselves, as you now deserve it, from all the race of man.

"You call the electors Jacobins, as a mark of contumely; in that view they despise you and ask, that a man shall avow himself. But why say, Jacobins? Are they not the authors of the greatest and most glorious revolution of which the annals of history can boast? Have they not loosed the shackles of slavery from thirty millions of people? Have they not fanned the sacred blaze of liberty, in every region of the earth? Have they not dethroned tyranny, monarchy, aristocracy, priestcraft, and all their satellites? Have they not set up and crowned the mighty majesty of human kind over the punyism of individuals? Yes! The Jacobins of France have done this. The French have no longer a king; they are no longer slaves; they are free; and therefore you despise them.

"But future ages, when they trace the history of man, when they contemplate the catalogue of woes, which blacken the pages of antiquity, will at this eventful epoch make a complacent pause, and drop a tear of gratitude to the memory of those who so much contributed to emancipate the human race.

"The revolution has blasted your hopes; the kings or tyrants of Europe have leagued against them; and why do you not go? The duke of Brunswick will receive you; he will embrace you, and you will show the ne plus ultra of human depravity; Americans aiding and abetting kings and tyrants to reduce to bondage thirty millions of people, whose blood and treasure were exhausted to purchase your country's freedom. Go hence and take with you the last seed, the last shoot, the last scion of your stock; and let that bold essayist, as your crusading champion, whose head, heart, and hand have been employed to sap the imprescriptible and defined rights of his countrymen be announced to kings and their cut-throats, by his herald as a voluntary fugitive from a country where men will cease to be, or live free.

"Thanks to you, electors; all the friends of human liberty will thank you; future ages will revere and venerate your names: Heaven and your own conscience will reward you.

"HENRICO."

Hartford, January 21st, 1793

> "Echo with transport turns her eyes
> "Where Old Virginia's realms arise;
> "Bright POKAHONTAS'* noble name
>   "Shall consecrate the lay to fame"

* POKAHONTAS, a celebrated Squaw, who married one of the first settlers of Virginia; and from whom some of the Virginians are proud to derive some of their most considerable families. It has not a little puzzled many American Politicians, in considering the political

With love of freedom, Mr. Carey! smitten,
In ancient realm was this Impromptu written,
Where Pokahontas left a noble breed
All other men in science to exceed;
On the report as Jacobins denoted,
Were our Electors who for Clinton voted.
    Having oft seen the offspring of the brain
Drop from your press, with small parturient pain,
Through your pure medium I have thought it right
To let my strange ideas see the light.
If any one a personal meaning smell,
I'll pack him off, or he shall me, to hell.

    REJOICE, ye Democrats! I say rejoice!
See fix'd secure your privileges choice!
Columbia's Genius has our cause espous'd,
Virginia's tutelary Saint * is rous'd,
That Saint so mighty whose extended sway
Ancient Dominion's wide domains obey,
Who while the War hover'd o'er our fertile coast,
Sent forth her reg'ments, an *unnumber'd* host,
Where *fifty* officers, in martial pride,

situation of Virginia, where the manners of the Planters are *naturally*
and *habitually* Aristocratic, to account for the greatest number of
our high-spirited Democrats having originated from that state. A
very ingenious Civilian, of our times, has thrown much light on this
subject, by deducing the origin of the Democratic part of the Ancient
Dominion, from the famous Pokahontas; and he gives two very
satisfactory reasons why her descendants should rather partake of
the Levelling, than of the Aristocratic principle, although the offspring of royal ancestors. For, *first*, he remarks, that the whites
were inclined to treat the *Natives* as an inferior order of beings; which
naturally created in *them*, and *their descendants*, a disposition to reduce all to one standard; and, *secondly*, which is a still more convincing argument, as being founded in the constitution of nature, he remarks, that the sovereignty among the Indians, was merely nominal;
and that they, universally, preserved the most perfect Democracy
in their Governments.
    * Saint Tammany.

Strutted with five poor soldiers at their side.
That saint who marks, with clear sagacious ken,
Low in the scale the gen'ral race of men,
While high his vot'ries stand—by him decreed
The guides of worlds—to follow where they lead.
Lo! fill'd with joy, he staggers o'er the land,
His *whiskey bottle* shaking in his hand:
To us he cries—"Behold this bottle big!
"Come on my boys, and take another swig!
"This magic juice will second-sight restore,
"And make you see things never seen before."
Waked by his speech Virginia's sons arise,
His grateful liquor sparkling in their eyes;
And her Electors, with consenting voice,
Have made George Clinton their united choice.
Him for our head we mount o'er every bar,
His voice our compass, nod our polar star.
For, with severe and unremitted hate,
We urge illustrious Adams on to fate;
Condemn his principles, his book detest,
Misquote his sentiments, his conduct wrest,
Charge him with loving what ourselves we love,
Charge him with hate of what we disapprove,
And load with vilest terms of reprobation
The very phantom of our own creation.
The monocrats, aristocrats lie low,
High-flying mushrooms sink in deadliest woe,
The toad-stool too, with sympathy opprest,
Feels his soft heart lie heavy in his breast,
And, as he hangs his head, he oft applies
The handkerchief to dry his moisten'd eyes.
While joyous sing the people's friends and prance,
And treat the Negroes to a royal dance,*

* The following description of the celebrated Equality Ball given
to the Negroes of Boston by Governor Hancock is extracted from
the New-Year's Verses for the American Mercury, for 1793:—
    "And lo! where o'er the Eastern shores,
    Bostonia lifts her haughty towers,

And loud to Anarchy their voices raise
In hallelujahs and in hymns of praise,
To the sweet Tune of *Freedom born anew*;
That Tune so charming, and so novel too,
That Tune by tinkers sung, by cobblers lov'd,

What motley scenes salute our eyes!
What wonders upon wonders rise!
There each succeeding day still brings
A mixture strange of various things.

*   *   *   *   *

There plays their *heathen names* forsake,
And those of Moral Lectures take,
While, thus baptis'd, they hope to win
Indulgence for all future sin.
Now, Hancock, fir'd with patriot rage,
Proscribes these morals of the stage,
Claps Harper under civil durance,
For having dared, with vile assurance,
By *Interludes* and *Plays profane*
Pollute the glories of his reign.
Now, prompt to assert the *rights of man*,
On Nature's most extensive plan,
Behold him to his splendid hall
The noblest sons of Afric call:
While as the sable bands advance,
With frolic mien, and sportive dance,
Refreshing clouds of rich perfume
Are wafted o'er the spacious room.
With keen delight the Sage surveys
Their graceful tricks, and winning ways;
Their tones enchanting raptur'd hears,
More sweet than music of the spheres;
And as he breathes the fragrant air,
He deems that Freedom's self dwells there.
While CUFFEY near him takes his stand,
Hale-fellow met, and grasps his hand—
With pleasure glistening in his eyes,
"Ah! Massa Gubbernur!" he cries,
"Me grad to see you, for de people say
"You lub de Neegur better dan de play."

Which to the Cow* of old so fatal prov'd,
That from this world with joy she took her flight,
And bade her ancient friends a long Good Night;
Those who his *Majesty of Mobs* disown,
And seek that *Holy Sovereign* to dethrone,
When Grandsire ADAM's *principles* shall fail,
And flesh and blood, from keeping long, grow stale,
May sing the funeral in mournal stave,
And get old Burkett † too to dig the grave.
   Rejoice! ye Pokahontian Tribes rejoice!
In loud *Te Deums* raise your clam'rous voice!
Proclaim from Anarchy what blessings spring!
"Shall CLINTON reign and HENRICO not sing?"
   Yes, men of Belial! had ye sense to feel,
You'd find Regeneration at your heel,
And not far distant is the awful day
When your base clan a reckoning dire shall pay,
When old Virginia shall resume the reins,
And yield a rich reward for all your mighty pains.
Then shall your dress, your mimickry of state,
Your chariots, servants, equipage and plate,
Your brilliant levees, and your gala-days,
Your court-parade, your frankincense of praise,
Your cries seditious 'gainst Virginia's sway,
Which all the other states were made to obey;
Against her Statesmen too, who're born to show
A truth which first or last the world must know,
That the best way a Government to raise
Is to destroy its pillars and its base;
All these to aid your sinking cause shall fail,
ADAMS *must* fall, and CLINTON *shall* prevail.
Soon, very soon, will every open'd eye
The fatal issue of *your* schemes espy;

    * There was a piper had a Cow—
      He had no hay to give her—
      He took his pipe and began to play—
      "Consider, Cow, consider."
† A well known Sexton.

While in equality *our* days shall flow,
And incense unrestrain'd its choicest gifts bestow.
   Rejoice! ye Anti-fed'ral Clan rejoice!
'Gainst *Bank* and Funding-system raise your voice!
Declare from *Ruin'd Faith* what honours spring!
"Shall CLINTON reign, and HENRICO not sing?"
   You call th' Electors Jacobins—what then?
Are not the Jacobins the first of men?
Most certainly they are, I do protest,
Of men the very first and very best;
With fist and stick this truth will I maintain;
For arguments I never rack my brain;
No—to poor drivelling souls I leave such things,
Whom right and reason hold in leading-strings.
The Jacobins, once more I say, are good,
Staunch, noble fellows, fond of letting blood—
The Jacobins—I dwell upon the name,
My admiration and my homage claim—
To wond'ring nations do they not display
A noble generous spirit every day?
With much politeness and with equal skill,
Do they not torture whom they mean to kill?
And fir'd with zeal to render man humane,
Bear high on pikes the heads of children slain?
Do they not curse that chosen man of God
Old David call'd, who shed Uriah's blood,
And swear, indignant, that they'll never sing*

   * This curious fact, among the multifarious events of the French Revolution, may still exist in the recollection of some of our readers. A member of one of the French legislative bodies, it was said, about this time seriously proposed the rejection of the psalms of David from the service of their churches for the reason above assigned. This reminds us of the story of the Cape Cod man who had removed to a town in Connecticut; and on the introduction of the psalms of Dr. Watts in place of the former New England Version into the Churches of that State, declared with much indignation to his clergyman, that he was determined never to attend Divine Service in his Church while he persisted in singing the psalms of that Isaac Watts,

The psalms compos'd by that adult'rous king?
And shall not we, inspir'd with equal hate,
Reject the Psalms of Brady, Watts and Tate?
Have they not heav'd Oppression's iron yoke
From off the necks of thirty million folk?
With strength Samsonian broke the chains of power,
And freed their legs, from long confinement sore?
Have they not fill'd Old Freedom so with fire
That the good Dame is ready to expire?
And e'en at length have worn her bellows out
In blowing Faction's flame the world about?
Have they not tumbled from his splendid throne
Our Ally, once so good, great Louis down,
And keep him closely in the *Temple* pent,
Like some fine stall-fed ox for slaughter meant?
Have they not plunder'd of their goods and cash
All those Aristocrats who *cut a dash?*
Have they not made the Priests renounce their vows,
And pluck'd the mitre from their hallow'd brows,
While their Satellites, the Monks and Friars,
Have furnish'd glorious fuel for their fires?
Have they not, fraught with sentiments refin'd,
Crown'd the big *Majesty of Human Kind?*
Set up, on high, that many-headed God,
And bade the world bow down before his nod?
So, wrought in gold, with dazzling jewels spread,
On Dura's plain the Image rear'd its head,
While awe-struck thousands at the King's decree,
Bow'd the proud head, and bent the stubborn knee.
All this the Jacobins have done and more,
And France no longer owns the monarchic power;
Set loose from law, from moral shackles freed,
Her sons have gain'd fair freedom's fullest meed.
　　Rejoice! ye pious Jacobins, rejoice!
Ye graceful Fishwomen strain high your voice!

whom he had very well known at Cape Cod, and who was the greatest
drunkard in the place.

Proclaim from bloody heads what transports spring !
"Shall CLINTON reign and HENRICO not sing?"
    But future ages when they come to trace
The varied history of the human race;
When they regard the list of woes so black,
That left such bloody weals on Time's old back;
Will at this epoch complaisantly pause,
And wet with tears their cheeks and drop their grateful jaws.
To those good souls, by charity inspir'd
And meek-ey'd pity's soft enthusiasm fir'd,
Who kindly clubb'd their wits and eke their power,
To speed poor Frenchmen on their saintly tour,
And, with a world of pains, so hard have striven
To boost their brethren o'er the walls of heaven.
Sons of benevolence! my heart o'erflows,
When I but think from what a weight of woes,
From what dread injuries, what pain, what grief,
Your neighbors, through your cares, have gain'd relief;
In Mr. Giles's classic phrase, though they
Had rather * manag'd matters their own way;
Had rather taken their own time to go;
Had rather staid a longer while below;
Had rather jogg'd more softly on their course;
And rather not have mounted Death's white horse.
    Cold are those hopes which once your bosom warm'd,
Those sanguine hopes that Order's sons had form'd,
O'er those bright scenes, which erst your fancies fed,
The Revolution's mildewing blast has spread.
Then why don't you to Europe's monarchs go,
And join those tyrants 'gainst your common foe?
The Duke of Brunswick will be glad, no doubt,
Of such strong aid the Jacobins to scout,
With tender Indian hugs he'll squeeze you to him,
For you can fully *ne plus ultra* show him.
Americans, abetting tyrants base

---

    * For examples of this elegant phraseology, see Debates in Congress—Article, Mr. Giles.

To bring in bonds the *virtuous* Gallic race,
Once more to make them wear their rusty chains,
And go to fiddling for their master's gains,
Those thirty million folk, whose sweat and blood
Stream'd in such torrents for your country's good;
I—by my power almighty—bid you hence!
Go—and take that with which we can dispense!
Take the last seed, shoot, scion of your stock,
Nor leave the poor old stump our nerves to shock!
Take every virtue with you as you go,
Leave us our Clinton, Jefferson and Co;
These shall amuse us in the daily papers,
And Johnny Hancock give us Negro capers.

Thanks be to you most wise and great Electors!
Freedom's old Cronies hail you her protectors!
Bald Father time, with mouldy tooth and nail,
In vain your fame, so bulky, shall assail!
Gabriel shall crack his trumpet with hard blowing,
And tell the names of folks so mighty knowing;
While your own consciences shall need new cases,
Grown thin and thread-bare in so many places.

Rejoice! ye noble Levellers rejoice!
Ye democratic Tribes exalt your voice!
Declare what joys from prostrate morals spring!
"Shall CLINTON reign, and HENRICO not sing?"

ECHO. NO. XX

[By Richard Alsop. A Federalist satire of Jefferson.—EDITOR.]

March 4, 1805

"ON taking this station on a former occasion, I declared
the principles on which I believed it my duty to administer
the affairs of our commonwealth. My conscience tells me
that I have, on every occasion, acted up to that declaration,
according to its obvious import, and to the understanding of
every candid mind."

"I have said, fellow-citizens, that the income reserved had enabled us to extend our limits; but that extension may possibly pay for itself before we are called on, and in the mean time may keep down the accruing interest; I know the acquisition of Louisiana has been disapproved by some, from a candid apprehension that the enlargement of our territory may endanger its union.

"But who can limit the extent to which the federative principle may operate effectively? The larger our association the less it will be shaken by local passions; and in any view is it not better that the opposite bank of the Mississippi should be settled by our brethren and children, than by strangers of another family? With which shall we be most likely to live in harmony and friendly intercourse?

"The Aboriginal inhabitants of these countries, I have regarded with the commiseration their history inspired: endowed with the faculties and the rights of men, breathing an ardent love of liberty and independence, and occupying a country which left them no desire but to be undisturbed, the stream of overflowing population from other regions directed itself on these shores: without power to divert, or habits to contend against it, they have been overwhelmed by the current or driven before it: now reduced within limits too narrow for the hunter state, humanity enjoins us to teach them agriculture and the domestic arts; to encourage them to that industry which alone can enable them to maintain their place in existence, and to prepare them in time for that state of society, which to bodily comforts adds the improvement of the mind and morals. We have therefore liberally furnished them with the implements of husbandry and household use; we have placed among them instructors in the arts of first necessity; and they are covered with the Aegis of the law against aggressors from amongst ourselves.

"But the endeavors to enlighten them on the fate, which awaits their present course of life, to induce them to exercise their reason, follow its dictates, and change their pursuits with the change of circumstances, have powerful obstacles to encounter, they are combated by the habits of their bodies, prejudice of their minds, ignorance, pride, and the influence of interested and crafty individuals amongst them, who feel themselves something in the present order of things, and fear to become nothing in the other. Those persons inculcate a sanctimonious reverence for the customs of their ancestors; that whatsoever they did must be done through all time; that reason is a false guide, and to advance under its counsel in their physical, moral, or political condition, is perilous innovation; that their duty is to remain as their creator made them, ignorance being safety, and knowledge full of danger; in short among them also is seen the action and counteraction of good sense and of bigotry: they too have their antiphilosophers, who find an interest in keeping things in their present state, who dread reformation, and exert all their faculties to maintain the ascendency of habit over the duty of improving our reason and obeying its mandates."

*　　*　　*　　*　　*　　*

"During this course of administration, and in order to disturb it, the artillery of the press has been levelled against us, charged with whatever its licentiousness could devise or dare. These abuses of an institution so important to freedom and science, are deeply to be regretted, inasmuch as they tend to lessen its usefulness, and to sap its safety: they might indeed have been corrected by the wholesome punishments reserved to and provided by the several states against falsehood and defamation; but public duties more urgent press on the time of public servants, and the offenders have therefore been left to find their punishment in the public indignation. Nor was it uninteresting to the world that an experiment should be fairly and fully made, whether freedom of discussion, unaided by power, is not sufficient for the propagation and protection of truth.—Whether a government, conducting itself in the true spirit of its constitution, with zeal and purity, and doing no act which it would be unwilling the whole world should witness, can be written down by falsehood and defamation. The experiment has been tried, you have witnessed the scene; our fellow citizens have looked on cool and collected; they saw the latent source from which these outrages proceeded; they gathered around their public functionaries, and when the constitution called them to the decision by suffrage, they pronounced their verdict, honourable to those who had served them, and consolatory to the friend of man, who believes that he may be entrusted with his own affairs.

"No inference is here intended, that the laws provided by the state against false and defamatory publications should not be enforced; he who has time renders a service to public morals and public tranquillity, in reforming these abuses by the salutary coercions of the law. But the experiment is noted to prove that, since truth and reason have maintained their ground against false opinion in league with false facts, the press, confined to truth, needs no other legal restraint."

*   *   *   *   *   *

"Contemplating the union of sentiment now manifested so generally, as auguring harmony and happiness to our future course, I offer to our country sincere congratulations.— With those too, not yet rallied to the same point, the disposition to do so is gaining strength; facts are piercing through the veil drawn over them, and our doubting brethren will at length see that the mass of our fellow-citizens, with whom they cannot yet resolve to act, as to principles and measures, think as they think, and desire what they desire; that our wish, as well as theirs, is that the public efforts may be directed honestly to the public good; that peace be cultivated, civil and religious liberty unassailed, law and order preserved, equality of rights maintained, and that state of property, equal or unequal, which results to every man from his own industry, or that of his fathers. When satisfied of these views, it is not in human nature that they should not approve and support them; in the mean time let us do them justice, and more than justice, in all competitions of interest: and we need not doubt that truth, reason, and their own interests will at length prevail, will gather them into the fold of their country; and will complete that entire union of opinion, which gives to a nation the blessing of harmony and the benefit of all its strength."

" Wak'd from long sleep her tuneful shell,
" Shall sportive Echo strike again,
" While loud its tones melodious swell,
" As nobler themes inspire the strain."

" 'Tis just four years, this all-eventful day,
Since on my head devolv'd our country's sway,
When at the undertaking's magnitude
With lowly rev'rence I most humbly bow'd.
You well remember with what modest air
I first approach'd the Presidential Chair,
How blush'd my cheek, what faultering in my gait,
When first I squatted on the throne of state!
But as, protected by my supernal power,
We all surviv'd that most tremendous hour,
Let us rejoice, and trust that not in vain
Four years have brought us to this place again.
A foolish custom forc'd me to declare
Off-hand what point of compass I should steer;
But knowing well that every Fed'ral eye
On me was fix'd some mischief to descry,
I tun'd my fiddle for the vulgar throng,
And lull'd suspicion by a soothing song.
An old companion in my bosom keeps
A constant watch, save when perchance he sleeps,
From early youth in friendship sweet we've play'd,
And hand in hand through life's vast circuit stray'd.
Last night I ask'd him freely to declare,
(And he was here before, and heard me swear)
How far I'd kept my first inaug'ral speech
And whether Candour could allege a breach.
He boldly answer'd—'Sir, on each occasion,
You've acted e'en beyond your declaration:
Thus, when you promis'd to be just and true
To *all*, and give to every man his due,
Could *Candour* possibly have understood
That the term *all men* could your foes include?
No, Sir, on me let all the mischief fall,

If aught except *your friends* was meant by *all*.
Nor shall the Fed'ralists, perverse and base,
On grounds like these lay claim to hold their place.
Again, when toleration was your theme,
What stupid mortal could a moment dream
You meant to drop at once your choicest grace,
The right to turn the Fed'ralists from place;
What though you said, with soft persuasive tone,
That Fed'ralists and Democrats were *one;*
Yet you, and I, and Candour fully knew
By *one* you meant no more nor less than *two,*
And shall a man of broad capacious mind
Be to one meaning rigidly confin'd?
The ancient proverb's wiser far, I trow,
'Tis best to keep two strings to every bow.'
This maxim oft, amid this world of strife,
Has prov'd the solace of your varied life,
Charm'd the rapt ear with soft and double tongue,
And gain'd applause by sweet ambiguous song.
Now, Sir, since I have set all matters right,
Conscience will bid the President good night.

*   *   *   *   *   *

"Among the deeds economy has wrought,
High rank the num'rous tracts of land we've bought;
Our country's limits constantly extend
O'er boundless wilds and rivers without end,
Nations are bargain'd for by sleight of hand,
We soon shall purchase old Van Diemen's land,
Beyond Cape Horn our speculations roll,
"And all be ours around the Southern pole,"
What though no boundary to our views is set,
And every bargain swells the public debt,
Unlike all other modes of gaining pelf,
Before we're sued this debt *will pay itself.*
And though our title deeds, by strange mischance,
Instead of Spain are sign'd and seal'd by France,
The limits too, not definitely fix'd,

Lie somewhere *this* and *t'other* world betwixt,
For fear some quarrel should hereafter rise
We've given our obligations for the price,
I grant some minds of weak and fearful mould,
Instead of buying think we'd better sold,
Lest first or last, by some unseen mishap,
So greatly stretch'd, our union cord should snap—
'Tis true, indeed, a leather string will break
If stretch'd too far; but much I do mistake
If ever mortal broke a string of leather
By tying first a dozen strings together.
And can it be that as we larger grow
At the same moment we grow smaller too?
This does not quadrate with dame nature's course;
She gives to pigmies weakness, giants force;
The mighty Mammoth stronger is by half
Than the slim stag, the bullock than the calf.
Thus should this great Republic once expand
From shore to shore and cover every land,
In like proportion would our strength abide,
And we could manage all the world beside.

And when our children leave our fost'ring arms
And roam the western wilderness for farms,
On banks remote to see them peaceful toil,
Lords of the stream, and masters of the soil,
Is better far than on the self same place
To meet with squatters* of a different race,
With whom, perhaps, possess'd of better right,
We cannot get along unless we fight.

     *   *   *   *   *   *

Oft have the dark-skinn'd natives of the wild
Our tenderest thoughts engag'd, Our love beguil'd;
At their sad story oft We've felt Our breast
With soft compassion's throbbing pangs opprest,
That story sad, by Fiction's hand adorn'd,

* Persons who settle on vacant lands in the wilderness, without title, and who are with difficulty removed.

Where hapless Logan for his offspring mourn'd,*
What time, by cruel Cresap's murd'rous knife,
Poor Squaw and Pappoose both were reft of life.
Long since We've prov'd from Philosophic ken,
That Squaws are women and their Sanaps men;
Though, far unlike our European race,
No bristly beards their polish'd chins disgrace,
O'er their smooth frames no hairs unseemly spread,
Nor aught displays that covering but the head,
Yet nature prompts them with the same desires,
And with like feelings and like passions fires.

When, fresh from Sovereign Nature's plastic hand,
Shone in the bloom of youth this blissful land,
Good simple, harmless, nor with blood defil'd,
Liv'd the poor Indian mid the desart wild.
Close by some crystal stream his wigwam stood,
The skins of deer his dress, their flesh his food;
Few were his wants, and his desires but few,
No bliss beyond his pipe and Squaw he knew,
Small as his wants his homely household gear
Inspir'd, from nightly theft, no cause of fear,
With various hues his deer-skin mantle dyed.
By night his covering, and by day his pride,
A pot of stone, his succotash † to boil,
And huge samp-mortar, wrought with patient toil,
These were his riches, these his simple store,
And having these, he sought for nothing more:—
Thus liv'd he blest, what time from Cambria's strand,
Advent'rous Madoc sought this unknown land.
With swords and bibles arm'd the Welch appear,‡

* For this story, see Notes on Virginia, and for its authenticity the
letters of Luther Martin, Esquire.

† The Indian name for the mixture of Indian corn, or maize, with
beans.

‡ One of these very bibles is said to have been discovered, not many
years since, in the possession of the Welch Indians, who have excited
so much curiosity, and who preserved with *a sanctimonious reverence*
this relic of their ancestors, although they were unable to read it and

Their faith to 'stablish and their empire rear;
Struck with surprize the simple savage sees
The pictur'd dragon waving in the breeze,
Hears with delight the harp's wild music play,
As sweet the strings respond to Gryffidd's lay;
But when th' advancing squadrons forward move,
Their arms bright gleaming mid the dusky grove,
Joy yields to fear, as now, approaching nigh,
Their dress and uncouth features meet his eye;—
And when their barb'rous Celtic sounds he hears,
That grate discordant on his *tender* ears,
Fill'd with wild terror from the scenes he scuds,
And seeks retreat amidst impervious woods,
While, in pursuit, behind th' affrighted man
'*The o'erflowing stream of population ran,*'
His wigwam swept away, his patch of corn,
Before the fury of the torrent born;
Drove him from wood to wood, from place to place,
And now for hunting leaves him little space.

   Then since, beneath this widely-spreading tide,
Sunk are the grounds that Indian wants supplied,
Few are the deer, their buffaloes are dead,
Or o'er the lakes with mighty Mammoth fled;
Humanity has whisper'd in Our ear,
Whose dictates ever have We held most dear,
To teach them how to spin, to sew, to knit,
And for their stockings manufacture feet,
Since by their energies' exertion's sole
Can they e'er figure on *Existence*' roll.
We therefore liberally to them have sent
Such household matters as for use are meant,
Pots, kettles, trenchers, dripping-pans, whate'er
Their kitchens lack, their victuals to prepare,
And with them skillful men to teach them how

ignorant of its use. It is to be hoped that the gentleman appointed
by the President to explore the western part of the Continent may,
in his researches, be so fortunate as to fall in with this tribe and
obtain from them this curious and invaluable deposit.

To still their whiskey, their tobacco *grow;*—
While, to secure them from domestic harm,
We've lifted o'er them with Our thundering arm,
The *Law's* broad *Egis,* under which as still
And safe they lie "as thieves within a mill."
  But vain th' attempt to this IMPERIAL DAY
To light their dusky souls with reason's ray,
To make them quit their guns and scalping knives,
And stay at home contented with their wives;
Most powerful obstacles this scheme prevent,
Thwart my fine plans and frustrate my intent:—
Firstly their bodies' habits different are,
And different med'cine claim, and different care,
No neutral mixture will for them suffice
Of gentle acids and mild alkalies;
But powerful *Blood-root, Oil of Rattle-snake,*
Jerusalem Oak, and *Gum of Hacmetac.*
Nor simple blood lettings their pain assuage,
Warm their cold chills, and quell their fever's rage,
Means far more potent their tough frames require,
And the free use of lancets and of fire.
Besides as ne'er the Indian's chin appears
Mark'd with a beard, howe'er mature his years,
Of course no *Barber's* hand, with razor keen,
No *Barber's pole* amidst the tribes is seen.—
Great marts of knowledge, form'd the world to bless,
The seats of scandal, politics and dress!
From *Barber's shops* what benefits we trace?
How great their 'vantage to the human race?
That source of civil culture unpossess'd,
What wonder reason slowly fills the breast?
Thou knight renown'd! possess'd of equal skill
The comb to flourish, or to ply the quill,
Whose bright effusions, wond'ring, oft I see,
And own myself in message beat by thee.
O would'st thou, HUGGINS, * to the Indians go,

* Though the Echo is disposed to allow a certain great philosopher
every credit for his zeal for political and moral reform, she has doubted

And on their chins give mighty beards to grow,
Soon should thy shop o'er all their wigwams rise,
And painted pole attract their *curious* eyes,
While the glad tribes would thither thick repair,
And claim in turn the honours of thy chair.
Methinks amid the newly-bearded band,
With brush and lather arm'd, I see thee stand,
And as each visage gleams with foamy white,
And wields thy dexter hand the razor bright,
Thy eloquence pervades, refines the whole;
And pours the beams of reason o'er their soul,
While the white-wigg'd savages, with loud acclaim,
Thee as the *People's Friend*, and *President* shall name.

Thrice happy time; when, freed from Error's night,
Reason's broad beam shall shed her mid-day light,
O'er realms regenerate ope unbounded day,
And bless the Indians with its brightest ray.
Drive the thick mist from their bewildered eyes
Give them their former habits to despise,
While they partakers of our equal right,
In civic feasts and whiskey shall delight.
But much We doubt that ne'er within Our reign,
Will Indian manners such refinement gain;
For ah! among them live some crafty dogs,
Change-haters, anti-philosophic rogues,
Chaps who, though something, are of nothing made,
Mere forms of air and phantoms of the shade:
Who say 'tis better in the ancient way
Safe to go on, than in new paths to stray,
Where bogs and precipices lurk beneath,

whether the solicitude expressed for the illumination of the savages
by this novel, though doubtless efficacious method, may not, in part,
have had its origin in the jealousy of the rival talents of the celebrated character, so strongly urged to this philosophic mission, and
a disposition to remove him to a greater distance, by this species of
honourable exile, as even the greatest men are not always entirely
devoid of that passion and "like the Turk can bear no rival near
the throne."

And *ignes fatui* point the way to death,
That civic feasts with Indians suit but ill,
And Rum and Whiskey are contriv'd to kill,
That what the whites the light of reason call
Is but another name for cheating all,
And that by *equal right* is meant, 'tis plain,
The right by force or fraud whate'er they list to gain.
Thus like the Feds to reason they pretend
Suspect Our motives, and decry Our end.

    Where *Action* too with counteraction jars,
And wild Misrule 'gainst Order fiercely wars,
Anti-Philosophers with scorn reject
Th' enlightening doctrines of our favour'd sect;
Bigots of mouldy creeds, that long ago
The Goddess Reason taught were idle show,
Their superstitious whims and habits hold,
Reject the new and cleave unto the old:
In vain Reform in Gallic mantle drest,
Unbinds her zone, and wooes them to her breast,
And Innovation's meretricious smile
Attempts their rigid firmness to beguile.
Strange that such Prejudice in chains should bind
In our enlighten'd days the human kind!
Fools must they be, by dullness sure possess'd,
In their old way contented to be blest,
When Novelty, with all-alluring charms
Of untried systems, lures them to her arms.

         *   *   *   *   *   *

    E'er since the day when first we took Our seat,
As Lord High Admiral of our nation's fleet,
The busy goose-quill has pursued its trade,
And the Press kept a constant cannonade,
Charg'd with the dreadful cartridges of wit;
Our head is batter'd, and Our heart is hit.
That scoundrel Scotchman, from his awful chest,
For weeks and months disturb'd Our nightly rest.
'Till freed from fear we heard the joyful sound
That Callender at last was safely drown'd.

Old Gabriel Jones the next in row appears,
And rings his story in Our tortured ears;
The old curmudgeon rummag'd up a feat
Of Ours, when fav'ring law allow'd to cheat,
Merely because We wish'd to pay, in trash,
A trifling quantity of borrow'd cash,
And makes as much disturbance at it *now*
As if it happen'd but a week ago.
Besides, the chance is even in Our mind
That Jones was anti-whiggishly inclin'd,
If so, it constitues Our brightest glory
To've done Our very best to trick a Tory.
Such tales with other things of trifling charge,
(For Us too tedious to detail at large,)
Mere peccadilloes, fir'd with deadly hate,
The paltry printers sound from State to State.

    Nor even here has ceas'd the thundering press,
But still invades Our quiet, "more or less;"
If from Our lips some contradictions fall,
These Fed'ral Warriors from their ambush crawl,
With direful War-whoop break upon Our ear,
And rend Our bosom with distracting fear.
Sometimes We're timid, other times too rash,
Penurious now, now prodigal of cash,
Sometimes We talk in hypocritic strain,
Sometimes we're hand in glove with atheist Paine,
Sometimes Our style is mere bombastic sound,
Sometimes 'tis mean and grovelling on the ground,
Sometimes We're sulky, insolent and proud,
And sometimes drinking cyder with the croud,
Now in imperial state beheld with dread,
Now seen with jack-knife slicing beef and bread.
So, the Old Man, to please the *many*, tried
His Ass to lead, to carry, and to ride,
While the base herd, from charity exempt,
Call'd *him* a Jack-ass for each vain attempt.
Nor stop We here—Our nerves receive a shock
Whene'er is nam'd that terrible *"dry dock;"*

That mount of salt, so monstrous high and long,
Is made the theme of many a '*caustic*' song,
Lead mines are laugh'd at, jeer'd are *horned frogs*,
And every booby sneers at *prairie dogs*.
These ills, too great for mortals to sustain,
Make Us at times most bitterly complain,
But then so far We've bolster'd up our cause
By loudly railing at Sedition Laws,
We've thought it prudent to entrust Our fates,
For kind protection to the sev'ral States.
Besides 'twas well to feel the public mind,
And know tow'rds Us how far it stood inclin'd,
To try if free discussion could remove,
Or aught impair the "sovereign people's love."
This has been done—and you have witness'd all
How vain th' attempt has been to work Our fall;
How round Us throng'd the *worthies* of the land,
"Ready, aye ready" at Our command—
"True Whigs of seventy-six," a goodly store,
Imported fresh from Erin's peaceful shore,
Time-serving changelings, faction's desperate band,
And all the *virtuous* refuse of our land,—
Thick as the flies that round some carcase pour,
Or lice that punish'd Pharaoh's sins of yore;
And kindly gave Us through their *patriot* cares,
In our own way to *gest** our own affairs.
No inference still must old offenders draw
That We dislike the vengeance of the law;
But being press'd with more important cares,
And loaded deep with national affairs,
We have not leisure now to throw away,
Nor wish for lawyer's fees our cash to pay;

---

* No apology, it is presumed, will be thought necessary by the
literary reader for the introduction of this very expressive word into
our language, as the use of it substantively, is sanctioned by such
high authority, in that elegant phrase, "the gestion of our public
affairs."

Yet he who loves in court his time to spend
Perchance the public morals may amend,
The slanderous Press of all its rage disarm,
And shield Our public character from harm,
To Fed'ralists a useful lesson teach
To drop their pens, and curb the use of speech;
And though, in Washington's and Adams' reign,
It was *Our* right 'gainst rulers to complain,
Though Freneau's labours faithfully were tried,
And year by year Duane and Cheetham lied,
Yet now the table's turn'd, we hold the sway,
Our lying Dogs at length have got their day;
'Tis therefore clear we cannot get along
Unless We shackle every Federal tongue,
Our fame in garb inviolable dress,
And bind in chains the Freedom of the Press.
And tho' with them 'twere base, with us 'tis fit
"Since one man's poison is another's meat,"
Nor does the adage in this case hold true,
"That sauce for goose is sauce for gander too."
But our success we merely note t' unfold
That since in reason's spite Our ground we hold,
All that the Feds can do We deem full light,
Though with opinions false,* *false facts* unite,
In league against Us harmless are they found,

---

* Next to invention, that first qualification of a writer, and the prime characteristic of genius, may be rank'd the happy talent of accommodating the *felicitous* thoughts or expressions of others to his own purposes; particularly when he possesses the art of giving them, by a light variation, the appearance and effect of originality. A rare specimen of this talent seems to occur in the above beautiful antithesis, for which, it is presumed the writer must have been indebted to the celebrated Ben Towne, a royalist printer in Pennsylvania, during our revolutionary war with Great Britain. . . . This noted character, in a confession of his politico-typographical sins, which he addressed to the good people of that state, acknowledged himself guilty of having, in imitation of his friend and model Jemmy Rivington, often stated in his paper, "*facts* that never happened."

These truths untrue a jingle mere of sound;
Nor need the Press, to Us devoted, e'er
Of harpy law the griping talons fear.

*   *   *   *   *   *

  Joy to Our friends, to all sincerest joy
Who share Our favours, or Our care employ,
Scarce can Our breast its load of joy contain
As ope to view the glories of Our reign!
Lo! all conjoin'd in one great bond of peace,
Contention dies, and oppositions cease!
Ourselves in social intercourse combin'd,
One spirit actuates, and one gen'ral mind,
Nor e'er shall varying systems rudely jar,
And 'midst Our bands excite intestine war,
Or furious Discord with unlovely mien,
Among *Fraternal Union's* sons be seen.
Hereafter free from care, Our skiff shall glide,
Its compass folly, theory its guide,
Adown the stream of state, no rocks t' impede,
No federal shoals to intercept its speed;
And should, perchance, from Eastern climes arise
The howling storm and darken o'er the skies,
Though the rent sails be driv'n before the blast,
The cordage snap and spring the groaning mast,
Yet on *one* anchor firm can We confide,
And all the perils of the storm deride;
The People's favour is that anchor sure,
With which, through every gale We ride secure,
And though, from want of skill, 'midst breakers cast,
That ever safely brings Us up at last.
As trout, by tickling so the Mob are ta'en,
This long we've known, and practis'd not in vain,
And now do what We may We need not fear,
Applause is sure to greet Our raptur'd ear,
For, should aught luckless pass, the stupid elves
Would shut both eyes and ears to cheat themselves.
O thou, to whom my present state I owe,
To whom whate'er of future hope I know,

Flatt'ry, great master, who, with magic art,
Mov'st at thy will, the springs of every heart!
O still propitious prove, still give my tongue
With honied sounds to lure the blinded throng!
Give them to trust, implicit, in my word,
Howe'er fallacious, and howe'er absurd!
Make them believe whatever I propose
From purest zeal for public welfare flows!
That those my fav'rite projects who decry
Are urg'd by malice, or mean jealousy!
That I alone the proper course can see,
That all of wisdom emanates from me!
That shall our *doubting brethren*, who, as yet,
To *rally* round Us have delay'd "a bit,"
When they so pleas'd and wonderstruck shall hear
That *all republican, all fed'ral* are;
That in all questions that betwixt us rise,
Where party passions clash, and interest vies,
Justice her scales holds so much more than even*
The balance ever to our side is given;

* The Echo acknowledges herself to have been at first not a little puzzled to discover the meaning of the expression *more than justice;* the explanation however fortunately presents itself in the first dramatic production of this country, the celebrated Mercenary Match of the Honorable Barna Bidwell; who puts into the mouth of his heroine, in addressing herself to her confidante, these striking and highly poetical words "My *more than maid*, my ever constant Betty." As more than maid must necessarily be there intended to mean something very different from that pure and icicle state of virginity, so finely described by Shakespeare, so it may fairly in the present instance, that *more than justice* signifies something widely different from that stern and unrelaxing principle, which, without regard, to friends or foes, perseveres inflexibly in the course of impartial rectitude; of this construction, the numerous removals from office, and other official acts of the present administration, will furnish a happy exemplification. At the same time the Echo is highly gratified in finding such respectable authority for the use of this expression, the ambiguity of which is so little in unison with the usual *plain* and *lucid* style of our Executive communications.

When they shall see this blissful state, 'tis plain
'Tis not in human nature to refrain,
Within Our fold in droves those sheep will run,
And joyful take Our ear-crop, every one,
And as a proof of love when safely penn'd,
Their silly fleece We'll sheer, their mutton vend.
So when in quest of game the Indian roves
Amid his native wilds and piny groves,
If chance, amidst the branches perch'd on high,
The yellow Wappernocker meets his eye,*
Instant, as if transform'd to powder'd beau,
He bows and cringes with politest show,
While, pleas'd, the simple beast wide opes his eyes,
And views the tawny juggler with surprize;
But, grown familiar with his antic feats,
He grin for grin and bow for bow repeats,
Drawing still near and nearer by degrees,
'Till in his reach his prize the savage sees,
When o'er his neck the treacherous cord he throws,
And closely draws the suffocating noose;
Then cease the bows, and drops the courtly air,
As the poor victim gasps within the snare;
While with stern joy he eyes th' expiring prey,
And bears elate his furry spoil away.

* Wappernocker, the Indian name for the marten. For this remarkable mode of taking that animal, see Peters's History of Connecticut, or some other work of equal veracity,——A similar device
is said to be practiced in the Bahamas for the taking of the Iguana.